Family Multinationals

T0291517

"A major contribution in the field of business history indispensable to understand the present of family-run multinationals."
—*Andrea Colli, Bocconi University, Italy*

This volume is one of the first to deal explicitly with family multinationals and the role of the family in internationalization. It situates itself at the crossroads of internationalization studies on the one hand and family business research on the other. Why do families continue to play such a large role in some of the most prominent firms in emerging and mature economies? How did they manage to maintain ownership control, yet divest of unrelated business ventures? How did they internationalize yet maintain control? This book identifies the idiosyncratic strategies and structures of family multinationals in different countries and at different points in time. A comparative historical and case study approach allows us to explore the role of the family through the firms' various internationalization pathways and understand long-term developments and path dependencies.

Christina Lubinski is Research Fellow at the German Historical Institute in Washington, DC. Her first book based upon her dissertation deals with corporate governance changes in German family firms since the 1960s and won the Prize for Business History by the Germany Society of Business History. As Harvard Business School Newcomen Fellow in 2010–2011, she compared German and U.S. family firms with a special focus on the process of internationalization. She has published on family business and multinationals in *Business History Review*, *Enterprise & Society*, and the *Journal of Family Business Strategy*. Her most recent research deals with German and U.S. companies in India since 1900 and asks how they dealt with the challenges of political risk.

Jeffrey Fear is the newly appointed Professor of International Business History at the University of Glasgow, Centre for Business History. He holds a PhD in history from Stanford University and has previously taught at the University of Pennsylvania, the Harvard Business School, and the University of Redlands. He is on the editorial board of the *Business History Review* and *Essays in Economic and Business History*. He writes on small and medium-sized business multinationals, international cartels, and management history. His articles have appeared in the *Business History Review*, *Jahrbuch für Wirtschaftsgeschichte*, the *Oxford Handbook of Business History*, the *Handbook of Organizational Learning*, and *Big Business and the Wealth of Nations*, among others.

Paloma Fernández Pérez has a PhD in history from the University of California at Berkeley and is Professor of Economic History at the University of Barcelona. She is coordinating a team of 21 scholars from 11 countries in a research that studies the origins and evolution of large family businesses in Latin America and Spain. Her research interests are family business, innovation, entrepreneurial networks, and lobbies. She has published *El rostro familiar de la metrópolis* (Unicaja, 1997) and *Un siglo y medio de trefilería en España* (Barcelona, 2004), has edited with P. Pascual *Del metal al motor* (Bilbao, 2007), and has published articles in *Business History*, *Enterprise & Society*, *Business History Review*, *Revista de Historia Industrial*, *Revista de Historia Económica*, and *Investigaciones de Historia Económica*. She is a principal researcher of a project on entrepreneurial networks in Spain and a member of the Centre d'Estudis Antoni de Capmany.

Routledge International Studies in Business History

Series editors: Ray Stokes and Matthias Kipping

Family Multinationals

Entrepreneurship, Governance, and Pathways to Internationalization

Edited by Christina Lubinski, Jeffrey Fear, and Paloma Fernández Pérez

NEW YORK AND LONDON

First published 2013
by Routledge
711 Third Avenue, New York, NY 10017

Simultaneously published in the UK
by Routledge
2 Park Square, Milton Park, Abingdon, Oxfordshire OX14 4RN

First issued in paperback 2016

*Routledge is an imprint of the Taylor & Francis Group,
an informa business*

Library of Congress Cataloging-in-Publication Data

Family multinationals : entrepreneurship, governance, and pathways
    to internationalization / edited by Christina Lubinski, Jeffrey Fear, and
    Paloma Fern?ndez P?rez.
        pages cm. — (Routledge international studies in business history ; 23)
    Includes bibliographical references and index.
    1. Family-owned business enterprises—Management. 2. International
business enterprises—Management.   3. Family corporations—
Management. 4. Enterpreneurship. I. Lubinski, Christina. II. Fear,
Jeffrey R.   III. Fern?ndez P?rez, Paloma, 1964–
    HD62.25.F377 2013
    658.1′149—dc23
    2012050788

ISBN 13: 978-1-138-21272-5 (pbk)
ISBN 13: 978-0-415-83671-5 (hbk)

Typeset in Sabon
By Apex CoVantage, LLC

Contents

Figures

Tables

1 Family Multinationals

Entrepreneurship, Governance, and Pathways to Internationalization[1]

Christina Lubinski, Jeffrey Fear, and Paloma Fernández Pérez

1.1 WHY FAMILY MULTINATIONALS?

Within a few years of Werner Siemens founding his eponymous German electrical company in 1847, it had developed a global presence. By 1913, for example, more than 30 percent of its 80,000 employees worked outside of Germany. By contrast, the medium-sized manufacturer Haitoglou Bros. S.A., a producer of high-quality Greek delicacies founded in 1924, only started exploring foreign markets after sixty years of leadership in Greece's domestic food industry.

Both Siemens and Haitoglou are examples of internationally active family businesses (FBs) whose internationalization pathways, strategies, and organizational structures have been shaped by family ownership and kinship relations. Werner Siemens utilized family ties to build his global empire in the nineteenth century, sending two of his brothers to England and Russia who jointly managed the company with him. They exploited the Siemens's "good name" internationally and expressly pursued the goal of building a lasting family dynasty.[2] Haitoglou, on the other hand, grew slowly and incrementally, choosing low-risk and low-capital strategies to maintain the family influence and avoid dependence on external funding. When the owning family eventually decided to go global, the company first targeted Greek diaspora markets in the United States and Australia, which helped it overcome "psychic distance" before broadening its product portfolio to include other high-quality Mediterranean food products. During its slow growth, Haitoglou accumulated specific and experiential knowledge that allowed it to grow from its low-risk strategy that built upon its Greek origin to an internationally adaptable corporate brand advocating healthy lifestyles in general.[3]

Siemens and Haitoglou are no outliers in today's global economy, nor are they relics of a bygone age. As in the late nineteenth and early twentieth centuries, one can now still find "born-global" FBs alongside those that internationalize cautiously, or not at all. FBs still constitute the vast majority of companies in market economies worldwide. Statistics vary greatly depending on data sources and definitions, but it is estimated that 96 percent of all U.S. companies are FBs, mostly in the smaller-size sector. In South America, FBs constitute between 90 percent of all companies in Brazil and 65 percent in Argentina. In Europe (all listed as percentages), they make up the majority in Belgium (70), Finland (80), France (65), Germany (60), Greece (80), the Netherlands (74), Italy (93), and Spain (75), to name but a few.[4] In most countries outside the United States, family ownership also prevails in larger companies.[5] While there is no conclusive quantitative data about how many of them are internationally active, families certainly have been important decision makers in the history of past multinationals and continue to shape international companies to this day.

This book explores such "family multinationals": companies active outside their country of origin that were significantly influenced by a family. More precisely, we seek to understand the degree to which family influence helps to explain internationalization pathways and strategies from the nineteenth century to the present. As historians, we reflect on how firm globalization has changed in light of underlying geopolitical conditions that have shaped global trading systems, as well as on how family kinship structures have changed over time in particular places.

The diversity of family multinationals—both historically and today—makes this topic challenging. Many unresolved issues derive from a lack of generally accepted definitions. We define multinationals as firms that control operations in more than one country as opposed to internationally active firms that merely export from a single home base[6] and family firms (or FBs) as companies significantly influenced by a family, usually through ownership and/or management. In the literature, majority ownership is often taken as a pragmatic defining characteristic, and many chapters in this volume follow this lead. However, in certain organizational structures, preferred voting rights, veto rights thresholds, the issuing of nonvoting shares, holding companies, or complicated cross-shareholding structures usually found in pyramidal business groups can result in a family having a high level of influence even without majority ownership.[7] Other FB characteristics discussed in the literature include key actors perceiving a company as a FB, a public image fusing firm and family, or attempts to maintain family influence for future generations.[8] This last quality has been described as a "dynastic motive" and as "the essence of a family business."[9] Such a vision may have a stronger impact on corporate structure and strategy than other aspects of governance, and it is certainly justified to call for a stronger focus on the family itself as a unit of analysis.[10]

Still, the range of possible corporate governance forms and cultural arrangements, especially in international contexts, means that these definitions can only serve as benchmarks against which to explore diversity.[11] Instead of creating a rigid dichotomy of global FBs and non-FBs, we follow Astrachan et al. in qualitatively assessing family influence, asking how a family influences a company and exerts control over it.[12] Companies change, family influences can dwindle and disappear over time, and we want to capture these dynamic processes. That is why we focus on the question of how families shape internationalization strategies and pathways, which would look rather different in the absence of the family.

Business research has so far viewed FBs and multinational corporations as opposing business models. FBs evoke an image of inward-oriented, small- to medium-sized firms that often lack financial and human capital and are hesitant to take on risk. Multinationals are usually associated with large-scale managerial professionalized organizations able to raise enormous amounts of capital for international expansion. With the growth of a company, Alfred D. Chandler Jr. argued, professionally trained experts who can act independently of family loyalties—as well as shareholders, as some critics lament—eventually replace founders and their families.[13] Within this oppositional point of view, these managerial companies are regarded as having more resources and being better prepared for internationalization.

However, over the last few decades, FB internationalization has received renewed consideration. Chandler's model has been criticized for being teleological and biased towards developments in the United States, despite his insistence that a diversity of organizational arrangements could appear in dynamic firms in different environments. Most countries had widely different experiences.[14] Even in the United States, the separation of ownership and management was never complete.[15] In a study of S&P 500 firms, Ronald C. Anderson and David M. Reeb discovered that 33.6 percent were FBs in which the founding family held, on average, 18 percent of firm equity. Moreover, they concluded that "family ownership is an effective organizational structure."[16]

This conclusion accords with at least three lines of research. First, La Porta et al. show that in the twenty-seven economies they analyzed, 30 percent of the largest companies were family controlled, while 36 percent were widely held and 18 percent state controlled.[17] While in the United States, United Kingdom, and Japan widely held ownership is the norm for the largest corporations, Argentina, Greece, Austria, Germany, Hong Kong, Portugal, Israel, and Belgium have hardly any such firms. Second, as Asli Colpan et al. have recently shown in their *Oxford Handbook of Business Groups*, most business groups in the world continue to be controlled by strong families.[18] Third, scholars investigating small and medium-sized multinationals have consistently demonstrated the importance of family influences.[19] However, the question of how controlling families influence internationalization pathways in different national and historical settings has seldom been posed.

We are well aware that family influence cannot be analyzed in isolation and that there are additional factors affecting strategies and structures for internationalization, such as a firm's age and industry, regulatory burdens, cultural barriers, and economic variables. Within the family and between families, religious or ethnic ties may impact internationalization pathways,[20] and company size is highly relevant, as well. We know very little about the differences between small and medium-sized international enterprises

(SMEs) and large-scale global corporations. Even leaving aside the family dimension—impossible in smaller firms—investigating the differences between small and large-scale firm internationalization has become an exciting new research field.[21] The contributions in this volume reflect on all of these variables and take pains to contextualize family multinationals. However, by focusing closely on different forms and degrees of family influence over time, we aim to explain how families have shaped the internationalization process in different historical periods.

1.2   CROSSING DISCIPLINARY BORDERS: FAMILY MULTINATIONALS IN MANAGEMENT AND HISTORICAL RESEARCH

This volume positions itself at the intersection of family business studies, international business, and business history. All three fields have dealt with FB internationalization in different ways. While both family business and international business studies are linked through strategic management literature, business history differs most clearly in its methodologies, its choice of topics, and its embeddedness in particular national research agendas.

When specialized family business studies emerged in the 1980s, scholars focused on theoretical models of the family and the firm.[22] The three-circle model, first presented by Renato Tagiuri and John Davis in 1982, understands a family business as the intersection of three separate circles: family, business, and ownership. Because FB members belong to more than one circle at the same time, they confront conflicting roles that can potentially generate tensions and conflicts.[23] Because much of this early research was devoted to internal FB dynamics, its explanatory power is strongest concerning the relationship between families and their businesses and in identifying potential conflicts. The most contentious issues in this phase of research were questions of definition, succession, family conflicts, and governance issues.[24]

Internationalization has only recently sparked the interest of family business scholars. Most peer-reviewed articles about FB internationalization have appeared since 2005, while the earliest contributions can be traced to the early 1990s.[25] FB internationalization research is closely related to and partly derived from previous studies in international business, and makes use of the same theories and methodologies.

International business studies are particularly strong in mapping and explaining internationalization processes and modes of entry into foreign markets. Recently, FBs have become an object for such studies as well. The focus, however, has largely been on small companies and elucidating the consequences of company size on internationalization rather than dimensions of family influence.[26]

Business history, by contrast, provides an array of in-depth longitudinal case studies that deal with family multinationals and contextualize them in specific historical settings, often lost to management studies with its focus on theory formalization. However, historians have neglected in the past to pay attention to management models and theoretical underpinnings of their work. Thus, while historians have dealt with FB examples for a long time, it was not until the mid-1990s that they began to explicitly focus on family influences.[27] Specialized family business research has since become a core genre in general business history. Single company studies, country studies, and comparative approaches have allowed in-depth comparisons, but theory development and generalizations have been slow.[28]

While all three disciplines deal with similar issues, there are few contacts between them—a situation that recently provoked Andrea Colli to implore scholars to conduct more research.[29] Similarly, several scholars have called for history and internationalization studies to be better integrated. In fact, Matthias Kipping and Behlül Üsdiken even argue that international business is one of the few fields in which business history continues to make empirical and theoretical contributions.[30] Similarly, Geoffrey Jones and Tarun Khanna put forward four reasons that greater cross-fertilization between the two disciplines would be desirable: 1) time series studies can be just as valuable as the oft-used cross-sectional variations to test conceptual issues; 2) many phenomena discovered in today's corporate landscape have historical predecessors; 3) the relevance of path dependency and the roots of a firm's unique resources can only be explored in historical studies; and 4) certain questions can only be asked and answered when considering firm development from a longer-term perspective.[31]

The relationship between international business and long-term economic development, for example, is inherently historical. Studies of international business need the tools of history to examine historical context, just as business history can adopt appropriate research methodologies and theories from international business studies.[32] Just as firms need market research on national developments and local preferences or behaviors before entering a specific market, international business studies require knowledge of firm and region interactions in time and place. Stage theories, kinship networks, organizational learning, and path-dependent theories imply an evolving process, often well captured by (historical) narratives that can deal with change over time.[33] In their renowned article, Bruce Kogut and Udo Zander stressed the importance of individuals' social-cognitive properties, which places a premium on understanding the distinctive aspects—the business history— of multinational firms since, as they emphasized, "strategies are made in social communities located in institutional settings. Strategy is a situated practice."[34] Family is the ultimate community that shapes the learning and strategy of such firms.

To be sure, some scholars have raised concerns about integrating international business studies with history. Mary O'Sullivan and Margaret Graham are skeptical that scholars can overcome the diversity of perspectives. They are most worried about the different meanings historians and management scholars attach to history and theory, and the lack of self-reflection and debate about these issues.[35] For instance, while archival research utilizing written sources is the main business of historians, management scholars are more skeptical that "what really happened" can be found in the sources. While management scholars regularly use oral interviews of main actors, historians are deeply suspicious about memory and biased self-representations about behavior. While historians often attempt to create "thick description" narratives, management scholars tend to think these are just (more or less interesting) "stories."[36] We believe, however, that this collection can spur a fruitful dialogue about such issues.

Despite the current lack of integration among the three research disciplines, it is noteworthy that they all address similar questions and utilize the same theories when it comes to FB internationalization. The most debated topics and theoretical frameworks, which will be elucidated in turn below, are

1   Transaction cost and agency relations
2   Mode of entry into foreign markets and choice of country
3   Scarcity of resources
4   Role of networks in internationalization
5   Attitudes and motivations for internationalization.

1.   Transaction Cost and Agency Relations. The concepts of transaction costs and agency relations are part of the larger framework of the so-called New Institutional Economics. Market transaction costs, such as search and negotiation costs, trigger firms to internalize transactions instead of contracting on the market.[37] Williamson refined this theory by identifying the concepts of bounded rationality, opportunism, and asset-specificity as incentives to internalize transactions. Because people cannot act fully rationally due to information asymmetries (bounded rationality), and because people act in self-interest and cannot be fully controlled (opportunism), certain transactions are cheaper when internalized within a firm; one can more efficiently order "by fiat" than negotiate a contract. The decision to use either market or hierarchy, furthermore, depends on the type of transaction (asset-specificity.) Some transactions necessitate investments in material and intangible assets, which can trigger a firm to replace market relations with hierarchical, internal ones.[38]

Transaction cost theory is one element in the eclectic paradigm model, first introduced by Dunning in 1980, that combines such internalization advantages with the concepts of ownership and location advantages of multinationals. According to this theory, multinationals exist because they possess advantages rooted in the firm's strength over local competitors. These ownership advantages include access to superior technology or knowledge, products, processes, or patents, better access to capital, and superior corporate governance. Some companies also derive ownership advantages from being multinational, for example, by realizing economies of scale or exploiting their superior coordination across national boundaries. Location advantages are rooted in the structure of the host country and include tariffs, governments, and regulations or size and income level of the host market. The eclectic paradigm argues that multinationals will engage in international activities if they possess ownership advantages, consider it better to exploit these advantages instead of selling them to foreign firms (internalization), and profit from location advantages.[39] Because it combines *ownership* and *location* advantages with the question of *internalization*, the model is some-times called the "OLI-model."

Internalization, information asymmetries, and opportunism are constant concerns in family business studies, as well. The principal-agent relation-ship, which highlights that owners lack complete control over their agents and have to cope with their opportunistic behavior, has a long tradition in this line of research. Family-owned and -controlled firms are widely under-stood to be companies with reduced or no agency costs because owners and managers pursue the same goals, and intimate trust-based relationships reduce information asymmetries. Agency costs, which include all actions by managers that contravene owners' interests plus firm investments made to align owner and manager interests, should arise less often.[40] While agency theory originally focused on the manager-owner relationship, agency costs also derive from transactions between any two groups of stakeholders or within a chain of suppliers. Agency problems occur particularly in large FB groups with minority shareholders who have voting power and control beyond their ownership stakes, permitting them to channel a greater share of the profits to the family ("tunneling") or to violate the ownership rights of the majority of shareholders.[41]

William Schulze et al. expand on agency theory in FBs and argue that they give rise to their own set of agency problems, which are hard to control if family members are already residual owners. For these authors, altruism emerges as a problem of self-control and allows some family members a free ride because the parents are biased in their perception of a child's per-formance or find it emotionally taxing to enforce a contract, for example.[42] Taking a more positive point of view, James Davis et al. offer the steward-ship theory to describe managers who act in the owners' best interest and manage the business with the same diligence and commitment one would expect of owners.[43]

John Ward, the FB expert, distinguishes nine potential variants of the relationship between firm and business ranging from stability-oriented fami-lies that run the firm with annuity-like goals to less growth-oriented "family first" types, from "stewards" to "business first," growth-oriented capitalist families.[44] Such varying family attitudes towards the firm, which can also differ among individual family members, greatly affect the firm's will to internationalize, contract, or enter into joint ventures with other foreign companies.

For companies conducting business over long distances, agency problems are particularly relevant because control mechanisms are less available and effective when there is no daily face-to-face contact to help align interests. Business history has offered several case studies identifying these problems in multinationals.[45] It is still an open question if agency and/or stewardship relations manifest themselves differently in global FBs than in other international companies.

2.   *Mode of Entry into Foreign Markets and Choice of Country.* Much research on FB internationalization follows the Uppsala model of internationalization, which argues that companies internationalize sequentially. They often start by exporting and gradually move on to establish sales offices and manufacturing plants abroad. Although firms engage in a range of different internationalization strategies, exporting is considered the most common foreign market entry mode, due to minimal capital requirements and risk. More cautious and risk-adverse firms, such as smaller ones and—presumably—many FBs, may prefer an incremental stage approach.

Anecdotal evidence appears to confirm that FBs are resistant to entering foreign markets whose "psychic distance" is far from their own culture. Instead, they seem to prefer to locate operations in culturally similar markets or close to where family members live.[46] This supports Shaker Zahra's finding that family influence correlates positively with international sales but negatively with the number of countries firms sell to.[47]

The recent swift expansion of knowledge-intensive firms, such as software companies, however, has given rise to a new category of "born-global" firms that calls the traditional stage theories into question.[48] Born-global companies have sometimes been described as a new phenomenon.[49] Yet a range of historical examples, such as the Rothschilds, Seligmans, or the Deutsche Bank—the latter with branch offices in Shanghai and Yokohama by 1873—show that the concept has historical antecedents. Historians also identified another type of internationalized firm, a free-standing company with headquarters in one country raising equity to invest in one or several other countries where it exerts management control or has the potential to do so.[50] Finally, researchers have described firms as "born-again" global firms if they internationalize rapidly to several countries after a trigger experience.[51] Typically, these are smaller entrepreneurial firms that internationalize either from inception or shortly thereafter. Smaller firms are also more dependent on external institutions and partners in both the home and host countries. Thus, it is implied that they are more inclined to engage in joint ventures or to use networks of relatives or people from similar cultural origins more often, thereby reducing psychic distance. Diaspora networks like those established by Jews, Indians, Chinese, Armenians, and Palestinians, for instance, have been studied to analyze some examples of FB internationalization.[52]

3.   *Scarcity of Resources.* Both FB and international business scholars have used the resource-based view (RBV) of firms to explain their subject of interest. With the aim of explaining why firms perform differently and how they realize competitive advantages, this view principally argues that firms possess valuable, rare, inimitable, and nonsubstitutable resources. Resources are defined as "all assets, capabilities, organizational processes, firm attributes, information, knowledge, etc., controlled by a firm that enable the firm to conceive of and implement strategies that improve its efficiency and effectiveness."[53] Management's role is to identify these firm-specific resources and to leverage advantages based on them.

Broadening the RBV, some scholars have called for a knowledge-based view of the firm (KBV) because knowledge and learning are any firm's most important resources. Considering that individuals and firms learn and enhance capabilities over time, the question of how firms learn is more important than investigating their access to specific nondynamic resource constraints.[54] In FBs, multinationals or otherwise, knowledge remains embedded in the specific community structures of families so that exploring the cognitive and social constructions of knowledge within families and firms becomes central to understanding these companies' available strategies and resources.[55]

The RBV and KBV have also specifically been used to describe FBs' idiosyncratic advantages. The bundle of resources distinctive to FBs that derive from family involvement is often called "familiness."[56] It is frequently considered a competitive advantage, albeit not in the context of internationalization.[57] A parallel argument can be found in studies of international businesses, which, scholars assume, need unique resources to outcompete rivals. However, familiness, to our knowledge, has rarely been seen as a potential advantage for internationalization, with the notable exception of historical studies dealing with periods prior to or during early industrialization. Studies in early industrialization highlight the family as the only possible structure for organizing business to compensate for the weak institutions and underdeveloped labor and capital markets of the time.[58] This perspective, however, has inadvertently led to the family's subsequent marginalization in the study of later periods. It is often assumed that the family's importance in economic and business activities diminished as institutions developed.[59] Consequently, scholars have not sufficiently investigated the family as a resource or as a bearer of knowledge and experience for internationalization in more mature economies.

Instead, international business scholars mostly argue that FBs face unique barriers to international expansion. This is especially true of firms that specialize in mature technologies and declining markets, and of multigenerational FBs where governance issues can affect the decision-making process.[60] Building on the RBV, such scholars see FBs constrained by more limited access to resources such as credit and capital, technology, human capital, and organizational capabilities. They regard FBs as less knowledgeable of the international marketplace, often entering international markets as a result of unsolicited orders,[61] and emphasize their less formal or structured ways of collecting information about global markets.[62]

Similarly, Chris Graves and Jill Thomas assume that FBs lack the managerial capabilities necessary to leverage a firm's resources in the international marketplace.[63] They build their RBV of the family multinational on previous studies about FBs that showed FBs frequently facing obstacles to developing their managerial capabilities as they grow.[64]

The overall tendency in the literature, therefore, is to see FBs as "reluctant internationalizers" and to interpret the family as an obstacle rather than an advantage or a resource that can be mobilized for internationalization efforts.[65] It is noteworthy that scholars have attributed the "scarcity argument" to the small size of many family SMEs, not to family nature. The family's role in internationalization, by contrast, is as yet little understood.

4.   *Role of Networks in Internationalization.* The importance of networks for FBs' internationalization has often been assumed but relatively poorly researched thus far. FB internationalization, particularly in the case of smaller firms, depends greatly on existing networks of clients and business contacts, including trade associations, cooperating firms, business clubs, distributors, relatives, and even competitors. All firms must build favorable relationships with external actors in their larger contexts. However, such relationships may be particularly relevant for FBs in light of families' embeddedness in specific local communities with their own idiosyncrasies and specific knowledge and resource bases, which FBs might leverage.

Again, the available literature, which focuses on SMEs, has tended to show that the choice of target countries largely depends on serendipity, a random order arriving from an unknown place, or on owners' opportunistic behavior.[66] Small FBs often group together in industrial clusters that form an important source of innovation, flexibility, and competitive advantages. According to Michael Porter, clusters enhance the informational advantages of firms within them so that assumptions about serendipity may not hold true, much like the phenomenon of chain migration wherein immigrants relayed information about opportunities abroad back home.[67]

Networks not only provide firms with new opportunities but can also help them overcome resource and knowledge constraints.[68] Business history, in particular, has shown that diaspora families furnish firms with an important means of exporting or expanding abroad by gluing together networks with family trust.[69]

Finally, networks are relevant to organizing collective action. Paloma Fernández and Nuria Puig have demonstrated this for the Spanish Institute of Family Firms, and Stéphanie Ginalski offers an example of close relationships among families in the Swiss metallurgy industry impacting cooperative agreements and cartels.[70]

5.   *Attitudes and Motivations for Internationalization.* Individuals' assessments of the desirability of international ventures largely depend on their entrepreneurialism or their family. This, in turn, is tied to family culture and the specific historical relationship between family and firm.

Chris Graves and Jill Thomas argue that making a long-term commitment to internationalization is crucial to the performance of family multinationals.[71] Multigenerational FBs can be considered to be more independent of shareholders than other corporations and often have longer-term planning that may help the internationalization process.

Business history is especially well equipped to track the attitudes and motivations for internationalization within one and across several generations. Longitudinal case studies have shown that multigenerational families make sense of the world as a negotiated social construct embedded in time and space, which shapes their entrepreneurship and corporate strategies. One does not belong to the family by birth as a matter of course but rather through a process of negotiation and renegotiation in everyday practices, communicative acts, and stories.[72] As different approaches to in-laws suggest,[73] contracts and intimate relationships, more than blood, determine this belonging.

Succession, the most debated topic in FB studies, is also regarded as influential concerning attitudes towards internationalization. However, the results are somewhat unclear. While Sam Okoroafo suggests that the second generation grows less committed to internationalization, Zulima Fernández and Maria Nieto find the opposite—that a new generation often spurs new entrepreneurial impulses.[74] The vision and managerial style of next-generation successors is a topic that seems to deserve more scholarly attention. While succession's overall impact on internationalization is not clear at this juncture, succession certainly has the potential to bring about change and regeneration. As entrepreneurship studies principally stress startups and IPOs, multigenerational multinational FBs have been neglected. *Interpreneurship*, a term that highlights strategy changes and innovations made by later generations—whose behavior is as entrepreneurial as that of the first-generation entrepreneur—remains a wide-open, exciting research field. It seeks to understand how families regenerate their business over the long run.[75]

Potential for Interdisciplinary Research of Family Multinationals

While there is considerable anecdotal evidence regarding family multinationals, the number of well-documented case studies is small. The broader theoretical and conceptual issues have only been addressed in a few stand-alone articles. The present volume fills this void by giving attention to the experience of individual family multinationals and groups of companies examined over considerable stretches of time since the nineteenth century. The book presents evidence from eight countries in a variety of sectors and from both born-global firms and late or slow "internationalizers." The contributions also set out to discuss theories often applied to multinationals or family business and contain critical discussions of the available literature. Most important, they show how international business theory, family business studies, and business history scholarship can mutually enhance one another.

As most of the authors are historians or historically informed scholars, their descriptions of pathways to internationalization are particularly strong in their consideration of "time" and periodization as a crucial and often neglected variable. This form of contextualization is indispensable to understanding global business. For instance, international business scholars focus, in particular, on entry modes into foreign markets, which have varied in ways dependent on the historical context. From the 1950s to the mid-1970s, Western economies experienced an era of relatively stable economic growth. The selection of the most appropriate entry mode into foreign (mostly Western European or U.S.) markets was then the most pressing concern, and the literature mirrored this status quo. The period before 1914 was, by some estimates, as globalized as the present; the period between the 1920s and 1930s was increasingly shuttered through tariff and capital controls; and the period after 1945 saw a considerable portion of the planet closed off under import substitution industrialization policies or communism. A theory of entry modes should consider these periods and geopolitical dimensions. The more turbulent external conditions of recent years make the question of how multinationals deal with external challenges more pressing. The historical experience of multinationals provides compelling insights into corporate response to shocks and transitions in the global economy at different points in time.

To this end, previous work by business historians can provide a temporal framework for understanding the changes and turning points in the global economy. Geoffrey Jones identifies at least three cycles of globalization since the Industrial Revolution: the First Global Economy (1880–1929), a period of disintegration (1930–1980), and the Second Global Economy (since 1979).[76] While different parts of the world were linked by strong trade long before the Industrial Revolution, globalization accelerated at an unprecedented pace in the nineteenth century. From the 1820s to the end of the century, international trade grew by around 3.5 percent annually.[77] The Industrial Revolution drove this growth, and exogenous circumstances, such as reduced transport costs, liberal economic policies, and the widespread adoption of the Gold Standard, which fixed the value of currencies to the price of gold, supported it. Multinationals made cross-border investments as never before.

With the beginning of the twentieth century, the First Global Economy saw signs of erosion. A shift towards trade protectionism and regulated immigration put an end to the free circulation of goods and people. For the first time in the history of multinationals, their nationality became an issue of major concern, when governments started sequestering "enemy-owned" company assets during World War I and the Russian Revolution.[78] Inflation and the suspension of the Gold Standard in the mid-1920s severely disrupted the international monetary system. The Great Depression was followed by the collapse of the international financial system. Multinationals were forced to deal with an increasingly unstable and unfriendly world economy.

By the 1950s, the Second Global Economy slowly emerged, but many restrictions on the flows of capital, trade, and people remained in place. After the collapse of the Bretton Woods system of fixed exchange rates in the early 1970s, international financial markets grew dramatically. World trade barriers were gradually reduced. At the same time, political unions created regional trading blocs that facilitated internal trade but created new obstacles for trade with other parts of the world. Technological innovations in transport and communication triggered further economic activities across borders. With these developments and new technologies, the pace of globalization quickened once more in the 1980s. Any description of international business cannot fail to consider these contextual factors for multinationals' investment decisions, which, at least partially, were responses to these changes.

Another theme prevalent in the literature is resource constraints for FBs going international—limits to their financial and human resources, organizational skills, and knowledge, to name but a few. The contributions in this volume acknowledge these challenges and constraints but do not conclude that FBs are, per se and across the board, "reluctant internationalizers." Instead, they strive for a more complete picture by investigating why some FBs internationalize successfully while others fail to do so.

Overcoming resource constraints is thus an underlying topic of all the contributions in this volume. FBs often mobilize family, or sometimes also ethnic, regional, or religious ties, to reduce transaction costs and profit from knowledge accumulated in these networks. While the contributions by Lombardi, Segreto, and Lubinski describe networks based on extended family, Gupta and Overbeck focus, in particular, on migrant communities as a unique pathway for FBs to go global, and Gutiérrez Poch and Overbeck also take regional communities and clusters into account. All of these communities nurture stewardship through cultural proximity, accumulate knowledge, shape motivations and attitudes, and have tested procedures for grooming, educating and supporting future generations. Several contributions, such as those by Gupta, Lubinski, Hilger, Fernández Pérez, and Popp, show how family members placed and/or trained abroad were an essential part of FB internationalization. Based on these findings, the authors of this volume argue that in some historical and national settings, FBs possess advantages for internationalization that can be leveraged. That this is not a foolproof affair, however, is also reflected. The contributions by Hilger, Gutiérrez Poch, Segreto, and Berghoff consider failures and setbacks that occurred during the internationalization process by showing FBs as vulnerable to conflict, conservatism, and reluctance to change, as well as illness or sudden death. Moreover, the contributions by Hilger, Fernández Pérez, Fear, and Hoshino, among others, shed light on how international businesses deal with changes in the environment from evolutionary change, such as technological change, to external shocks, such as wars or economic depression—a topic that is timely and certainly deserves further attention.

Several authors, such as Gupta and Hoshino, suggest that FBs can either have open or closed governance, which both have their pluses and minuses. Opening up firms to external capital and knowledge may enhance their ability to internationalize but simultaneously threaten their independence, as new decision makers and investors seek to have their say in the business. Being too rigidly closed to external resources, on the other hand, is likely to impede growth and ultimately threaten companies' survival.

Historical contextualization is pivotal to capturing how business functions in society. It also helps minimize the faulty impression that individuals and individual companies are atomized and devoid of links to the surrounding environment. Fernández Pérez's and Hoshino's contributions most pronouncedly demonstrate the visible hand of governments in China and Mexico and their influence on internationalization. Fear's and Lombardi's highlight the role of banks in encouraging or discouraging internationalization. Moreover, Fear underscores the importance of supporting institutions in Germany—often government-funded—that play a decisive role in helping internationally active Mittelstand firms overcome some of their most blatant resource constraints. These predominantly small and medium-sized firms profit from the market knowledge and expertise of external institutions instead of having to bear the costs of internalizing these functions. This is particularly relevant for smaller companies with less financial and human capital.

Company size—SMEs versus large companies—is certainly an important factor because it shapes the challenges firms face in internationalization. However, we also found it valuable to contrast small business internationalization with that of large-scale companies. Fear's, Overbeck's, and Gutiérrez Poch's findings on small family multinationals could be turned into relevant research questions for studies on larger firms or for comparative research. To better understand the similarities and differences between large and small firms—which are often presumed rather than investigated—scholars would have to investigate them more systematically, for example, by comparing internationalization pathways of matched pairings of large and small companies going international from the same country to the same country.

Management scholars have devoted much energy to the question of how companies enter foreign markets, yet they often neglect the actual management process of globalized business. Do FBs govern their overseas operations differently than managerial corporations do? A number of authors deal with market entry strategies; however, they do not limit themselves to how firms find and first access foreign markets. Instead, Hilger, Fear, Berghoff, and Segreto offer long-term historical perspectives that allow us to understand the actual management process of international businesses over time.

The theoretical review in this introduction, as well as several contributions, acknowledge the important role of *interpreneurship*—a term referring to firms' efforts to organize and support business revitalization just prior to or during the next generation's tenure.[79] It is related to the idea of *intrapre-*

neurship in the sense that it refers to in-house entrepreneurial activities but focuses specifically on the intergenerational ones and looks at how knowledge and skills can be passed on to future generations. Most contributions emphasize that knowledge accumulation and transfer across generations is a pivotal point in FB internationalization. Longevity, an aim often attributed to FBs, may be an advantage in this respect because it stimulates the development and testing of knowledge transfer mechanisms. These results prompt us to see further research potential concerning the combination of RBV and KBV and a more nuanced analysis of different FB strategies, such as an "open" strategy, including outside professionals and resources, or a "closed" strategy, focusing on independence and autonomy.[80] Both how families "embed" their firms in their emotional strategies and generational lifecycles and how firms can rely—or not—on family members are major variables for understanding firm strategy.[81] FBs often strive for long-term success and maybe even prioritize business survival or the family's well-being over economic gains, as several cases in this volume show. This "dynastic motive" (Casson) shapes strategies and pathways for internationalization if we acknowledge that entrepreneurs and members of entrepreneurial families are not just economic beings but "people with particular social identities and histories."[82] Such a motive, however, is not a timeless constant but rather a collective ideal that family members and other shareholders negotiate and renegotiate, about which individuals can well have different opinions, as Lubinski argues.

Attitudes towards internationalization are thus embedded in larger life concepts and emotional relationships, as Popp and Overbeck most clearly show in their contributions. We agree with cultural anthropologist Sylvia Yanagisako that family relations and sentiments are elements of all forms of capitalism, not just family capitalism; however, it seems that FBs bring emotions and sentiments more clearly into view.[83] Instead of attributing certain emotions to the family and others to the firm, thereby separating both entities—one as the emotional, irrational realm; the other as the rationalistic, calculative realm—we understand both entities as interwoven in the social practice of individual actors. Feelings about kinship and gender are important in understanding intergenerational transfers through inheritance, which, in turn, are crucial to firm development and internationalization. Popp and Gupta highlight the importance of gender, and Fear and Gupta see changing gender norms in their relationship to FB internationalization, opening up spaces for women but also allowing men to rely on their support and spend larger time periods abroad. Both Gupta and Lubinski, moreover, point out that successful FBs also serve as role models that other companies can imitate, giving examples for what sociologists DiMaggio and Powell called "mimetic institutional isomorphism."[84] In moments of change and conflict, therefore, FBs have also had to adjust their attitudes and reinvent themselves, their global business, and their "imagined community" (Anderson). The family as a social community may also affect marketing strategies, as many of the family multinationals analyzed in this volume use the family name for marketing and PR purposes, such as Bat'a, Bertelsmann, Siemens, DuPont, and others.

As indicated, many open questions remain. However, we believe that investigating changes over time and in different historical environments of the role of the family in international business is a worthwhile exercise that opens up new perspectives and generates new questions. Based on our experience, we believe that more comparative research on large and small firm internationalization may be necessary to better understand the role of families. Studies could analyze pairs of SMEs and large businesses undergoing internationalization to explore whether and how their internationalization processes are qualitatively different. It also seems that greater sensitivity to time and context can enhance research on family multinationals in at least two ways. First, historical contextualization helps scholars counteract the danger of isolating an individual firm's experience. It allows us to better understand the role families play and the ways that family, market, and political power are entwined, as well as how these interrelationships change over time. Some authors, among them Hoshino (in this volume), suggest that diversified business groups are a product of emerging economies. But do families lose their influence as countries develop? Do conglomerations dwindle while families remain? Second—and this may be particularly relevant for businesses with a dynastic self-concept—company development often follows path dependency, with past decisions limiting future choices. A family's accumulated knowledge and the mechanisms developed to pass it on may be resources that deserve more attention and can be linked more closely to business expansion processes and internationalization pathways. The twelve contributions in this volume are intended as a first step in this direction.

NOTES

1. The editors gratefully acknowledge the support of the German Historical Institute, Washington, DC, and the Gerda Henkel Foundation, Düsseldorf. We would also like to thank Patricia Sutcliffe for her diligent copy-editing and support.
2. Feldenkirchen, 1999.
3. Plakoyiannaki and Deligianni, 2009.
4. International Family Enterprise Research Academy, 2003. Cf. also Casillas, Acedo and Moreno, 2007. http://www.ffi.org/?page=GlobalDataPoints.
5. La Porta, Lopez-de-Silanes and Shleifer, 1999.
6. Jones, 2005, 5.
7. Cf. Colli, 2003. Morck, 2005. Barca and Becht, 2002. Colpan, Hikino and Lincoln, 2010.
8. Westhead and Cowling, 1998. Howorth, Rose and Hamilton, 2008.
9. Casson, 1999. Chrisman, Chua and Sharma, 2005.
10. Zachary, 2011.

11. For multiple-context definitions, see also Colli and Rose, 2007, 194. Morck, 2005.
12. Astrachan, Klein and Smyrnios, 2002. Klein, Astrachan and Smyrnios, 2005.
13. Chandler, 1977.
14. Jones and Rose, 1993. Church, 1993.
15. Lipartito and Morii, 2010.
16. Anderson and Reeb, 2003. Morck, 2005. Barca and Becht, 2002.
17. La Porta, Lopez-de-Silanes and Shleifer, 1999.
18. Colpan, Hikino and Lincoln, 2010.
19. Jones, Dimitratos, Fletcher and Young, 2009.
20. Popp, 2012. Lee, 2011.
21. Hollenstein, 2005. Kontinen and Ojala, 2010. Graves and Thomas, 2005. Fernández and Nieto, 2005. Jones, Dimitratos, Fletcher and Young, 2009. A new journal, the *International Journal of Globalisation and Small Business*, launched in 2004.
22. Dyer, 1986. Dyer, 1989. Lansberg, 1988. Lansberg, 1999. Ward, 1987. Gersick, Davis, Hampton and Lansberg, 1997.
23. Tagiuri and Davis, 1996, Original: 1982.
24. Sharma, 2004. Zahra and Sharma, 2004. Chrisman, Chua and Steier, 2003. Poutziouris, Smyrnios and Klein, 2006.
25. Kontinen and Ojala, 2010.
26. Hollenstein, 2005. Kontinen and Ojala, 2010. Graves and Thomas, 2005. Fernández and Nieto, 2005.
27. Jones and Rose, 1993. Rose, 1995. Hannah, 1983. Church, 1993.
28. Colli, 2003. Colli and Rose, 2003. Colli, Fernández Pérez and Rose, 2003. Colli and Rose, 2007. Fear, 2005. Colli, 2011.
29. Colli, 2011.
30. Kipping and Üsdiken, 2007, 112. This was recently confirmed by a special issue in *Business History* on "Business History and International Business," with an excellent introduction by Buckley, 2009a.
31. Jones and Khanna, 2006.
32. Buckley, 2009a.
33. Fear, 2001.
34. Kogut and Zander, 1993, 509–510. Kogut and Zander, 2003.
35. O'Sullivan and Graham, 2010.
36. See the introduction to Rivoli, 2009.
37. Coase, 1937.
38. Williamson, 1975.
39. Dunning, 1993.
40. For agency costs, cf. Jensen and Meckling, 1976.
41. For family firms, additional agency problems between majority and minority shareholders are of special importance. Cf. Morck, Shleifer and Vishny, 1988. Morck, 2003. Morck, 2005. Colpan and Hikino, 2010, 57–58.
42. Schulze, Lubatkin, Dino and Buchholtz, 2001. Schulze, Lubatkin and Dino, 2003. Jensen and Meckling, 1976.
43. Davis, Schoorman and Donaldson, 1997.
44. Ward, 2004.
45. Jones, 2005. James, 2006.
46. Kahn and Henderson, 1992.
47. Zahra, 2003.
48. Calof and Viviers, 1995. Prasad, 1999. For a critique, see Gankema, Snuif and Zwart, 2000.
49. Knight and Cavusgil, 2009.
50. Wilkins, 1988. Wilkins and Schröter, 1998.

51. Bell, McNaughton and Young, 2001.
52. See Gupta (in this volume). Klich and Lesser, 1998. Black, 2004.
53. Barney, 1991, 101. See also Eisenhardt and Martin, 2000.
54. Cabrera-Suárez, Saá-Pérez and García-Almeida, 2001.
55. Kogut and Zander, 2003.
56. Habbershon and Williams, 1999.
57. Hoy and Verser, 1994, 19.
58. Kocka, 1999.
59. For the separation of family and business, see also Weber, 1978. For a critical review Yanagisako, 2002, 18–22.
60. Fernández and Nieto, 2005.
61. Okoroafo, 1999.
62. Ibid.
63. Graves and Thomas, 2006.
64. Gibb Dyer, 1989. Hoy and Verser, 1994.
65. The term *reluctant internationalizers* has been used by different scholars. Vipin Gupta uses it for family businesses and questions their reluctance to internationalize. Anna Morgan-Thomas and Marian Jones use it to describe a specific kind of newly internationalizing firm. Gupta (in this volume). Morgan-Thomas and Jones, 2009.
66. Musteen, Francis and Datta, 2010. Loane and Bell, 2009. Tang, 2009. Meyer and Skak, 2002. Chetty and Blankenburg Holm, 2000. Coviello and Munro, 1997. Kahn and Henderson, 1992.
67. Colli, 1998. Porter, 1998.
68. Fernández Pérez and Rose, 2010.
69. Godley, 2001. Ampalavanar Brown, 1995.
70. Fernández Pérez and Puig, 2009. Ginalski, 2010.
71. Graves and Thomas, 2008.
72. Davidoff, Doolittle, Fink and Holden, 1999. Lubinski, 2010.
73. Davidoff, 1995.
74. Okoroafo, 1999. Fernández and Nieto, 2005. Recent evidence seems to confirm the argument by Fernández and Nieto. See the examples of Chinese successors learning abroad and bringing outside knowledge to some of the largest Chinese FBs in Fernández (in this volume), or the modernization of the automobile supplier Brose in Fear, 2012.
75. Hoy and Verser, 1994, 19.
76. Jones, 2005.
77. Ibid., 18.
78. Jones and Lubinski, 2012. Kobrak and Hansen, 2004.
79. Poza, 1989, 28.
80. Lubinski, 2011.
81. Popp, 2012.
82. Yanagisako, 2002, 5.
83. Ibid., 13.
84. DiMaggio and Powell, 1983.

Part I

Internationalization Pathways and Governance Choices

2 Are Family Firms "Reluctant Internationalizers"?

Insights from the History of Indian Family Businesses

Vipin Gupta

Several recent studies suggest that family businesses (FBs) tend to be reluctant internationalizers. A study using a longitudinal Australian database finds that FBs had lower levels of internationalization than nonfamily firms.[1] Even among internationalized firms, the extent of internationalization was lower for FBs.[2] Internationalization poses many resource challenges to them[3] because there are limits to their financial and human resources, broad-based organizational networking, and knowledge of international markets.[4] First, FBs prefer internal funding to avoid the influence and control of external stakeholders. Thus, the benefits of such external stakeholders shaping their vision and presenting them with the opportunities, resources, and confidence to internationalize are also limited. Second, FBs privilege internally trained successors and loyal, long-serving employees—groups with weak experience and confidence in dealing with new external paradigms in diverse contexts.[5] Third, FB culture tends to be characterized by limited cooperation only with other, similar FBs,[6] which restricts their knowledge base for competing internationally.[7] Finally, FBs generally strive to defend and protect their niche, which generates a problem-solving focus in internal operations.[8] Consequently, their organizational learning concerning the pursuit of new markets is also circumscribed.[9] That makes them reluctant internationalizers, since internationalization requires motivation to change and pursue new opportunities.

Though many FBs find internationalization challenging, many others internationalize successfully. Understanding how they do so contributes to international business theory. Research on international business highlights that a firm's specific ownership advantages in competing across borders are key to successful internationalization.[10] One usual FB ownership advantage is family relations—family and ethnic community members either assigned abroad or already present in foreign markets who help mobilize resources, reduce transactional uncertainty, and bring specialized knowledge for evaluating opportunities and risks and managing and governing activities.[11] These family relations tend to be a critical trigger factor in choosing specific countries and acquiring locational advantages; they offset potential liabilities related to the firm's foreignness. FBs can also uniquely leverage country-specific ownership advantages with their families' deep embedded-ness in their home country and creatively hybridize these with locational advantages acquired through cultivation of knowledge and social capital in other countries. Thus, key ownership advantages recently identified for many Indian FBs are their accumulation of skills for managing large multilocation operations across diverse Indian cultures and their "frugal engineering skills"—honed while catering to the larger part of India's income pyramid—which allow them to deliver value for money.[12]

Overseas family businesses (OFBs)—FBs set up by international migrants—have been a unique historically popular organizational solution for families seeking to do business across borders. They allow families to overcome resource challenges by utilizing the entrepreneurial skills of migrant family members, thus, reducing—or sometimes completely eliminating—other resource demands on starting such businesses. Only relatively recently have management scholars grown interested in the internationalization of FBs, although OFBs have existed for several hundred years. Therefore, a historical study of OFBs can provide useful insights into the pathways of internationalization other FBs have used.

Historically, several groups of OFBs have been prominent internationally, including Jewish, Arab, Lebanese, Chinese, and Indian ones. This chapter focuses on the historical experiences of Indian OFBs, which are of particular interest because they share several distinctive features. First, in Indian culture, going overseas was historically considered a religious taboo, making most FBs and families highly reluctant to migrate overseas or internationalize. Though Indian merchants are known to have been very active in maritime trade since ancient times, many Brahmans believed that if one ventured into the oceans—resting places for the gods (referred to as *kala pani* or black waters)—one would incur their wrath and face fierce demons.[13] In medieval times, Brahmans imposed very expensive penalties and penances on anybody who ventured into the oceans. This belief paralleled similar sea taboos practiced in the Confucian Ming dynasty of China and in Tokugawa Japan.

A second distinctive feature of Indian OFBs is the absence—not the presence—of ownership advantages as a key to which families or FBs internationalized. Specifically, families belonging to peripheral social groups (i.e. a disproportionate number of Muslims), hailing from peripheral geographical regions (primarily coastal areas), and most adversely impacted by British colonial rule were more likely to be "pushed" overseas and become OFBs. Conversely, families from more mainstream social groups with more successful businesses were less inclined to be "pulled" by overseas opportunities.

Third, India presently has the highest percentage of FBs in Asia. They account for 67 percent (663 of 983) of the total of listed companies with market capitalization of more than $50 million. They also account for half of all corporate hiring and 46.8 percent of the total market capitalization in India.[14]

These distinctive features suggest that the ownership advantage under-pinning the success of disadvantaged families was their skill at managing the space of disadvantage, which they occupied both in their older and new adopted homes. These OFBs knew how to transform the disadvantage into advantage, especially in the context of British colonial rule dismantling the incumbent business powerbases in those overseas markets and opening new opportunities for those without a privileged position. The OFBs' advantage perhaps lay in their skill at engaging with the local communities, thereby gaining deep and direct insights into people's shifting needs, as local spaces were transformed. These skills sustained their advantage as they successfully contested the dominance of Jewish and Arab businesses over the nineteenth and twentieth centuries in two distinct geographical clusters: Africa and Southeast Asia. The Indian OFBs' parallel experiences in these regions strengthen the historical methodology not only by enabling comparisons but also by identifying common factors that may have broader relevance.

The analysis begins with a review of recent literature to identify key factors in the internationalization of FBs. Then, we examine the pathways for the launch and development of Indian OFBs up to the 1980s, paying special attention to the identified factors. Thereafter, we reexamine the pathways with an eye to these firms' evolution in the 1990s. We, finally, discuss the implications of our findings for the received perception of FBs as "reluctant internationalizers" and conclude with the implications for the research and practice of FB internationalization. Our analysis shows that the received view of FBs as reluctant internationalizers is an overgeneralization; each OFB needs to be looked at in its own right to see if it was reluctant to internationalize, and it will become clear that, in many cases, FBs had particular advantages for internationalizing.

2.1   LITERATURE REVIEW: FACTORS INFLUENCING FAMILY BUSINESS INTERNATIONALIZATION

While FBs as a group have been found to be reluctant internationalizers, recent research demonstrates that some FBs are fairly active and successful in internationalization and is beginning to uncover their distinctive features.

The first strand of studies focuses on the role of open corporate governance, strategic intent, and partnerships in enabling FBs to overcome their resource challenges particularly by bringing about a change in their conservative mindset. Research in several national contexts shows how a conservative mindset, such as fear of loss of control, risk-taking, and change, discourages FB internationalization.[15] Using a sample of Finnish and French FBs, Basly suggests that this results from conservatism constraining FBs' accumulation of international competence.[16] Accordingly, recent research on Swedish firms has examined and found empirical support for this thesis that opening all levels of a firm's governance structure to nonfamily resources—by having external ownership, external board members, external CEOs, and a large top management team—helps FBs achieve internationalization not only on a greater scope (spread across nations) but also on a greater scale (penetration within nations).[17] Similarly, another study on Australian firms found that FBs whose strategic intent prioritizes growth, networking, and innovation are more likely to internationalize than those with a conservative lifestyle orientation.[18] Case studies of FBs from the emerging markets of China, Mexico, and Turkey suggest that appropriate partnerships are key: firms achieve accelerated internationalization by forming and leveraging strategic partnerships with established Multinational Enterprises (MNEs) to develop their own design, branding, and marketing capabilities; move into more profitable industry segments; and adopt strategies that turn latecomer status into a source of competitive advantage.[19]

A second strand of studies has challenged the myth of FBs as reluctant internationalizers, finding that, in many historical and national settings, they have actually demonstrated higher levels of internationalization than other firms. Historically, various Jewish, Lebanese, and Asian FBs used the help of family members and ethnic communities—by assignment through migration, or designation of already present immigrants—to effectively evaluate international opportunities and risks, mobilize resources and market knowledge, and manage and govern activities. The shared family and ethnic bonds nurtured stewardship through cultural proximity, natural honesty, and confidence-building, which reduced trust barriers inherent in cross-border commercial transactions and investments.[20] Zahra attributes FBs' stronger internationalization—identified in terms of ownership and family-member involvement—in a sample of U.S. manufacturing firms in a recent period to family members acting as good stewards of existing resources. While these findings were replicated in the Australian sample, they have not been replicated for Europe.[21] These conflicting results suggest that family ownership and involvement in a business may not be a sufficiently decisive factor in FBs' internationalization. Diaspora research studies ascribe accelerated FB internationalization to the role of the ethnic social network and "internationally spread family." Thus, one ought to consider family members' and the ethnic community's commitment and involvement in internationalization, as well.

A third strand of studies underlines the institutionalized privileges FBs enjoy in certain contexts, which help activate and support their accelerated internationalization. Institutionalized privileges include special consideration from the state, either directly or through the leading firms or other actors that it preferentially supports. Studies on China show that Chinese state-owned banks offer substantial lines of credit at subsidized interest rates to support competitive bidding by large state-owned enterprises for large infrastructural and resource projects in Africa.[22] The credit is tied to the Chinese firms' investments, which utilize Chinese inputs and skills in Africa. It also involves subcontracting the smaller parts of the integrated project to various private Chinese enterprises, which are predominantly FBs. Chinese FBs are able to use this institutional sponsorship as a test-bed for overseas investments because these investments in Africa also offer a protected space with limited competition and few behavioral regulations, similar to China.[23]

A fourth strand of studies points to the role of gender in FB internationalization. Globalization and liberalization encourage women from Indian business families to also go abroad for education.[24] These women have taken over leadership roles in a growing number of FBs and driven internationalization. A 2005 amendment to the Hindu Succession Act gave women equal succession rights. Women's leadership of flagship enterprises has allowed men from many FBs to migrate temporarily or permanently to other nations and expand their firms internationally. In other cases, women's leadership in finance and marketing has allowed men to focus on operations to more effectively defend their FBs from the onslaught of MNEs and global competition. Women, in the meantime, have creatively and patiently recast finance and marketing to develop new opportunities to launch the internationalization of their FBs. In yet other cases, women have chosen to migrate overseas after education and/or marriage and opened international marketing and development offices for their FBs.

Historical studies also point to women's role in accelerated FB internationalization in other contexts. After World War II, Femmes Chefs d'Entreprises Européennes—the European Association of Women Entrepreneurs—was important in promoting women's succession in FBs and in helping these women internationalize FBs through pan-European networking, training, and mentoring.[25] As part of a vacation-exchange program started in 1962, the daughters of women entrepreneurs spent their vacations with the families of association members in other nations to develop their international contacts and language skills. Daughters also had opportunities to do internships abroad and gain experience in their own business sector. Further, the association helped find potential cooperation partners for international business and for financing international capital investments.[26]

In sum, one can identify four key factors in accelerated FB internationalization: (1) corporate governance and strategic intent open to nonfamily resources, and their broader and international connections and partnerships with key international players; (2) family and ethnic community commitment and involvement in FB internationalization; (3) institutional privileges and direct or indirect state sponsorship; and (4) opportunities and power enjoyed by women to champion and support FB internationalization. Next, we review the history of the Indian OFBs over the nineteenth and twentieth centuries, with a particular attention to these four key factors.

2.2 INDIAN OVERSEAS FAMILY BUSINESSES (OFBs)

Indian FBs have been engaged in international trade and investments since prehistoric times.[27] Up through precolonial times, many South India–based FBs maintained trade contacts throughout Southeast Asia. Trade took place within the broader sharing of Hindu and Buddhist cultural elements, although, among the Indians, only Tamil-speaking Chettairs settled permanently in Southeast Asia.[28] In Africa, by contrast, some Gujarat (Western India)–based families have resided and conducted business since ancient times. McNeil, for instance, notes the presence of such families in Egypt as early as 500 bc,[29] and Tinker observes how locally settled Indian business families guided many early European explorers into Africa during the eighteenth century.[30]

In the middle of the nineteenth century, when the colonial era began, Indian OFBs grew rapidly. As the British were investing their colonial trade surplus in mines and plantations in Asia, Africa, and other regions, there was a great demand for labor against the backdrop of growing European opposition to slavery. The onset of the transportation and communication revolutions and the opening of the Suez Canal, thus, catalyzed large-scale migration of Indian families.[31] From 1830–1930, about 27 million people migrated overseas from India (primarily South India). Millions of Indians migrated under the indenture system to Southeast Asia, East Africa, and the West Indies to work on plantations, roads, railway lines, and ports. Muslims, a disadvantaged group, formed a disproportionate number of these migrants—half or more. Voluntary migration also occurred, mostly among impoverished peasants suffering from exorbitant land taxes, but about 5 percent of the total comprised traders who migrated—particularly from the mid-1880s onwards—to extend their FBs overseas.[32]

Indian OFBs in Africa

In Africa, the most prominent OFB founders had a limited history of business success in India and limited capital in hand. A large group of founders adopted the entrepreneurship pathway by taking up self-employment either directly or after initially acquiring relevant skills and capital through employment. Typically, those who became self-employed directly used the start-up mode, while those who initially sought employment used the acquisition mode. Groups adopting the entrepreneurship pathway were motivated by a strategic intent for a better life, self-control, and independence. Many began as start-up traders, initially specializing in selling goods to the Indian laborers as a captive ethnic market. Other founders began in the employment mode, working initially as salesmen or supervisors in stores, or doing skilled work such as tailoring, and then decided to move into their own business—often by using their savings to buy out established businesses and set up small shops selling clothing, food, and general merchandise. These parallel entry channels gave the Indian community two distinct skills: the former group honed their proficiency in doing business in Africa, while the latter group learned about Africans' needs because their workplaces catered to the locals. Gradually, both these skills fused into a distinct competitive advantage, as Markovits (1999) notes: "Thus in South Africa Indian traders increasingly specialized in selling goods to the natives, a field in which their low operating costs and knowledge of the market allowed them to make rapid inroads to the detriment of European competitors, mostly Jewish merchants. The same was true of East Africa."[33]

Another group of founders adopted the network extension pathway, building on the foothold and relationships in trade outside India that their FBs already had. Most of these hailed from a few coastal regions, primarily Gujarat and Tamil Nadu, and, secondarily, the Punjab, Sind, and Kerala. Their communities had international trading networks, many of which dated back several centuries, and most of which specialized in industry niches and had their community's interest-specific industry associations in host nations; these played an important role in their success.[34] The Bhaiband Sindworkies, who concentrated on silk and curios sales, had an established FB branch network comprising 5,000 members in 1900–1910. It extended to all major ports along the two main sea routes: India-Japan (via Sri Lanka, Singapore, Indonesia, Vietnam, China, Philippines) and Bombay-Panama (via Sudan, Egypt, Malta, and Spain, or, alternatively, via Mozambique, South Africa, and Sierra Leone). In the big Sindworkie firms, the telegraph was the main means of communication, yet the principals made regular months-long branch "inspection tours."[35]

The fusion of intraregional and interregional trading capabilities of the first two groups of start-up traders and the latter group of network extenders, respectively, endowed them with a unique competitive advantage. Some Indian OFBs developed integrative capabilities, becoming general dealers, engaging in money-lending, banking, and/or cotton or grain trade, and creating networks linking large coastal Indian wholesale houses and hundreds of small traders in Africa. They kept low overhead, offered low-cost products, and assured consumers of fair business dealings to fill the vacuum left by the fall of the Arab traders under the British Empire. They soon dominated the local retail trade, controlling it up to 70 percent, especially in the rural areas of East and South Africa.[36] In general, they reserved the top leadership roles for their family members and children. Members of their ethnic community took on less senior but supervisory roles, while native Africans occupied lower-level roles.[37] In Africa, Indian FBs thus "constituted the vital middle class, which served as the connecting link on the eastern side of the [African] continent between the African peoples and the peoples of Europe, America and Asia."[38]

In due course, network reconfiguration—punctuated by the pressures from local or international institutions—became a prominent pathway for the development of Indian OFBs. Host governments initially ignored or even welcomed Indian FBs. By the early 1950s, however, their growing prosperity, and their penetration of the commercial and residential areas monopolized by local elites, began attracting local government restrictions, including commercial and residential segregation and limitations on their rights to maintain family and business relationships in India.[39] After the 1950s, many withdrew from commerce and trading to accommodate the locals and moved into manufacturing, construction, and services, including expansion to neighboring nations.[40] While native entrepreneurs lacked the skills and contacts they needed to succeed as large enterprises in the commercial and trading space, they were still able to form microenterprises.[41] Similarly, in the 1970s, several Indian families that had been residing in Africa migrated to the United Kingdom (UK) after they were expelled from Uganda or faced expropriations in Kenya and Tanzania. Simultaneous developments in the UK spurred this remigration: the UK government made Indian immigrants' commitment to establishing a base in the UK a condition of retaining their colonial-era UK passports and induced them to invite their family members to settle there.[42]

Gender intersected with the pathways in significant ways. Women as spouses played an important role in the early development of new businesses. Patriarchal attitudes kept husbands from frequently acknowledging their wives' contributions; they either consciously moved the business away from their wives or otherwise expanded their businesses beyond their wives' life-balance needs and interests. Wives' role in FBs resurfaced when the children grew older and found their mothers to be knowledgeable and supportive mentors as the children made formative decisions on whether to join the FBs, learned about opportunities for development or change, and considered how they might prepare for such shifts.[43]

Indian OFBs in Southeast Asia

In Southeast Asia, a majority of Indian OFB founders adopted a network extension pathway by leveraging the support of the community's international business networks. These founders were predominantly from the South Indian states of Tamil Nadu and Kerala. Though family members would sometimes migrate themselves, usually nonfamily employees or partners became the managers, supported by clerks and salesmen hired from the family's home region in India.[44] Many Indian FBs initially entered Southeast Asia to expand their India-based wholesale trading businesses, which operated in textile, fancy goods, and sporting goods for a colonial and elite clientele.[45] As their products were popular among the British in India, they wished to tap the opportunity in other British colonial markets in the late nineteenth and early twentieth centuries. Moreover, colonial pressures and laws limited opportunities in India.[46] The success stories of previous migrants encouraged additional "chain migration" of business families from the same region in India, who started similar businesses using the credit and networks of the early movers.[47]

The Tamilian Nattukottai Chettiar FBs internationalized from the mid-1880s to become major financiers of commercial agriculture in Southeast Asia, using temples as clearinghouses. They were the main providers of rural credit to the farmers of Sri Lanka, Myanmar, and Malaysia, with operations extending also to Vietnam, Indonesia, Thailand, and South Africa. The biggest of the Nattukottai Chettiar financial houses had more than a hundred overseas branches, controlled from their headquarters in India.[48] Indian families were prominent in insurance, banking, and money-lending, as the only source of mid- to long-term credit. Many Chinese entrepreneurs started their businesses with loans from these families, as the colonial banks would lend only against first-rate securities.[49]

Network servicing was another salient pathway for the Indian FBs, often characterized by mergers, spinoffs, and buyouts. Many migrants who came to work as clerks and salesmen gradually founded their own businesses servicing larger Indian FB networks as vendors. Sometimes, these vendors became sufficiently wealthy to be able to partner with other co-ethnic businesses and form larger businesses. In due course, these partnerships broke into smaller firms, or resulted in one partner buying out the others.[50] Though many FBs were thus interconnected, there was no formal coordination among FBs of different Indian ethnicities. For instance, the Kutchi Memons exported rice grown by Burmese farmers with advances from Chettiar moneylenders; the Burmese farmers discounted the bills from Chettiar firms through Shikarpuri bankers, who in turn discounted them again with bankers in Bombay.[51]

Institutional forces alongside collaborations underpinned the network reconfiguration pathway. During the 1960s, growing American assistance to the Asian region gave Southeast Asian–based Indian FBs the opportunity to reconfigure their networks beyond trading and retailing.[52] For instance, some started schools teaching English and commercial subjects, and some in textile trading diversified into textile manufacturing. A classic success story is that of a bullock-cart driver rising to a position of wealth. In the late 1800s, Tamils and Sikhs in Malaysia began giving up coolie work to become bullock-cart drivers. When the road had been constructed, some traded their bullock-carts to become lorry drivers, becoming prominent transporters in the latter half of the twentieth century.[53]

Ongoing national economic development also gave locally hosted Indian FBs opportunities to secure know-how from India and other nations. Many used their intimate knowledge of local trade and markets to enter new sectors through joint ventures with Indian firms that provided capital, machinery, and technical know-how. Some formed overseas collaborations to secure technical know-how. These collaborations allowed them to diversify and enter even nontraditional areas, such as filmmaking (using local talent), shipping, furniture-making, and the dairy industry.[54] They acquired large blocks of land, department stores, hotels, wholesale businesses, and factories, and internationalized with the help of the local and global Indian diaspora.[55] Unlike the network extension pathway, the network reconfiguration pathway was driven by the availability of trusted managers who had the skills to manage new ventures successfully rather than by the intimate knowledge of a new sector.[56] In the 1970s, the network reconfiguration pathway took a different shape. Many Indian FBs in Indonesia were forced by the government to sell their local businesses and real estate at throwaway prices, some responded by reconfiguring their businesses in Singapore, which offered a more welcoming environment. In a few cases, they were able to avoid confiscation because of their collaborative relationships with local elites.

Gender again intersected with the pathways in important ways. Business-men tended to leave their wives and children in India unless they had become sufficiently successful. With success, those who had gone overseas invited additional members of their family, village, or religion to manage expansions and diversify their investments into real estate and manufacturing. After migration, wives and daughters helped in the business but were generally not recognized as being employed.[57] Moreover, women's involvement was usually limited to micro-enterprises, such as selling cooked food and spices from home or in the local market or through their children.[58]

2.3   INDUCTIVE ANALYSIS OF THE FAMILY BUSINESS INTERNATIONALIZING PATHWAYS

Four pathways are identifiable in the development of the Indian OFBs in Africa and Southeast Asia over the nineteenth and twentieth centuries:

The entrepreneurship pathway was driven by a strategic intent to improve one's life and gain a sense of self-control and independence. This pathway entailed either starting up a new enterprise—often with limited capital, presumably with some related, previously acquired skills, or purchasing an existing enterprise—often after gaining some capital and skills through employment in a related domain.

The network extension pathway was supported by the FBs' already established international footholds and relationships. This pathway required either family members or trusted employees to extend the FB into new geographies.

The network servicing pathway involved a business-to-business (B2B) opportunity to participate in the value chain of other established businesses. This pathway entailed founding a feeder business to serve other businesses in which the founder or a collaborative partner may have worked earlier as an employee. Initial collaborations eventually resulted in splits or buyouts, giving the FB new shape and form.

The network reconfiguration pathway comprised a shift of resources from one market to another, usually influenced by institutional constraints and incentives. FBs often collaborated to gain footholds and build relationships in new areas, which enabled them to shift their networks into new geographies and/or new sectors.

Gender intersected with these pathways. Even in a patriarchal culture centered around men as the primary business leaders, women offered a helping hand, supported the family and the children, and/or helped open new network opportunities in unchartered and unexplored areas.

Each of the four pathways contributed to the Indian OFBs' evolution. The entrepreneurship and network extension pathways were formative in their establishment. The former helped build host country–specific and intraregional trading capabilities, while the latter augmented home country and interregional trading capabilities. The network servicing pathway was more normative as it deepened and broadened various OFBs operating capabilities across different parts of the value chain, helping to create new competitive norms. Finally, the network reconfiguration pathway was transformative, helping to alter FBs' capabilities in light of new opportunities or constraints presented by the institutional forces. Women and collaborations played significant roles in helping FBs seize new opportunities or manage constraints.

The four pathways were neither independent nor linear. Instead, they coalesced to shape the competitive advantage of the OFBs, individually and as a loosely connected group. Network research underlines the significance of "weak ties" in the competitive advantage compared to "strong ties" within a particular group.[59] Weak ties offer access to distinct resources and opportunities that cohesive networks with strong ties tend to withhold access to. In this way, entrepreneurs gained an edge in intraregional trade because they were closer to the network extenders who operated interregional trading networks in complementary domains. Similarly, network extenders were able to expand their interregional trading networks because they had loose ties to entrepreneurs who were acquiring deep intraregional connections. The value chain networks of each of these groups had plenty of gaps that those taking the network servicing pathway rapidly filled. Finally, FBs that were able to connect these resources within the various institutionally mediated constraints and opportunities generated transformative capabilities to successfully move into new domains that were not necessarily related to the initial Indian OFB networks.

2.4 VALIDATING INDUCTIVE ANALYSIS WITH INDIAN OFBs' MORE RECENT HISTORY

Successor education was the predominant theme in Indian OFBs' experience in the 1990s. *The power of education, and not the force of institutions, became the primary driver of the network reconfiguration pathway for their development.* In response to the changed local and global environments, many Indian business families sent their children to UK or Western-style local universities for higher education.[60] Enhanced wealth and changing social attitudes made similar educational opportunities available to daughters also, so that many daughters were also prepared for significant leadership roles in their FBs.[61]

These educational paths made it essential for nonfamily senior managers to get involved in strategic decisions for several reasons, First, family members spending time becoming educated were not available to work in their families' firms. Moreover, potential successors, when they returned from their educational sojourns, lacked business and firm-specific experience. Thus, nonfamily managers helped make strategic decisions involving the entry and roles of potential successors to smooth transitions and allow for experience-sharing.[62]

Having spent more of their formative time on education in multi-ethnic settings rather than socializing with the family within ethnic conclaves, the new leaders had fewer emotional bonds with the co-ethnic community. They were more willing to reward locals with senior management positions for their loyalty, hire consulting firms, and build connections with various organized lobbies, which helped them adopt some formalized FB management methods. A few Indian FBs, such as Universal Print Group in South Africa, even embraced missions to empower less privileged indigenous communities through employment and vendor and distributor partnerships. The new young, educated leaders revolutionized the management of their FBs by introducing formal frameworks for regulating family members' role in the business; allowing access to external human capital, private equity and debt, and public equity; and facilitating acquisitions and organic growth. Those who failed to do so, such as Damjee Jewellers and Mistry's/Dash Supermarket, consequently suffered erosion in their business interests.[63]

Another salient feature of Indian OFBs that emerged in the 1990s was women taking on more central roles. A significant number of educated Indians, including those from the business families that had settled in Africa and Southeast Asia, began migrating to North America. Several gained employment in the retail and hospitality sectors, such as gas stations, motels, fast food franchises, restaurants, and jewelry stores, often owned by South Asian families who had migrated there in previous generations. As they accumulated experience, they created profit-sharing partnerships with their employers to set up new units with the option of buying out their former employer's share. Typically, wives worked with these founders as a copreneurial team running all aspects of business; sometimes, parents or siblings also joined in as the business grew. With still further expansion, such FBs often hired help and women frequently withdrew from the primary business, although they kept an eye out for any new business opportunities. Once women established new businesses, their husbands either sold off the earlier businesses—usually to siblings or co-ethnic members—or brought in their older children as successors to lead further growth.

Finally, creating cross-border business ties with India and other home nations was a significant theme for network extension and network servicing pathways. After completing their higher education, children of the North America–based business families tended to first work in outside professional organizations before joining the FB to help take on different opportunities.[64] Some children even ventured to set up their own businesses in the high-tech sector, using the help of co-ethnic ties formed through professional and social activities.[65] Often, these ventures were born-global firms as their partnerships, offices, and other support services were situated in India or other home nations in Africa or Southeast Asia.

2.5   DISCUSSION

The experiences of the Indian OFBs challenge the notion of FBs as reluctant internationalizers. Many early Indian OFBs faced significant resource challenges, including limited financial and human resources, lack of broad-based organizational networks, and limited knowledge of international markets. While these resource challenges did influence the pathways for their start-up and development, they did not discourage specific Indian families from starting and growing overseas operations.

One of the unique features of FBs is commitment to local communities, where the family also has a stake, and stakeholders. When Indian FBs internationalized by sending either employees or family members abroad, they also transferred unique capabilities to engage with the new local communities and stakeholders. Similarly, when family members migrated on their own, they started engaging with local communities and stakeholders, whether as self-starting entrepreneurs or employees. Initially, their networks tended to be within the same ethnic community. Gradually, though, other ethnic businesses that originated in India and other local businesses, vendors, and customer discovered the unique capabilities of these OFBs. Interactions with these different groups deepened and broadened the OFBs' knowledge of the market, enhancing the competitive advantage of all the linked FBs.

Institutions played an important role in shaping the strategic intent of the OFBs. Various institutional incentives or constraints sometimes spurred the OFBs to drastically shift entire networks. For example, entire families might move to new countries with new businesses. OFBs were less likely to embrace other drastic changes, not because they avoided change, but perhaps because they did not know how to go about pursuing them. Since the 1990s, international education has allowed OFB successors to bring new approaches to reconfiguring networks and internationalizing. With potential successors spending more time getting educated, nonfamily employees had greater opportunities to participate in firms, both when successors were away for their education and when they returned and were ready to learn the FB.

Maintaining the integrity of internal operations oriented towards their immediate community and stakeholders and the dynamism of external initiatives directed towards opening new markets and internationalization was also a challenge for these OFBs. Nonfamily businesses facing this challenge are better able to prioritize the latter—even if it implies dramatic internal restructuring and shifts in internal competencies and community. For FBs, however, the internal operations founded on a deep engagement with local communities and stakeholders are an integral source of perceived competitive advantage. To pursue change and accelerated internationalization, OFBs needed pathways that would strengthen, not weaken or replace, their operational competencies.

Indian OFBs pursued several such pathways. Collaborations with members of the co-ethnic community alleviated the resource challenges of extending into new markets. OFBs often pursued this network extension pathway by temporarily assigning key employees or family members abroad, hiring new employees from the co-ethnic community to lead or run overseas assignments, or having some family members migrate to other nations. Similarly, cross-border ties with the home nation allowed some OFBs to deepen their advantages and become more valuable partners within their broader value chain networks.

Finally, educating female family members facilitated the entrepreneurship pathway for internationalization in various ways. Men could more confidently manage internationalization by migrating to new markets and working with their spouses as copreneurial teams. Educated women could support internationalization by taking on the external roles of creative marketing and financing, as well as new business opportunity development, while men focused on core internal operations. The changing perceptions of core competencies and core businesses among such OFBs are also interesting. Often, women's success in externally oriented activities led men to sell off their earlier businesses rather than defend their entrenched niches, and to refocus their energies on new opportunities the women had opened up. These new opportunities were frequently large enough to require the involvement of additional extended family members to exploit them fully. In other words, the OFBs' key challenge does not appear to have been a lack of human resources but rather the lack of viable opportunities linked to their current competencies. Since FBs were an important lifeline for the survival and well-being of the family, which included planning for the children's future, FB owners may have been reluctant to pursue opportunities not immediately related to their current operations. Thus, they may have seemed to be protecting and defending their entrenched niches. Educated women, however, demonstrated how families' competencies were sufficient at their core to successfully operate in new domains, thereby facilitating the reconfiguration, growth, and/or internationalization of their FBs.

2.6 CONCLUSIONS

This historical analysis complements the major empirical findings in FB research that emphasize FBs' culture of conservatism and the importance of open strategic intent and corporate governance in their successful internationalization. Specifically, it suggests that another factor, their ability to engage deeply with their local communities and stakeholders, also constitutes a key ownership advantage when they seek to internationalize. One of FB owners' key motivations is to support their families' well-being and to preserve its wealth and investment in the FB. Most FBs seek to defend their incumbent niches and are reluctant to voluntarily embrace major change or reconfiguration because their owners have focused stakes in the business. To make such dramatic changes, therefore, they find it essential to have demonstrable capabilities and confidence for succeeding in a new domain or internationally.

There are several ways FBs may discover and develop demonstrable capabilities, and families may offer support. Families are likely to be more confident of their FB's capabilities if they see other co-ethnic families with similar business experiences operating internationally who are willing to collaborate, as in the network extension pathway. Similarly, if some family members are educated overseas or are willing to migrate temporarily, they can start up new operations either directly or after accumulating some experiences in local businesses, as in the entrepreneurship pathway. The government and other facilitating institutions can also help to enable cross-border connections and/or visitations, especially when there may be benefits to having FBs move into emerging domains of advantage of high national priority, as in the network reconfiguration or network servicing pathways. Finally, women's education and participation can be powerful catalysts for FB change and internationalization. Women can bring new depth and breadth to FBs' existing capabilities, take existing capabilities in new creative directions, and discover new ones to complement or even replace the old. The result is a better future for both the FB and the family, whether or not the family continues to own and manage the prior business.

In sum, prior research that has focused on FB internationalization has assumed that families are conservative and inhibit such internationalization. The present research on Indian OFBs suggests that both the families and their businesses need to be studied together. A family's deep engagement with local communities, its ethnic relationships and partnerships, institutional priorities, successor education, and gender dynamics within the family are all important factors in an FB's ability to internationalize. Adding these factors demonstrates that families and their businesses may have more ownership advantages and capabilities for accelerated internationalization than many FB managers and research scholars perceive.

NOTES

1. Graves and Thomas, 2008.
2. Ibid.
3. Tsang, 2001.
4. Basly, 2007. Naldi and Nordqvist, 2009.
5. Basly, 2007.
6. Gray, 1997.

7. Basly, 2007.
8. Gallo and Sveen, 1991.
9. Basly, 2007.
10. Dunning, 1997.
11. Fan, 1998. Basly, 2007.
12. Kumar, 2008.
13. This belief was recorded in *Manu Smriti* (Chapter 3, verse 158, dated ca. 200 bce).
14. "Asian Family Business Basket," *Research Report*, ed. *Credit Suisse*, November 4, 2011.
15. Casillas and Acedo, 2005. Fernández and Nieto, 2005. Gallo and Sveen, 1991.
16. Basly, 2007.
17. Naldi and Nordqvist, 2009.
18. Graves and Thomas, 2008.
19. Bonaglia, Goldstein and Mathews, 2007.
20. Basly, 2007.
21. Zahra, S. (2003). International Expansion of US Manufacturing Family Business: the Effect of Ownership and Involvement. Journal of Business Venturing, 18(4), 495-503.
22. Kaplinsky and Morris, 2009.
23. Hilsum, 2005.
24. See knowledge@wharton, *New 'Right-Hand Men': The Growing Role of Women in Indian Family Business*, November 5. Retrieved from knowledge.wharton.upenn.edu/india/article.cfm?articleid=4424.
25. Eifert, 2006.
26. Ibid.
27. Markovits, 1999.
28. Jayaram, 2004.
29. McNeil, 1963.
30. Tinker, 1977.
31. Jayaram, 2004.
32. Klein, 1986. Markovits, 1999.
33. Markovits, 1999, 90.
34. Ibid.
35. Ibid.
36. Hiralal, 2001.
37. Janjuha-Jivraj, 2006.
38. Patel, 1997, 9.
39. Hiralal, 2001.
40. Himbara, 1994.
41. Janjuha-Jivraj, 2006.
42. Ibid.
43. Ibid.
44. Markovits, 1999, 86.
45. Mani, 2006a. Mani, 2006b.
46. Markovits, 1999, 86.
47. Ibid., 90.
48. Ibid.
49. Sandhu, 2006.
50. Mani, 2006a.
51. Markovits, 1999.
52. Chanda, 2006.
53. *Sikh Review 51*, nos. 595–600, Sikh Cultural Center, Calcutta, 2003.

54. Mani, 2006a.
55. Arkin, 1981. Ginwala, 1977.
56. Gidoomal, 1997.
57. Markovits, 1999.
58. Mani, 2006a.
59. Granovetter, 1973.
60. Hiralal, 2001.
61. Janjuha-Jivraj, 2006.
62. Ibid., 37.
63. Hiralal, 2001.
64. Janjuha-Jivraj, 2006.
65. D. Clark, "South Asian 'Angels' Reap Riches, Spread Wealth in Silicon Valley," *Wall Street Journal* (Eastern Edition), p. B1, May 2, 2000.

3 A Family Multinational's Quest for Unity
Siemens's Early Business in India, 1847–1914

Christina Lubinski

Multinational companies face the issues of bridging space and time and of controlling agents at great distance. Problems of communication make this task challenging even today, yet during the first rise of globalization in the decades before World War I, these issues were particularly pressing as the available technology made communication slow, and, thus, control difficult.

Based on the example of the German electrical company Siemens from its foundation in 1847 to World War I, I will show that ownership and kinship relations were crucial in dealing with these issues, shaping internationalization pathways, strategies, and organizational structures. The corporate governance choices that allowed Siemens to go global cannot be understood without taking a close look at the kinship relations. The company's founder aimed to create a lasting company that would provide income for himself, his family, and future generations. He was fully committed to his "dynastic" vision,[1] which had a strong impact on the internationalization pathway he advocated. By placing his brothers and other relatives in strategic positions in different countries, he hoped to profit from social ties, intimate trust-based relationships, and open lines of communication, thus—in modern management parlance—reducing agency cost.[2] When few modern communication and mobility technologies were available or in their infancy, this was a very reasonable—and perhaps indispensable—business strategy.

However, a dynastic ambition is not a timeless constant but a negotiated social construct that is reinterpreted, reinforced, or put to rest by a group of individuals with differing ideals and understandings of it. A close look at the family dynamics reveals that the family and firm continually debated and contested the founder's vision. Based on primary sources, in particular, the frequent letters between Werner Siemens and his brothers, I explain how the first and second generation discussed and kept alive the dynastic ambition of this early family multinational. The frequent disputes over Siemens's early business with India concerning whether they were striving for a unified global family business and, if so, what shape it should take, are especially revealing of the family dynamics.

While Werner Siemens saw the Siemens family as a dynastic transgenerational community and the international business as *one global entity*, his brothers and other stakeholders held different views. I will contextualize the dynastic vision as an act of sense-making—individual and subject to change over time—that continually resulted from sociocultural negotiations. It was individual because different members of the Siemens family and company stakeholders held different opinions. It changed over time as these people changed their minds due to external conditions or changing personal preferences. While Werner believed in the family multinational as a dynastic transgenerational community, his brother William advocated separating the multinational into several smaller companies, each independently managed by a family member, and his second brother Carl argued that whatever strategy generated the most profits was best. Thus, the sources show that questions related to centralization versus decentralization regularly arose, such as how much power should be removed from the center and how independent affiliates of the firm and individual family members should be.

Finding the right balance between centralization and decentralization remains a hot topic for today's multinationals.[3] There is no "one-size-fits-all" solution. For most of the nineteenth century, doing business in remote corners of the world—in the absence of widely available communication and transport technologies—essentially required a decentralized organization. The East India Company and the J.P. Morgan and Rothschild banking houses exemplify businesses with a decentralized organization. With the major inventions in communication technologies (telegraph, telephone) in the late nineteenth and early twentieth centuries, however, more centralized business forms became popular.[4] This case study reflects a major dispute on this issue, which may have been typical for multinationals in that time period. It observes an oscillation between centralization and decentralization and shows that the specific balance depended on both the historical environment and the negotiations between organizational actors from within and outside the family.

My argument is structured in three steps. I first discuss how the Siemens family helped solve some of the most urgent problems of the early multinational, focusing on Siemens's overseas business with India. One of its first big transnational projects was the Indo-European Telegraph Line constructed between 1867–1870, which brought tensions over unity versus decentralization to the fore. Second, I argue that the Siemens family added a significance to the work and helped create a collective identity and community during the debates over strategy. This act of sense-making, however, also subordinated various individual interests to the collective idea. Third, I discuss the family tensions that arose as the multinational evolved—some of which even survived into the second generation of managers comprising both Siemens family members and externally hired professionals.

3.1   THE EMERGENCE OF A FAMILY MULTINATIONAL

Siemens was one of the earliest and best-known family multinationals in Germany. In its start-up phase, it successfully exploited telegraphic communication technologies in Germany and abroad. Founder Werner Siemens (1816–1892) was born into a highly educated upper-middle-class family living in relatively humble economic conditions: his father practiced agriculture on a leased estate. Werner applied to the Prussian Army in 1834, studied mathematics, physics, and chemistry during the following years, and attended lectures at Berlin University.[5]

In 1839 and 1840, respectively, Werner's father and mother died, so that he became the head of the household by age 23, responsible for six underage siblings. He supported them financially and advised them in their career choices. His brother Wilhelm (1823–1883) visited a commercial school in Magdeburg, where Werner was stationed at the time. Together, Werner and Wilhelm engaged in scientific studies, and Werner was granted his first patent for electrolytic plating with silver and gold in 1842.[6] Wilhelm then traveled to England in 1843 and patented the process for Britain and its overseas colonies.[7] One year later, Wilhelm relocated permanently to Great Britain, changing his name to William, although he continued to work with Werner.

In Germany, Werner built on his success as an inventor. Thanks to his previous achievements, the Prussian Army tasked him with researching new telegraphic communication technologies, which were then on the verge of becoming commercial. The history of the telegraph reputedly began when Frenchman Claude Chappé coined the term (from the Greek roots for "far writer") in 1791. The first electric transmission was performed by Samuel Thomas von Sömmerring in 1809 in Munich, Germany.[8] In 1832, Michael Faraday experimented with electromagnetic induction, and the inventors Wilhelm Weber and Carl Friedrich Gauss used the procedure for message transmission. Further progress was made in Great Britain, where William Cooke and Charles Wheatstone patented the first pointer telegraph in 1837. It was not before the 1840s, however, that the first commercial line was launched in Europe. Around the same time, in 1838, Samuel Morse constructed his single-line telegraph in the United States, where the telegraphic industry grew rapidly.[9] By 1858, a transatlantic cable already connected the United States and Britain. Despite initial success, however, frequent failures resulted from poor insulation and cables being destroyed by the weather, animals, or human beings.

Werner devised a number of new products in this and related fields, receiving, among other things, a patent for major improvements to the Wheatstone needle telegraph. To better exploit the inventions commercially, he started cooperating with engineer Johann Georg Halske (1814–1890) in 1845. In 1847, Werner Siemens and Georg Halske established the "Telegraphen-Bauanstalt von Siemens & Halske" (hereafter, S&H) for pointer telegraphs in Berlin. Werner's cousin, Johann Georg Siemens (1839–1901), made a significant investment in the business, receiving 20 percent of the profits over the following six years in return.[10] The two men ran the company as a partnership and split the remaining profits equally. In 1848, S&H landed its first big contract with the Prussian military commission to build a telegraph line between Frankfurt, the meeting place of the newly elected German National Assembly, and Berlin. This highly symbolic project, which S&H successfully finished, put the start-up company on the map of the German communications industry.

In many respects, S&H was "born global," pursuing international ambitions early on. Instead of first building a stable domestic position and then expanding internationally in gradual and sequential stages, as the literature would predict, S&H started internationalizing from the beginning, entering relatively distant markets and multiple countries at once.[11] The company sold its main products, telegraph equipment, principally to central authorities and administrative bodies. Although it led the German domestic market, this was naturally limited. It quickly became obvious that it could only achieve growth by expanding beyond Germany's borders. However, there were considerable obstacles to building and managing a multinational in the mid-nineteenth century.[12] Finding and controlling senior staff was particularly challenging: First, the tasks that managers abroad had to cope with were hard to standardize and changed rapidly. Siemens's agents abroad, for example, needed the power to negotiate with public authorities, who were the company's most important customers. Second, there was no organized market for managerial staff at this time, which made recruiting particularly difficult. Third, as communication and transport were slow and often unreliable, it was hard to supervise far-away agents. Inevitably, a certain degree of decentralization of responsibility and control emerged.

To overcome these obstacles, Siemens relied heavily on the cohesion and loyalty of the family. As early as the 1850s, Werner Siemens and his brothers established a multinational business based on three pillars: the main company of S&H in Berlin headed by Werner Siemens and Georg Halske, a branch in London managed by Werner's brother William, and a branch in St. Petersburg, Russia, headed by a third brother Carl.[13] Thereafter, William and Carl acted as agents for S&H, selling the inventions of the German mother company abroad. The contract with William of March 1850 stipulated that S&H receive two-thirds of the profits and William one-third.[14]

Allowing Siemens to expand worldwide, this organizational structure had several advantages. Each of the three brothers had the power and—as a member of the Siemens family—symbolic capital to interact with the authorities within his reach. Each of them built a social network in his sphere of influence. Yet the pull of the geographical distance between the three branches was balanced by family loyalty and the close contact and intimate communication among the three brothers, mainly through letters. In this first stage of the firm's development, the unity of the nuclear family that formed the basis for the development of dynastic ambitions guaranteed the unity of the multinational.

Frequent correspondence between Werner, Carl, and William (and occasionally other family members)—in which business and personal matters were interwoven—ensured that the firm was managed in a noncontradictory manner.[15] The letters show that in this first stage, the brothers were emotionally close and had privileged, intimate, and open lines of communication that facilitated the running of the multinational based on family trust. This structure enabled S&H early on to be quite profitable abroad, for example, in Russia where it laid a cable between Oranienbaum and Kronstadt and set up a state telegraph network in the European part of the empire. It was also commissioned to do the maintenance of the Russian lines, which provided continuous income for Siemens. Until the early 1860s, the Russian business exceeded in both sales and staff figures the business in Germany, which did not experience continuous growth until the late 1860s.[16]

3.2   ACCESSING INDIA

One of the biggest and most symbolic projects in Siemens's start-up phase was the construction of an Indo-European telegraph line between Calcutta and London. A constant point of contention between the brothers, this India project mirrors the issues that family members and external managers debated regarding the multinational's structure and operations. In 1856, Siemens first considered doing business in India. William Siemens delivered equipment for the telegraph line from Bombay to Calcutta to the director of the Anglo-Indian Telegraph, William O'Shaughnessy (1809–1889), who had been building an extensive telegraph network in India since 1839. His work contributed to the rapid increase in Indian telegraph miles from 82 in 1852 to more than 10,000 in 1860.[17]

While the domestic network in India grew, the connection to Europe was rattled with difficulties. Since 1843, gutta-percha, a natural plastic formed from the sap of a Malayan tree, had been used to coat the cables, significantly improving the quality of submarine telegraphy. In July 1854, the brothers John Watkins and Jakob Brett, who had laid the first cable across the English Channel in 1850, suggested a telegraph line between England and its colonies via France and North Africa. However, the cables could not be laid successfully despite repeated attempts.[18]

Siemens was not a cable manufacturing company, so it started cooperating in 1854 with an expert British cable company, R. S. Newall & Co. based in Gateshead. In 1856, Werner and William met with Newall's managers in Berlin to discuss the business in England and the overseas colonies.[19] Werner Siemens took part in Newall's deep-sea expedition of 1857 and assisted in laying a cable from Bona to Cagliari in Sardinia.[20] Further expeditions were supported by other Siemens employees. In 1858, Siemens's London business was turned into an independent subsidiary with William as a partner and Newall & Co. as an investor.[21] Simultaneously, S&H and R. S. Newall &

Co. made a five-year cooperation agreement about which Werner confidently wrote: "officially united with N.[ewall] we are a power that cannot be easily dissolved or overtaken."[22]

Political events pushed the India telegraph line high on Great Britain's political agenda. On 10 May 1857, Indian soldiers serving in the British East India Company's army, so-called *sepoys*, mutinied, threatening the company's power. The rebellion was contained on 20 June 1858. In its aftermath, the Government of India Act transferred power from the East India Company to the India Office, a department of state, making the Queen of England the highest political authority in India.[23] The telegraph had been vital for the containment of the rebellion as it allowed for rapid message transmission and helped the British to move their troops quickly and efficiently.[24] Shortly after the uprising, historian Edward Nolan argued that the telegraph "was of more importance than the presence in India of 10,000 additional soldiers."[25]

On 8 July 1858, a peace treaty was signed and the rebellion ended. The last rebels were defeated in Gwalior on 20 June 1858. By 1859, rebel leaders Bakht Khan and Nana Sahib had either been slain or had fled.

In autumn 1859, Newall went on an expedition to India to extend its cables from Aden to Karachi. Thirteen Siemens employees, among them Werner Siemens, participated, gaining experience with the geographical and climatic conditions.[26] The so-called Red Sea Cable that resulted delivered seven to eight words per minute. However, when it was connected to the Indian network, there were frequent disturbances. Insufficient insulation allowed the cables to rust and deteriorate rapidly. Newall's image as a cable manufacturer and expert for submarine cables was badly damaged: "We cannot get a telegraph to India by British enterprise (thanks to official folly and the blunders of manufacturers)," remarked *Mechanics Magazine* in 1860.[27] Siemens ended its cooperation with Newall at the end of that year, and Newall withdrew its capital investment from British Siemens. Despite William Siemens's marriage to Anna Gordon, the sister of Newall's partner, the partnership between the two firms was dissolved. In 1861, the "Telegraph to India Company," which tried to repair the damaged lines, was founded. Experts, however, quickly agreed that only a landline could guarantee reliable service.

During the 1860s, Siemens's British operations suffered losses from failed cable expeditions in the Mediterranean Sea. Consequently, Werner Siemens's partner, Georg Halske, withdrew his partnership, considering the business too risky.[28] Werner, conversely, regarded the London business as vital to the survival of the family multinational. Without London, he believed, Siemens would "disappear from the world market" and would not be able to exploit the "asset" of its "telegraphic renown."[29] William reinforced this perspective by informing his brother that the good business with India allowed him to remain "economically flexible."[30] Although Werner saw great potential in the London business, he was also concerned whether William would be able to manage the business by himself.[31]

Around the same time, Siemens took on one of its biggest and most symbolic projects: laying a telegraph line from London to Calcutta, the planning for which began as early as 1856.[32] In a published business proposal, Siemens called for investors and highlighted the location advantages of India. It argued that India, with its enormous population and growing production, was one of the largest markets in the world and, moreover, a gateway for Europeans to the large markets of China, Japan, and Australia. Furthermore, it explained that a direct line to India was actually more important than the already existing transatlantic line to the United States. India had a population of 136 million on 44,000 square miles, whereas the United States only counted 32 million people on 133,000 square miles. Finally, letters from London usually took eleven days to New York and about thirty to Calcutta.[33] Even a telegram on the existing lines between London and Karachi typically took four days and sometimes as many as thirteen.[34] As different companies had previously tried to build a new line, it is not surprising that many were skeptical about the Siemens project, the "Indo." "We dare not anticipate much benefit from Mr. Siemens' line," announced the editor of the *Times of India* on 26 November 1869.[35] Werner Siemens, by contrast, was excited "to show what telegraphy can achieve."[36]

The success of the Indo not only depended on technical savvy but also on diplomatic maneuvers because different authorities had to grant permission for it to be built. In this, the size and geographical distribution of the Siemens family helped the multinational achieve its goal. Carl in St. Petersburg, William in London, and Werner in Berlin worked on the different permissions and used their respective contacts with local authorities. Georg Siemens, the son of Werner's cousin, traveled to Persia to obtain necessary permissions there.[37] Between 1867 and 1870, the Indo line was built from England via Russia and Persia to the British submarine cable in the Persian Gulf to India. It was completed in April 1870 and was in use until 1931.[38] At the same time, British competitors invested in a second connection from England to Gibraltar, Malta, and Alexandria, and from Suez to Aden and Bombay. Between these two lines, Britain and India had, by 1870, a reliable telegraphic connection that transmitted messages in about five hours.[39] Combined with the opening of the Suez Canal the previous year, which reduced the travel time from Europe to India by half, this line significantly improved English and European business with India.[40]

3.3   UNITY OR DECENTRALIZATION? TENSIONS IN THE FAMILY MULTINATIONAL

Only the cooperation of the three brothers across countries for permissions (along with other members of the extended family) made the big multinational project of an Indo-European telegraph line possible. However, this project also generated considerable conflicts between William, Carl, and

Werner. In essence, the tensions arose because they held different views of the relationship between the family and the business. While William wanted to separate the Berlin and the London business and Carl opted to maximize profits by whatever means necessary, Werner's main goal was "to found a lasting firm, which perhaps one day, under the leadership of our boys, could become a world firm like Rothschild, etc., and bring our name to the notice of the world." The eldest clearly prioritized the family firm's survival, also pointing out that "[t]he individual must be willing to accept personal sacrifice for this great plan, if he thinks it a good one."[41]

When the first contract between the three brothers ended in 1863, William pressured his brothers to separate the London business from Berlin, which would give him a more independent and powerful position. The London-based engineer and nonfamily manager Ludwig Loeffler also lobbied for the separation.[42] While William, who had become a British citizen in 1859, considered England a grand colonial power entitled to doing business overseas, Werner believed that the German and British companies could only be "completely free or completely united,"[43] though if they were united, they ought to cooperate in a brotherly manner and trust each other completely. However, Werner argued, if they decided to separate, Berlin could unreservedly and freely serve the world market so that the companies would come into competition.[44] Up to that point, Werner explained, the Berlin company had refrained from competing with Siemens London in the overseas business: "Not even to India, despite articulated requests, have we made offers because we did not want to damage the London business."[45] Although it was not a contractually fixed agreement between the brothers that London take on the overseas business, it was clearly a long-standing business practice. "The business here [in Germany] cannot see the British business as anything other than a part of its own body, because it would otherwise be forced to be a fierce competitor for it."[46]

Instead of separating the companies, Werner suggested that they start a new company with three relatively independent firms in Berlin, St. Petersburg, and London. Each brother would manage the day-to-day business independently and only consult with the others on big and risky ventures. He explained the "guiding principle" behind this proposition as founding "a lasting company."[47] Werner had clearly ascertained that the company could not survive without William's activities in London and close cooperation between the brothers. In 1867, the three brothers met in Berlin to discuss the company's future and agreed to Werner's proposal. British Siemens was renamed "Siemens Brothers" under William's management in 1865.[48] In the following years, several big projects occupied the brothers, including the construction of the Indo line until 1870 and of six transatlantic cables between 1874 and 1884. These left little time for debates about general business strategy but gave Siemens a glorious reputation worldwide.[49]

In December 1880, at the peak of its success, the London business was transformed into a limited company. The engineer Loeffler became a partner

Table 3.1   Profit Distribution in the Siemens Family

	Werner	William	Carl	Total
Berlin	50%	25%	25%	100%
London	35%	45%	20%	100%
Petersburg	35%	20%	45%	100%

Source: SAA Lm 910 *Dir. i. R. Wolfram Eitel, Die historische Entwicklung des Übersee-Geschäftes des Hauses Siemens und seine Organisation, 1957/58*, 21.

with a small percentage. The brothers signed a new contract stipulating that the new Siemens Brothers & Co. Ltd. and the German S&H would not compete against each other "as far as practicable."[50] Each brother was a partner in all three companies, with profits distributed among them according to Table 3.1.

While Werner hoped to achieve unity with this structure, conflict with the London business, headed by William and Loeffler, continued. Both argued that the overseas business had been and continued to be the exclusive business of the London firm.[51] In 1879, Werner wrote William that it was impossible to stay out of the world market because competitors were taking over in many parts of the world. He observed that other German companies were exporting their machines to India, Japan, and China. "Your technical power is not sufficient to distribute our diverse products all over the extra-European world, and it is a loss in total if we stand in each other's way."[52] However, Werner agreed to let London deal with the British colonies, first and foremost India, if William agreed to let Berlin engage in business with other overseas countries.

Before they could reach a compromise, William died unexpectedly in 1883, and the Siemens's family influence on the London business decreased. Right after William's death, Werner and Carl were forced to offer some of his shares to Loeffler, whom they depended on to continue the business. Over time, Loeffler managed to increase his percentage to one-fourth of the shares, garnering considerable influence.

The conflict between the London and Berlin firms mirrors the changes in the world economy at the time. During the last third of the nineteenth century, an era of German nationalism, the German state and German entrepreneurs started expanding into different parts of the world, and Germany acquired colonies in Africa.[53] In the economic sphere, German traders and entrepreneurs increasingly competed with their British counterparts. As Werner explained to Loeffler in 1884: "Once England governed the overseas world business almost exclusively, and the economies of other countries, namely Germany, could only participate by English mediation. . . . Now the world looks completely different! . . . [T]he English industry has to fiercely compete with foreign industries all over the world."[54]

However, Loeffler continued to claim Siemens London should serve the whole world, except for Germany, Austria, and Russia. As the branch had previously lost important business with British crown agents in India because of higher prices, this claim was sharply criticized.[55] Only crown agencies could purchase goods for government use within the colonies of the empire, so this represented a considerable loss for the British company. Although Siemens Berlin could manufacture at lower cost, London insisted on having exclusive rights in India. Werner concluded: "It is the old English arrogance *[Übermut]* that Bismarck will hopefully manage to break."[56]

In the changing world economy and after heated debates, both companies agreed to free each other from their previous arrangement concerning overseas business in October 1885. Werner voluntarily refrained from exporting to British colonies and France, although he wanted acknowledgment that "[t]he [German] business would be significantly better if we could freely export to England, America, and the overseas countries. . . ."[57] The London firm profited from the new agreement. While 1886 was still a bad year, 1887 and 1888 were reasonably good, and 1889 was quite successful with profits of over £100,000 and a dividend of 22.5 percent.[58]

In 1887, at age 71, Werner once again reminded Carl of his larger goal: "Ever since adolescence I have dreamt about the foundation of a world business à la Fugger, which brings worldwide power and prestige not only to me but also my offspring."[59] The Fuggers were a large and prominent German business family during the fifteenth and sixteenth centuries whose worldwide activities as bankers and venture capitalists had become legendary. Evoking this image, Werner argued: "I understand the business only secondly as a financial investment. It is for me more an empire, which I founded and which I want to pass on undiminished to my offspring."[60]

After William's death, Werner tried to convince Carl that their different opinions were a matter of perspective: "You have always attached greater importance to material goods than I, whereas I have chased after phantoms and ideas. . . . You look at the business with the eye of a capital investor, whereas I see it from the perspective of a 'spiritual worker' *[geistigen Arbeiters]*."[61] Werner devoted his "spiritual work" to creating a lasting family multinational, his grand plan and legacy. Because both Carl and Werner reaped the profits of the London business, Carl was not concerned about London having exclusive rights to parts of the world as long as the firm's overall performance was good. Werner, in contrast, focused primarily on the future and longevity of the family business, not its day-to-day profits. To avoid further conflicts with Loeffler, the brothers eventually considered selling him the London business. However, Loeffler requested that Siemens once and for all forgo its rights to exporting overseas. While Carl was willing to consider it, Werner refused to "cripple the business," which he wanted to pass on to his children.[62] For the sake of the unified global family multinational, Werner decided instead to make a significant investment and buy Loeffler's shares back in 1888. He appointed his cousin Alexander Siemens (1847–1928) manager of the London business. With its new ownership structure and management, Siemens London started cooperating more closely with Germany, and the relationship was rather harmonious during the following years.[63]

Around the same time, in 1890, the German business began changing its legal form from a partnership to a limited partnership. Firms often underwent this process to guarantee that they would have greater independence from the family and that family members would not have to take on the risk of unlimited liability. Carl Siemens and Werner's sons Arnold and Wilhelm were personally liable shareholders; founder Werner Siemens, at age 74, remained a limited partner with holdings of 6.2 million marks. His will stipulated that his shares be divided equally among his six children upon his death. In 1897, the company went public. Instead of clearly separating business and family, however, the Siemens family took steps to prevent outside influence and remained the most influential shareholder. All members of the first supervisory board came from the Siemens family. Moreover, company statutes granted far-reaching power to the supervisory board and especially to its chairman, who could not only supervise management but also issue instructions to the management board—a highly unusual and often criticized structure.[64] Siemens was committed to keeping the business a family firm; the chairmanship of the supervisory board, with its contractually fixed influence, was held by family members until 1981.

In the 1890s, the overseas business gained speed, and both the London and Berlin companies profited from it. In December 1892, Werner Siemens died and left his company to his brother Carl, who became president of the London business, and his two sons Arnold and Wilhelm. Alexander Siemens continued to manage the London business.

3.4   HIERARCHY AND CONTROL: TRANSFERRING THE "SPIRIT OF SIEMENS"

After the founder's death, his relatives continued the business. While conflicts about the overseas business were mostly resolved, Alexander Siemens did not support the idea of a unified family multinational but rather tried to establish clear boundaries between the firms. Werner's son Wilhelm, on the other hand, lobbied for closer cooperation, noting in his diary in 1899: "The foundation of a unified technical department for Berlin, London, Petersburg and Vienna is in preparation. The firms shall cooperate like an international unit."[65] At the turn of the century, the Siemens family bought back all shares not held by family members.

Around the same time, technological changes made it necessary to review the company's general business strategy. While Siemens had focused primarily on "light-current" products and processes (so-called at that time), most importantly telegraph equipment, it now shifted increasingly to so-called heavy-current products based on the invention of the dynamo. The rapid development of the dynamo business expanded its customer base significantly. While it offered telegraph equipment mainly to the public sector, it sold dynamo products to a range of consumers, including other companies and individuals. Thus, a sales organization became indispensable. Siemens had worked with agents before but now started to build a system of "technical offices," first in Germany during the 1890s and then abroad.

In 1903, Siemens merged its heavy-current operations with the Nuremberg EAG, founded by Sigmund Schuckert, to form the Siemens-Schuckertwerke GmbH (hereafter SSW). The merger gave Siemens, which had always had a strong position in the market for light-current products, a leadership position in the heavy-current sector, as well.[66] Joint departments were set up for financing, personnel, patents, and for managing the agencies in Germany and abroad. The merging companies S&H and SSW were structured quite differently, reflecting the differences in manufacturing and selling telegraph equipment as opposed to heavy-current products with a broader customer base. While the former called for a structure combining development, manufacturing, and marketing for specific projects, the latter required a divisional structure because of its more diverse customers.

These structural differences, in turn, necessitated the revision of the sales organization. After the merger, in 1903, Siemens had 44 technical offices serving the domestic and foreign markets. Wilhelm Siemens and nonfamily manager Robert Maass had previously developed this system and were known within the company as the "father" and "mother" of the offices. Since Robert Maass had personally known the company's founder Werner Siemens, he had significant authority. He claimed to know what he called the *Siemensgeist* (spirit of Siemens), which for him meant prioritizing long-term development over short-term gains. "To transfer the spirit of Siemens to the staff at the technical offices abroad was my primary field of work in the following years," he stated in his memoirs.[67] The technical offices often started with a single engineer who sold the products and provided services to the customer. If necessary, Siemens employed an additional businessperson to take care of the sales activities and administration.

In 1901, Wilhelm's younger brother Carl Friedrich relocated to London and became a member of the board of directors. Like his father and his brother, he corresponded with Wilhelm on a regular basis. Shortly after his arrival, he wrote to his brother in Berlin: "You wrote in your letter that the different Siemens companies do not sufficiently work hand-in-hand. Well, that is the old wound. . . . According to Uncle Carl's stories, this is not a fact of modern times but the conflict is almost as old as the company itself."[68] The problem persisted and was particularly problematic for the overseas business, for which Siemens used some technical offices but also import-export firms and agents, some of which had been hired by S&H, some by SSW, and some by the London firm Siemens Brothers & Co. In some countries, Siemens even worked with three different agents after the merger because each of the former companies had its own representative.

In the first step of reorganization, Siemens separated the light- and heavy-current business in England by building a new plant in Stafford for the heavy-current business. In 1906, the German SSW leased that plant and named it "Siemens Brothers Dynamo Works Limited," which worked alongside the original Siemens Brothers but was now exclusively responsible for the light-current business.

Shortly afterwards, Carl Friedrich and some of Siemens's top managers met in London to discuss a new structure for the overseas business. The meeting was first initiated to talk about the Siemens business in India, where Siemens had been cooperating with a Bremen-based agent, Schröder, Smit & Co., in Calcutta since 1903.[69] Previously, they had discussed turning the office into a corporation with an English-language name under Indian corporate law. This suggestion was approved and a technical office in Calcutta with offices in Bombay and Madras took over the business with India in 1907. The Siemens managers considered using the same model for other overseas markets, such as China and Japan, but this triggered a more general discussion about a centralized structure for the international business.

Up to this point, Siemens Germany and Siemens England each had two export departments: S&H and Siemens Brothers for the telegraph business, and SSW and Siemens Brothers Dynamo Works for the dynamo business. In restructuring, the company aimed to make all four of these departments accountable to a single unit that would develop and secure a unified strategy for the foreign business. Robert Eitel, a manager of Siemens's overseas business, later assumed that the biggest challenge during this process was to find a suitable general manager for the unit. According to him, a family member was absolutely necessary because "only he possesses a priori the necessary authority to deal with the independent offices both in London and in Berlin that, up to then, wanted nothing to do with such an export structure."[70] It was expected that a family member would evoke the respect needed to best overcome internal opposition to the reorganization. The strong family influence since the company's founding and Werner Siemens's express commitment to forging a dynastic global family firm shaped top managers' position on this issue. Moreover, the recent reorganization of the Siemens firms as public corporations allowed the Siemens family to secure its ongoing influence mainly through personnel decisions based on the far-reaching power that the supervisory board of the German company possessed. It was, thus, logical to appoint Carl Friedrich von Siemens, who had relocated to London in 1901 and taken a seat on the board of the London business at age 29. It is reasonable to assume that Wilhelm Siemens was grooming him for the position as a general manager for the new foreign business unit, a highly influential and important post within the family multinational.

The Central Administration Overseas (*Central-Verwaltung Übersee*, hereafter CVU) became operational in 1908.[71] Headquartered in Berlin, it oversaw four export offices—two in Germany and two in England—and was responsible for all Siemens's overseas activities. It delegated these to various export offices according to geographical and historical criteria. Orders from abroad were transferred to the CVU, whose managers further distributed them to the different Siemens departments and supervised their timely fulfillment. One of the CVU's first acts was to establish that the name *Siemens* would be used for newly established corporations all over the world, a symbolic decision meant to highlight the unity of the family multinational and the visibility of the founding family.[72]

With the establishment of the CVU and the positive economic environment, the overseas business expanded greatly between 1908 and 1914. Turnover increased from 19 million marks in 1908/09 to 35 million marks in 1910/11 and 51 million marks in 1913/14.[73] At the time, Siemens had a workforce of 82,000 employees, a quarter of whom worked outside of Germany.[74] Siemens was the largest electrical company worldwide and the third-largest company in Germany.[75] With the outbreak of World War I, however, the era of expansion abruptly ended. Siemens's market collapsed, and the majority of its foreign assets and patents were expropriated. The British government took over financial control of Siemens Brothers and Siemens Brothers Dynamo Works and sold them to a British finance group. Consequently, large parts of the international business came to a standstill and the prewar structure of the family multinational ceased to exist.

3.5 CONCLUSION

The German multinational Siemens relied heavily on the cohesion and loyalty of the family in its international business. Family structures and family resources helped solve problems of the early multinational but were also responsible for some of the greatest tensions within the family and the company. In the first stage of the firm's development, the unity of the multinational was linked to the unity of the nuclear family. Werner Siemens, company founder and *pater familias*, promoted the unity and long-term survival of the dynastic family business for the benefit of later generations. The trade-off between centralization and decentralization, as well as the role of the family within the multinational corporation, were heavily debated issues from the foundation of the company to World War I.

During the founding years, Werner's brothers supported his plans, which proved to be advantageous for creating a family multinational. However, Werner's brothers and other company stakeholders later began to contest his explicit focus on long-term survival. William, who lived most of his life in Britain, asked to have the exclusive right to do business with India for his London company and lobbied for a clear separation of both entities; Carl, based in Russia, argued that monetary rewards should guide the strategic choices of the Siemens multinational.

No harmonious solution was found during Werner's lifetime. Rather, the conflict was handed over to the next generation of (family) managers, who ultimately decided to create a dynastic family multinational, as promoted by Werner. Werner's goal of an internationally active unit came to be known as "the spirit of Siemens" and was transferred to Siemens offices around the world. The Siemens managers who built this structure often referred to Werner Siemens as the spiritual father of this idea and were able to invoke and thus support the "imagined community" Werner had been so eager to create.

Siemens's commitment to internationalization and the early debates on the relationship between the family and the firm generated a great deal of tension up to World War I but allowed Siemens to develop a strategy for the family multinational and a structure that preserved the idea of a dynastic and globally active family firm. The example of Siemens shows how creating a dynastic family multinational is an act of sense-making within the family and the firm that results from communication and discussions between different family members and family firm stakeholders.

NOTES

1. Casson, 1999.
2. See the introduction (this volume).
3. Child, Faulkner and Pitkethly, 2000.
4. For an excellent recent study of the impact of the telegraph on diplomacy with frequent comparisons to business organizations, see Nickles, 2003. Yates, 1986.
5. Feldenkirchen, 1994, 28–29.
6. Ibid., 35.
7. British Patent No. 9741, 29 May 1843. Weiher, 1990, 18.
8. Beauchamp, 2001.
9. John, 2010.
10. Feldenkirchen, 1999, 15.
11. For the "born-global" concept, see the introduction (this volume.) For an early discussion of the issue at Siemens, see *Siemens Archiv-Akten Brüderbriefe*, letter Werner to Carl, 22 November 1854.
12. Jones, 2005. Wilkins, 1970.
13. See Kocka, 1999. Lutz, 2011, 83.
14. Weiher, 1990, 21.
15. Approximately 7,000 letters survived and are in the Siemens Archives in Munich. They are quoted as *Siemens Archiv-Akten*, hereafter, SAA, BB [*Brüderbriefe* (brother letters)]. On multipurpose letters, see also Andrew Popp (this volume). Popp, 2009. Boyce, 2010.
16. Feldenkirchen, 1999, 35. For the Russian business, see also Lutz, 2011.
17. Statistical Department India Office, 1867, 72.
18. SAA 35.LK 232 *Dr. Hans Pieper: In 28 Minuten von London nach Kalkutta (2 Bände)*, 1976 (hereafter, Pieper, 1976), 50–52.
19. SAA BB letter Werner to Carl, 5 June 1856.
20. Pieper, 1976.
21. SAA BB letter Werner to Carl, 22 November 1854.
22. SAA BB letter Werner to Carl, 12 May 1858.
23. Webster, 2009.

24. Headrick, 1981, 158–159.
25. Nolan, 1858, 335. The rebellion officially ended with a peace treaty in 1858; the mutiny was finally put down in 1859.
26. Pieper, 1976, 64–65.
27. *Mechanics Magazine* 1860, part II, 185, quoted in Pieper, 1976, 65.
28. Ehrenberg, 1906, 161.
29. SAA BB letter Werner to Carl, 3 March 1864.
30. Quoted in Ehrenberg, 1906, 167.
31. SAA BB letter Werner to Carl, 27 June 1863.
32. SAA BB letter William to Werner, 26 March 1866. For the earlier discussion see SAA BB letter William to Werner, 12 September 1856.
33. Reprinted in Pieper, 1976, 306–311.
34. Pieper, 1976, 86; based on a publication of the Indo-European Telegraph Department Office in Karachi, 1868.
35. "Editorial Article," *Times of India*, 26 November 1869.
36. SAA BB letter Werner to Carl, January 1867.
37. Feldenkirchen, 1994, 95.
38. Bühlmann, 1999.
39. Headrick, 1981, 160.
40. Ibid. Wenzlhuemer, 2013.
41. SAA BB letter Werner to Carl, 4 November 1863.
42. SAA BB letter Werner to Carl, 17 April 1863.
43. SAA BB letter Werner to William, 16 April 1863.
44. Ibid.
45. SAA BB letter Werner to Carl, 7 December 1864.
46. SAA BB letter Werner to William, 13 May 1863.
47. SAA BB letter Werner to Carl, 4 November 1863.
48. Scott, 1958, 65–68.
49. Ehrenberg, 1906, 286.
50. While the contract of December 1880 did not survive in the Siemens archives, §6 was quoted repeatedly in the letters between the brothers. See also Weiher, 1990, 136.
51. Scott, 1958, 65–68.
52. SAA BB letter Werner to William, 28 June 1879.
53. Conrad, 2010.
54. SAA BB letter Werner to Ludwig Loeffler, 21 December 1884.
55. SAA Lm 910 *Die historische Entwicklung des Übersee-Geschäftes des Hauses Siemens und seine Organisation, von Herrn Dir. i. R. Wolfram Eitel 1957/58* (hereafter, Eitel, 1957/58), 46; SAA BB letter Werner to Ludwig Loeffler, 21 December 1884.
56. SAA BB letter Werner to Carl, 20 October 1884.
57. Ibid.
58. Scott, 1958, 68.
59. SAA BB letter Werner to Carl, 25 December 1887.
60. Ibid.
61. Ibid.
62. Ibid.
63. Weiher, 1990, 166–169.
64. Feldenkirchen, 1999, 41–44.
65. SAA Li 219 Excerpts from Wilhem von Siemens's diary [*Auszüge aus den Tagebüchern Wilhelm von Siemens.*]
66. Feldenkirchen, 1999, 49–52.
67. Memoirs of Robert Maass, quoted in Eitel, 1957/58, 65.
68. SAA Lh 299 letter Carl Friedrich to Wilhelm, 8 June 1901.

69. SAA 13092 Contract with Schröder, Smit & Co., 1903.
70. Eitel, 1957/58, 82.
71. SAA 8110 *Rundschreiben betr. Übersee-Organisation, 22 July 1908. SAA 8188 Historische Entwicklung des Übersee-Geschäftes und seine Organisation, Hermann Reyss.*
72. Eitel, 1957/58, 59.
73. Ibid., 76.
74. See www.Siemens.com/history.
75. Hertner, 1989, 145–159.

4 Family Capitalism and Internationalization

The Case of the Czech Family Firm Bat'a up to the Early 1940s

Susanne Hilger

Crossing national borders is among the crucial challenges for corporate business. Geoffrey Jones once pointed out that it has become imperative for firms "to move with the customer," especially since the industrial growth of the markets.[1] The internationalization of family-owned companies from the late nineteenth century onwards, however, is still relatively unexplored territory in this field of research, although recent publications have begun to probe the early internationalization of family-owned companies in Germany. For example, Angelika Epple, Hartmut Berghoff, and Patrick Kleedehn in their studies of the family businesses Stollwerck, Hohner, and Bayer, respectively, highlight the fact that these companies began to internationalize early on, and, thus, followed a path similar to that of other multinational enterprises.[2] Epple characterizes the Stollwerck chocolate company's approach to internationalization as "fraternalistic" (in contrast to "paternalistic"). In this approach, having a horizontal executive level and following the tradition of "consensual decision-making" are particularly important; this was the case in several businesses run by brothers at the end of the nineteenth century. This corporate governance concept that emerged in family firms was based on consensus, which was sometimes difficult to explain to nonfamily members. This strategy helped to reduce transaction costs, particularly those associated with information and communication. At the same time, the lack of hierarchical decision making triggered new conflicts when consensus could not be achieved among the family members.[3] Hartmut Berghoff describes a similar "fraternalism" in his study on the German harmonica manufacturer Hohner.[4]

However, these studies have only begun to raise the question of the role of the family in the internationalization process. While European family-owned companies crossed national borders to gain access to foreign markets, the way they did so depended on the means they had at their disposal and how they structured their companies to take this step. Studies on Early Modern trade history have already highlighted the importance and strategic positioning of family members in the creation of international trading networks.[5] Can a particular organizational structure of "friends and families" be identified with the internationalization of family firms in the late nineteenth and early twentieth centuries, as well? This chapter will explore these issues by looking specifically at the development of the Czech shoe manufacturer Bat'a up to World War II, which even today is one of the world's largest family-owned companies.[6]

This chapter offers initial insight into a comparative research project. In addition to investigating Bat'a, this chapter also provides insight into broader changes in the shoe-making industry by comparing Bat'a's case to those of two other European, family-owned shoe companies, Bally and Salamander. Similar to the Swiss Bally and the German Salamander shoe companies (all founded between 1851 and 1894), Bat'a, by the 1930s, had already developed from a small family-owned craftsman's workshop set up under difficult economic conditions into a family-owned global player. Around World War I, the firm—which adopted mass production methods from the United States very early on—developed innovative strategies for corporate organization and marketing; for example, it turned to international markets by exporting its organizational model all over the world. This involved founding industrial satellite towns for shoe manufacturing.

In accordance with the theme of the present volume, the following questions will be addressed: What role did the family play in the organization of this kind of business? How did the family finance and manage corporate growth? How were family members involved in the process of international expansion? The chapter begins with brief corporate histories of the companies and the development of the shoe market from the late nineteenth century to the mid-twentieth century. Afterwards, it focuses on the questions of corporate organization and internationalization, using the example of Bat'a. This history will show that the company can be seen as an extraordinary example in the internationalization of a family business, one that stresses the link between "familiness" and internationalization in the wave of deglobalization in the 1930s.

4.1   ON THE CORPORATE HISTORIES OF EUROPEAN SHOE MANUFACTURERS

Thanks to Anne Sudrow's ambitious dissertation of 2010, the making of shoes is no longer one of "the blank spots" in the European history of industrialization.[7] Her work, however, deals with the history of the technology behind shoe manufacturing and is intended to be a "product history" of shoes during the era of National Socialism; it is not really about the firms (and families) "behind" this industry. Towards the end of the nineteenth century, shoe manufacturing developed into a growth market on the basis of mechanized work processes, though only a select number of companies benefited from this. Among the European family-owned companies in the shoe industry, Bat'a can be regarded as extraordinary, in part because the shoemaker and company founder Tomáš Bat'a (1876–1932) focused on economies of scale early on, swayed by study trips to the United States in the early twentieth century. This move was unusual for a small craftsman's workshop in a rural area. Together with his brother Antonín and his sister Anna, Tomáš founded a shoe factory in the small Moravian town of Zlín (then in Austria-Hungary) in 1894. The small village of only 300 inhabitants grew quickly due to Bat'a's influence and success (it had up to 43,000 inhabitants in 1938).[8] In 1923, Tomáš Bat'a became its mayor and contributed to accelerating its urban development.[9] Bat'a's business at first profited from the increasing demand for military boots during World War I. Bat'a started to enter international markets in the 1920s, and its company motto reflected this international orientation: "half the world's population walk barefoot."[10] Employing several thousand workers by the 1920s, Bat'a had long since left the European shoe industry behind, where the average staff numbered 50.[11]

Marc Casson's definition of family business as a "family-owned and -controlled" company seems at first glance to fit Bat'a's corporate history. From the very beginning, Bat'a family members were engaged in both the strategic management and daily transactions of the business. When his older brother Antonín died in 1908, Tomáš alone took over the role of chief executive.[12] Anna, by contrast, invested her inheritance in the company, providing necessary financial support.[13] A few years later, Tomáš's half-brother Jan Antonín Bat'a (1898–1965) joined the company.[14]

If we compare Bat'a to other European shoe companies, it becomes apparent that Bat'a's success was not an isolated case, particularly in light of its unfavorable starting conditions (it was a small family businesses in a rural area). Two other European companies with similar roots took a leading role in the European shoe business even earlier than Bat'a: the German company Salamander Shoes (founded in 1887 and located in the southwest of Germany) and the Swiss shoe company Bally. Although there is no indication that Bat'a imitated these companies' strategies, they can be seen as strong competitors. Bally, for instance, had already turned itself into a large-scale enterprise before World War I with an output of more than 1 million shoes a year.

As early as 1854, Swiss entrepreneur Carl Friedrich Bally and his two brothers founded a *fabrique des chaussures* in Schönwerd, in the Swiss canton of Solothurn. They wanted to bring fresh ideas into the knitwear company they had inherited from their father. In the 1870s, the company had already begun to set up sales offices in several European as well as South American cities.[15] It opened agencies in numerous cities, such as Hamburg, Berlin, Beirut, Lisbon, Barcelona, Marseilles, Bucharest, Smyrna, Constantinople, Alexandria, Cairo, Madrid, and Brussels. Even before the turn of the century, Bally had become an international corporation with a several thousand employees.[16] Meanwhile, on the local level, factory-scale production turned the rural area and modest resources of Solothurn into a small "kingdom."[17]

Similar to Bat'a and Bally, Jacob Sigle's German shoe company Salamander was a start-up. The young shoemaker began doing business in 1885, with his brothers Ernst and Christoph as partners. Again like Bat'a and Bally, it took Salamander only one generation to make the step from a one-man shop to a global business. As in Schönwerd and Zlín, Kornwestheim, Salamander's hometown, experienced industrialization and growth thanks to the dedication and investment of the Sigle family.[18]

In all three cases, the entrepreneurial families not only spurred local growth but also engaged in local social and policy issues. The founding families, patriarchal entrepreneurs, their relatives, successors, and close family friends played a crucial role in the three companies throughout the period under consideration. Moreover, although each of these firms operated on a family consensus basis, each also had a clear leader, at least for the decisive stages of development. These were Carl Friedrich Bally, Jacob Sigle, and Tomáš Bat'a (later Jan Antonín Bat'a). Chandler's "quasi law of nature" on the transition from family-owned to professionally managed businesses contends that the founding family loses influence when the business comes to be run by managers. These three cases, however, run counter to this law: By the early 1930s, all three companies had become stock corporations (Bally in 1907, Sigle in 1915, and Bat'a in 1930). Nonetheless, the capital stock as well as managerial and oversight functions largely remained under the control of family members (at Salamander up to the 1960s, at Bally up to the early 1970s, and at Bat'a up to the present day. Yet only Bat'a has remained a "family-owned and -controlled" business to this day, mainly because the family has always been able to provide leaders who performed well under economic pressure.

4.2   CORPORATE ORGANIZATION AND MODERNIZATION IN THE SHOE INDUSTRY

Bat'a's extraordinary growth has been attributed to a variety of strategies, only some of which had to do with the family. The "Bat'a system of management," or "Bat'aism," is typically seen as the precondition for the company's extraordinary expansion.[19] The "Bat'a system" replaced traditional and patriarchal corporate policy in a process analogous to a rationalization of operational procedures. The German journal *Soziale Praxis* discussed this system as early as 1928, explaining the four elements on which it was based:[20]

technical organization: integrated production allowing for different types of products, better known as Sloanism in the automobile industry;

labor relations: self-administration of departments (profit-center organization);

sales system: low-price policy, ubiquity;

welfare system: incentives, integration and control.

In the sense of genuine Fordism, Bat'a continually integrated production from early on. With mechanization and assembly-line work, Tomáš Bat'a succeeded in reducing production costs up to 20 percent. Bat'a caused a "price revolution" in Europe and on the world market as well, whereas Bata's workforce earned more than any shoe workers in Czechoslovakia or elsewhere in Europe because of the Fordist "five-dollar day" and piecework pay.[21] Another key to Bat'a's success also seems to have been the implementation of self-administered divisions for the different lines of production, which fostered entrepreneurial thinking among the employees.[22]

Given the influence of American production methods on Bat'a, we need to address the concept of Americanization, which I have referred to formerly as the "express way to globalization."[23] The central impetus for Bat'a's global development was the reorganization of shoe manufacturing following an "American system of production," that is, standardized mass production. In the United States regional shoe production clusters, which had developed on the East Coast in Lynn and Brockton, Massachusetts, served as a model for Tomáš's corporate policy.[24]

The limited availability of labor in the United States prompted shoe manufacturing—a complex and labor-intensive process (involving cutting, stitching, punching, lacing, and soling)—to be mechanized there in the first half of the nineteenth century. New machine-based manufacturing processes, such as industrial sewing machines and the Goodyear system for welted shoes, then spread to continental Europe. Thus, the essential preconditions for reorganizing operating processes utilizing time-efficient and cost-cutting line production were given. By shifting from manual to machine production, segmenting the manufacturing process, and standardizing the product line, output increased while the cost of making shoes declined considerably. The economies of scale that shoe manufacturers were thereby able to achieve gave them a significant cost advantage over their nonindustrialized competitors. Most important, with increased output and lowered costs, they were able to pass the cost advantages on to the consumer by lowering prices.

In view of rising output, it became essential for shoe manufacturers to develop effective distribution systems to realize economies of scale. Thus, branch systems became one of the central components of the large-scale distribution of shoes during the first decades of the twentieth century.[25] By setting up their own networks, big shoe manufacturers took over retail and tried to push independent shoe retail businesses aside. Cost advantages arose from eliminating the retail intermediaries (premiums for sales representatives did not have to be paid, shoes could be produced in larger quantities and at more competitive prices) and also from outfitting the "shoe palaces" (what Bat'a called "houses of service") with the standardized but unique design of a corporate store.

At Bat'a, the standardized design for the sales branches explicitly aimed at a process of branding:

With regard to the exterior of the sales rooms [. . .], which are spread all over the republic and the whole world—in Belgrade, Cairo, Singapore [. . .] it needs to be said that they are always in prime locations, easily accessible to the customer, sporting a sign made of white glass that bears the four typical black letters 'BAT'A.' The entrance, which is straight and without steps, is of a standard design, made of glass and iron and has large display cabinets. These facilities very much caught the eye of the public and to a certain extent [Bat'a's] brands dominated the market.[26]

In all three of the family-owned shoe companies discussed here, the family played a central role in modernizing production and corporate organization and overcame knowledge constraints with the help of an international family-networking strategy. For centuries, it had been customary in many family-owned businesses for the sons and brothers to go abroad to investigate the latest promising developments in manufacturing. Nineteenth-century shoe manufacturers engaged in this practice as well. In 1869, for example, Carl Bally's eldest son, Eduard, initiated the purchase of pioneering Goodyear sewing machines for the Swiss location after having visited modern shoe factories in the United States, the homeland of the "American System of Manufacturing." Similar to Bally, Swabian entrepreneur Jacob Sigle sent his brother Ernst to the United States in the mid-1890s to bring technological innovations to his own company.[27]

It was not until a few years later that company founder Tomáš Bat'a dared to go to the United States. In 1904, he got a job as a mechanic at the Boston-based United Shoe Machinery Company, the market leader for shoe production machinery, in order to study the American machinery during assembly and operation. He was obviously free to stay away from the Zlín plants for long stretches as he was able to count on relatives and close family friends at home. Such family-based knowledge transfer ensured that American corporate organization, with its use of special machinery and the segmentation and simplification of the production processes, took hold on the European continent before World War I. Adopting this organization was the precondition for mass production and the internationalization of business, first on a European scale and later also outside of Europe.

More than Bally and Salamander, the Czech Bat'a group is regarded as a prototype of an "Americanized" company since it seemed to utilize the principles of Fordist production (productivity and wage policy) in their "purest" form. Tomáš Bat'a's fascination with machines culminated in his meeting Henry Ford in Detroit in 1919, where he gained insight into Model T production.[28] Afterwards, he took over a small shoe factory in Lynn, Massachusetts, the center of the American shoe industry, in the early 1920s. Headed by the company founder's half-brother and subsequent successor, Jan Antonín Bat'a, this factory takeover served to transfer essential know-how.

Tomáš Bat'a pursued a more dramatic modernization policy than Bally and Salamander. Unlike traditional family-owned businesses, Bat'a focused on a realistic perception of "the employee," combining intricate wage and premiums systems and self-administered profit centers with comprehensive social welfare and social control measures (for which he received his due share of criticism). In his standardized planning in Zlín during the 1920s and 1930s, Jan A. Bat'a, in particular, followed models of contemporary modern architecture such as Bauhaus and Le Corbusier, which made him one of the corporate pioneers in Europe.[29]

Quite unlike other well-known model villages that had been built in Europe and the United States since industrialization, such as Pullman (now part of Chicago) or Port Sunlight in the Western part of England, Zlín had no patriarchal or romanticized traces but mirrored the New Objectivity. The architecture was also intended to reflect the rational and standardized principles that dominated production and working conditions.[30] Mirroring a new trend in management, it objectified the relationship between the owner family and the staff and lacked any sense of emotional ties.

Research on other twentieth-century (family) businesses has also identified this tendency toward objective management. In Siemens factory towns, for example, Carl Friedrich von Siemens sought to structure workmen's housing for maximum quality and quantity in production. He claimed that the housing projects in Berlin's "Siemensstadt" should not be based on philanthropic or romantic objectives but should aim to achieve hygienic standards and the reproduction of labor force, and to solve social disaffection. These projects were built in the 1920s without Siemens's financial support.[31] By contrast, Bat'a contributed to the construction and expansion of infrastructure, including social, cultural, residential, and even administrative buildings in Zlín, not least because Tomáš Bat'a was the town's mayor up to his death in 1932.[32]

However, Bat'a's company village practices were regarded with ambivalence: On the one hand, the company was viewed as an example of modern, forward-looking management. Contemporaries like leftist publicist Egon Erwin Kisch, on the other hand, condemned Tomáš Bat'a for the overbearing control to which he subjected his staff, both in the Fordist production halls and in private life.[33] Not only were workers ruled by the tyranny of the stopwatch and/or piecework pay, but they also had to conform to company ideals in their leisure time, participating in company-organized recreational activities. The company, thus, seemed to exercise "total control." Such criticism can be interpreted as anticapitalist, but Bat'a's welfare system (organized leisure time, sports) also resembled the prefascist activities of the Italian organization, the Opera Nazionale Dopolavoro (OND, National Recreational Club), and the Deutsche Arbeitsfront (DAF, German Labor Front).

More recent studies, like Martin Marek's, have pointed out that the company actively built up the "Bat'a" myth. From the 1920s on, Bat'a put a lot of resources into press and public relations, thus communicating the entire range of company policy measures.[34] However, there seemed to be no sense of patriarchalism, nor the idea of the corporate community as a "family." Rather, it was a kind of social rationalization of industrial production that connected the technical processes of work with the workers' psychological state.

4.3   CORPORATE INTERNATIONALIZATION STRATEGIES: THE CASE OF BAT'A

Family business, with its own particular decision-making characteristics, has long been viewed as an opposing model to larger, multinational firms. Earlier research shaped an image of family enterprises as small, conservative, and rather cautious in their business approach and strongly embedded in their home regions. The Bat'a example underlines the limits of such generalizations. The firm's growth and international orientation were always seen as a key to its success. It was the family (mainly in the person of Tomáš Bat'a and later his half-brother and successor Jan A.) that paved the way to modernization and internationalization.

Bat'a started this path in the early twentieth century with the production of "Batovky" shoes. Made of canvas with rubber soles, these were already mass produced and became very popular in the markets of Austria-Hungary. During World War I, Bat'a's good connections to the Austrian government helped make it one of the main suppliers of military boots. When this main client fell away after the war, Bat'a at first drastically decreased prices and wages. After the crisis-ridden period in the early 1920s, it recovered by means of automatization, rationalization, and specialization. One of the new products it focused on was fashionable shoes, including fancy ladies' shoes.[35] During the Great Depression, Bat'a suffered dramatic losses and a steep decline of its home and European markets. Globalization offered an opportunity to escape from this.

Indeed, Bat'a experienced an international boom in the decade of the Great Depression, despite Tomáš Bat'a's death by plane crash in 1932. Under his successor Jan A. Bat'a, the number of Bat'a companies worldwide rose from 24 in 1931 to 120 in 1942. Whereas Bat'a had manufacturing units operating in 18 countries and had established shops in more than 25 countries in 1931, this number grew under Jan's leadership to 40 production sites and shops in more than 35 countries around the world—an amazing story in the middle of this economic slump. In addition, new production plants and shops opened mainly in Central and South America and in parts of Africa as well. By the early 1940s, the number of Bat'a employees worldwide had climbed to more than 100,000 (from approximately 16,000 in 1931).[36]

Tomáš Bat'a, with his aim "to shoe the world," has often been characterized as a "visionary entrepreneur." Undoubtedly, the company can be seen as an outstanding example of corporate globalization prior to World War II as Bat'a's rapid growth far exceeded that of its competitors in both Europe and the United States. A few key facts illuminate Bat'a's exceptional effort to expand its international business. By the early 1930s, the company managed an annual output of 4.5 million shoes, and Czechoslovakia had overtaken the world's leading shoe-producing nations such as Great Britain (3.4 million) and the United States (1.1 million).[37] With such high productivity, a small domestic market, and a limited supply of raw materials, Bat'a had no choice but to access foreign markets, beginning in Europe and then expanding overseas. Bat'a's share in the overall Czech export of shoes rose from 50 percent to more than 88 percent between 1929 and 1935.[38] Asian and African markets apparently interested it most.

The introduction of mass production was the primary push factor in Bat'a's entry into foreign markets as it had to look outside its home market to find new demand. In contrast to the typical image of rather cautious international expansion in family enterprises, Bat'a was continuously willing to internationalize and modernize. Given the family's readiness to assume risk and the pressure of the crumbling markets, the firm passed through the stages of internationalization rather quickly. Bat'a's activities—in particular, its massive price-dumping strategy—met with considerable resistance among European shoe producers during the crisis-ridden 1920s. As mass production lowered costs and lowered Bat'a's prices, the company challenged local manufacturers by offering shoes often for about half the price of local products.[39] Consequently, in many foreign markets, the strategy engendered calls for boycotts, protest actions, protective tariffs, and import bans against the Czech company. To avoid these import bans, Bat'a soon worked hard to launch production facilities and sales branches, setting up subsidiaries in the Netherlands (1921), Denmark (1922), Yugoslavia (1922), Poland (1922), and England (1924).[40]

The Great Depression, which is generally seen as a cornerstone of deglobalization, led to even more restrictive protective foreign trade measures that forced Bat'a to open manufacturing subsidiaries abroad, behind tariff walls. The German Reich, France, Italy, Austria, Denmark, Norway, Finland, Latvia, Lithuania, Estonia, Egypt, and Canada all introduced protective tariffs in 1929 to safeguard domestic industries, and Great Britain followed suit in 1931. Import quotas on shoes were also in place for Switzerland, Belgium, and Holland, and Hungary and Poland had systems for restricting imports on shoes. The tight market and protective tariff policies led to a drop in Bat'a shoe sales in Europe—from 83 percent of all exports in 1928 to 40 percent in 1933.[41]

Against this backdrop, Bat'a bought manufacturing companies not only in Germany (such as Ottomuth in Upper Silesia) but also in Chelmek, near Cracow in Poland, Möhlin in Switzerland,[42] Bataville, near Hellocourt/Strasbourg in France,[43] and Borovo, near Osijek in Yugoslavia, all established in 1932. Best, near Eindhoven, and East Tillbury, near London, followed in 1934. Stockholm in Sweden, Bucharest in Romania, Vienna, and Alexandria, as well as Batovany in Slovakia (today's Partizánske) were later added to the list.[44] Additional sites were set up in Fiume, Italy, Helsinki, Brussels, Luxembourg, and Bat'ov (Otrokovice) in what is now the Czech Republic. Clearly, tariff barriers shaped the company's internationalization strategy.

As some of the names of the company towns might indicate, the family-driven Czech company Bat'a served as a model that was transferred to various locations all around the world in a one-to-one manner. Following the "shoe hometown" Zlín, Bat'a constructed numerous factory towns prior to World War II in Europe and overseas. In 1931, Bat'a built a production facility and residential quarters on the model of Zlín in Borovo on the Danube, near Vukovar. This would become the most important shoe manufacturing site in Yugoslavia after the war. The town of Best in the southern Netherlands would literally be turned into a Bat'a town (Batadorp). By 1939, the number of Bat'a's foreign subsidiaries had risen to 33, containing a mixture of sales and production sites. Apart from the European subsidiaries, Bat'a was now present in Egypt, Tunisia, Algeria, Morocco, Western and Eastern Africa, as well as Syria, Palestine, Indochina, British India, Singapore, Shanghai, Hong Kong, China, Malaysia, Indonesia, the Philippines, Thailand, and Belcamp, Maryland (1937), on the West Indies, Guyana, and Tahiti.[45]

Whereas Bat'a had focused on the European markets up to the early 1930s, thereafter it shifted to overseas markets, particularly in Africa and Asia, to compensate for European losses. The satellite town of Batanagar was built near Calcutta in 1934, again following the model of Zlín. In Africa, Bat'a founded subsidiaries in Johannesburg and Cape Town as well as in the Belgian Congo. In 1934, it founded subsidiaries in Tangiers, Casablanca, Algiers, and Tunis, as well as the "Chaussure Bat'a S.A. de L'Afrique Occidentale" in Dakar.[46] Bat'a's main interest was "to supply the local population with shoes" since these countries were seen as "juicy markets"[47]—justifiably so, because in some parts of the globe like India and Africa, the name Bat'a became synonymous with "shoes."[48] Thus, within a few decades, Bat'a turned into a "global player" using economies of scale as well as innovative strategies of marketing (chain stores) and personnel management that were essentially just like those of joint stock companies.

Additionally, political developments in the 1930s not only accelerated the company's international expansion but also lay behind the family's decision to leave its Czech home. Jan A. Bat'a was very interested in ensuring "greater safety for his capital deposits" outside Europe, especially since, as Léhar put it,

> the trend of development in Zlín was approaching its zenith . . . a further expansion . . . could no longer be directed from Zlín, but only from abroad where, for one thing, there was a sufficiency of raw materials . . . and, for another, greater possibilities for side-lines of production and the extension of marketing activities to the whole globe.[49]

Probably seeing the way the wind was blowing before the Munich Agreement was signed in September 1938, which allowed Germany to annex the ethnic German territories of Czechoslovakia, Bat'a began negotiations the previous spring to move the company headquarters from Prague to Ontario,

Canada. The family network enabled further expansion when Jan A. headed for the Brazilian market in the late 1930s. Bat'a's South American overseas business, established some time earlier, started to flourish as Jan A. became very active in founding new company towns. The shoe towns of Batatuba (1939) (today, a district of Piracaia) and Bataguassu (1959) were founded in the federal states of São Paulo and Mato Grosse do Sul. Following the example of Zlín, Jan A. adapted the concepts of the ideal industrial town to the newly founded Bat'a settlements.[50]

4.4 FINANCING CORPORATE GROWTH ABROAD AND EXERCISING FAMILY CONTROL

Bat'a's expansion was extraordinary, begging the question of how the company managed to finance it. How could a family do this and be so profitable in the midst of the Depression and huge international tensions? Léhar and others assumed that Bat'a managed to achieve "financial independence from bank capital."[51] He mentioned the Swiss proprietary company (Schweizer Holdinggesellschaft, Leader AG, St. Moritz), where Tomáš Bat'a had invested reserve funds in the 1930s and which served as the financial base for the new parent company in Canada.[52] In his critical reflections, Léhar assumed that the capital surplus of the parent company was invested abroad: "All . . . foreign companies were financially dependent on the owner of the founding company, Tomáš Bat'a, who owned either the whole or the majority of their shares."[53]

As a family entrepreneur, Tomáš Bat'a also controlled the personnel policy from the headquarters in Zlín with the help of close associates and his half-brother Jan A. Rather than hire foreign managers who did not listen to what the center wanted them to do, Bat'a reproduced the home model by deploying executives from Czechoslovakia who stayed in close contact and seemed crucial to Bat'a's ongoing international success.

Throughout the twentieth century, Bat'a remained family-owned and family-controlled with the exception of the part of the company that remained where it all started—in Czechoslovakia. This part was put under state control in 1948 and renamed "Svit,"[54] precipitating a protracted dispute about the company inheritance that embroiled the family for a decade during and after World War II, some of which was also fought in court. Tomáš Bat'a's widow Marie, their son Thomas Bat'a Jr., and Tomáš's half-brother Jan A. raised the question of property, holdings, and heritage several times, leading to "a war of attrition, fought through the courts, for the ownership rights of the Bat'a Shoe assets."[55] After Jan A.'s death in 1965, Thomas Bat'a Jr. (1915–2008) further expanded the company. In 1946, Thomas had married the Swiss architect Sonja Wettstein (b. 1926), who got involved in the company, building a Bat'a shoe organization in Canada. Gordon and Nicholson rightly call her "a key person of decision making."[56] In contrast to Anna and

Marie (the sister and the wife of company founder Tomáš Bat'a), who did not appear on the corporate level, Sonja can be identified as the first female family member to actively influence the business's performance (although Bat'a otherwise maintained the conservative view "that there was no place for women in management").[57] To this day, she represents the Bat'a family at public events and cultivates awareness of shoe-manufacturing heritage in the Bat'a Shoe Museum in Toronto.[58]

The extraordinary story of Bat'a raises the question of how the family managed to expand the company in prewar times during a period of strong deglobalization and how it survived in the postwar period despite ongoing "family wars" of succession in the late 1980s/1990s.[59] As Gordon and Nicholson conclude, "The Bat'a case is living proof that even serious succession conflicts don't have to destroy a business. Bat'a Shoes was undoubtedly helped by the fundamental strength of the business. Without that the business and family harmony might have collapsed altogether."[60] More detailed accounts of the difficulties of succession, how the family fared as a family over the long term, as well as more precise information about the family's

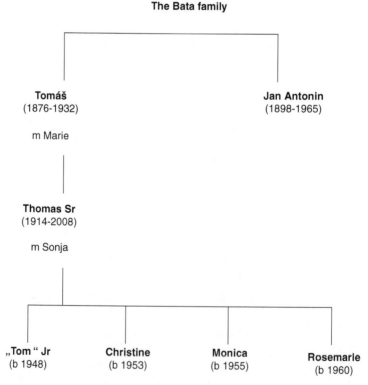

Figure 4.1   The Bat'a Family
© By the author.

role in the enterprise remain key issues for further research. Particularly in regard to the problem of succession in the third generation, Bat'a resembles most other family-owned businesses.

4.5 CONCLUSION

One of the main questions of this volume is whether "familiness" hinders or helps businesses in their path to globalization at different periods of time. Since Bat'a's success stretches over more than a century, including several waves of globalization and deglobalization, one could reflect on how the Bat'a family helped to manage the major impediments to global trade after 1918, particularly because Bat'a is a still a family firm whereas other European market pioneers such as Bally and Salamander have become corporate-owned and were much more affected by structural changes in the shoe industry. Why did Bat'a remain a family firm while the others did not? What kept the Bat'a family robust?

There is no easy answer to these questions. Bat'a's success in expanding internationally during the rise of European shoe manufacturing after World War I demonstrates that there is not necessarily a contradiction between "family entrepreneurship" and international expansion on the basis of technological and organizational progress. Bat'a, Bally, and Salamander illustrate that several Central European family-owned companies adopted modern American production techniques and sometimes even refined them, taking on additional risks and preparing for the challenges of reorganization and internationalization. Bat'a's success, in particular, rests not so much on family networks as on its adoption of standardized mechanization. The founder's interest in Fordism and family travels facilitated this development, as they paved the way for the transfer of technological and organizational know-how.

The reason Salamander and Bally lost "family control" whereas Bat'a "did right" obviously has to do with the different leagues of expansion in which they played. Based on the Americanization of production and sales, Bat'a developed a global system for expanding shoe markets under the hard conditions of the Depression. By 1938, the company had already become a global shoe-manufacturing company with more than 65,000 staff, a third of whom worked abroad.[61] Bat'a made use of the Great Depression and its protectionist influences on international trade "to found dozens of production and trading companies all over the world, set up a widely branching network of sales points in every corner of the globe, and expand export to the most distant overseas countries."[62]

"Familiness" in and of itself neither hindered nor fostered Bat'a's internationalization because the main "family resources" involved the particular knowledge of the global shoe market of its founder, Tomáš Bat'a, and the resulting transfer of the Zlín company model to various geographic markets around the world. Although the Bat'a family has retained complete ownership and control up to the present, the company cannot be seen as a family enterprise in a classical sense. The "family" never served as a small, stable, and harmonious environment. In terms of labor relations, Bat'a did not emphasize personal patriarchal relations but rather the principle of an "objecitified management."

Bat'a is more than a family enterprise. In contrast to generalized opinions about predetermined characteristics of family capitalism, it must be considered a successful example of innovation, modernization, and early internationalization. Large-scale, modernized production, standardized satellite towns, and a global perspective were the family's response to growing local market pressures. In Bat'a's case, "family" ownership and control did not lead to a particular "familiness" in the business. Rather, the development of the "Bat'a system" derived from Tomáš Bat'a's particular convictions concerning market development ("to shoe the world"). This can be seen as the "real mission" of the family's global business, passed on with the help of family bonds.

In his work *Aufstieg der Kleinen* [The Rise of the Small], Harm Schröter points out that "small" countries such as Belgium, the Netherlands, and Switzerland were able to expand on an international scale very successfully.[63] A number of successful multinational, family-owned companies are located in these countries, such as Nestlé, Philips, Unilever, and Suchard. As domestic markets in these countries were small, manufacturers had to concentrate on expansion and export. This situation applied to Czechoslovakia, too. Bat'a's highly cost-oriented corporate policy, an expression of the standardized American manufacturing culture of "economies of scale"—transferred all over the world via the company's satellite towns—clearly distinguishes Bat'a from many other family-owned companies. The present efforts of Thomas Bat'a's widow Sonja, as head of the Bat'a Charity Foundation, to preserve the "Bat'awa" site in Canada underlines the Bat'a family's commitment to this strategy and its achievements.

NOTES

I would like to thank John Nash and Jeff Fear for support and helpful comments.
1. Jones, 1996.
2. Epple, 2010. Berghoff, 2006b. Kleedehn, 2007.
3. Epple, 2010, 321–324 and 414–415.
4. Berghoff, 2006b, 143–145.
5. Schulte Beerbühl, 2007. Weber, 2004.
6. There is still no comprehensive corporate history of Bat'a, although a number of recent conferences have been dedicated to the history of Bat'a sites, including the international conference on "Company Towns of the Bat'a Concern" organized by the Institute of Philosophy of the Academy of Sciences of the Czech Republic in Prague on March 24–25, 2011. For older Czech research, see Léhar, 1960. For a recent literature review, see Marek, 2009.

7. Sudrow, 2010.
8. Nerdinger, 2009, 6.
9. Ibid., 42.
10. Cekota, 1968. Erdély, 1932. Henning, 1949.
11. Ausschuß zur Untersuchung der Erzeugungs- und Absatzbedingungen der deutschen Wirtschaft, 1930. Bräutigam, 1997, 26.
12. Gerslová, 2011, 281. Léhar, 1963, 150.
13. Casson, 1999.
14. Jan stemmed from the second marriage of Tomáš, Anna, and Antonín's father Anton.
15. Sales offices were opened in Paris (1879), Montevideo (1870), and Buenos Aires (1873) in that decade. Later, offices were added in London (1882) and Vienna (1914).
16. Schmid, 1939.
17. Heim, 2000.
18. Sturm, 1967. von Klaß, 1961. Bräutigam, 1997, 59–64.
19. Bat'a, 1992. Zeleny, 1998. Dubreuil, 1936.
20. Schwenger, 1928. For an opposing point of view, see Devinat, 1930. Internationales Arbeitsamt, 1930.
21. Erdély, 1932, 52. Gerslová, 2011, 285.
22. Schwenger, 1928, 1137–1140. Erdély, 1932, 90–99.
23. Hilger, 2008.
24. Zahavi, 1988. Zahavi, 1983.
25. Sudrow, 2010, 114–116.
26. Kallai, 1936, 94.
27. Sturm, 1967, 316.
28. Erdély, 1932, 50–51.
29. Nerdinger, 2009. Klingan and Gust, 2009.
30. Chikugo, 1991.
31. Sachse, 1990, 149–154.
32. Erdély, 1932, 162–163.
33. Kisch, 1969. See also Philipp, 1928.
34. Marek, 2009, 418.
35. Gerslová, 2003, 301.
36. Total Survey, Prof. Dr. Frederick Haussmann, November 30, 1947, Personal Archives of Jan A. Bat'a, John Nash, Hampton, New Hampshire, USA.
37. Roth, 1932, 64.
38. Léhar, 1963, 151.
39. Sudrow, 2010, 123–125. Bräutigam, 1997, 40–42.
40. Léhar, 1963, 149.
41. Sudrow, 2010, 108. Léhar, 1963, 154.
42. On this, see Brändle, 1992.
43. On this, see Gatti, 2004. Le Bot, 2005, particularly 135–137.
44. Moravčiková, 2009.
45. Gerslová, 2003, 301. Léhar, 1963, 149–153.
46. Léhar, 1963, 152–153. Hlavková, 2006.
47. Erdély, 1932, 169.
48. Gerslová, 2003, 295.
49. Léhar, 1963, 176–177.
50. Bat'a, 1951.
51. Léhar, 1963, 158. Also Erdély, 1932, 186.
52. Léhar, 1963, 153 and 158. See also Hier spricht der Chef, 1953.
53. Léhar, 1963, 151.
54. Gerslová, 2003, 311.

55. Gordon and Nicholson, 2008, 91. See also Hier spricht der Chef, 1953.
56. Gordon and Nicholson, 2008, 91.
57. Ibid., 92.
58. For example, she did this recently to mark the 80th anniversary of Bat'a in Möhlin, Switzerland: "Sonja Bat'a besuchte Möhlin," http://www.moehlin.ch/Bat'a/index.php?news_id=854&id=12, accessed February 23, 2012.
59. Gordon and Nicholson, 2008, 91–92. Miller, Steier and Le Breton-Miller, 2003, 519.
60. Gordon and Nicholson, 2008, 94.
61. Gerslová, 2003, 311.
62. Léhar, 1963, 155.
63. Schröter, 1993.

Part II

The Visible Hand of Governments and Supporting Institutions

5 Globalization from a 17mm-Diameter Cylinder Perspective
Mittelstand Multinationals

Jeffrey Fear

In his 2011 State of the Union Address, U.S. President Obama made a commitment to doubling America's exports by 2014 to help rebalance America's longstanding trade deficit. Yet most large American Fortune 500 companies already have significant overseas presence and export capabilities. Hollywood banks on international sales that amount to roughly 60 percent of its $27 billion in revenues.[1] Apple manufactures all of its products abroad through contract manufacturers, which famously adds to the American trade deficit even though Apple captures most of its products' value.[2] UNCTAD found that General Electric was the world's largest "transnational" firm (with more than 50 percent of sales, assets, and employees abroad) so that its "transnationality" index (TNI) was 52.2 percent. The TNI rating of other quintessentially "American" firms is high: Procter & Gamble's (P&G) was 60.2 percent, Coca-Cola's 74.3 percent, Ford's 54.3 percent, General Motors' 48.7 percent, and Wal-Mart's, though just 31.2 percent, is increasingly rapidly. General Motors fell just below the 50 percent threshold, but in 2010 GM sold more cars in China than in the United States.[3]

Exporting or establishing a global presence is apparently less a problem for large American-headquartered companies, but the ability of a broad swath of American businesses—particularly small and medium-sized ones—to export successfully is questionable and they have little presence overseas. Only 1 percent of American firms export—of those, 58 percent export to only one country, most often NAFTA members Canada or Mexico. U.S. Commerce Secretary Gary Locke admitted that large—but not smaller—firms receive the "full force of government" to assist them. Traditionally, American firms have been able to rely on a large, wealthy domestic market. Going abroad is also potentially hazardous: while small and midsize companies can easily chase after nonpaying domestic customers, international ones are harder to track down. Locke recommends better contacts with the Export-Import Bank to guarantee payments so that an "owner of that company in Maryland [can] sleep at night."[4] Locke frames internationalization as a fear of being defrauded rather than as an opportunity.

Contrast America with Germany, the world's leading exporter in *absolute* terms between 2003–2008. (China surpassed Germany in 2009, but

Germany remained number two). Just 1 percent of American firms export, compared to 11.3 percent of German firms and—importantly—*not* just to other EU countries. According to official criteria, a *Mittelstand* firm is simply a small (under 9 employees) or medium-sized business (up to 500) with up to €50 million in revenues. While most SMEs are naturally oriented to local, regional, or national markets, they accounted in 2008 for 20 percent of Germany's export sales (ca. €200 billion out of €1.02 trillion). Moreover, about 44 percent of total German exports went to non-EU countries; SME firms also exported to non-EU countries in roughly the same proportion as large enterprises. On average, 26 percent of the revenues for all exporting German firms derive from exports, while exporting SMEs with revenues between €17,500 and €50 million derive only a slightly smaller proportion (21 percent) from exports. Manufacturing SMEs exported even higher proportions of their revenues: 28 and 36 percent for firms employing 100–249 and 250–499 people, respectively.[5] Bottom line: German SMEs are as oriented to global markets as large German firms—unlike American SMEs.

Overall, Germany's export surpluses were based on long-term wage moderation, improved overall productivity and labor market flexibility, the relative weakness of the Euro, and the increasing competitiveness of its *manufacturing* products—precisely in the *Mittelstand* (the family-owned small and medium-sized [SME] sector). Moreover, this occurred in an environment with high wages, social benefits, taxes, and regulation.[6] Many Nordic countries—Switzerland, Austria, and northern Italy—manage to do the same.

In 2011, *Time* highlighted the country's "backbone" of family businesses such as STIHL, the global leader in chainsaws, as an exemplar of why the export ratio relative to GDP increased from 33 percent in 2000 to 41 percent in 2009 for Germany (a growth of 22 percent compared to a measly increase of 1 percent in the United States during the same period.[7] Even midsize businesses from obscure little towns in Germany saw the globe as their marketplace. For example, located in Nienhagen near Celle, Micon is a 60-employee firm specializing in precision equipment designed to keep deep-drilling machines vertical. It exports 90 percent of its products and was in the news in the summer of 2010 because its equipment helped to save the 33 trapped Chilean miners.[8]

The export performance of Germany's midsize family firms is even more impressive if one employs the common-sense understanding of *Mittelstand* Germans use, which elastically includes almost all independent, unlisted family firms with often relatively large revenues and employment figures, such as STIHL (€2 billion with 10,800 employees worldwide in 2009) or TRUMPF, a leader in laser-cutting technology (€1.34 billion with 7,900 employees worldwide in 2010). Almost 31 percent of total German exports derive from such "upper-class" (*gehobene*) family-owned Mittelstand firms.[9]

Under this conception, Mittelstand connotes a set of attitudes that includes a strong corporate identity, hands-on owners, financial caution, a long-term orientation rather than shareholder value maximization, a deep embeddedness in regional or community life, loyalty to a core group of highly skilled workers, and, finally and most important, intergenerational continuity whereby sons (and increasingly daughters) are expected to continue the family tradition. Under this most elastic definition, even Robert Bosch considers itself a "Mittelstand" firm.[10] Such firms have allegedly relied on conservative growth paths, but as I will demonstrate, many are bold multinationals exhibiting a remarkable ability to combine family control with global operations such as STIHL or TRUMPF.[11]

Finally, large, publically listed firms in Germany usually have a controlling bloc owner, often a family with a relatively low degree of free float, that is, available shares for purchase on equity markets.[12] Many Germans consider this family anchor of even the largest companies—such as the Quandts in BMW, the Mohns in Bertelsmann, the Haniels in Metro, or the Piëchs in Volkswagen—a corporate governance virtue, not a vice.[13] Although debatable, this view argues that family control ensures orientation to the long term rather than to short-term shareholder value.[14] Bernd Venohr, one of the leading analysts of German export leaders, believes that a sort of "enlightened family capitalism" was at work. Family lies at the heart of German capitalism.

Hermann Simon's *Hidden Champions of the 21st Century* (2009) best outlines these considerable strengths of such midsize export champions with their tight focus on niche strategies combined with a commitment to high quality and innovation. Remarkably, Simon found about 2,000 world market–leading companies, two-thirds stemming from the German-language area (Germany, Switzerland, Austria), followed by the Netherlands, Scandinavia, northern Italy, the United States, and Japan.[15]

Less appreciated is the degree to which many of these "hidden champions" are pocket multinationals or micromultinationals with a significantly high transnationality index. For example, Mustang Jeans, located in Künzelsau near Heilbronn, was among the first European producers of jeans after its owners swapped six bottles of schnaps for six American jeans in 1948. In 2009, it was a third-generation family firm employing a whopping 480 people, 350 still in Germany; nonetheless, many of its nine production sites were outside Germany—in Portugal, France, Russia, Hong Kong, China—and it had a joint venture with a department store operator in India. Arri, a world leader in professional camera and film equipment, is based in Munich but has subsidiaries across Europe, Canada, and the United States; globally it employs 1,200 people, about one-half outside Germany. A third-generation family firm owned by the Niedeckers, PolyClip System, has a 50 percent world market share in fastening clips for sausage and other food packaging (a 90 percent export share in terms of revenues). It is headquartered in Hattersheim outside of Frankfurt yet has 20 subsidiaries run by local managers including production sites in the United States and Brazil since the 1970s; it employs 700 globally with 350 in Germany.[16]

The list could go on, but such firms' internationalization process has been neglected in explaining their world market leadership. In the first part of this chapter, I highlight a few key firms that have internationalized since the 1970s for which published interviews, sufficient secondary literature, press coverage, and/or archival material on their internationalizing process could be found. I also utilized major business journals, *Wirtschaftswoche* and *Handelsblatt*, to embed these individual stories in a broader pattern. Most remained committed to maintaining family control (not always successfully).

The second part focuses on a few key barriers smaller firms face when internationalizing. The Bank of Reconstruction and the Institute for Mittelstand Research found that insufficient financing capacity, difficulty finding qualified personnel, and legal/regulatory barriers are SMEs' largest hurdles for international engagement.[17] I will concentrate on the tension between finding new forms of financing to go abroad and retaining family control. The examples below also show that reorganizing firms and bringing in outside executives with significant international experience are key moments in overcoming the "liability of foreign inexperience." Finally, I argue that the internationalization process for such SMEs *was* different than for larger corporations, first, because of their reliance on *external* institutions (Chambers of Commerce, Foreign Chamber of Commerce, and banks) for knowledge and resources.[18] A robust array of supporting institutions meant that such family-owned midsize firms did not have to internalize such resources yet still had access to them.[19] Internationalization potentially called firms' family ownership and/or control into question so that owning families either relied (or tried to rely) on retained earnings for their growth or invented novel corporate governance solutions to maintain family control. Again, such possibilities depended upon local/national corporate governance laws, making the quality of the home institutional environment a crucial variable in SME internationalization.

5.1   GLOBALIZATION FROM A 17MM PERSPECTIVE

The following examples highlight some of the most frequent dilemmas family firms encounter when internationalizing. The Swiss Kaba Group turnaround was particularly dramatic as the firm's internationalization effort was saved by a 17mm perspective. This example also highlights common issues and trends midsize firms have faced since the 1970s.

Kaba Group

Founded in 1862, the family-owned Swiss Bauer AG (now the Kaba Group), a manufacturer of safes, steel furniture, locks, and other security products for banks, found itself near bankruptcy almost exactly a century later. A new energetic executive brought in to liquidate the firm instead turned it around after a decade of struggle. He kept it in business in the 1970s despite a series of expensive flops such as diversifying into wooden furniture. But the decisive moment for Kaba was technological. In the late 1970s and 1980s, electronics altered the playing field for mechanical engineering firms. Because electronic locking and security systems were clearly the wave of the future, Kaba engineers began developing products that linked electronic sensors to traditional mechanical keys. In 1983, Kaba had its breakthrough, a "mechatronic" key lock that electronically detected different sorts of metal alloys in the key and could be reprogrammed, enhancing security.

Kaba executives saw great potential in the new type of key combined with European efforts to create a single European market, but Switzerland had a 22mm standard. Although Kaba had sales and production subsidiaries in Austria and England as early as the 1960s, it could not export to other European countries because their standards did not accommodate the 22mm design. Varying national standards acted as a nontariff trade barrier. Switzerland alone could not generate the necessary sales volume to lower costs. Kaba responded by creatively changing its standard lock cylinder, reducing the core part to 17mm, the smallest diameter extant in Europe, and then customizing the surrounding lock cylinder to accommodate different national standard diameters around this common core. The 17mm core or module eventually became a common *mental* platform for expanding more swiftly across Europe, then across the rest of the globe.

In certain respects, Kaba had to stop being "Swiss," built on a "22mm-diameter cylinder perspective," and shift to a more focused, tighter core—call it a new "17mm perspective"—with greater systems integration that unlocked new markets. With this, a key became an integrated system that controlled entry to the building, and access to its security and electronics (fire, climate controls, other doors, even personnel and work time information). Computer-integrated manufacturing not only helped make the "mechatronic" key in all its global permutations but enabled it to link to the customer's computerized building administration. Kaba began to redesign banks' entire security, locks, safes, and building sensors into a single platform for "intelligent buildings": "Total Access" (in English). From locks and keys emerged a locking *system*. This trend parallels that of automobile suppliers who also moved in the 1980s and 1990s from supplying "parts" to complex systems. Today, such keys contain microchips, enabling the Kaba to enter various ticketing markets.

The metaphor of a 17mm perspective exemplifies how many smaller firms succeeded. First, they moved into a widening Europe in response to the Single European Market initiative of the 1980s, then into Eastern Europe after the fall of communism, then they went global by both thinking smaller in niches (the cylinder size of locks) and by thinking wider (exporting to the world rather than just Switzerland and a few countries). Many midcap firms gained stunning world market shares by thinking in niches.[20] The Swiss Bauer AG's old 22mm-diameter-cylinder perspective proved both a barrier to thinking across borders and to rethinking the old Swiss Bauer family firm, which was subsequently transformed in 1995 into the Kaba

Group (named after the firm's longstanding product) and by being listed on the Zurich stock exchange. "Going global" from a 17mm perspective meant reinventing the firm.

Parallel to these internal innovations, the Kaba Group became a pocket multinational, opening wholly owned manufacturing sites, starting joint ventures, and acquiring firms overseas. The 1995 public offering generated additional capital for such expansion. By 2000, this classic, regionally embedded and nationally oriented firm employed about 2,800 workers—only 850 in Switzerland. In 2001, financed by a large capital increase, Kaba acquired Unican outright, a Montreal-based key, lock, and security company, for over a billion Swiss francs to gain access to Canadian and U.S. markets. By 2010, it employed around 7,700 with over SFr1 billion in revenues, and ranked first in the world in its specialties. Kaba has production sites in Germany, Austria, the United States, Japan, and Malaysia and recently acquired the Wah Yuet Group in China and two JVs in India.[21] While still anchored in Switzerland, the Kaba Group is arguably no longer "Swiss."

Unlike many other firms that managed to retain family control, Kaba made a classic transition from a family firm to a managerial enterprise because of its late 1960s bankruptcy, the turnaround executive's success, and the rapid capital increase generated by issuing shares. The last family remnant rests in a 15 percent share owned by the heirs of Leo Bodmer, who had purchased Bauer in 1915. Nonetheless, the family had little active influence on the firm's strategy or internationalization process.

5.2   MITTELSTAND MULTINATIONALS

Kaba's transformation and internationalization parallels a great number of (former) SMEs that started in the 1970s but accelerated their global expansion after the economic recession of the early 1990s. Many firms maintained family control such as STIHL (chainsaws), TRUMPF (laser-cutting), Siegwerk (specialty inks), Elektrisola Dr. Gerd Schildbach (fine, enameled wire), and Krawinkel/PWM (electronic gas station price signs). By contrast, Nordenia, a film-packaging producer best known for the thin porous film inside P&G's Pampers baby diapers, like Kaba, could not maintain family ownership and sold out to a private equity group. However, even if they did retain family ownership, these firms represent a transformation away from a classic Mittelstand firm to a new sort of globally active, family-owned company.

After the exchange rate shocks following the collapse of Bretton Woods in the early 1970s, STIHL, TRUMPF, Siegwerk, Elektrisola, and Nordenia internationalized, but each had slightly different drivers. Located in Waiblingen (Württemberg), STIHL earned over €2 billion in revenues—88 percent abroad (about 30 percent in the United States alone)—and employed about 10,800 employees across the globe with just under 4,000 employees in Germany. Consequently, its transnationality index is quite high. Yet in 1972, it was a classic, export-oriented family firm employing 2,500 employees—all in Germany—with revenues of DM 220 million.

STIHL opened its first overseas plant in São Leopoldo, Brazil, in 1973 in reaction to the falling dollar of the 1970s and oil crisis, which helped it by raising the demand for wood. In 1974, it opened further plants in Wil, Switzerland, and Virginia Beach, United States. The Virginia Beach plant hedged against currency fluctuations. STIHL also diversified into related goods such as helmets, outdoor apparel, and trimmers and blowers. By the beginning of the 1990s, STIHL produced more saws in the United States for the non-professional small U.S. chainsaw market than it did in Germany. After the fall of communism, STIHL opened sales subsidiaries across Eastern Europe and Russia, as well as in Japan (1990), Mexico (1995), Hong Kong (1995), South Africa (1996), China (1995), and Argentina (1998). STIHL's expansion fit with the remarkable, decade-long wave of globalization in the 1990s, one of the main periods of internationalization for German business.[22] Like Kaba, STIHL activated huge new foreign investments in the mid-2000s by expanding its American plant, opening a new chainsaw factory in Switzerland, but opened a further factory in Quingdao, China, in 2006. Some figures provide some sense of this twenty-first-century expansion wave: in 1999, STIHL employed roughly 6,000 people worldwide, with just under 3,000 in Germany, yet by 2010 it employed 10,000 people globally with 4,000 in Germany. All of the plants remained wholly owned.[23]

TRUMPF, led by the legendary Berthold Leibinger, one of the most respected spokespersons for the German machine-tool industry, was the Gold Standard for the Mittelstand. Although Leibinger continually stressed the virtues of Germany as an industrial location, by 2009/2010 TRUMPF, which earned €1.34 billion, generated 71.8 percent of its revenues overseas with about 44 percent of its total 7,928 employees located outside Germany in 59 worldwide subsidiaries and branch offices. Yet in 1967, TRUMPF was a classic Mittelstand firm employing 440 employees, all in Germany, with sales of just DM 20 million. It specialized in machines that cut metal but became most famous for developing laser-cutting of sheet metal, introduced in 1979. Electronics, computerization, and laser-cutting, like the mechatronic key at Kaba, transformed TRUMPF as it began producing its own lasers by 1985. Already in 1968, TRUMPF was among the first firms to introduce numerically controlled, computer-guided production systems, which spread throughout the machine-tool industry during the 1970s and 1980s.[24]

Like Kaba, TRUMPF established its first sales subsidiary in Baar (Zug), Switzerland, in 1963, but jumped swiftly across two oceans to the United States (Connecticut) in 1969 and Japan (Yokohama) in 1977. As reasons, Leibinger stressed TRUMPF's desire to acquire competitors' technological expertise and to pay closer attention to major markets. The first laser-cutting machine, for instance, was borrowed from the United States. Leibinger had lived three years in the United States and was comfortable with Japanese culture as his parents and the founder of TRUMPF, Christian Trumpf, were serious Japanese art collectors. Though most subsidiaries handled sales and service, the American site integrated production operations. TRUMPF initiated manufacturing in Japan in 2008 in Fukushima. By the 1980s, an inadequate number of skilled workers at home pushed TRUMPF to begin manufacturing parts in 1980 in Grüsch (Switzerland) and Haguenau (France). After the 1993/1994 German reunification crisis, TRUMPF turned to outside consultants to redesign its production operations and global strategy. At first, TRUMPF was wary of moving manufacturing to other locations, mostly for reasons of product quality, but it became increasingly confident that localism anywhere in the world was important for serving local customers. TRUMPF emphasized geographic proximity as a main driver of global expansion because localism sped decision making. In order to go global, many such companies simply had to go local to be near clients.[25]

In response to cheaper, mostly Japanese and Asian competition, TRUMPF created simpler machines and lowered prices while still remaining a premium brand, especially when moving into emerging markets. In 1999, TRUMPF began working with Taiwanese partners then opened a new plant in 2001 in Gueishan Shiang; by 2005, it launched a new series of machines produced there. In 2007, TRUMPF opened another facility in Apodaca (Monterrey), Mexico, to produce frames for its American subsidiary in Connecticut; in 2006, it opened a new factory in Liberec, Czech Republic; in 2009, it opened another factory in Taicang, near Shanghai, which became known as Little Swabia because so many German firms moved production there.[26] TRUMPF expanded entirely through retained earnings, and Leibinger kept complete control and ownership by stressing that TRUMPF would remain a family business; his successor was his daughter, Nicola Leibinger-Kammüller.

Siegwerk, which specializes in packaging ink for frozen foods and chocolate bars, and even supplied specialty ink for the 1957 Treaty of Rome and the seventh hardcover volume of the Harry Potter series, remains a sixth-generation family firm. As an intermediate supplier (one of its main clients was Nordenia below), its fate was tied to the 1950s color-magazine publishing industry. Siegwerk employed around 100 people then. By 2010, it had become the third-largest producer in the global ink industry and first in Europe with sales in 2010 of €874 million, more than doubling from €387 million in 2004 through massive acquisitions after 2000 (like Kaba). In 2010, it employed 4,400 employees worldwide, less than 950 employees, in its home headquarters in Siegburg, down slightly from its peak employment of 1,200 people in 1995.[27]

Siegwerk's internationalization accelerated after the collapse of communism; but like TRUMPF and STIHL, it went multinational in the United States in the 1970s by following its main publishing partners to Iowa, Virginia, North Carolina, and Arizona. Its German publishing partner supplied 40 percent of the American joint venture's equity to finance the expansion. Like the above firms, Siegwerk invested greater attention in

R&D, digitized colored-ink production, electronically steered engraving equipment, improved testing and measuring equipment, and computerized ink manufacturing. After the 1990s, all the big German publishing houses moved into Eastern Europe, pulling Siegwerk along with them, although Siegwerk remained an exporter from its Siegburg base, which by the mid-1990s employed 1,200 people and had revenues of DM 700 million.

The game changed, however, as globalization and Single European Market initiatives consolidated the global print industry into larger firms and the Japanese entered the European market through aggressive acquisitions (150 acquisitions in the 1990s including the print division of Siegwerk's main home rival BASF). Siegwerk was pressured to broaden its scale and international presence as American and Netherlandic firms also expanded throughout Europe. Surprisingly, Siegwerk's U.S. partner suddenly sold its 40 percent stake in its subsidiary to a rival printing firm, which Siegwerk managed to buy back at great expense in 2002. By the late 1990s, Siegwerk had hired an outside executive with significant international experience, reorganized into a joint-stock company (AG), and hired additional managers with international experience. As at TRUMPF, the new executive brought in management consultants to improve marketing, procurement, and logistics, which enabled Siegwerk to launch a major push to "go global" with plans to invest €200 million between 2003 and 2008. Revenues jumped to €874 million by 2010 after a wave of mergers and acquisitions between 2004 and 2006. After 2000, Siegwerk then expanded to Thailand, Poland, England, Portugal, Brazil, France, Turkey, Spain, South Africa, India, China, Malaysia, Mexico, and Argentina. The core of the new expansion resulted in two major acquisitions in 2003 in the United States (Color Converting, Inc.) and Switzerland (Sicpa Packaging). Siegwerk acquired Sicpa, which gave it a presence in over 30 countries, partially out of fear that without sufficient scale, it would lose its independence as private equity and investment banks consolidated the industry.[28] Unlike STIHL or TRUMPF, which moved to the market, Siegwerk's expansion was in part defensive as the global ink industry consolidated around it. But it, too, depended on a sort of localism throughout its history whereby being close to its main clients permitted customized solutions and speed of service. In this case, that meant following abroad.

As with STIHL, Kaba, Siegwerk, and TRUMPF, Elektrisola Dr. Gerd Schildbach engaged in its first tentative overseas ventures because of currency fluctuations and new trade agreements. Market opportunities pulled Elektrisola abroad. Elektrisola specialized in super-thin enameled copper wire it could manufacture seven times thinner than a human hair; these were used in electronic watches, electronics, and even the Mars Rover explorer. Unusually, Elektrisola's Malaysian and Swiss plants, but not its German one, could produce such fine wire. Although overall revenue figures are not known, in 2010 it earned roughly €99.6 million in Germany and about $90 million in the United States and employed 2,600 globally but just 300 in Germany. Elektrisola is a particularly hidden multinational.

Trade agreements drove Elektrisola's global expansion. Italian import tariffs and a desire to be closer to its main clients, who lay in Italy, prompted it to move production to two sites to Italy after 1964. When Switzerland joined the EFTA, raising tariff rates 10 percent, it opened a production subsidiary in 1968 in Escholzmatt. The rise of the DM and fall of the dollar led it to establish a production subsidiary in New Hampshire. With its largest customers in Asia, it opened its largest manufacturing operation in the early 1990s in Bentong, Malaysia, employing around 1,000 employees. After NAFTA was signed in 1994, it moved in 1995 to Cuauhtémoc (Chihuahua), Mexico. Finally, as established electronics companies moved production to China, Elektrisola followed its main clients in 2006 to Hangzhou. As Elektrisola describes it, "we deliver enameled wire to customers across the whole world from factories in Europe, America, and Asia because by reducing the distances between the production site and our customers, we can make possible shorter transportation lines and therefore create flexible and faster delivery times."[29] Psychic distance was less important than proximity to clients and servicing the local/regional market.

The Nordenia Group was founded in 1966 by Peter Mager as a private company to produce flexible packaging, safety or technical films for industry and consumer uses (such as wrappings for candy, ice cream, or diapers). Nordenia tended to follow its largest customers (Henkel, Proctor & Gamble, and Unilever) abroad. It founded its first subsidiary in the United States in 1988 to cater to P&G (especially for its diapers). In 1997, it expanded into China (again to follow P&G after just three weeks of intensive debate and planning); it also started a joint venture with the Dalian Shengdao Group through a chance encounter. Abroad, it had to rely on a different network of suppliers and even build palettes and shelving that would have come complete in a more developed country. It had to send specialty-skilled workers to explain technical issues but despite a slew of translators had difficulties conveying precise specifications. It then turned to external sources, discovering a Mandarin- and German-speaking Chinese consultant who had lived in Bielefeld for 15 years. In other areas of the world, it often hired outside experts from other firms to help with the start-up process.[30] After 2003, Nordenia further expanded into Russia and Malaysia. At each juncture, it had to find outside experts, translators, partners, and financing to continue expansion.

Unlike the above firms, financing proved Nordenia's ultimate limitation. Nordenia formed a financial holding and transformed into a joint-stock company in 1992 to secure additional capital for its further expansion into Spain and Hungary (following P&G). Ownership and control remained united with the owner. It aligned itself with joint-stock company corporate governance rules but did not issue shares; instead, it relied on its banks ("whose loans were not always the cheapest") until a Los Angeles–based private equity firm, Oaktree Capital Management, bought it out in 2006. According to Mager, financing expansion proved the main "bottleneck," so that the firm's continued expansion required Mager to cash out to the highest bidder, though he still controlled 15 percent of the equity. Revenue jumped from €670 million in 2005 to €800 million by 2010.[31]

A true SME with just 65 employees in 2010, PWM, led by seventh-generation manager Max Krawinkel, practically symbolizes the changes in the German economy since early industrialization. Symbolically, in 2010 PWM remained housed in the defunct textile mill of the first generation. Founded in 1806, the company began with a single weaving loom for socks. Eventually, the Krawinkels built two spinning and weaving factories in and near Bergneustadt, about 50 kilometers east of Cologne. It shifted to cotton socks and by 1914 employed about 1,400 people and exported about 50 percent of its production as far away as China and South Africa. Succession issues and fraud by the adopted son nearly bankrupted the firm in the 1920s, but it almost accidentally acquired a basalt rock quarry in the process. By the 1950s/1960s, profits from the crushed rock business, prosperous because of road and streetcar line building, essentially carried the loss-making textile business.

Sensing that textiles might not ever recover, the Krawinkels diversified widely in the 1960s into fertilizer, specialty chemicals, a Ford dealership, a Canada Dry soft drink distributor, a traffic light company, electronic coils for telephones, and plastic advertising signs (Plastikwerk Müller & Co.), the basis for PWM. Ironically, while the family retained complete ownership, as a diversified family conglomerate, it was run by professional managers, except for Plastikwerk Müller, which the sixth-generation Krawinkel tried in vain to turn into a profitable business from the late 1960s to the early 1980s.

The family nearly went bankrupt once again as one of the salaried executives convinced the family that the crushed rock business could be successful in Nigeria. To save the family firm, they "amputated" the venture in the late 1970s, got rid of the salaried executive, and, fortunately, found a deep-pocketed buyer for the crushed rock business, which still exists in Nigeria.

That left only a thin ray of hope for Plastikwerk Müller, which struggled to find a successful product for its plastic molding skills. It luckily gained a large order for lottery signs in the mid-1970s but concentrated on moving into the insulated plastic window frame business. Not until 1984 did Karl-Adolf Krawinkel hit upon the bright idea that gas station attendants could change the price signs of gas stations electronically rather than manually did the business take off. By encasing the price signs, now using LEDs, in near indestructible plastic, the overall operating costs of the signs dropped, and they allowed for swift price changes in response to market rates. Having conquered the German domestic market with a 90 percent market share, PWM turned to exports and divested itself of most its other subsidiaries. By 2000, it opened a sales subsidiary in Houston and began targeting the American market, capturing a nationwide contract for Texaco and Chevron in 2007 and becoming a true SME micromultinational.[32]

Together, these collective mini-portraits illustrate, at the firm level, some general patterns of transformation and challenges of internationalization over time. Structurally, the 1970s saw many firms such as STIHL, TRUMPF, Elektrisola, and Siegwerk make significant commitments abroad. As large firms suffered disproportionately, the proportion of industrial employment in sectors like electrical and machine-engineering rose for medium-sized firms, with firms like TRUMPF or STIHL leading this trend; overseas investments helped maintain employment at home.[33] The 1980s were less a period of internationalization per se than a period of reengineering products and firms. Computers, microelectronics (microprocessors, chips, miniaturization), computer-assisted design (CAD), and electronics revolutionized manufacturing processes and final products such as gas station signs, laser-cutting, and locks and keys. The cycle of innovation sped up. In the electronics industry, a *"Know-how-Defizit"* appeared alongside a shortage of personnel trained in information technology. Simultaneously, Japan appeared "unbeatable." Japan (and to a lesser extent South Korea, Taiwan, Singapore, and Hong Kong) managed to produce quality machines that were durable, and reliable but simpler and at a much lower price point, which eroded the traditional competitiveness of products "Made in Germany." To avoid competition, many German firms escaped further into narrow niches of high-quality goods, so-called diversified quality production (DQP). The business weekly *Wirtschaftswoche* concluded in 1991 that Germany would only receive a "bronze medal" in global competition.[34] Finally, the overall cost base of German firms rose in the 1980s so that by 1994, the Association of Mechanical Engineering Firms in Germany estimated that about 24 percent of the surveyed firms stated that they already had a production site abroad and 11 percent planned to open one.[35]

The 1993/1994 unification crisis proved another major turning point, primarily because of Eastern Europe's potential as a market and an "extended workbench," as well as the fast growth of the Pacific Rim rather than the crisis of cost and reunification at home. The *opportunity* of global markets and the expansion of the single European market, not sickness at home, propelled such firms abroad. Internationalization was driven by client and service needs that permitted such firms to leap oceans relatively easily without an Uppsala-type stage process (see Introduction). The late 1980s and early 1990s saw a remarkable transformation of global supply chains, probably none more dramatically than that of the automobile industry; "shipping" transformed into "logistics." In particular, two major trends hit automobile subcontractors. As with automobiles, Japanese automakers changed the rules of the game by challenging Germans' craft-based production process with just-in-time production and quality circles. The second trend was price pressure on automobiles themselves as original equipment manufacturers pushed for greater cost efficiencies from their subcontractors, all the while demanding greater technological innovation. Closer coordination with original equipment manufacturers regarding designs, production cycles, and timing became imperative. Information technology systems were upgraded. As original equipment manufacturers moved abroad such as

BMW, subcontractors had to follow. Siegwerk and Nordenia—intermediate suppliers for larger consumer product firms—did so, too. On top of these challenges, the postreunification recession hit firms hard as craft-based Porsche slipped near bankruptcy and Robert Bosch lost money. In Würt-temberg, the state provided emergency liquidity loans through its state bank to hundreds of small and medium-sized firms, one-third alone to automobile, electronics, and machine-engineering firms. A reading of two leading German business periodicals, *Wirtschaftswoche* and *Handelsblatt*, between 1986–2001 reveals that their coverage shifted its attention from the preparation for a single market and logistics between 1986–1992 to an increasing emphasis on the challenges of internationalization and finance between 1993–2001. These technological and logistical innovations placed great pressure on financing, which *Landesbanken* (federal state banks), savings banks (*Sparkassen*), and cooperatives readily supplied to the Mittelstand.[36] In 1997, the OECD published a survey on the motives of German SMEs for moving abroad, see Table 5.1, which overwhelmingly demonstrated that they moved abroad to access new markets or to secure existing markets.

As with Eastern Europe, Asian markets became just as important as a target market that could only be accessed by actually moving production there (STIHL, Elektrisola, TRUMPF, Nordenia). The famed eyeglass wear producer, Rodenstock, had already built production sites in Thailand to improve its international competitiveness. Elektrisola moved to Malaysia. In 1996, Berthold Leibinger of TRUMPF stressed that Germany was too far away to properly service customers; exports from home would simply be too expensive.[37] Another 1996 article emphasized that German firms would have to cater to the "special expectations" of these new markets and that this would require delegating more responsibility to knowledgeable people from those areas. Mittelstand family firms would have to significantly rethink their operations.[38] Kaba, STIHL, Siegwerk, and Nordenia all re-formed themselves as joint-stock companies to access capital markets and raise equity; all four significantly revised their organizational structures, and all brought in outside management talent with knowledge of global operations. *Wirtschaftswoche*

Table 5.1   Motives for Internationalization of German SMEs

Expansion into New Markets to Enhance Revenue	72 percent
Securing Existing Markets	53 percent
Lower Labor Costs	27 percent
Tax Advantages	12 percent
Following Important Customers	11 percent
Potential Advantages of Reimporting	10 percent
Lower Environmental Expenses	5 percent

Source: OECD, Globalisation and Small and Medium Enterprises (SMEs), V. 1, 1997, 47.

thought German firms were simply too expensive, did not have enough financing capabilities to expand globally, and lacked qualified people who could work abroad. Yet, as it noted, globalization was not so much an option as "the only chance" for subcontracting firms.[39]

In retrospect, the tone of this analysis in this time period sounds dire, a product of the "sick man" rhetoric pervading Germany between the mid-1990s and early 2000s, yet many German Mittelstand firms were actually aggressively asserting themselves and developing overseas connections, manifesting positive results after 2005.

Since the mid-1990s, SMEs have increasingly engaged in foreign direct investment. The Bank for Reconstruction (KfW) estimated that between 2003 and 2007 about 3 percent of all SMEs (ca. 100,000 firms) did so. Between 1996 and 2006, German FDI grew around 250 percent. Although official statistics do not break down FDI by the size of the firm, the KfW carried out a survey of 600 firms that already had some foreign direct investment and another 200 that planned to engage in it soon. It found not only that the overwhelming reason for moving abroad was to access new markets, particularly in Eurozone countries, but also that China was just as important. Thirty-six percent mentioned financing issues as the most significant problem, followed by personnel dilemmas (24 percent), then legal or bureaucratic barriers (24 percent).[40]

Another survey by the German cooperative central bank (DG BANK) of 500 Chinese subsidiaries of German SMEs found that about 60 percent were wholly owned, but personnel and organizational issues were once again listed as the paramount challenges.[41]

The next section focuses on the role of key external institutions that helped SME/midsize firms overcome such barriers so that they often internationalized as swiftly and effectively as larger firms.

5.3   FAMILY CONTROL VERSUS FINANCING

The selected firms were by no means reluctant internationalizers but definitely reluctant to relinquish family control. Except for Nordenia, whose owner sold 85 percent of his stake to a Los Angeles–based private equity group to raise new capital for expansion, and Kaba, whose original owner lost most of his control in its bankruptcy process *prior* to internationalization, all of the above firms retained family control.

TRUMPF insisted that it "will remain an internationally active family business" on its website. Elektrisola described its management in its overseas Malaysian subsidiary as still that of a family company: "Since then [1948], no one has ever been laid off. Elektrisola is an extremely stable company that is very much committed to its employees. We practise this worldwide. We would rather the shareholders take a short-term loss than any worker. This is still very much a family company in spirit and action."[42]

PWM remained entirely in the hands of the Krawinkel family. Now in its seventh generation, it has little desire to "go public."

But all these companies had to significantly alter their corporate governance structure and add more personnel with international experience, the second biggest problem in various surveys. In order to internationalize, four of the above companies turned to equity markets and went public. Kaba went public in 1996 and then raised more equity as it acquired Unican and split its shares. The merger meant absorbing Unican, which took around three years, and reorganizing the company into three global product divisions, albeit keeping a small board of just eight directors. STIHL remained a private partnership under Hans-Peter Stihl and his sister Eva Mayr-Stihl until 1997 when it was reorganized as a joint-stock company to raise new capital as STIHL AG. Family ownership and control remained via the STIHL Holding KG, a private partnership, which was founded in 1995 as an umbrella organization for its original firm, its Swiss subsidiary, and its marketing headquarters. They formed a separate limited liability corporation, STIHL International GmbH, to restructure all of its international subsidiaries. Hans Peter Stihl stepped down from active management in 2002, although he remained influential on the supervisory board as chair until 2012 when his son, Nikolas Stihl, took over after he retired. Bertram Kandziora became chief executive in 2003, and the board expanded to a tight five people by 2008.

TRUMPF too had to significantly reorganize its business. Like Siegwerk, it turned to external consultants to design its global strategy. It tended to keep core R&D and high value-added production at home with tight, centralized headquarters supervision. It created "Centers of Excellence" (like General Electric) to ensure quality high enough, wherever production took place, so that those manufacturing subsidiaries could export products anywhere in the world. Cash flow and profitability remained so high that the family has retained full ownership through a foundation of the two TRUMPF holding companies, one organized as a private partnership and the other as a limited liability (GmbH) corporation. This reorganization in 2000 meant that Berthold Leibinger stepped back more but created clearer competencies globally among TRUMPF's four main product lines. Managing a global company changed TRUMPF, although the family remained in full control.

In 1999, threatened by global consolidation in the ink industry and after the retirement of its chief executive, the Keller family of Siegwerk hired an outside executive with significant international experience in the United States, Mexico City, and Paris. He hired more managers with international experience, brought in management consultants to advise the greater professionalization of management across the board, and created a new international division of labor. In 2002, with global expansion looming, the private limited liability partnership (GmbH & Co. KG) was transformed into a public limited company, in case it needed to raise additional capital quickly. The Keller family's lack of desire to "go public" showed in its decision to turn the company in 2011 back into a private limited joint-stock company (KGaA).

These examples demonstrate that even firms retaining family control had to significantly reimagine their companies and creatively resort to different corporate governance solutions, as well. They brought in outside advisors or executives with international expertise. Many raised equity—reluctantly. The examples also demonstrate that families might not be reluctant internationalizers if creative ways of maintaining significant control stakes through corporate governance options could be found. These options depend upon the external legal framework, making securities law a crucial variable in families' eagerness or reluctance to internationalize. The quality of equity markets, which improved in Germany for start-ups and midsize firms in the mid-1990s, also coincided with Mittelstand internationalization. Indeed, *established* family firms raising equity dominated German IPOs around the turn of the century.[43] Such firms might have been reluctant to go public, but not reluctant to internationalize.

5.4   KEY EXTERNAL INSTITUTIONS

Without resorting to the obvious manner of raising more capital, which dilutes family ownership, how does one "go global" with limited capital, organizational and personnel resources, and knowledge of other countries?[44] One of the keys to internationalizing Mittelstand firms is the quality of *external* agents and institutions (other firms, partners, banks, consultants, local, regional, and national governments) to substitute for weak or missing internal competencies that larger corporations have internalized. Independent consultants are one possibility, but German SMEs have stated that the two most important institutions are their regional Chambers of Industry and Commerce (*Industrie- und Handelskammer*, IHK) combined with their associated Foreign Chambers of Commerce (*Auslandshandelskammern*, AHKs) established by the national umbrella organization called the Diet of German Industry and Chamber of Commerce (*Deutscher Industrie- und Handelskammertag*, DIHK), and banks. Slight differences among firms arose concerning which institution was most effective. Firms over 500 employees ranked banks number one, while firms of 100–499 workers—classic SMEs—ranked their local IHK as most helpful.[45]

One distinctive aspect of the German economy is its rich associational life of intermediary institutions that blur the boundaries between the public and private, between markets and politics, providing midsize firms with a thick ground cover of export support. One critic called this a "fragmentation of export promotion agencies," while another spoke of a "jungle of export promotion agencies."[46] However, the eighty regional IHKs were judged most effective by Mittelstand firms in numerous surveys. These public bodies by law represent the interests of all firms in the region and are particularly focused on Mittelstand needs; participation was mandatory and collected contributions by firms according to size. These chambers acted as quasi-public institutions for the "self-government" (*Selbstverwaltung*) of the regional economy. Their responsibilities went well beyond interest group representation or lobbying (more the American model): they acted as consulting organizations, carried out research projects regarding the locational advantages and disadvantages of their region, acted as a research and statistical agency, promoted new start-ups and regional innovation initiatives, helped organize international contacts and delegation trips, arranged partners abroad, brought in outside experts and consultants for common projects, and acted as a central information source and clearinghouse for regional business. Finally, it acted as a policy-coordinating forum for all businesses in the region, paying special attention to local training, educational, and certification programs.[47]

The umbrella organization of the regional chambers was the National Association of Chambers of Industry and Commerce (DIHK), which established Foreign Chambers of Commerce (AHKs) in around 80 different countries with about 120 local branches. Over 40,000 German firms and local partners were voluntary members in these private associations, which were DIHK-certified and financially supported by the Federal Ministry for Economics and Technology. These AHKs, among the most important channels offering a range of services (often for fees) and establishing contacts in particular places around the world, were, nonetheless, often viewed as the "most important pillars" or "core" of export promotion. From the DIHK website, with a simple drop-down box, one can access the contact information of each individual AHK around the world with a list of German-speaking contacts with varying sorts of expertise.[48]

Friendly banks provided a second base of external support. Traditionally, many family firms did not necessarily have sophisticated financial controlling, especially as financial advice could be "outsourced" to local banks. Thus, banks were not only a source of credit but provided consulting advice, as well as contacts worldwide. Banks offered such an advisory or service center as it attracted the business of many successful SMEs. Relationship banking also permitted families a degree of discretion not possible if they issued equity. SMEs in Germany (but also across Europe, for example, in Italy) were quite sensitive to legislation or economic downturns that questioned lines of credit. The level of controversy surrounding Basel II and Basel III financial market legislation was astounding because legislation might have constricted lending.[49]

Moreover, German SMEs often could rely on banks rather than internalizing market research. All of the Big Three banks (Deutsche Bank, the former Dresdner Bank, and Commerzbank) catered, in particular, to the export-oriented, "upper-class" (*gehobene*) Mittelstand firms such as a TRUMPF or STIHL, especially those with revenues above €50 million. Small to midsize SMEs tended to rely on savings banks, state public banks (*Landesbanken*), or cooperatives.

If banks provided comprehensive consulting services, they could bind together long-term financial planning along with foreign market analyses and "how-to" advice on finding business partners, starting up subsidiaries, and finding political contacts. In the mid-1990s, for instance, the Deutsche Bank established 260 "centers of competence" to provide in-house consulting services (and sometimes used specialized external subsidiaries). Often large banks, both private and state public banks, established commercial centers in Asia or Latin America to gather information about potential export partners or establishing local production subsidiaries. This help also rebounded to their own business interests as these banks dominated export finance. Baden-Württemberg was especially aggressive at founding public-private partnerships among public entities, banks, and firms as information sources for Mittelstand firms seeking to "go international." In 1999, for instance, the Federal Ministry for Economic Cooperation and Development (BMZ) started a program entitled Public Private Partnerships (PPP) that brought together public development agencies in various countries with mostly Mittelstand firms. This gave German firms some public support to smooth market access and provide local knowledge, especially in countries with "unfavorable framework conditions," while the individual countries' public agencies gained access to critical industrial knowledge. By 2010, the BMZ enabled 3,000 development partnerships in about 70 countries worth about €21.4 billion. Such public partnerships took on part of the financing costs but also reduced companies' risk of going it alone.[50] Certain public-private banks such as the *Kreditanstalt für Wiederaufbau* (KfW) and the *Industriekreditbank* (IKB)—before it went bankrupt in the 2008/2009 financial crisis—led the way in securitizing Mittelstand loans then sluicing funds back to Mittelstand firms.[51]

After its near disastrous forays into complex financial securities and investment banking after the dot.com boom, the Commerzbank reoriented its basic strategy for becoming the number one bank for the Mittelstand. It offers a particularly good example of the role—and profitability—of catering to this sector. Commerzbank created a distinct "Mittelstandsbank" as its own distinct segment; just under 10 percent of its employees work specifically for Mittelstand firms. A 2010 survey ranked Commerzbank as the "favorite institution for international business." It had representation in more than 50 countries but made a strategic decision to focus on the German Mittelstand by providing consulting advice, strategy formulation, specific suggestions and contacts for different countries, as well as an "International Desk" in Germany. Commerzbank advertised that firms "would feel abroad like at home" (*Im Ausland wie zu Hause*).[52] The Deutsche Bank tended to concentrate mostly on the "upper-class," export-oriented firms, which fit its classic profile as an export financing bank.

However, Germany's ubiquitous savings banks, its single largest banking sector, were the greatest banking "friend" for the broad base of Mittelstand firms. In 2003, the umbrella financial organization of German savings banks established "S-CountryDesk," which brought together all of its export and international business experts in the service of the Mittelstand. Every savings bank, along with its client, had access to the service; with more branches and more assets than any other group, the savings bank system provided a powerful means of supporting "going global." By the end of 2003, this service "accompanied" over 30,000 foreign transactions. The idea was that "going international" (the words of the savings bank group) required "access to information, access to financing, and processing financial transactions with foreign banks and the corresponding extra organizational efforts." As local banks could not judge the credibility of German firms and local German banks could not necessarily judge the value of foreign collateral, the savings bank service created partners with similar banks in foreign countries. This eased the entry of individual Mittelstand firms into foreign markets and lowered their transaction costs. It also provided full-service advice for setting up subsidiaries, managing foreign financing, and for direct currency transactions. The direct contacts with local foreign banks kept the savings banks from having to lend relatively expensive capital to finance supposedly riskier foreign ventures as the local banks were often eager to bring foreign investment into the locality and lent the money themselves. The savings bank group's CountryDesk service found English- and German-speaking partners, provided lists of firms and potential partners, as well as legal and judicial advice, economic, tax, and investment information, and even translation services for individual firms. A drop-down box on its Internet site listed already vetted and trusted partners. Naturally, all this extra help was supposed to bring additional business to the local savings banks by managing financing for local companies.[53] Such services solved U.S. Commerce Secretary Gary Locke's "will I get paid" problem as noted in the introduction.

5.5 CONCLUSION

Smaller firms may have different internationalization processes than larger firms because of their reliance on external institutions. Moreover, national and institutional contexts with coordinating institutions permit smaller firms *not* to internalize business functions that larger firms do. This is not "export promotion" per se. By *not* internalizing such functions, smaller firms reduce their capital needs (not only for international expansion), which enables them to maintain family or ownership control. This, in turn, makes them less reluctant to go global even as they remain reluctant to go public. The "resource constraint" or "knowledge-based" perspective, which focuses on atomized individual firms, falls short in this case because it presumes internalization of resources or competencies *within* the firm. This external support system helps minimize some of the risk of moving overseas with its inevitable missteps. This argument implies that "liberal market economies" like the United States, with less well-developed intermediary organizations or institutions than "coordinated market economies" like Germany, might be less successful in developing a robust SME export sector. State support and export promotion could fill the gap but depends on more robust government programs—unlikely in a cash-strapped and anti-big-government culture. One corollary hypothesis is that "coordinated market economies" as described in the "varieties of capitalism" literature, including Germany, Switzerland, and Austria, can better launch SME internationalizers, while "liberal market economies" require individual firms to "go it alone," making them weaker, slower internationalizers. This perspective could help to explain why Hermann Simon found such an overproportionally powerful group of "hidden champions" precisely in this region of "alpine capitalism." The irony, however, is that with these champions, *home* institutions support production offshoring and the growth of jobs and international revenue that might question the traditional alignment among community, firm, and family over the long term. Will they maintain the same longstanding commitment to their home region if they are just at home in the world, with often more sales and employees abroad than at home?

But there are other questions. Many of Hermann Simon's "hidden champions" are also "hidden multinationals" whose workings and internationalization processes still need closer analysis. For instance, all the firms discussed here have corporate websites in English and German. Perhaps *mittelstand* will become an English word just like *kindergarten*. But, more important, these firms have gained competencies around the world, contradicting the traditional "rootedness" in a particular locality or region that the classic Mittelstand implies. In STIHL's words, all these firms are "global players." What makes them still Mittelstand? Even firms that remained "all in the family" still had to reimagine and reorganize themselves as firms. Are they halfway between a family enterprise and a managerial enterprise that might dissolve in the next generation, as is the case with Kaba or Nordenia? Does that mean that they are becoming "ordinary" multinationals? Or can they retain their "familiness" that so many desire?

A final paradox that emerges from this discussion is how much Mittelstand firms utilized the "sick man" phase of Germany in the 1990s to strengthen their global positioning, providing the basis for Germany's tremendous export success after 2002. While the *Financial Times* and *The Economist* were labeling Germany the "sick man of Europe," German firms were actively repositioning themselves globally—quite healthily—directed particularly toward Asian Pacific/Chinese markets. After the bursting of the New Economy bubble in 2001 and the financial crisis of 2008–2009, German Mittelstand firms were well positioned to cater to some of the fastest-growing, emerging markets in the world—"like at home."

NOTES

1. "Universal Zooms in on Foreign Box Offices," www.ft.com, Nov. 23, 2007.
2. Greg Linden, Kenneth L. Kraemer, and Jason Dedrick, "Who Captures Value in a Global Innovation System? The Case of Apple's iPod," Personal Computing Industry Center, University of California, Irvine (June 2007), http://escholarship.org/uc/item/1770046n.

3. UNCTAD, Largest TNCs, *World Investment Report 2009*, www.unctad.org/ Templates/Page.asp?intItemID=2443&lang=1. The TNI Index combines the ratio of foreign to domestic assets, sales, and employment. "Asia: Poised for a Shift," *Financial Times*, www.ft.com, Nov. 22, 2010.
4. Quoted in Sudeep Reddy, "Trade Officials Urge Small Businesses to Export," *Wall Street Journal*, blogs.wsj.com, Feb. 25, 2011.
5. Schlüsselzahlen/Kennzahlen zum Mittelstand 2009/2010 in Deutschland, Institut für Mittelstandsforschung, www.ifm-bonn.org; "Abbildung 3: Auslandsaktivitäten," *Ergebnisse zum Export aus der Umsatzsteuerstatistik*. www.ifm-bonn.org. *Die Bedeutung der außenwirtschaftlichen Aktivitäten für den deutschen Mittelstand*, Institut der Mittelstandsforschung, www. ifm-bonn.org/assets/documents/IfM-Materialien-171.pdf.
6. WTO, www.wto.org. For example, "Germany's Surprising Economy," *Economist*, Aug. 20, 2005, 9. " 'Sick Man' Is Picture of Health," *Financial Times*, www.ft.com, Dec. 11, 2006.
7. Michael Schuman and Claudia Himmelreich, "How Germany Became the China of Europe," *Time*, Mar. 7, 2011, 52-55.
8. "German Mittelstand Gives Chilean Miners, Economy Escape Route," *Bloomberg News*, Sept. 30, 2010, www.bloomberg.com/news/2010–09–30/ german-mittelstand-gives-chilean-miners-economy-escape-route.html. Fear, 2012.
9. Langenscheidt and Venohr, 2010, 10–19.
10. "The German Drive to Globalize," May 31, 2011, www.ft.com.
11. Lubinski, 2010. Berghoff, 2006a. Hauser, 2007. Fear, 2003.
12. Barca and Becht, 2002.
13. Wimmer, Domayer, Oswald and Vater, 2005. Braun, 2009. Michler, 2009.
14. Haunschild and Wallau, 2010.
15. Simon, 2009, esp. 285–313. Also Wolfgang Mewes Beratergruppe Strategie, 2000. Rommel, 1995.
16. Langenscheidt and Venohr, 2010. Combined with individual corporate websites. On PWM, see below.
17. KfW Bankengruppe, 2009. Haunschild, Hauser, Günterberg, Müller and Sölter, 2007, 21–26, 53–61, 91–112, 209–217.
18. A full review of the literature about small firm and family firm internationalization cannot be provided here. See the introduction to this volume and the literature review in Fear, 2012, 134–142. Hauser, 2006, 32–68. Some key articles are Hollenstein, 2005. De Clercq, Sapienza and Crijns, 2005. Chadwick, Ghafoor, Khail, Khan and Hassan, 2011. Graves and Thomas, 2008. Graves and Thomas, 2005. Fernández and Nieto, 2005. Winch, 2006.
19. Winch, 2006. Hollenstein, 2005.
20. Simon, 2009. Wolfgang Mewes Beratergruppe Strategie, 2000.
21. Graf, 2000. *Security in a Dynamic World, Investors Handbook 2010/2011*, Kaba Group, www.kaba.com.
22. Gutmann, 2000.
23. STIHL, 2002. "STIHL beginnt Produktion im neuen Werk Qingdao, China," Sept. 15, 2006, www.stihl.de/stihl-beginnt-produktion-im-neuen-werk-qingdao-china.aspx; "STIHL Breaks Ground on New Manufacturing Plant," RP News Wires, 2006, www.reliableplant.com/Articles/Print/2694; "Stihl to Open Plant in China," *Financial Times*, www.ft.com, Feb. 28, 2005. More articles available on the STIHL corporate website.
24. Geschäftsbericht 2009/10, TRUMPF Group, www.trumpf.com. Leibinger, 2010.
25. Fear, 2012. Mathias Kammuller, director of TRUMPF machine tools, quoted in "Industry Left High and Dry," *Financial Times*, www.ft.com, Apr. 12, 2011.

26. These were independent subsidiaries. See, for example, TRUMPF Taiwan Industries Co. Ltd., www.tw.trumpf.com, or TRUMPF Sheet Metal Products (Taicang) Co. Ltd., www.cn-taicang.trumpf.com.
27. Heimerzheim and Siegwerk AG, 2007. Siegwerk website, www.siegwerk. com; "Schwarz für Harry Potter, Gold für Haribo," *General-Anzeiger* (Bonn), www.general-anzeiger-bonn.de, Dec. 5, 2008.
28. Heimerzheim and Siegwerk AG, 2007, 84–89. "Siegwerk steht vor Kauf eines US-Druckfarbenherstellers: Konzernschef: Keine Kurzungen am Standort Siegburg," *General-Anzeiger* (Bonn), www.general-anzeiger-bonn.de, Nov. 25, 2003; "Erfolg bekennt Farbe," *Wirtschaftsblatt Westfalen, www. e-pages.dk/wirtschaftsblatt/86/105,* 1 (2010), 105.
29. Elektrisola corporate website, www.elektrisola.com. Elektrisola: "To the Sun, Mars, and Back," TAGALink, July 3, 2008, 12–15, www.tnb.com.my/tnb/application/ uploads/tenagalink/4e8f549cc983048f6f6d5a363bdb0d49. pdf.
30. Nordenia Company website, www.nordenia.com/article,navsub_id-lang, 3-en.html. Mager, 1999.
31. "Familienunternehmer vor der Wahl," *Handelsblatt*, Feb. 15, 2011, www. handelsblatt.com.
32. For more detail and sources, see Fear, 2012, 157–166.
33. Wimmers and Wolter, 1997.
34. "Wettbewerbsvergleich: Wie gut ist das Made in Germany?" Keine Übermenschen, *Wirtschaftswoche*, Feb. 8, 1991, 34-38.
35. Wimmers and Wolter, 1997, 55–57, 68–75. Deeg, 1999, especially 157–187.
36. Winkelmann, 1997, 73–108. Deeg, 1999, 166–177.
37. "Globalisierung: Mittelständler berichten—BDI/DIHT Forum: Strategien für den Einstieg in das Asiengeschäft," *Handelsblatt*, www.handelsblatt. com, June 26, 1996, 11. Other surveys found that 69-85% of German SMEs moved abroad to access new markets, see Gutmann, 2000, 38 and KfW Bankengruppe, 2009. 6.
38. "Mittelstand: Herausforderung für Familienunternehmen: Globalisierung im Visier," *Handelsblatt*, Sept. 19, 1996, 27.
39. "Mittelstand schmoren im eigenen Saft," *Wirtschaftswoche*, July 17, 1997, 58.
40. KfW Bankengruppe, 2009. Also Haunschild, Hauser, Günterberg, Müller and Sölter, 2007, 21–26, 53–61, 91–112, 209–217.
41. Hennerkes and Pleister, 1999, 197. Weber and Kabst, 2000.
42. Elektrisola: "To the Sun, Mars, and Back," TAGALink, July 3, 2008, 12–15, www.tnb.com.my/tnb/application/uploads/tenagalink/4e8f549cc983048f6f 6d5a363bdb0d49.pdf.
43. Franzke, Grohs and Laux, 2004. Kolbeck and Wimmer, 2002.
44. Many German family SMEs have notoriously low equity ratios on average, just 20–30 percent around 2000. Fear, 2003. Berghoff, 2004, 124–126.
45. Hauser, 2006, 205.
46. Cited in Hauser, 2006, 94.
47. http://www.dihk.de/ or http://www.dihk.de/en or individual regions, for instance, Württemberg, http://www.bw.ihk.de/.
48. See http://ahk.de/. Quotes from Hauser, 2006, 105–106.
49. Fear, 2003. Hommel and Schneider, 2003.
50. "Partnerschaften zur Entwicklung," *Handelsblatt*, www.handelsblatt.com, Dec. 26, 2010.
51. "Schätze Nützen," *Wirtschaftswoche*, Nov. 9, 1995, 66-78. Deeg, 1999, 114–121.

52. Commerzbank corporate website: www.firmenkunden.commerzbank.de/de/international/start.htm. Fear, 2003; "Die Deutsche Bank und ihr Kampf um den Mittelstand," *Handelsblatt*, www.handelsblatt.com, Feb. 9, 2011.

53. "Schlüssige Antworten auf die fortschreitende Globalisierung: Sparkassen begleiten Mittelstand mit 'Countrydesk' ins Ausland," *Handelsblatt*, www.handelsblatt.com, March 23, 2005. See www.countrydesk.de for further information.

6 Fast Learning

Business, Kinship, and Politics as Determinants of the Growth and Internationalization of the Largest Chinese Family Businesses

Paloma Fernández Pérez

6.1 INTRODUCTION

Large Chinese family businesses do not follow the Uppsala model at all,[1] but overcome ownership disadvantages by acquiring global knowledge. This chapter presents evidence to support this claim, representing a critique of the ownership, location, internalization (OLI) and Uppsala models about firms' internationalization. It will show that Chinese families use "social and political capital" (real estate, public banks, stock markets, connections to the Communist Party and provincial governments) to overcome their lack of knowledge and resources. The chapter also indicates that resource-view perspectives on the internationalization of firms (examining an individual, isolated firm) may fall short as these Chinese family firms and groups can rely on public institutions (development policies, Communist Party networks, "business angels"). The family's crucial role in the largest Chinese family businesses analyzed here is for the family heir to either go abroad for experience or occupy critical external roles in China.

It is well known that Chinese companies have used joint ventures and foreign direct investment (FDI) by foreign firms to build their knowledge capacity. Less known is how a growing class of Chinese family firms has been internationalizing to access and accumulate world-class knowledge. Considerable social and political capital supports this process, which is creating the first multinational Chinese companies. These firms train heirs to improve their internationalization in the next generation.

International business theory in the 1960s concentrated on portfolio capital transfers to explain firms' international activity, but after that decade, the field experienced a major theoretical breakthrough.[2] Particularly well known are the "Scandinavian" model of stages of internationalization and the eclectic paradigm. The first approach,[3] which has been criticized,[4] describes an ordered globalization process whereby firms first export, then establish agencies, sales and production subsidiaries, and possibly forms of licensing. The second maintains that firms internationalize if they have ownership advantages, if it is more efficient to internalize these advantages in foreign markets than sell them to local firms, and if the foreign market presents more locational advantages (e.g., labor costs, taxes) than the home market.[5] The resource-based and knowledge-based approaches add an additional perspective: internationalization may start with the acquisition of global knowledge rather than exports. In some countries, firms utilize joint ventures and acquisitions more as learning tools than as entrance platforms. Some governments have provided significant support to public and private businesses in the process of knowledge production or transfer necessary in a globalized economy.[6]

This chapter focuses on the internationalization of the largest family businesses in China in the last few decades using the knowledge-based perspective. It will show that most internationalization theory has not considered firms' internationalization to accumulate learning. Many firms make large leaps to key areas around the globe less to access markets than to access sources of knowledge. Evidence about seven of the largest current Chinese family businesses supports this thesis of knowledge accumulation as an important first stage for latecomer economies. Chinese government development policies provide strong support and encouragement for such internationalization.[7]

6.2 HYPOTHESES AND GOALS

Literature on family business (FB) internationalization indicates that internationally oriented individuals and their heirs are key to understanding this process.[8] Consequently, this chapter looks at the relationship between the internationalization pathways of the largest Chinese FBs over the last few decades and the personal and family background of internationally oriented entrepreneurs. The cases gathered here suggest that large Chinese FBs have not often followed the Uppsala model but rather a less risky strategy, the peaceful acquisition of foreign knowledge, to become global corporations.

Several key characteristics of the individuals and companies can be discerned:

1. Most of the entrepreneurs and families in top management have very humble origins; very few could attend secondary school or university, but all had excellent connections to their local communities, professional associations, and local and national Communist Party organizations. All had outstanding individual entrepreneurial attitudes and leadership before becoming CEOs.
2. Local, provincial, and national political institutions rewarded these entrepreneurs, helping them get promoted within their corporations.
3. Such internal promotion and institutional support allowed these individuals to access three key financial resources that helped their companies expand internationally: real estate investments, public banks, and the stock market.
4. In several cases, institutions promoted fast acquisition of foreign knowledge in production, distribution, and organization. Heirs incorporated into top management are crucial to continuing fast knowledge transfer from abroad.

This chapter shows the relationship between these characteristics and firms' international growth on the basis of seven Chinese FBs. It begins with a discussion of sources and methodology followed by a section summarizing the information about the origins, backgrounds, values, and main internationalization processes of the largest Chinese FBs. Finally, it concludes that humble, entrepreneurial individuals with strong ties to local communities and the Communist Party have been key drivers in the internationalization process of the largest Chinese FBs in the last three decades. The political and cultural context—strong supervision of authorities and a common philosophy of creating wealth for China, families, and individual entrepreneurs—have also been influential.

6.3   SOURCES AND METHODOLOGY

Sources on Chinese businesses and business groups are very scarce,[9] and there are even fewer on Chinese FBs.[10] More particularly, several Asian and Western scholars have studied the internationalization process of Chinese multinationals between 1912 and 1949[11] and, above all, from the 1980s to 2010.[12] Studies that concentrate on listed firms have also recently focused on the rise of large Chinese FBs.[13] Knowledge about nonlisted FBs—particularly about those with the most sales and employees, and about the qualities of the growth and internationalization of such firms—is quite limited. It derives primarily from diverse case studies.[14]

Sources for this study are the rankings of the top 500 firms elaborated by the Chinese government and the Chinese Confederation of Enterprises in 2005; corporate websites of 79 Chinese FBs; Asian business and economics journals; the Orbis database on ownership; and others listed in the bibliography. Here, *family firm* follows the Grupo Europeo de Empresas Familiares/European Group of Owner Managed and Family Enterprises GEEF definition, adapted to Chinese reality: a business in which at least two members of the same family—not necessarily from different generations—have strategic control of decisions. Firms with only one such person do not qualify as FBs. While this surely excludes many firms in the founding stage, it does seem to better predict family control in the absence of more reliable information.[15] A concentration of significant shares and control of strategic seats on the council board indicate family control.

I used the 2005 database of the largest Chinese FBs to build another database of large FBs with at least one international activity, such as exports, joint ventures, or subsidiaries. Thereafter, I gathered biographical data on the founders and heirs alongside the history of internationalization of the seven largest internationalized firms in this database, aiming to discern other signs of internationalization and key drivers of international activities.

First, I analyzed the 2005 "Top 500 Enterprises of China," a ranking of the top enterprises in the People's Republic of China created by China

Table 6.1 Top 28 Largest Chinese Family Firms and Groups (2005)

Ranking among China Top 500 Companies in 2005	Company Name	Province	Revenues ($ million)	No. Employees	Sector	Creation	Family
117	Suning Appliance Chain Store (Group) Co., Ltd.	Jiangsu	2,739	46,000	Wholesalers and retailers of electronic implements for daily use	2001	Zhang
123	Guangsha Holding Venture Capital Co. Ltd.	Zhejiang	2,638	54,627	Construction	1992	Lou
127	Wanxiang Group Co., Ltd.	Zhejiang	2,584	32,947	Car and motorcycle manufacture	1969	Lu
173	Hengdian Group Holdings Ltd.	Zhejiang	1,763	48,668	Electrical machines and equipment manufacture	1975	Xu
175	Youngor Group Co., Ltd.	Zhejiang	1,728	24,000	Textiles	1979	Li
204	Chint Group Corp.	Zhejiang	1,481	14,500	Electrical machines and equipment manufacture	1984	Nan
212	Hangzhou Wahaha Group Co., Ltd.	Zhejiang	1,414	17,361	Beverage manufacturing industry	1987	Zong
217	Jiangsu Sanfangxiang Industry Co., Ltd.	Jiangsu	1,376	5,682	Chemical fibers	1980	Bian
229	Delixi Group Co., Ltd.	Zhejiang	1,329	14,200	Electrical machines and equipment manufacture	1984	Hu
250	Nanshan Group Corp.	Shandong	1,264	35,581	General manufacture	1978	Song

Ranking among China Top 500 Companies in 2005	Company Name	Province	Revenues ($ million)	No. Employees	Sector	Creation	Family
295	Hailiang Group Co., Ltd.	Zhejiang	1,054	3,115	Metal products	1989	Feng
302	Rockcheck Steel Group Co., Ltd.	Tianjin	1,023	6,500	Ferrous metal foundries and presses	1994	Zhang
306	Tangshan Baoye Industry Group Co., Ltd.	Hebei	1,014	13,870	Ferrous metal foundries and presses	1987	Han
318	Hongdou Industrial Co., Ltd.	Jiangsu	980	13,329	Textiles	1957	Zhou
336	The Home World Hypermarket Co., Ltd.	Tianjin	895	18,861	Supermarket	1997	Duxia
338	Shanxi Haixin Iron and Steel Group Co., Ltd.	Shanxi	881	10,175	Ferrous metal foundries and presses	1987	Li
343	Cosun Group	Guangdong	878	7,620	Electronic implements for daily use manufacture	1992	Wu
346	Haicheng Xiyang Refractories Materials Corp.	Liaoning	871	14,087	Chemical material and products	1988	Zhou
355	Lifan Group	Chongqing	843	4,507	Car and motorcycle manufacture	1992	Yin
392	Ren Ren Le Hypermarket	Guangdong	768	10,900	Supermarket	1996	He

394	New Hope Group	Sichuan	764	22,000	Food	1982	Liu
426	Long Yuan Construction Group	Zhejiang	687	76,589	Construction	1980	Lai
431	Century Golden Resources Group	Beijing	682	6,518	Real estate	1986	Huang
451	Geely Holding Group	Zhejiang	639	10,358	Car and motorcycle manufacture	1986	Li
463	SANY Group	Hunan	623	17,400	General machine building	1989	Liang
484	Wu Yang Construction Co., Ltd.	Zhejiang	590	2,500	Construction	1999	Cheng
486	Dahua Co., Ltd.	Shanghai	587	4,363	Real estate	1988	Jin
500	Zongshen Industrial Group	Chongqing	567	41,061	Car and motorcycle manufacture	1992	Zuo

Note: Revenues with exchange rate as of 2005.

Source: Own elaboration.

Enterprise Confederation (CEC) and China Enterprise Directors Association (CEDA),[16] two governmental institutions. This predated the current crisis. According to this source, state-owned and state holding enterprises, with 356 entries (71.2 percent), dominated the list; there were 27 collectively owned and cooperative enterprises and 70 private ones (several were former town village enterprises and very few were founded by individuals disconnected from local institutions or businesses).

Firms in the dominant category were the least productive and efficient, whereas Hong Kong, Macao, Taiwan, and foreign investment enterprises had the highest rates of profit, assets turnover, and revenue per employee, and the second-highest asset profit ratio.

Second, I searched for FBs among these 500 Chinese companies. No official sources give this information. I derived ownership structure from the Orbis database, which provides the names and immediate holdings of all owners with more than 5 percent of a company's stock. I double-checked this ownership information with data from the national and international business and financial press, companies' websites, and stock market watchdogs (for public companies). With this information, I was able to apply the GEEF definition of family business. Table 6.1 shows the 28 largest Chinese FBs among the 500 largest Chinese firms in 2005.

Third, I created the list of international companies from the 28 largest Chinese FBs. The main activities and pathways of internationalization of six of these were included in official records. A seventh was based in Hong Kong. I summarize these activities and pathways in Table 6.2.

6.4   INTERNATIONALIZATION DETERMINANTS IN SEVEN OF THE LARGEST CHINESE FAMILY-CONTROLLED MULTINATIONALS

These seven case studies aim to analyze three key internationalization drivers: the founder's background and values, the role of public administration in providing crucial support (local, regional, or state), and the environmental circumstances that prompted the entrepreneurs and their families to seize business opportunities that could expand overseas. The Hong Kong case, Hutchison Whampoa, and the six continental China cases, Hengdian Group, Suning Appliance, Guangsha Group, Wanxian, Youngor Group, and Wahaha, are described briefly below.

1. Hong Kong–based Hutchison Whampoa, founded in 1866 by British entrepreneurs and bought by Li Ka Shing in 1979, is a multinational with operations in 54 countries and approximately 220,000 employees worldwide. Of the seven, it has the most foreign revenues and the greatest international experience. It is also the only one whose family heirs have Western citizenship with strategic implications in global trade (Canada).

Table 6.2 Internationalization Pathways of the Largest Seven Family Business Firms and Groups of China (2005)

Company	Family	Province or Region	MainActivities	Start business	Start intzon	Countries	Typologies/ stages intzon
Hutchinson Whampoa	Li	Hong Kong	Ports/TICs/ Perfumes/Hotels/Real Estate	1866/ 1979	1866/ 1979	Argentina, Australia, Bahamas, Belgium, Egypt, Germany, Indonesia, Italy, Malaysia, Mexico, Myanmar, Netherlands, Oman, Pakistan, Panama, Poland, Saudi Arabia, South Korea, Spain, Sri Lanka, Sweden, Tanzania, Thailand, United Kingdom, Vietnam	Worldwide Subsidiaries/Joint Ventures/ Mergers and Acq
Suning (Chinese Wal-Mart)	Zhang	Jiangsu	Chain stores home appliances	1990	2009	Japan, Australia	Mergers and Acq
Guangsha	Lou	Zhejiang	Construction	1973/ 1992	Recent	Algeria, Angola, Qatar, Malaysia, Pakistan, Libya, Congo, South Korea	Joint Ventures
Wanshiang	Lu	Zhejiang	Auto components	1969	1980s	United States, Great Britain, Germany, Canada, Australia	Subsidiaries, Joint Venture
Hengdian ("China wood")	Xu	Zhejiang	Electronics, chemical, film and entertainment	1975	2007	Austria, Italy, Japan, United States	Joint Venture, Subsidiaries
Youngor	Li	Zhejiang	Textiles (branded garment manufacturing and marketing); property and real estate	1979	1998	Japan, France, Italy, United States	Mergers and Acq, Subsidiaries
Hanzhou Wahaha	Zong	Zhejiang	Beverages and food industries	1987	1996	United States, France, Germany, Japan, Italy	Joint Venture with Danone; in 1999 Danone sold the share.

Source: Own elaboration, from 2005 "Top 500 Enterprises of China" compiled by China Enterprise Confederation (CEC) and China Enterprise Directors Association (CEDA), http://www.cec-ceda.org.cn/english/, plus Orbis database to confirm shares and ownership.

2. Hengdian Group, a well-known movie-making company, was established in 1975. It has owned a subsidiary in Milan since 2007.
3. Founded in 1990, Suning Appliance is the leading consumer-appliance, computer, and communications company. It is also the largest home appliance retail chain in China, with subsidiaries in Japan and Australia.
4. Guangsha Group started business in 1973, and though it specializes in construction, it is a large, diversified modern corporation. It now has more than 50,000 staff and 80 subsidiaries (in Mainland China, Hong Kong, Southeast Asia, the Middle East, Europe, North Africa, and South America).
5. Wanxiang Group, an auto-components manufacturer founded in 1969, has more than 60 subsidiaries in China, 18 subsidiaries overseas, more than 30,000 employees, and serves customers in 40 countries.
6. Youngor Group, founded in 1979, has a specialized core business in branded garment manufacturing and marketing.
7. Hangzhou Wahaha Group Co., Ltd., established in 1987 and specializing in food and beverages, was formerly a sales department in a school-run business in the Changsheng district. It now has 150 subsidiaries in 29 provinces, 17,000 employees, and is exploring nearby Southeast Asian and a few Western markets.

These firms are very diverse in size and international orientation. Their corporate websites and the few references that address their origins show that, with the exception of Hong Kong–based Hutchinson Whampoa, they typically evolved after the 1980s as follows:

a. First, workers of town village enterprises, or peasants and farmers who demonstrated excellent management skills on the local level, became CEOs when local or provincial authorities legally transformed the enterprise into a corporation.
b. Successful CEOs (able to lead remarkable and fast innovation processes, conquer provincial and national markets, and include their corporation in Chinese stock markets) were allowed, with some restrictions, to buy large portions of shares and appoint family members, and, of course, colleagues to top management positions (thus providing them with enough earnings to become large shareholders).
c. These closely linked, highly motivated managerial teams with controlling shares undertook international activity.
d. Some firms in sectors with very dynamic markets (logistics and TICs, auto components, consumer electronics), and others in more mature sectors (food and beverages, textiles) were more cautious in their internationalization.

Now, we will look at each of the seven FBs in turn. Hutchinson Whampoa now has five core businesses: ports and related services (50 ports in

Argentina, Australia, Bahamas, Belgium, Egypt, Germany, Indonesia, Italy, Malaysia, Mexico, Myanmar, Netherlands, Oman, Pakistan, Panama, Poland, Saudi Arabia, South Korea, Spain, Sweden, Tanzania, Thailand, and Vietnam);[17] property and hotels; retail (8,700 stores in 31 countries including Marionnaud and the Perfume Shop); energy and infrastructure; and TICs (many operating in Southeast Asian countries like Indonesia, Vietnam, Sri Lanka, and Thailand.[18] In 1977, Hutchinson Whampoa was one of Hong Kong's major trading houses. Listed on the Hong Kong Stock Exchange in 1978, it came into serious financial difficulties, becoming an interesting investment for someone with cash, connections, and global ambitions, and in 1979, wealthy Hong Kong entrepreneur, Li Ka Shing and his property group Cheung Kong Holdings, bought it.

Li Ka Shing was born in Chaozhou in the Guangdong Province (China).[19] His father Li Yunjing was a primary schoolteacher who emigrated to Hong Kong with his family in the winter of 1940 (when it fell under Japanese control) after the Japanese invasion of the village in 1939 suspended schooling there. In 1942, Li's mother returned to Chaozhou with her younger son and daughter, while Li stayed in Hong Kong with his father in a wealthy uncle's house. His father died of tuberculosis when he was a teenager, and he had to leave school at 14 to become an apprentice in a plastic watchstrap company on Ko Shing Street. He worked 16 hours a day, and bought second-hand books to educate himself. In 1947, he became manager. After marrying his cousin Chong Yuet-Ming (the wealthy uncle's daughter) and creating a new family, he was motivated to become an entrepreneur. By 1950, aged 22, with money from friends, relatives, and trading contacts, he founded Cheung Kong Plastics Co., which manufactured high-quality plastic products (toys, daily household items, and, above all, flowers). In the 1950s, Li's company was successful in Asia, but in the 1960s, political instability and riots broke out in Hong Kong.

Together with the birth of his sons, Victor in 1964 and Richard in 1966, this chaotic situation made him see opportunities and provided incentives; he invested with his savings and loans from relatives and friends in Hong Kong real estate. He foresaw not only that property values would fall because of the riots and problems in 1967, but also that they would go up again when the economy recovered. To organize this new business, he founded Cheung Kong Industries in 1971, which soon became a leading Hong Kong real-estate investment company. It was listed on the Hong Kong Stock Exchange in 1972.

In the 1970s, incentives caused real-estate investments to exceed plastics investments (the Ten-Year Housing Plan of 1972 called for quality housing for almost 2 million people to be built). In 1979, Li acquired an important stake in Hutchinson Whampoa (from HSBC), which specialized in handling containers in ports throughout the world, making him the first Chinese owner of a British-style trading company. The main strategies he employed in the 1980s involved overseas expansion and investment in telecommunications and natural resources. To reinforce its international dimension Hutchinson opened a European office in London,[20] and then created Hutchinson Telecommunications. It also acquired a percentage in Cable and Wireless, an English telecommunications group,[21] launching a telecommunications satellite over China as a joint venture.[22] In 1987, it created Cavendish International Holding to be its investment and natural resources arm. In 1990, it acquired Nokia Mobira (to reinforce the UK branch) and Cluff Resources UK mineral and mining company.[23] In 1991, the UK branch Hutchinson Telecommunications acquired BYPS Communications, the UK telepoint consortium,[24] one of a series of UK acquisitions as Hutchison planned to develop a range of wireless personal telecommunications products in the United Kingdom.[25]

Hutchison's strong financial position allowed it to seize new business opportunities, but the growth strategy of overseas expansion had problems in 1992 with overseas companies performing worse than the core Chinese and Hong Kong business. Consequently, Hutchinson returned to its core business of infrastructure and property in Hong Kong and China during the 1990s. Li began to prepare for post-1997 Hong Kong (which would formally end British rule there) and China. In 1992, Hutchison acquired 50 percent of Shangai's container port.[26] Li emphasized efforts to invest in mainland China in 1992, and focused particularly on retailing, manufacturing, and property development projects in selected cities (Guangzhou, Shanghai, and Qingdao).[27] This new strategy marked a major management reshuffle. In 1993, Simon Murray stepped down as managing director, replaced by Canning Fok. This symbolized the group's evolution from a British-style trading company to a Chinese corporation.[28] Fok was regarded as short-term stand-in for Richard Li (then 26), who was simultaneously promoted to deputy chairman.[29] In the early 2000s, Li returned to the overseas-expansion strategy, but now in the beauty sector. In 2005, the group acquired the French company Marionnaud Parfumeries SA and became the world's largest health and beauty chain.

Li Ka Shing is actually the chairman of Cheung Kong (Holdings) Ltd. and Hutchison Whampoa Ltd. He bought an international company and made it still more global. His two sons have been trained to extend this globalization further. Both have served as company directors in different areas, and both have Canadian citizenship. Victor (b. 1964) is the official successor. He is managing director and deputy chairman of Cheung Kong (Holdings) Ltd., deputy chairman of Hutchison Whampoa Ltd.,[30] and chairman of Cheung Kong Infrastructure Holdings Ltd. and CK Life Sciences International (Holdings) Inc. He obtained a BS in Civil Engineering, an MS in Structural Engineering, and an honorary degree.[31] He serves as a member of the Standing Committee of the 11th National Committee of the Chinese People's Political Consultative Conference of the People's Republic of China and of the Commission on Strategic Development, the Greater Pearl River Delta Business Council, and the Council for Sustainable Development of the Hong Kong Special Administrative Region. He is also vice-chairman of the Hong Kong General Chamber of Commerce. These positions strengthen networking with the Chinese government and businessmen. Such connections are always fundamental, but especially in countries where trust is a critical business resource. The concept of *guanxi*—broadly translated as "personal relationship" or "connections"—pervades the Chinese business landscape.[32]

Victor's preparation as the future heir of Li's empire included study and work abroad and developing cross-border networks of personal and business relationships. After studying in Stanford, Victor needed to be prepared for the company's interests in Canada—it had high stakes in Husky Oil (Victor served as its director), one of Canada's largest energy and energy-related companies. Victor, aged 22, was appointed president of Concord Pacific, the company responsible for developing the Pacific Place project on the former site of Expo '86 in Vancouver.[33] Victor's Vancouver experiences helped him gain understanding in property development (in the global market, not only in Hong Kong); establish connections with Vancouver's elite social network, and build a strong personal and financial basis for his future career.[34] Victor actively established business networks and informal ties and learned from businessmen with strong links to the community, which facilitated informal business deals wherein "the word is the bond."[35]

Victor's brother Richard (b. 1966) is chairman of PCCW, one of Asia's leading information technology and telecommunications companies.[36] He went to Menlo Park School in California and attended Stanford University, but did not graduate.[37]

Hengdian Group is a rather different story. Established in 1975 as a silk factory before the economic reforms, the firm was transformed into a diversified group focusing on electronics, pharmaceutical and chemical, and film and entertainment activities. The transformation pathway began with supply shortages in the silk factory prompting the decision to diversify into electronics and chemical products. The creation and fast-growing activity of Hengdian World Studios, today often known as "Chinawood," brought success. Group-controlled Hengdian DMEGC is listed on the Shenzhen Stock Exchange.

In 1975, Xu Wenrong, the president of Hengdian Group, set up Hengdian Silk Factory. In 1980, Hengdian took the lead in the magnetic materials industry, establishing a basis for electronic components manufacturing thereafter. In 1989, the company entered the pharmaceutical and chemical industry. From 1975 to 1980, to acquire strategies and know-how for long-term development, Hengdian had to select and send young staff with relatively high cultural qualifications to the state-run enterprises; today, these young staff have become the experts and backbones of various industries. Between 1980 and 1990, the company sent outstanding young staff to domestic institutions for further education in groups and by stages. From 1993–1995, Xu Wenrong was deputy of the Eighth National People's Congress and received several awards and distinctions. In 2004, the First Cooperative Association for Film & TV Shooting Bases in China—Association for Film & TV Shooting Bases across Zhejiang Province—was founded, and a joint venture between the Chinese Film Group Corporation with Hengdian Group and Warner Brothers was initiated.

In 2007, Hengdian established a subsidiary company in Milan, Italy, relatively late compared to other Chinese companies. The owning family, then under the control of Xu Yong'an, the founder's son (president since 2004), decided to move abroad to "gradually learn the marketing skills required to export and to identify potential new areas for investment, particularly related to port sales assistance and customer care."[38] Thus, internationalization began with investments in education and knowledge. Interestingly, European investment started in Milan because the CEO of the Europe group was an Italian citizen with personal ties to the Chinese founder's son.[39]

Hengdian has invested heavily in the film industry, from urban movie theater chains to a joint production company with China Film and Warner Brothers. Xu Yong'an wants Hengdian, now a sizable town of 100,000 people, to be the next Hollywood. This, he said, "cannot be done by one person or one company. We must have the support of the government and society. Only when foreign producers swarm here will we move closer to our goal of becoming the movie capital of the East." This case again shows owners of leading Chinese FBs understanding internationalization as something that starts by bringing products, services, and business models into China from outside, not as outsiders entering foreign markets.[40]

Up to 2009, Suning Appliance Company Ltd. ran 1,000 chain stores covering more than 300 cities in 30 provinces and municipalities throughout China with 120,000 employees. Suning Appliance cooperates closely with nearly 10,000 famous home appliance suppliers at home and abroad, with logistics an area of core competitiveness. Currently, Suning has a national distribution network composed of regional distribution centers, city distribution centers, and cross-docking operations. In 2009, Suning acquired LAOX, a Japanese appliance chain with 80 years of history, and Critical Retail Management Ltd. (the third largest appliance retailer in Hong Kong).[41]

Suning's founder Zhang Jindong was born in the Anhui Province in 1963. He studied Chinese literature, graduating from the Nanjing Normal University in 1984. Zhang first worked in a cloth factory named Haowei Group between 1985–1989. In 1990, together with his older brother Zhang Guiping, he opened a small shop in Nanjing called Suning Electrical Appliance, selling air-conditioning and related products. Zhang Guiping later quit, shifting into real estate. As with Hutchinson Whampoa, cash and social capital Suning accumulated through real estate seems to have provided the resources to launch the Suning Appliance Group. Realizing that the core competitive advantage of the new venture should be "service," and that basic innovation involved more than products, services, and business models, Zhang developed the strategy of "informationalization, standardization and specialization," that is, using computers and promoting standard rules to reduce inefficiencies. In 2004, Suning Appliance was listed with medium- and small-sized enterprises on the Shenzhen Stock Exchange, making it the first appliance chain of this kind in China. As it was listed and reformed to be public with directional transfer of shares, Zhang retained only about one-third of the total shares. With Suning, the one national enterprise in the domestic appliance chain market, Premier Wen Jiabao encouraged its leaders to strive to make it the Walmart of China. Zhang has received many state-level honors.[42]

Guangsha Group concentrates on construction and real estate, and public authorities have supported and rewarded its success—as in the previous cases. With more than 50,000 staff members, it is one of the 26 large enterprises specifically selected for a development experiment by the government of Zhejiang Province. The corporation and its industries are spread all over mainland China, Hong Kong, Southeast Asia, the Middle East, Europe, North Africa, and South America. While construction and real estate are Guangsha's two leading industries, it has expanded in recent years into media, energy sources, finance, tourism, education, and medical care. Its origins are closely tied to the 1973 Dongyang Guanxiu Building Association, which changed its name several times before becoming a provincial enterprise (Zhejiang Guangsha Construction Enterprise Group) in 1994. It was listed on the Shanghai stock market in 1997, and registered as Guangsha Holding Ltd. in 2001, and as Guangsha Holding Venture Capital in 2002. Lou Zhongfu is the official founder and is still the chairman. Nevertheless, he has integrated two sons into the business, the eldest being the designated heir. Lou Zhongfu (b. 1954) of Han nationality, a native of Dongyang in Zhejiang Province, attended college and joined the China People's Congress (CPC) in 1984, becoming a delegate of the 10th National People's Congress, and deputy chairman and director of numerous professional and regional associations. His eldest son, Lou Ming, has been chairman of the board of Guangsha Construction Group, CEO of Guangsha Holding Venture Capital Co. Ltd., chairman of the board and secretary of the Party Committee of Guangsha College of Applied Construction Technology, a delegate of the Fifth National People's Congress of Jinhua Region, and vice-president of a number of professional associations.

Wanxiang Group supplies universal joints, bearings, and other car supplies to 40 countries. The main foreign customers include Delphi, Arvinmeritor, Dana, Visteon, TRW, Caterpillar, Timken, NSK, ZF, Rockford Powertrain, John Deere, and NTN. Currently, it has 350 design engineers and more than 300 national patents. The Chinese government authorized Wanxiang to operate independently at the provincial level in 1990, when city authorities still directly controlled most Chinese businesses. Wanxiang's founder, Lu Guanqiu, has been the subject of many articles on emerging Chinese capitalism. Featured on the May 1991 cover of *Newsweek*, he told his story of raising Wanxiang from a small bicycle repair shop to its present position as a major auto parts producer and a diversified multinational company. He decided to explore the U.S. market himself rather than relinquish control to an American franchiser, obtaining the necessary financial resources by listing the company. Like some other Chinese companies, Wanxiang trains employees internally to become export professionals, through international mergers and acquisitions and joint ventures. This internationalization path based on strategic alliances enabled it to accumulate managerial competencies.[43] The State Council supports Wianxiang as a selected experimental enterprise. It took its current form in 1990 when the Zhejiang provincial government approved Lu Guanqiu's proposal to formally establish the Zhejiang Wanxiang Machinery & Electronic Group (the "Wanxiang Group"). In 1994, a subsidiary, Wanxiang Qinghai Co. Ltd., was listed on the Shenzhen Stock Exchange and Wanxiang America was founded in Chicago's Industrial Park, becoming the center of Wanxiang's overseas strategy. This was the first step in Wanxiang's globalization strategy and the beginning of a series of international acquisitions with a clear focus on the United States. From 1994 to 2006, Wanxiang America took control of Zeller, ID Co., LT C, QAI Co., American Universal Automotive Industries Inc. (listed on NASDAQ), and Rockford Powertrain, using majority or minority shareholding, or cross-shareholding. Wanxiang America employs only 5 Chinese expatriates among a staff of 60 and earns $200 million more than double its Chinese counterpart. Key strategies in America are adapting to local regulations, the business environment, and merging with local business culture. Wanxiang America maintains close relationships with leading U.S. financial institutions such as Citigroup and Merrill Lynch; it plans to list in the United States to gain access to a large financial market. Since its foundation, the Wanxiang Group has created, acquired, or invested in 30 companies in eight countries, including the United States, Great Britain, Germany, Canada, and Australia.

Lu Guanqiu was born to a peasant family in Hangzhou, in the Zhejiang Province, in 1945. When he was 15, he dropped out of school and became an blacksmith, later opening a bicycle repair shop. In 1969, with six other peasants, he cofounded a factory that produced small agricultural machines. Eventually, his success made him president of Wanxiang Group, located in the district of Xiaoshan in Hangzhou; he was also appointed part-time professor at Zhejiang University. The current president is his son, Lu Weiding, who, as a rebellious teenager, loved racing jeeps and motorcycles in rural China. His father sent him to Singapore to be trained to succeed him. In 2003, Time and CNN named Lu Weidung one of the 20 most influential figures in global business. That year, Lu was appointed to the Central Committee of the Communist Youth League—one of only 129 persons from private industry to receive this honor. Said to control 2 percent of the world's automobile joints industry, Wanxiang increased its U.S. sales 78 percent to $98 million in three years.[44]

The Youngor Group, alongside its core business of branded garment manufacturing and marketing, focuses on property development and equity investment. Li Rucheng and his brother Li Rugang are president and vice president. A pig farmer, Li Rucheng (b. 1951) suffered hardships in his youth, including the imprisonment of his parents and only seven years of schooling. During the Chinese famine of 1959–1961, Li lost four family members, including his mother. From a mere license to import and export obtained in 1994, Li developed Youngor into a major multinational corporation employing over 50,000 people. It was listed on the Shanghai Stock Exchange in 1998. Youngor shirts were the first in China to be exempted from export quality inspection. For eight consecutive years, Youngor's fashion business achieved the highest revenue and profit in the Chinese garment industry. Youngor has won many awards from Chinese associations. In 2008, it purchased Smart Shirt from the American company Kellwood, further enhancing its design and management capabilities. This purchase gained it a U.S.-wide distribution network, making it one of the biggest integrated textile and garment businesses in the world. Youngor also branched out into the hospitality, tourism, and international trade sectors.[45] Youngor's primary goal for years has been to position itself within the high-end market and pursue a path towards internationalization. Since the 1990s, Youngor has used multiple resources to raise funds and has acquired modern clothing production lines from Germany, Italy, Japan, and other leading fashion-industry nations. By December 2004, Youngor had opened a branch office in the United States, taking its first true steps towards becoming an international company. When Li signed the 2005 garment development deal with Japan's Itochu and Italy's Marzotto, Youngor became truly global.[46]

Finally, Hangzhou Wahaha Group Co., Ltd., has developed into China's largest and most profitable beverage company. Zong Qinghou (b. 1945), Wahaha's founder, together with two other retired teachers, started a business selling frozen juice in a school-run sales department with a loan of 140,000 RMB. Zong has been the chairman and CEO of Wahaha and a deputy to the 10th and 11th National People's Congress; he has been honored with many titles in his career. He received secondary schooling and then worked at the Zhoushan salt farm. In 1979, he returned home when his mother retired from teaching. In 1987, he sold milk in a school grocery store in Shangcheng, acquiring know-how in beverage distribution at a micro-level. His wife, Shi Youzhen, and daughter, Zong Fuli, collaborate in the business: Shi is Wahaha's purchasing manager.

In 1989, Wahaha Nutritional Food Factory was founded to produce "Wahaha Oral Liquid for Children." The year 1991 marked a turning point when the Hangzhou government supported a merger between Wahaha Nutritional Food Factory (with 100 employees) and Hangzhou Canning Food Factory (with over 2,000 employees), forming Hangzhou Wahaha Group Corp. In 1994, Wahaha merged with three companies in Fulin to support the construction of the Three Gorges area, efforts highly valued by the party and the State Department. National leaders, such as Jiang Zhemin, Li Peng, Wu Bangguo, Wen Jiabao, and Zhou Jiahua, have visited Wahaha's sites several times. In 1998, after large investments in innovation, Wahaha launched China's own cola: Wahaha Future Cola, challenging Coca-Cola and Pepsi-Cola. Wahaha has aimed at internationalizing its capital structure to facilitate the development of its international operations and globalization. This involved cooperation and a joint venture with Danone, through which both companies learned a lot although there were difficulties.[47] The two companies decided to invest jointly in Indonesia in 2004. Currently, Wahaha has 150 subsidiaries in 29 provinces and 30,000 employees. In 23 years, Wahaha has grown to have 360 world-class automatic production lines, imported from the United States, France, Germany, Japan, and Italy. The main products include milk, juice, tea, and carbonated soft drinks, drinking water, health and canned food, and snacks.

6.5   CONCLUSION

Large FBs do not always follow the orderly 1960s Uppsala model of internationalization. In China, Hengdian in movie-making, Suning in electronic appliances, Youngor in branded garment manufacturing, and Wahaha in beverages all began internationalizing by going abroad or establishing joint ventures to buy knowledge that would change their business models and enable them to go global. Support from local, provincial, and party-level administrations, entrepreneurship, and high social and political capital, combined to alter labor qualifications and training processes in human resources in just a few years. Internationally oriented teams and managers, with political support and financing, have driven specialized technological transfers from abroad. In many cases, exporting occurred in a second stage, sometimes with strength (as with Wanxiang's auto components, or Hutchinson Whampoa in logistics and information technology [TICs]), most often constituting a small percentage of the group's total sales, possibly to curb big losses in unknown markets. Hengdian, Suning, Youngor, and Wahaha seem to have taken this route.

The study has identified the chronology and typology of the foreign investments of the seven largest FB groups in China, including Hong Kong. Concerning chronology, only Hutchinson Whampoa already had an internationalization history (since 1866) and a presence in more than five foreign countries before Deng Xiaoping's 1978 reforms. The other six groups explored foreign markets after these reforms, buying much less abroad than Hutchinson Whampoa and preferring joint ventures and commercial branches abroad after an export stage.

The common elements identified here that motivated firms to go abroad fit in Dunning's classical framework (1993). Seeking natural resources was a less common motivator for FBs than for large public Chinese groups. These FBs basically went abroad and started joint ventures to seek markets, strategies, efficiencies, and above all, knowledge. Another significant motivator for these large FBs suggested by the results is the creation of internationally oriented heirs who can manage the transformation of Chinese giants into global giants.

Back home, the visible hand of the state and party promotes growth, transformation, and even the creation of FBs, though the sources do not always provide clear details. Since 1978, Chinese public institutions have often utilized funds, loans, or diplomatic support to generate the incentives and resources necessary for private firms to go abroad. Conversely, entrepreneurs or companies that pursue official goals successfully can, in exchange, be invited by public institutions to help design new rules of economic activity in China, much in economist William Baumol's entrepreneurial style.[48] Li Ka Shing of Hutchinson Whampoa and his two sons, or Zong Quinghou of Wahaha Group, for instance, were appointed deputies to the National People's Congress. Deng Xiaoping approached Li about promoting China's continental development, and Li served as a member of the Hong Kong Special Administrative Region's Basic Law Drafting Committee, the Preparatory Committee for the Hong Kong Special Administrative Region, and was a Hong Kong Affairs Adviser. Li was also appointed a member of the CITIC, the most important Chinese conglomerate involved in the country's economic development and 41 percent government-owned.

Concerning finances, government actors, and agencies were fundamental "business angels of internationalization" for large FBs in continental China over the last three decades. All the continental Chinese FBs under study received the financial resources they needed to expand and internationalize from local community or town institutions, with the private founder usually working at the upper managerial level of a local factory. Availability of local credit, which was restricted and difficult to obtain, usually promoted mergers and acquisitions among local companies and factories. When these companies had individual shareholders and decision-making boards and named a private CEO, they could create local giants with a mixture of public and private management. Increasing their share of regional or national market power facilitated going public and attracting private capital (domestic and/or foreign) to invest in innovation and internationalization. The CEO, with board approval, attracted family members (typically sons, and sometimes the daughter and the spouse as with Wahaha) as shareholders and members of the board, producing a de facto family-controlled business group.

The origins of the FBs analyzed here were generally humble and rural; most of the founders were common people with little formal education: only two undertook university studies, three had experience in village enterprises (Suning, Wanxiang, Wahaha), three belonged to peasant families or had worked as farmers (Hengdian, Wanxiang, Youngor), three were members of important regional or provincial professional associations (Guangsha, Hengdian, Wahaha), and four held relevant positions in political organizations or directly in the Chinese Communist Party (Hutchinson Whampoa, Guangsha, Hengdian, and Suning). Li Ka Shing of Hutchinson Whampoa, for instance, abandoned studies at 14 after his father's death and worked in the street, and the founders Xu, Lu, and Li Rucheng also had primary schooling. Only founders Lou and Zhan Jindong had some advanced formal training. In all cases, however, when the company's size and market power grew, so did the pressure on the CEOs to professionalize management and achieve excellence. Founders clearly privileged their heirs in the succession track, and used internationalization to gain know-how and train their heirs to become global managers. Thus, Hutchinson Whampoa's heirs became Canadian citizens right when the group expanded its oil industry investments in NAFTA-member Canada and then studied in Canada and the United States, acquiring firsthand knowledge of these markets. On the other hand, heirs who did not behave as expected could be excluded from succession until they resumed accepted behavior, as happened to Wanxiang's heir Lu Weiding. His father sent him to get trained in Singapore after he crashed his motorcycle, after which Lu returned to work alongside his father and succeed him as CEO in 2003.[49]

Taken together, these Chinese case studies confirm three strands of research. First, from internationalization studies, they confirm that internationalization involves continual learning about competition practices on the international scale, something that requires time, risk, and accumulation of experience.[50] Second, from the born-global perspective propounded by Oviatt and McDougall (1994) and the international entrepreneurship views of Shane and Venkataraman (2000) and Zahra and George (2002), they emphasize the concept of opportunity and individuals' role in discovering and choosing to take advantage of opportunities in foreign countries. Third, from a family business literature approach, they reinforce that families, as stakeholders in the FBs, are essential to understanding these firms' decision to go global.[51]

Finally, the sample shows that the influence of politically correct notions of fatherhood and the relationship between business and politics are very strong, conditioning business strategies both domestically and abroad, resource allocation, and the succession process within these large Chinese FBs. Both the firms' survival and the wealth of coming generations depend on Chinese FBs including the state and social commitments in the community as permanent and influential stakeholders, at all times, in all the firms' actions and organizational structures. In other words, kinship, culture, and politics have all highly conditioned the internationalization of large Chinese FBs.

ACKNOWLEDGMENTS

Research and writing has been possible with financial support of public Spanish research project ECO2008–00398/ECON and an ICREA Academia 2008 award. Comments from Matthias Kipping, Vipin Gupta, and Jeffrey Fear to previous versions are greatly appreciated. Also helpful were email conversations with Professor Zhang Weijiong from the Chinese Europe

Business School of Shanghai (November 23, 2009). Special thanks must go to research assistants Hui Li and María Fernández Moya, and to Patricia Sutcliffe for wonderful and patient editorial assistance.

NOTES

1. See the introduction, this volume.
2. Buckley, 2009b, 309–311.
3. Johanson and Vahlne, 1977.
4. Buckley, 2009b, 313.
5. Dunning, 1979. Dunning, 2001.
6. Since the early 1990s, governments have played a key role in the production and transfer of knowledge-based economic activities in the world. References in Organisation for Economic Cooperation and Development, 1996.
7. Chinese outward FDI accounts for less than 1 percent of world FDI stock, but these investments are rising fast. MOFCOMs (Ministry of Commerce People's Republic of China), 2010. Pietrobelli, Rabellotti and Sanfilippo, 2010. This increase in China's participation in the world economy marks a great change since its relative isolation between 1950 and 1970. Three initiatives changed this: the opening reforms of December 1978, the policy of being a good neighbor to Southeast Asian countries since 1990 (doing treaties and investments with the ASEAN countries), and the "be global" strategy initiated in 2002 to promote foreign investments and activity outside China.
8. Casillas, Acedo and Moreno, 2007.
9. Lee and Kang, 2010.
10. Pomeranz, 1997. Yeung, 2000. Ding, Zhang and Zhang, 2007; Ding, Zhang and Zhang, 2008. Köll and Goetzmann, 2005. Nie, Xin and Zhang, 2009. Wu, 2009.
11. Wu, 2009.
12. Larçon, 2009.
13. Ding, Zhang and Zhang, 2007. Ding, Zhang and Zhang, 2008.
14. Pomeranz, 1997. Yeung, 2000. Wu, 2009. Larçon, 2009. Nie, Xin and Zhang, 2009.
15. GEEF (http://www.geef.org/definition.php) defines a family enterprise as one that has the following characteristics: 1. The majority of votes is in possession of the natural person(s) who established the firm, or in possession of the natural person(s) who has/have acquired the share capital of the firm, or in the possession of their spouses, parents, child or children's direct heirs. 2. The majority of votes may be indirect or direct. 3. At least one representative of the family or kin is involved in the management or administration of the firm. 4. Listed companies meet the definition of family enterprise if the person who established or acquired the firm (share capital) or their families or descendants possess 25 percent of the right to vote mandated by their share capital.
16. Website of China Enterprise Confederation (CEC) and China Enterprise Directors Association (CEDA): http://www.cec-ceda.org.cn/english/. Doctoral student Hui Li kindly provided assistance translating from Chinese. The tables in this section are based partially or totally on this source.
17. The map of H.W.-owned ports is almost identical to the map of ports controlled in early modern times by Portuguese and Spanish colonial empires in Asia, Africa, Europe, and America.
18. http://www.hutchison-whampoa.com/eng/index.htm.

19. This biographical material is taken from the Li Ka Shing Foundation website (http://www.lksf.org/en/about/timeline).
20. "Managing Director at Hutchison Whampoa," *Financial Times* (London), November 20, 1985, 43.
21. David Dodwell, "Hutchison Whampoa Lifts Earnings and Dividend," *Financial Times* (London), March 30, 1988.
22. Ibid.
23. Angus Foster, "Hutchison Whampoa Lifted by Property," *Financial Times* (London), August 24, 1990, 22.
24. John Elliott, "Hutchison Whampoa Buys into Telepoint," *Financial Times* (London), February 8, 1991, 19.
25. Ibid.
26. Simon Davies, "Hutchison Whampoa Takes Half Share in Shanghai Container Port," *Financial Times* (London), September 4, 1992, 26.
27. "Hutchison Whampoa Declines 5%," *Financial Times* (London), March 19, 1993, 24.
28. Simon Davies, "MD of Hutchison Whampoa Steps Down," *Financial Times* (London), September 1, 1993, 19.
29. Ibid.
30. He has been Executive Director and Deputy Chairman of Hutchison since 1995 and 1999, respectively. http://www.hutchison-whampoa.com/eng/index.htm.
31. Ibid.
32. Wong and Leung, 2001.
33. Yeung, 2000.
34. Ibid.
35. Ibid.
36. http://www.hutchison-whampoa.com/eng/index.htm.
37. http://www.richardli.com/bio.html.
38. Pietrobelli, Rabellotti and Sanfilippo, 2010.
39. Ibid.
40. Quotations from www.zjhddx.net/site/en/pop_news.asp?id=2261.
41. "Suning Appliance Intends to Become Walmart," http://en.21cbh.com/HTML/2010-2-22/yOMDAwMDE2NTgyOQ.html.
42. http://www.cnsuning.cn/include/english/Z-jianjie.html.
43. Chen, Dong and Hull, 2009. Zhanming, 2009.
44. http://www.answers.com/topi/lu-9.
45. http://en.youngor.com/news.do?action=detail&cid=200811190204341243&id=200909170957097978.
46. Zhang and Alon, 2009.
47. Zhanming, 2009.
48. Baumol, 1990.
49. Larçon, 2009.
50. Jones and Khanna, 2006. Buckley, 2009b. Buckley, 2009a.
51. Casillas, Acedo and Moreno, 2007.

7 Multinationalization Strategy of Mexican Family Business

Taeko Hoshino

7.1 INTRODUCTION

Family multinationals have been emerging from Mexico rapidly since the 1990s, a phenomenon closely related to their growth in a late-industrializing country: family-owned and -controlled business groups (FBs) are a representative organizational model of economic agents in such a setting.[1] They form in response to traits of late-industrializing economies, including market failures,[2] underdeveloped economic institutions,[3] and a close relationship between businesses and the state, making them predominant in firms of all sizes.[4] The distinctive features of FBs in late-industrializing countries deserve a separate analysis.

Large Mexican FBs are particularly interesting because they did not internationalize sequentially as the Uppsala model describes as an ordinary course.[5] Their internationalization was not incremental but accelerated, skipping some steps.

There are two main reasons Mexican FBs did not follow the process described in the model. First, they fall into the exceptions implied by the model, which presupposes three conditions wherein additional market commitment is not made in small steps: when firms have large resources, considerable experience of markets with similar conditions, and can gain market knowledge other than through experience.[6] Large Mexican FBs are an exceptional case because they had significant resources that they utilized in advancing into markets of similar conditions in other late-industrializing countries. The literature on business groups in late-industrializing countries explains their growth in terms of specific resources acquired in the growth process, including the capability of combining foreign and domestic resources,[7] and the project execution capability acquired through repeated new investments for business diversification.[8]

The second reason is that changing economic conditions, such as intensified competition, expansion of international financial markets, and rapid technological development since the 1990s, forced and also enabled large Mexican FBs to accelerate and skip over predicted steps of internationalization. This suggests that radical changes in the global economy since the 1990s have reduced the Uppsala model's explanatory strength.

So how did the internationalization of large Mexican FBs proceed? Of the several steps of internationalization such as regular and nonregular export, opening sales and production subsidiaries, I will focus on multinationalization, which means opening production subsidiaries in more than one foreign country, because this step most clearly reflects the characteristics of these businesses.

Two factors are salient in these firms' multinationalization: the first is liberalizing external conditions. In the 1990s, the Mexican economy was fully immersed in the worldwide trend toward globalization because of Mexico's liberalization policy on trade and inward foreign direct investments (FDI), and the privatization policy of state-owned enterprises, which were started in the mid-1980s and completed by the mid-1990s. This process affected multinationalization of large FBs by pressuring them to internationalize to survive and by offering opportunities for business expansion, including improved accessibility to foreign markets, international fund-raising, and strategic alliances with multinationals from industrialized countries (shown below).

The second factor relates to large FBs being the predominant economic agents in late-industrializing countries. I hold that Mexican family multinationals have competitive advantages in the international markets such as the Latin American advantage, the first mover advantage, monopoly rents accrued by possessing a controlling power on the Mexican market, strategic alliances with multinationals from industrialized countries, and resources acquired in the process of multinationalization. These derive principally from their role as the predominant economic agents. I will analyze the ten largest Mexican family multinationals of 2010 to show how these advantages played out.

The analysis is divided into four sections. Section 1 deals with the external economic conditions in which large Mexican FBs multinationalized, focusing on how the liberalization of the Mexican economy affected this process. Section 2 provides information on the ten largest Mexican family multinationals of the year 2010. Based on this sample, Section 3 examines the competitive advantage of large Mexican family multinationals. Section 4 considers the relationship between the competitive advantages—their sustainability—and familism.[9]

7.2   CHANGE OF COMPETITIVE CONDITIONS AND REDEFINITION OF STRATEGY

Globalizing the Mexican Economy

Large FBs are the principal economic agents in the Mexican economy. The majority form business groups, making large FBs and business groups almost identical in Mexico. During the period of import substitution industrialization after World War II, they experienced steady growth, facilitated by two favorable conditions. First of all, government policies—such as a restriction on imports and the regulation of inward FDI—protected Mexican producers from competition with imports and foreign multinationals.[10] The government also spurred their growth by encouraging them to invest in lucrative industries.[11] The other favorable condition was the rapid expansion of the Mexican market, which enhanced business opportunities. As long as the Mexican market was protected and expanding rapidly, large FBs had little incentive to internationalize.

Around 1980, Mexico experienced an investment boom induced by petroleum export during which the government and large FBs took out tremendous loans with international commercial banks. Accumulated external debt provoked an economic crisis in 1982 when the international petroleum price fell, the interest rate in the international financial markets rose, prompting investors to flee with their capital.

The 1982 external debt crisis was epoch-making for the Mexican economy because it ended import substitution industrialization and sparked economic reforms such as radical trade liberalization (in 1985), deregulation of inward FDI (in 1989), and the privatization of state-owned enterprises (1988–1993), including those of telecommunication, petrochemicals, television broadcasting, and banks.[12] Although the de la Madrid administration (1982–1988) initiated the reforms, the Salinas administration (1988–1994) accelerated and consolidated them. The North American Free Trade Agreement (NAFTA), which came into effect in 1994, exercised institutional constraint, which made reversing the direction of reforms difficult.

Redefining Strategy

The 1982 external debt problem was also epoch-making for large FBs in several ways. First, FBs lost the favorable protection from international competition when trade was liberalized and inward FDI deregulated. Second, the domestic market stopped expanding because of the severe recession of the 1980s. Third, FBs with external debt were driven into insolvency because successive devaluations in the 1980s rapidly increased their debts and payment levels valued in foreign currencies. Under these adverse conditions, large FBs needed to be restructured. Some groups succeeded in this, but others failed. Also, newly formed FBs emerged by seizing business opportunities such as the privatization of state-owned enterprises and the acquisition of troubled firms. Consequently, the composition of dominant FBs in the Mexican economy was reshuffled.[13] One common strategy of the surviving and emerging firms under these changing competitive conditions was internationalization.

Globalization as an Opportunity to Internationalize

Changing competitive conditions not only pressured firms into change, but also facilitated their internationalization by bringing them new opportunities. These included fund-raising on international financial markets, acquiring firms, and forging strategic alliances with multinationals from industrialized countries.

The rapid growth of international financial markets under globalization made firms from late-industrializing countries, which previously lacked creditworthiness, a target of investment and financing. During the petroleum boom around 1980, large Mexican FBs first acquired access to financing in the international market. Although the external debt problem caused financing to stop in the 1980s, it resumed in the 1990s after the Brady Plan of 1989 stabilized the debt problem. Soon thereafter, large Mexican FBs began to raise funds actively in the international market by issuing shares and bonds and by contracting bank loans. Access to the international financial market liberated business groups from growth-restricting capital limitations; access to finance also made acquisitions possible. In the 1980s when economic reforms were enacted, bankruptcies of firms, disintegrations of firms of highly indebted FBs, and the privatization of state-owned enterprises created opportunities to reshuffle firms' ownership. This fluid situation helped large FBs restructure to improve their competitiveness and other newly formed FBs emerge within a short period through acquisitions.

7.3   EMERGENCE OF MEXICAN FAMILY MULTINATIONALS

After the mid-1980s, large Mexican FBs began to internationalize by means of exports, overseas direct investment, and international fund-raising, though FBs chose various methods.[14] I focus on FBs that selected overseas investment as a principal internationalization method.

Table 7.1 shows the ten largest FBs with subsidiaries in more than one foreign country extracted from a list of the twenty largest Mexican business groups in 2010 that I identified. Of these ten, Carso and Alfa are diversified FBs with more than two multinational companies in different sectors. Consequently, Table 7.1 contains thirteen multinational companies that belong to ten FBs.[15]

Evolution of Large Mexican Family Multinationals

Analyzing Mexican multinationals at the end of the 1990s,[16] C. Garrido pointed out that, at this stage of their evolution, they principally confined their activity to mature industries on the American continent, with only a few exceptions. Compared to Garrido's analysis, Table 7.1 shows considerable progress in multinationalization.

These reinvented family business groups functioned not only in mature industries, such as cement, beverages, and foods, but also in industries that utilize advanced technologies, such as autoparts supply and petrochemicals. At the same time, they extended their geographical reach by investing in a greater number of countries. Of the thirteen identified companies, seven

Table 7.1   Overseas Direct Investment of Mexican Family Businesses (2010)

Name of Family Business	Controlling Family	Name of Multinational Company	Principal Activities	% of Overseas Sales (Including Export)	Number of Invested Countries (Excluding Mexico)	Geographical Distribution					
						North America	Latin America & Caribbean	Europe	Asia	Australia	Middle East Asia
Carso	Slim	América Móvil	telecommunication	57%	17	1	16	0	0	0	0
		Grupo Carso	retail, autoparts	13%	4	0	3	1	0	0	0
Cemex	Zambrano	Cemex	cement	77%	31	1	9	12	6	0	3
Femsa	Graza Lagüera	Coca Cola Femsa	beverage	62%	8	0	8	0	0	0	0
Alfa	Garza	Nemak	autoparts	94%	11	2	2	6	1	0	0
		Sigma	foods	24%	5	1	4	0	0	0	0
		Alpek	petrochemical	54%	2	1	1	0	0	0	0
Bimbo	Servitje	Bimbo	foods	51%	16	1	12	2	1	0	0
Grupo Mexico	Larrea	Grupo México	mining, railroad	87%[1]	2	1	1	0	0	0	0
Gruma	González Barrera	Gruma	foods	67%	14	1	7	3	2	1	0
Salinas	Salinas	Grupo Elektra	retail, finance	n.a.	7	0	7	0	0	0	0
Mabe	Berrondo	Mabe	electrical appliance	n.a.	12	1	10	1	0	0	0
Mexichen	Del Valle	Mexichen	petrochemical	n.a.	17	2	12	1	2	0	0

[1]Grupo México also has a domestic railroad division (16% of total sales), which is not included in the total sales in calculating percentage.

Sources: Annual reports for the year 2010 of respective companies presented to the Mexican Stock Exchange. In the case of Mabe, information was taken from the company's home page, http://www.mabe.com,mex.

have subsidiaries in more than ten countries, and another seven extended their activities beyond the American continent. As a result, in eight of the ten companies whose data were available, overseas sales accounted for more than half of total sales by 2010. Alfa-Nemak, Alfa-Sigma, and Mexichem were among those who started overseas expansion in the 2000s. All the data show that the multinationalization of Mexican large FBs that started in the 1990s accelerated in the 2000s.

This acceleration resulted from changes in the underlying driving forces. Until the end of the 1990s, competitive pressure in the internal market, combined with benefits of business expansion, acted as pushing and pulling drivers of overseas investment for such firms. In addition, improved access to international financial markets acted as a strong pull factor in the 2000s. Excess liquidity in these markets from the late 1990s prompted a drop in interest rates, a global hunt for yield, and declining risk aversion among investors.[17] This situation made it possible for emerging multinationals from late-industrializing countries, including Mexico, to raise funds in international financial markets with favorable conditions relatively comparable to those of their counterparts in developed countries.[18]

Acquisition as a Principal Method of Foreign Expansion

The principal method of foreign expansion was acquiring existing companies. These companies preferred this method for three reasons: First, existing companies had operational facilities and markets allowing market entry in a shorter time. Alfa-Alpek acquired three U.S. PET (plastic resin) and PTA (material of polyester fiber) plants from Du Pont in 2001, making it a leading producer of PET and PTA in North America. In 2011, Alpek acquired further U.S. PET and PTA plants from Eastman for $600 million. Although Alpek produces diversified petrochemical products in Mexico, its foreign investments concentrate on PET and PTA.

Second, existing companies had resources that complemented their own resources. Alfa-Nemak, an original engine-parts manufacturer established in 1979 as a joint venture of Alfa (60 percent), as well as the Ford Motor Company and an Italian company, Teksid (40 percent), provides an example. Although Teksid left the joint venture early on, Nemak began foreign expansion in 2000 by acquiring a Ford plant in Canada in exchange for Ford's increased participation in Nemak, which had been decreased by Alfa's large-scale investment in Mexico. This acquisition gave Nemak not only a plant in Canada but also its advanced technologies. Thereafter, Nemak made more large-scale acquisitions, including in 2005 the German company Rautenback with plants in two European countries, in 2007 the Norwegian company Norsk Hydro with plants in four European countries, and also plants in six countries from Teksid. These acquisitions improved Nemak's technological capabilities and extended its client list—which had previously been limited to U.S. automakers—to European automakers.

Another example is Mexichem, which used acquisitions to fill missing links in its products' value chain. Mexichem's business is built on the two pillars of PVC (polyvinyl chloride, plastic resin) and fluorine. Both rely on global vertical integration, ranging from the extraction of materials to the manufacture of high-value-added products, such as from salt to PVC products, and from fluorite to refrigerant gas. Mexichem's strategy is to stabilize the usually volatile petrochemical industry through full vertical integration. It implemented this globally and vertically integrated business model through successive large-scale acquisitions between 2007 and 2011. In 2010, it acquired a fluorochemical business owned by the Ineos Group of the United Kingdom with sites in four countries for $354 million, and in 2011, it bought a company owned by Rockwood Specialties Group with PVC manufacturing plants in two countries for $326 million. These acquisitions secured Mexichem's position as a world-leading petrochemical producer.

The third reason acquisitions were preferred in the 2000s was the above-mentioned access to the international financial markets, which made them possible. Between 2005 and 2010, the scale of acquisitions rose in response to the expanding scale of business and improved accessibility to funds. The most outstanding example is CEMEX, which began multinationalizing in 1989. Successive acquisitions made it a world-leading cement multinational. In 2007, CEMEX acquired Rinker of Australia with plants in Australia, the United States, and China for $14.2 billion. Unfortunately for CEMEX, the Lehman shock hit the world economy after this acquisition. Major losses in derivative deals and a drop in sales caused by the economic recession brought the company to insolvency. Although creditors agreed to reschedule debts in 2009, CEMEX presently (in 2013) continues to suffer from huge external debts.

If abundant acquisition opportunities exist, then there are likewise abundant opportunities to be acquired. In fact, some Mexican family multinationals were acquired by other multinational and domestic companies or retreated from foreign markets by selling off their foreign assets. Of the thirteen multinational companies Garrido studied, one was bought out, one retreated from foreign markets, one decreased foreign assets, and one fell into bankruptcy afterwards.[19] With competition so intense, how can Mexican family multinationals expect to compete in the global market?

7.4   COMPETITIVE ADVANTAGE OF MEXICAN FAMILY MULTINATIONALS

There are five competitive advantages of the largest ten Mexican family multinationals: the Latin American advantage, the first mover advantage, monopoly rents accrued in the Mexican market, strategic alliances with multinationals from industrialized countries, and resources acquired in the process of multinationalization. They constitute a package, whose composition varies among family multinationals. It is safe to say that all ten of these family multinationals enjoy the Latin American advantage, but the most important factor differs among them. For example, monopoly rents in the Mexican market are considered to be the most important factor for América Móvil, a Carso telecommunications business, while strategic alliances with multinationals from industrialized countries are the most important for Femsa, Gruma, and Mabe. It seems that the most important competitive advantage depends on conditions in the Mexican and foreign markets for respective sectors, but also on the respective family multinationals' strategies.

Latin American Advantage

The Latin American advantage is the favorable position Mexican companies enjoy when competing in the Latin American market, as it is more similar to other countries' lower level of industrialization; similarity in language, culture, and historical background; and geographical proximity.[20] In markets with lower levels of industrialization than Mexico, Mexican companies can use resources and knowledge acquired during their growth in Mexico. The similarity in language, culture, and historical background facilitate communication with suppliers, distributors, clients, workers, and government officials. They also make building business networks, addressing the needs of consumers, penetrating trademarks, and negotiating with unions and government officials proceed more smoothly and effectively. Geographical proximity fosters the accumulation of information by frequent exchanges, so that Mexican companies have a higher quantity and quality of information.

Bimbo specializes in the production of bread and confectionaries. Its products are nondurable consumer goods, so marketing plays a decisive role in its growth. Bimbo was able to grow successfully in Mexico by making use of the latest technologies, maintaining a well-equipped distribution system, and vigorously utilizing trademarks and advertising. The similar language and culture made it easier for Bimbo to penetrate Latin American markets by applying comparable strategies in them.[21]

In the early stage of its foreign expansion, CEMEX chose developing countries because it could then utilize resources it acquired during its growth in Mexico. A peculiarity of the cement market in developing countries is that homeowners building their own homes constitute a very large part of it, so that cement is sold in packages as a consumer good.[22] By contrast, in developed countries, cement is mainly sold in bulk as an intermediate good. The marketing capabilities required in each case differ. In a consumer good market, the capacity to build distribution networks of retailers and diffuse trademarks, for example, is important. As CEMEX possessed this skill, it had a competitive edge over multinationals from other developed countries when competing in developing countries, especially Latin America.

The Latin American advantage is also effective in the United States, where the Hispanic population is expanding. Sigma, Alfa's food business, started investing in the United States in 2006. It aims to penetrate the Hispanic market in the United States, calculating that it already has an advantage because its trademarks are familiar to the Mexican community and it is familiar with the Hispanic population's tastes.[23]

The First Mover Advantage

Large Mexican family multinationals have often had a first mover advantage over companies from other Latin American countries. That is, they were the first movers in their respective sectors in Mexico and had already attained a predominant position in the market. They stand out in terms of scale by Latin American standards. In a list of the 500 largest companies in Latin America in 2010, América Móvil, CEMEX, and Bimbo held the first position in the telecommunications, cement, and bread and confectionaries sectors, respectively. In the beverage sector, Femsa was the third-largest producer. In petrochemicals, Alfa-Alpek and Mexichem held the second and third positions. In electronic appliances, Mabe was third.[24] To compete with first movers, followers need to make comparable investments in production, distribution, and management. With their existing resources, first movers can initially compete favorably with latecomers if they continue to invest in improving their capabilities.

Support from Monopoly Rents Accrued in the Mexican Market

Although competition in Mexico has intensified, large family multinationals still maintain dominant positions in their respective sectors. A notable indicator for gauging monopoly rents accrued by monopolistic positions in the Mexican market is a greater operating margin (the ratio of operating profit to sales) for Mexico than outside Mexico, suggesting that competition is higher abroad. Operating margins in and outside Mexico for 2010, respectively, were 0.38 and 0.13 for América Móvil, 0.29 and 0.06 for CEMEX, 0.17 and 0.10 for Bimbo, and 0.14 and 0.05 for Gruma.[25] Thus, these firms seem to get monopoly rents in Mexico, which helps them compete favorably internationally where competition is fiercer.

A representative case is América Móvil. A former government monopoly telephone service, it was privatized in 1990 and competitors entered the market. Nonetheless, América Móvil still maintains a monopolistic position with market shares of 70 percent in the mobile-phone and 80 percent in land-line markets. Telecommunications service is a licensed business regulated by the government. Licensees are obliged to offer open network structures— that is, they have to allow other providers to connect to their networks for a connection fee. América Móvil's balance of connection-fee proceeds is overwhelmingly favorable because of its large domestic market share.

In addition, América Móvil was able to unilaterally set the connection-fee rates. The Federal Telecommunications Law established that licensees would negotiate the rate and, if no agreement was reached, the Federal Commission for Telecommunications (Cofetel), a government regulatory body, would set rates. However, to keep regulatory rates from applying, which were at all times much lower than América Móvil's expected rate, the company usually sought *amparos* (legal injuctions) in courts, obtaining a judicial suspension of regulatory decisions. While the appeals were underway, América Móvil could apply its higher rates. América Móvil's abuse of *amparos* has been criticized—a product of Mexico's weak legal system resulting in the nonapplication of laws and regulations.[26]

Strategic Alliances with Multinationals from Industrialized Countries

Mexican family multinationals have also improved their competitiveness by combining their resources through strategic alliances with foreign multinationals. Partners also expect to exploit the resources of their counterpart, so alliances require that both parties have something to offer. Equity participation generally makes alliances more persistent and solid. Of the thirteen companies under examination, five have equity participation from multinationals from industrialized countries. AT&T has a 29-percent equity stake in América Móvil. The Coca-Cola Company holds 37 percent of Coca-Cola Femsa. BASF and LyondellBasell have equity participation of 49 percent in two Alfa-Alpec subsidiaries. Archer Daniels Midland (ADM) has equity participation of 23 percent in Gruma. General Electric has equity in Mabe of 48 percent.[27] Here, we will examine the cases of Coca-Cola Femsa and Gruma more closely.

In 2010, Coca-Cola Femsa was the largest bottler in the world, measured in sales, for the Coca-Cola Company. Coca-Cola provides Femsa with drink concentrate, the right to use its trademark, and marketing support. It also holds greater bargaining power in the alliance because it has the right to set the price of concentrate, the right to refuse if Femsa wishes to produce other drinks, and the right not to renew the contract, which is periodically revised. Coca-Cola Femsa began going multinational in 1994 with an acquisition in Argentina and accelerated this process in a 2003 burst when it acquired Panamerican Beverage of Panama with plants in seven countries including Mexico. As Coca-Cola had 25 percent equity in this company, the acquisition took place with its consent.[28] Coca-Cola is believed to have selected Femsa as a partner for two reasons. First, at that time, Coca-Cola was competing with Pepsi in Mexico, where Panamerican Beverage earned almost 40 percent of its sales.[29] Coca-Cola needed to strengthen its Mexican business, so it preferred a Mexican company as an alliance partner. Second, Femsa could offer favorable conditions as a partner such as a good record as a Coca-Cola bottler, a nationwide distribution network for soft drinks and beer, another pillar of its business, and a good reputation as one of the prominent older business groups in Mexico. Femsa was Coca-Cola's best possible, eligible partner.

Concerning the ADM/Gruma alliance, ADM is a multinational of U.S. origin involved in agribusiness. Gruma had already started investing in the United States as early as 1977 in corn flour milling. The two multinationals initially competed in the U.S. market. In 1996, they agreed on a strategic alliance under the following conditions: (1) ADM acquired 23.2 percent of Gruma's shares; (2) Azteca Milling was established with Gruma putting up 80 percent of the capital and ADM 20 percent; the U.S. flour-milling plants of both companies were integrated into it; and (3) Gruma acquired 60 percent of Molinera de Mexico, an ADM wheat flour-milling subsidiary in Mexico. After 2004, Gruma accelerated foreign expansion by entering Europe, Australia, and Asia.[30] For Gruma, the merits of the alliance with ADM were, first, to minimize competition with ADM and to expand its American tortilla business by acquiring control of ADM's assets, and second, to secure a stable supplier of corn, which would facilitate the expansion of its tortilla business on a global scale. ADM allied with Gruma, first, because corn flour-milling was of little importance in the U.S. market, and second, to secure a stable client of corn, as corn was one of its principal commodities. ADM's principal competitor is Cargill, another multinational of U.S. origin, which expanded into Mexico in 1972 and has businesses in grain trading and manufacturing of agricultural products. The ADM/Gruma alliance represents a vertical integration of the trade and distribution sector and the manufacturing sector of corn. Cargill also moved into corn flour-milling in Mexico in 2005. In other words, Cargill chose internal vertical integration rather than an alliance like that of its main competitors, ADM and Gruma.

Resources Acquired in Multinationalization

Of the thirteen companies, Grupo Carso, CEMEX, Alfa-Alpek, Bimbo, and Mexichem expanded to industrialized countries through their own efforts. Alfa-Nemak also belongs in this category because Ford's equity participation is decreasing. In industrialized countries, the Latin American advantage, the first mover advantage, and strategic alliances may lose effectiveness. However, the companies remain competitive in industrialized countries because the resources they acquired in the growth process in Mexico attained world-class levels. This explains the success of multinationals in technologically mature industries, such as Bimbo in the bread and confectionery industry. They also acquired new resources by internalizing those of acquired companies and enhanced their learning through repeated acquisitions and the implementation of new projects. This was the case with Alfa-Alpek's PTA and PET business, Alfa-Nemak, and Mexichem. CEMEX exemplifies a case of acquiring new resources by learning in the internationalization process. CEMEX improved its technology and delivery systems and became famous for integrating the management of acquired companies into its worldwide business network. It also maintains the capacity utilization of plants around the world by adjusting cement's export and import on a global scale through its newly started cement trade business and its own transportation vessels.[31]

7.5 COMPETITIVE ADVANTAGE AND FAMILISM IN MEXICAN MULTINATIONALS

How Familism Affects Multinationalization

How are these competitive advantages related to these Mexican multinationals being FBs, owned and controlled by a family? From the previous discussion, we can see two common sources of this competitive advantage. One is the large scale of business, which enables the firms to engage in international fund-raising, acquisitions, and strategic alliances. Another is their trajectory of growth in a late-industrializing country, which affects their resources and their position in the market. It is hard to see any direct relationship between familism and these sources of competitiveness.

In order to multinationalize their businesses, large Mexican FBs made two changes in their long-standing family-related features. One was to open ownership to outsiders to raise funds in stock markets and forge strategic alliances. Another was to appoint family outsiders to some top management positions as the expansion increased their need for qualified managers. Despite these changes, however, the families maintained overall control of their businesses by adopting a hierarchal control structure.

In a hierarchal control structure, companies in FBs form a pyramid tied from the top to the bottom by one-way equity participations. A holding company, usually listed, forms the pyramid's peak. The principal merit of this structure is that it saves on the economic cost of control because the family controls the whole pyramid by holding a controlling share of the apex company. Dual class shares further reduce the cost of holding shares. In addition, the holding company prevents a dispersion of family shares, and voting trusts unite the family's vote.[32] Another merit of the structure is that it facilitates a division of labor between family managers and nonfamily managers. The apex company's role is mainly fund-raising, resource allocation, and strategic planning. The family holds key managerial positions only in the apex company and is scarcely observed at the subsidiaries level.[33] By holding the apex of the hierarchal management structure and delegating top management to nonfamily managers, the controlling family tries to balance the family's limitations as a pool of human resources and the expanding business's increasing need for qualified managers.

The sustainability of this control structure seems to depend on three conditions. First, it depends on family cohesion for uniting the vote. Maintaining family cohesion is a survival issue in the long run, because family shares can now be traded in stock markets and ownership of shares will be dispersed through successions. Second, it depends on the durability of the institutional framework of corporate governance in Mexico, which allows for the actual control structure. Third, it depends on the family's capacity to provide family managers qualified enough to lead an increasing number of qualified nonfamily managers.

The presence of such a hierarchal structure indicates that a controlling family—especially members in key managerial positions in the apex company—decided to multinationalize; here in particular one can observe the relationship between familism and multinationalization. The mode of multinationalization often directly reflects families' initiative. Typical cases are CEMEX and Mexichem.

Behind CEMEX's early start in foreign expansion in 1989, the family's managerial leadership experienced a generation shift. Multinationalization progressed under the initiative of Lorenzo Zambrano, the leader of the new generation who inherited the top managerial position in 1985 from his uncle. It was a time when Mexican cement companies were hard hit by the external debt problem, and cement multinationals from developed countries were looking to acquire troubled companies. Although CEMEX had no debt problem thanks to the uncle's conservative management style, there was concern that CEMEX could be acquired if it failed to remain competitive. Thus, Zambrano adopted multinationalization through acquisitions as a survival strategy, making him decisive in CEMEX's multinationalization.[34]

Mexichem's vertical integration on the global scale was initiated by Antonio del Valle, the head of the controlling family.[35] He had formerly owned a bank that was expropriated in 1982 when the Mexican government nationalized private banks to curb capital flight provoked by the external debt problem. With the indemnity for the bank, he purchased a caustic-soda manufacturing company. He reentered the banking business with other investors when the government reprivatized banks in 1992, but he sold his shares in 1994 and bought a fluorite mining company. These two companies formed the basis of Mexichem's vertical integration, which continued through acquisitions first in Mexico and later in other countries.

Sustainability of Competitive Advantages

The resource-based view maintains that, to sustain its competitive advantage, a firm must have valuable and rare resources that cannot be imitated or replaced.[36] If it does not, its competitors will duplicate the resources, gradually eroding the advantage. If a firm does have such resources, how sustainable is its competitive advantage? How sustainable are the competitive advantages of large Mexican family multinationals?

Reviewing the five advantages of these firms, we can assume that the Latin American advantage and first mover advantage would be lost over time, because they can be duplicated. Mexican FBs improved their resources by acquisition, but their rivals could pursue the same path. A good example is CEMEX. It changed its target markets from less industrialized to industrialized countries in the 2000s. To compete in industrialized countries, it had to deliver freshly mixed concrete at construction sites, so it also had to build a network uniting cement manufacturing plants, concrete mixing plants, and construction sites. CEMEX achieved this through acquisitions, yet multinationals from industrialized countries, CEMEX's major competitors, likewise expanded aggressively into less industrialized countries. Consequently, its rivals' resources and assets grew similar to its own through the competition for shares in the global cement market.

It is also likely that monopoly rents would be lost in the long run, because global competition is extending into the Mexican market. Multinational rivals of América Móvil and CEMEX have already invested in Mexico and are ready to undermine these firms' dominance. A Supreme Court decision of 2011 marked América Móvil's first heavy blow: the company's competitors had complained of its use of *amparo* to continue charging higher connection fees, and the court ordered that Cofetel's arbitrated rate should be applied while *amparo* appeals processes were underway. This now prevents América Móvil from abusing the *amparo* system to delay or effectively nullify the application of Cofetel's much lower rates.[37]

As for strategic alliances, they are not a stable source of competitiveness because they can be dissolved. In addition, as alliances are reciprocal, FBs must have an original competitive advantage to become partners.

If these four competitive advantages cannot be maintained in the long run, then large Mexican family multinationals will have to rely on the fifth—acquiring new resources through multinationalization—to remain competitive. They will continually need to seek new combinations of existing competitive advantages and to acquire new resources. Frequent changes in the list of leading Mexican family multinationals show that this is not an easy task.

7.6   CONCLUSION

The multinationalization of large Mexican FBs began in the 1990s and accelerated in the 2000s. These firms moved into technologically advanced sectors and well beyond the Americas, rapidly expanding the rate and scale of investment.

Two factors affected the process: globalization, and the fact that these large Mexican FBs acted as the predominant economic development agents in this late-industrializing country. Major economic reforms in response to the external debt problems of 1982 opened the Mexican economy to the full flood of globalization's effects in the 1990s, which, in turn, affected the internationalization of large Mexican FBs in two ways. First, trade liberalization and deregulation of inward FDI pressured them to internationalize by creating more competitive conditions in the Mexican market. Second, it facilitated internationalization by providing new opportunities for international fund-raising, acquiring firms, and forming strategic alliances with multinationals from industrialized countries.

As predominant economic development agents, large Mexican FBs enjoyed various competitive advantages, including the Latin American advantage, the first mover advantage, monopoly rents accrued in the Mexican market, strategic alliances with multinationals from industrialized countries, and resources acquired in the process of multinationalization. The first four of these five elements derive from resources the firms acquired in the growth process in Mexico by adopting and taking advantage of conditions of a late-industrializing country.

Examining the basis of these firms' competitive advantage, familism does not seem to be directly related to it. Familiness is merely reflected in the controlling families' decision to multinationalize in the face of increased competition, and also in the families' role in determining how to multinationalize. Most controlling families opened ownership of their businesses to outsiders and delegated some top management positions to family outsiders for the sake of fund-raising, forging strategic alliances, and addressing their increasing need for qualified managers. They, nevertheless, still maintain control of their businesses by adopting hierarchal control structures. The sustainability of a family's control depends on its cohesion, the durability of the institutional framework of corporate governance in Mexico, and the family's ability to provide managerial talent.

The analysis in this chapter shows that Mexican FBs were extraordinarily adaptable to the changing environment. One important pillar supporting their adaptability is their demonstrated ability to combine various sources of competitive advantage and acquire new resources, and to redefine their organizational structure within Mexico's institutional settings. Their survival seems to depend on whether they can continuously renew this ability.

NOTES

1. Khanna and Yafeh, 2007, 331.
2. Leff, 1978, 666–667.
3. Khanna and Palepu, 1997, 41–48. Khanna and Palepu, 2000, 868.
4. Haber, Maurer and Razo, 2002, 28–36. Schneider, 2009. Morck, Wolfenzon and Yeung, 2005, 695–699, 708.
5. See the introduction (this volume) and Kontinen and Ojala, 2010, 104.
6. Johanson and Vahlne, 1990, 12.
7. Kock and Guillén, 2001. Guillén, 2000.
8. Amsden and Hikino, 1994.
9. I use Colli and Rose's definition of *family business* as "one where a family owns enough of the equity to be able to exert control over strategy *and* is involved in top management positions." It is because this definition explains the nature of large Mexican FBs after the modification of control structures

in the 1980s. *Business group* refers to a large-scale business entity consisting of large companies under common control, in many cases, of an owner family. Colli and Rose, 2007, 194.

10. Hansen, 1971, 44–55. Story, 1986, 73–74.
11. Hoshino, 2001, 77–114.
12. Aspe, 1993, 156–158, 166–168. Hoshino, 1996.
13. Hoshino, 2010, 434, 438–439.
14. Salas-Porras, 1998.
15. The information on companies referred in Sections 3, 4, and 5 was taken from the annual report for the year 2010 of respective companies presented to the Mexican Stock Exchange, when it is not specifically noted.
16. Garrido, 1999.
17. Bracke and Fidora, 2012, 190–191.
18. Santiso, 2008, 13.
19. Of the thirteen multinationals studied by Garrido, Geo does not have overseas assets at the point of 2010, Vitro sold its assets in the United States in 2011 due to an external debt problem, Consorcio G Grupo Dina bankrupted in 2001, and Seminis of La Moderna was acquired in 2003.
20. Tavares, 2007, 57.
21. Hoshino, 2001, 72–75.
22. According to the annual report of CEMEX for the year 2007, 60% of CEMEX's sales in Mexico was attained through 5,800 sales agents spread over the country.
23. The information was taken from the annual reports of Alfa for the year 2008.
24. The data was taken from "Las Mayores Empresas de America Latina" of *America Economía*, which is a ranking of the largest 500 companies of 19 countries of Latin America at the point of December 2010, http://rankings.americaeconomia.com/2011/500.
25. Figures are calculations by this author based on financial statements taken from annual reports of the respective companies. "Operating profit" and "sales" in Spanish are *utilidad de operación* and *ventas*, respectively.
26. Organisation for Economic Cooperation and Development (OECD), 2012, 26.
27. The information on Mabe was taken from *Directorio Industridata empresas AAA 2010* edited by Mercametrica Ediciones, Mexico.
28. The information was taken from the annual reports for the year 2008 of Fomento Económico Mexicano.
29. "Las jugadas de las colas," *Expanión*, February 17, 1993.
30. The information was taken from the annual reports for the year 2008 of Gruma.
31. Hoshino, 2002, 51–52.
32. Hoshino, 2006.
33. Hoshino, 2005, 7–8.
34. Hoshino, 2002, 54.
35. Adolfo Ortega, "Antonio Del Valle, el empresario del año," *Expansión*, January 21, 2008.
36. Barney, 1991, 102.
37. Organisation for Economic Cooperation and Development (OECD), 2012, 58.

Part III
From Local Base to Global Expansion

8 Carving out a Place in International Markets

Success and Failure in European Family Papermaking Firms (1800–2010)

Miquel Gutiérrez Poch

8.1 INTRODUCTION: FAMILY BUSINESSES, HISTORY AND GLOBAL MARKETS[1]

Family businesses (FBs) are typically thought to be less likely to go global than large firms. This tendency is explained in terms of their generally risk-averse nature, limited growth aspirations, poor financial strength, and weak managerial capabilities. The situation leads Mark Casson to claim that, within the conventional neoclassical framework, the family firm is an anachronism.[2] Yet, family firms can be highly successful, and even adopt international strategies and cultures.[3] FBs have "traditionally focused on their domestic markets"[4] but, they also "increasingly find themselves obliged to internationalize, in order to survive in a market that is becoming more and more globally competitive."[5] This chapter supports the hypothesis that "family ownership and management is not in itself an obstacle for the growth and internationalization of a firm."[6] FBs might have their weaknesses, but they enjoy sufficient strengths to operate globally.

Casson identifies in-depth customer knowledge and very specific technical know-how as the particular strengths of most family firms that allow them to internationalize. According to the OLI-Framework, which highlights firms' ownership, location, and internalization advantages, the firms with the highest productivity rates are most likely to invest in foreign countries. For Michael E. Porter (1998), the strengths of firms under family ownership and management lie in sector specialization and clustering. FBs use niche markets with high-value-added components (though not solely) and their firm rootedness in regional or local communities to become competitive in global markets. However, they also rely on a number of related factors that include networking and strategic alliances. Most global family businesses fit this portrait. It is assumed that a firm's internationalization depends less on its size or type of ownership than on national and international (historical, social, and economic) contexts and the sector in which it operates. The literature distinguishes three main theoretical models in the internationalization process: the stage, born global, and born-again global models. And, indeed, examples of family businesses can be found that match each of them.

This chapter seeks to analyze the successes and failures in the internationalization processes of European family papermaking firms. As a firm's competitive strategy depends on the particular sector and the firm's position within it, sector analysis is a good way to examine the links between global markets and family businesses. Therefore, this study undertakes a long-term analysis of the papermaking industry; however, the results must be considered provisional as the database is still under construction.

Information comes from around 200 primary and secondary sources not individually listed in consideration of space. The first historical section is based on company monographs (Drewsen Spezialpapiere), specialized historical articles (like the ones published by the *British Association of Historians of Paper*), and statistical yearbooks of the papermaking industries (like the *Internationale Papier-Statistik* by Franz Krawany between 1910 and 1927). For the remaining sections, the most important sources include papermaking and chemical industry journals (*Pulp & Paper International, Perini Journal, Tissue World Magazine, Recupera, Kemira Solutions, Results Pulp & Paper, Paper Technology, FiberSpectrum*); yearbooks of the sector associations (ASPAPEL, ASSOCARTA, etc.); statistical reports from the Confederation of European Paper Industries (CEPI); sectoral websites (like www.letsrecycle.com, www.convertingtoday.co.uk), and regional websites (www.klmagazine.co.uk, www.calvados-strategie.com, www.invest-in-bavaria). In addition, corporate websites (like those from Palm, Europac, Sociedad Anónima Industrias Celulosa Aragonesa [SAICA], Van Houtum, Papierpabrik Scheufelen, Fedrigoni, Ahlström, Koehler Paper Group, Lucart) and corporate publications (*Z-Info* for Ziegler Papier), as well as the political and economic press from different countries (*El País, La Vanguardia, Cumbria Life, Irish Independent*, etc.) proved useful. Finally, the selection of companies benefited from the well-known business databases AMADEUS and SABI.

8.2   THE FAMILY FIRM AND INTERNATIONALIZATION: FROM PREINDUSTRIAL TIMES TO THE SECOND INDUSTRIAL REVOLUTION

The family unit and the paper mills were at the heart of the productive and commercial structure of the papermaking industry during the preindustrial period. Location and kinship were the mainstays of the whole production system; the papermaking families of Italy, France, Germany, and Spain built their businesses on these foundations. During the sixteenth and seventeenth centuries, Genoese papermakers established strong ties to the trade routes developed by the city's merchants throughout the Mediterranean. They exploited this commercial network to sell their paper and to ensure a good supply of raw materials (mainly old rags). Spanish papermakers began trading with the Latin American colonies in the late eighteenth century (where paper for official uses was in demand), but they did not require a sophisticated export structure as they enjoyed privileges granted by the Spanish government. However, difficulties arose developing a system flexible enough to supply the growing demand from the colonial market. At this time, the industry's whole productive structure was cemented by marriages arranged between leading papermaking families.

Following the introduction of the Fourdrinier machine, it was mostly firms under family ownership and management that championed technological change. This confirms the "importance of family business in early industrialization,"[7] with the Didot and Montgolfier (in France), Godin (Belgium), and Dickinson and Cowan (United Kingdom) families playing leading roles. Indeed, the British papermaking industry at this time was characterized by "its family concerns and close personal ties."[8] Throughout the 1830s and the 1840s, new technology was widely adopted with hundreds of machines operating in the United Kingdom, France, and Germany, although more peripheral countries were slow to adopt the modern process. Interestingly, modern technology did not eclipse old methods; some family businesses survived for decades by adhering to a niche strategy and producing handmade specialty paper.

During the nineteenth century, papermaking firms followed three possible pathways to internationalization: via the emigration of skilled workers, product exports, or raw material supply. In all three instances, the existence of networks cemented by family ties was essential. The emigration of skilled workers allowed firms to learn more about foreign markets. Thus, a number of French papermakers, after working in Spain, used their knowledge of the Iberian market to export and even open their own warehouses there. However, in the mid-nineteenth century, increasing production led to a bottleneck in and rising prices for raw materials, prompting firms to seek substitutes for old rags. One option was esparto grass grown in the Mediterranean area. Various British family businesses invested there to guarantee the supply. Edward Lloyd, the owner of paper mills and newspapers, purchased warehouses for esparto grass storage in Algeria and Spain during the late 1860s and early 1870s. Lloyd also owned land in Algeria. William McMurray, a British papermaker, likewise invested in Spain and North Africa during the late 1870s. His foreign assets comprised esparto fields, warehouses, and factories for processing the fiber, and his nephews managed the Spanish business.

Foreign direct investment was not significant in papermaking during the first industrial revolution. Bryan Donkin, owner of the first workshop to build continuous machines for paper production, invested in factories in different countries in the early nineteenth century, although he was mainly interested in selling engineering. Members of the Donkin family traveled around Europe, overseeing their investments and monitoring their customers. French papermakers also invested in Spain and Italy. In such foreign investments, a family member would typically remain in the foreign country to manage the new factory. This was the case for Alfred Motteau, a paper-making engineer who, together with local partners, invested in Spain in the early 1860s, with his son appointed manager of the mill. Usually, however, these investments had little continuity.

The introduction of wood pulp changed the industry's situation as it, alongside growing mechanization, increased capital requirements. From about 1880 to 1920, the big corporations took center stage. The leading firms were International Paper Co. Ltd. (U.S.), Zellstoff Waldhof AG (Germany), and Kymmene AB (Finland). Yet even in this new landscape, small and medium-sized enterprises (SMEs) survived and some leading firms remained family-owned and -managed, such as Weyerhaeuser in the United States.

Foreign investment rose to meet the growing need for wood pulp; this included some FBs that invested in foreign countries to ensure their raw material supply. In 1883–1884, the French firm Darblay *père et fils* set up a pulp factory in the Austrian Tyrol, which it owned until 1931. The Belgian papermaker, de Naeyer, made pulp with Nordic wood and built factories in France, Spain, and Russia. The Spanish branch, opened in 1890, resulted from a "joint venture" with locals. De Naeyer kept its French factories until the 1920s. In the United Kingdom, some of the most internationally active firms were also family businesses. Edward Lloyd invested in Norway in 1892 and owned two pulp factories there in the early twentieth century. W. V. Bowater and Sons, founded in 1881, began as a newsprint wholesaler but turned to papermaking in 1923. This British firm started expanding internationally by opening commercial offices in the United States (1914) and Australia (1919). During the 1930s, Bowater also purchased shares in Swedish and Norwegian pulp mills and in 1938 acquired a newsprint factory in Newfoundland, which enjoyed access to enormous timber resources. Newsprint specialists Albert E. Reed & Co. Ltd., founded in 1894, invested just before World War I in pulp factories in Norway and in Newfoundland, with the Newfoundland factory managed personally by the owner's son. Also newsprint specialists, Van Gelder Zonen of the Netherlands, began its international expansion in 1912 by opening an office in Saint Petersburg to buy Russian wood. In 1914, it opened a further office in London to sell newsprint. Yet the Great War interrupted both projects. In sum, from about 1880 to the onset of World War I, some FBs were engaged in projects of international expansion, trading in the standard newsprint and pulp.

At the same time, other family businesses continued to operate principally in niche markets, producing cigarette paper (Miquel y Costas & Miquel (MCM) of Spain; L. Lacroix et Fils and Braunstein Frères of France), hand-made paper for official use (Miliani of Italy; Canson of France; Guarro and Vilaseca of Spain), and high-quality printing and writing paper. Some of these firms established themselves as veritable global leaders. MCM typifies the "born-global" model, since it exported most of its production from the beginning, chiefly to Latin America given the obvious trading advantages of a common language and similar tastes. Its Havana office opened when the firm went into business in the late 1870s; shortly thereafter, it opened commercial offices in the Philippines, Chile, Argentina, Mexico, and the United States. In most cases, the office managers had ties of kinship or origin with the Miquel family. MCM also appointed sales agents in Colombia and Brazil and purchased workshops in Cuba and Mexico. By 1900, L. Lacroix et Fils was selling around two-thirds of its output on foreign markets. Anciennes Manufactures Canson & Montgolfier, an old French family firm that established itself as a corporation in 1880, had commercial branches in New York and Geneva in the mid-1920s. In addition to its own network, Canson had representatives in more than 20 countries.

Modernizing business structures facilitated the next generation's entry into family firms. In countries with longer papermaking traditions, many family businesses chose to go public. W. V. Bowater adopted limited liability as a private company in 1910, which smoothed the transition after its founder's death. By contrast, Reed & Co., registered as a public company in 1903, experienced numerous problems upon its founder's death in 1920. Reed's sons sold some of their shares to Lord Rothermere, their primary customer and the owner of a media conglomerate. Rothermere also purchased a controlling share in Bowater in 1928, but the founding family bought it back in 1932.

In 1914, with the outbreak of World War I, the first global economy disintegrated, derailing the process of internationalization and culminating in the Great Depression.[9] This shift in the economic climate prompted family firms to focus on the domestic front rather than on international markets.

8.3   FAMILY BUSINESS AND GLOBALIZATION: PRESENT-DAY REALITY AND HISTORICAL DETERMINANTS

The evolution of papermaking during the "second wave of globalization[, which] began during the 1950s and intensified after 1979"[10] was characterized by two main changes. The first was the geographical shift in the axis of world paper production. In 1961, North America produced 52.2 percent of the world's output, Europe 32.1 percent, South America 1.7 percent, and Asia 11.9 percent. By 2009, this scenario had changed radically with the above areas producing 22.5, 27.2, 3.9, and 42.9 percent, respectively; this trend away from North American towards Asian predominance is expected to continue. Interestingly, Europe is holding its own, responding to new challenges with changes to its business structure.

The second change concerns the intensive rationalization of the papermaking sector. The crisis of the 1970s and early 1980s saw the demise of a great many family firms. The number of companies in the Confederation of European Paper Industries[11] (CEPI) shows how this process has intensified over the last two decades: it fell from 1,052 (1991) to 683 (2010)—see

Number of firms (CEPI countries)

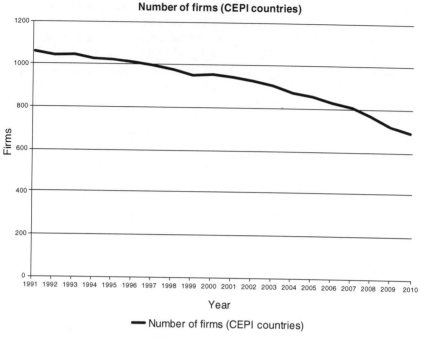

━ Number of firms (CEPI countries)

Figure 8.1   Number of Firms (CEPI Countries)
© By the author.

Figure 8.1—while the number of paper and pulp factories dropped from 1,601 to 998. In Spain, about 280 factories operated in the mid-1960s, but by 2010 this number was just 85 (including paper and pulp mills). In Italy, 304 paper firms were in business in 1950; by 1998, 171 firms operated a total of 207 factories, and by 2008, these numbers were down to 139 and 180, respectively. SMEs—above all, family-owned businesses—have been the main victims in this process. Reasons for closures include misguided production specialization decisions, failure to introduce technological change, the very small size of the firms, and the problems encountered at the time of intergenerational handovers. Once more, the advance of the big corporations seemed to condemn SMEs (including family-owned firms) to oblivion, although some of the big firms also closed.

A number of highly competitive family firms did manage to survive this process of rationalization, some of which can be regarded as big firms today. The following family firms (at least until recently) rank in the world's top 100 papermaking firms in 2010, according to *Pulp & Paper International* magazine: Oji Paper (ranked 4th), Smurfit Kappa (9th), Smurfit-Stone Container (13th), Daio Paper (19th), Cascades (22nd), Suzano Papel e Celulose (32nd), Burgo (33rd), Mayr-Meinhof Karton (36th), Lee & Man (41st), Klabin (44th), Palm (60th), Prinzhorn (61st), Ahlstrom (63rd), Fedrigoni (74th), LEIPA Georg

Leinfelder (78th), Koehler (81st), Europac (92nd), and Exacompta Clairefon-taine (93rd). The majority of these companies are European—see Table 8.1. Other firms that can also be considered family-owned on the basis of the size of their investment holding might be added to this list, such as Stora Enso (ranked 3rd), owned by the Wallenbergs and Sequana (11th) forming part of the Agnelli holding. SAICA, a Spanish firm, should also be included but does not appear as the magazine did not have access to the available data. *Pulp & Paper International* also publishes the RISI Top 50 Power List, a ranking of the most influential people in the global pulp and paper industry. In 2009, the big corporations dominated the top positions but not to the exclusion

Table 8.1   European Family Businesses (Including Groups) Among the World's Top 100 Papermaking Firms in 2010

Rank	Company (Country)	2010 Sales ($ million)	Production 2010 (1,000 tonnes)		Employees	CEO
			Market Pulp	Paper & Board		
33	Burgo Group, Italy	2,546.1	823	2,562	4,793	Girolamo Marchi*
36	Mayr-Meinhof Karton, Austria	2,356.5		1,579	8,679	Wilhelm Hörmanseder
60	Palm, Germany	1,324.7		1,890	3,000	Wolfgang Palm*
61	Prinzhorn Holding, Austria	1,272.8		1,600	4,000	DI Thomas Prinzhorn*
74	Fedrigoni, Italy	950.7		400	2,035	Claudio Alfonsi
78	LEIPA Georg Leinfelder, Germany	874.3		850	830	Hubert Schödinger*
81	Koehler, Germany	849.7		492	1,708	Kai Fürler*
92	Europac, Spain	710.7		868	1,400	J. M. Isidro Rincón*
93	Exacompta Clairefontaine, France	702.5		219	3,230	François Nusse*

*Member of the owning family.

Source: Pulp & Paper International Top 100 of 2010. Ahlström and Smurfit Kappa Group are not included as they are no longer family firms.

of various family firms in Asia, North America, and Europe. Teguh Ganda Wijata, CEO of Asia Pulp and Paper (APP), was ranked first. In Europe, the two highest-ranking leaders from family firms were Michael Smurfit (36th) and Wolfgang Palm (40th in 2009 and 30th in 2010). Wolfgang Palm is the president of Verband Deutscher Papierfabriken e. V, the German papermaking employers' association.

A close inspection of the leading European papermakers reveals a dense network of family businesses. From a provisional list of the 350 largest firms (excluding multinational enterprises [MNE] branches, the number is roughly 180 to 200), around 30 are family businesses. The majority are based in Italy (13), Germany (11), and Spain (6), with the first two countries presenting the highest densities. The case of Germany is demonstrative of the strength of the *Mittelstand*.[12] Family businesses can also be found in the Scandinavian countries, France, the Netherlands, and the United Kingdom.[13]

8.4 FROM HISTORICAL ORIGINS TO THE DYNAMICS OF INDUSTRIAL DISTRICTS

Longevity is an essential advantage of family businesses. Many FBs can to trace their roots to the initial stages of industrialization, making their history an important, intangible value even in their marketing. Some authors consider FBs to be short-lived ventures lacking the capacity to survive into a second or third generation. Yet, other kinds of business often fail to survive the equivalent of even one generation.[14] Most of the papermaking firms discussed here have survived for several generations. The Kohlers, the owners of Büttenpapierfabrik Gmund, and the Hamelins, the owners of Groupe Hamelin, Palm Papierfabrik, are in their fourth generation; Ziegler Papier AG is in its fifth; James Cropper, Exacompta Clairefontaine, and LEIPA Georg Leinfelder Gmbh are in their sixth; Papierfabrik August Koehler is in its eighth; and Gumà Camps is even in its tenth. The motto of the UK family firm James Cropper captures this idea perfectly: "A family business. Seven Chairmen. Six generations. One family."

Longevity ensures the accumulation of both technological and commercial know-how. The factories of these FBs were (and are) places of informal learning, while some firms, mainly in Germany, offer formal training programs. Papierfabrik Palm has signed agreements with local technical schools and universities to train its employees. The British staff of its new factory, opened in 2009, were trained in the "firm's culture" in Germany. The Austrian firm, Mayr-Melnhof, also opened its own internal training institution, MM-Academy, in 2006.

The family firms analyzed here date from four different periods: (1) the eighteenth and early nineteenth centuries;[15] (2) the mid-nineteenth century;[16] (3) either side of World War II (when a significant number were founded);[17] and (4) the Golden Age (1950–1973).[18]

The founding dates of these firms seem to correlate closely with their chosen specialization so that the oldest are less standardized and adhere more closely to a niche strategy, reflecting path-dependence mechanisms. Thus, family businesses with more standardized production more often failed, since in these cases economies of scale and large production units (such as those operated by British newsprint producers) were more important. The newsprint industry was affected by the curtailment of price-fixing arrangements and the tariff changes introduced by the 1960 European Free Trade Association agreements. The British newsprint producers had problems competing with Scandinavian firms, and some of the families were forced to sell.

Most family papermaking businesses are located in industrial districts, exemplified by Lucca (Italy) and Baden-Württemberg (Germany). This geographical clustering enables them to profit from a shared, skilled labor market; common input suppliers; and technological spillover. Furthermore, as they have sought to expand their international markets, they have enjoyed the support of the local authorities and banks.

The Tuscan province of Lucca has made paper for centuries, but since the mid-1960s, it has specialized in tissue production. The Lucca district is responsible for 70 percent of Italy's tissue production, which amounts to 20 percent of Europe's total output, making it the center of the global tissue industry. The basis of its productive and business structure is a network of SMEs—many family owned, like Sofidel (owned by the Stefani and Lazzareschi families), Papergroup (Vamberti), Cartoinvest and Carma (both owned, at different times, by the Carrara family), Kartogroup (Toccafondi and Dianda families), Lucart Group (Pasquini), and Industrie Cartarie Tronchetti Spaa (Tronchetti). Foreign groups recently acquired some of these, including Kartogroup, purchased by the German firm WEPA, and Cartoinvest, bought by the Swedish company SCA. At Cartoinvest, the Carrara family sold 11 of its mills but retained ownership of three Italian factories (the core of Carma). However, because outsiders do not adapt easily to the business forces in these traditional regions, some of these acquisitions have since returned to the family groups. SCA has sold back some of its Lucca assets to the Carrara-owned Carma Group. Likewise, Lucart Group took over the large corporation Georgia-Pacific Italia in January 2012 and included a factory in this district.

As well as being a leading center for tissue-making, Lucca is also a center for converting machinery, boasting 25 specialized mechanical workshops. Its engineering sector has forged a symbiotic relationship with tissue producers, for example, the pioneering Fabio Perini Spa founded in 1966 and owned since 1993 by the German group Körber. Today, Fabio Perini owns Faper and its subsidiary Futura, a tissue-paper-converting machinery firm with industrial branches in Brazil and the United States. Most of the engineering firms are also owned and managed by families with a background in papermaking: Tostotec (owned by the Menuccis), Recard (Cardinottis and the Renieris), A. Celli (Cellis), and Costruzioni Meccaniche Gambini (Gambinis). These firms are important actors on the global market. Between 1990 and 2009, around 17 percent of all tissue-making machines installed worldwide were produced in Tuscany. Tuscan tissue-paper producers typically buy machines for their new foreign factories at the "nearest corner" workshop, as it were. A key element in the industrial dynamics of Lucca is the MIAC, the paper industry's international exhibition, devoted to the technological updating of the papermaking and the paper transformation industries. The Tuscan firms also enjoy the support of the local authorities, who back technologically innovative projects.

In Germany, the industrial dynamics of the Baden-Württemberg region also help explain the competitiveness of family papermaking businesses head-quartered there: Papierfabrik Palm GmbH & Co., Koehler Paper Group, Papierfabrik Scheufelen GmbH, and so forth. Like Lucca, Baden-Württemberg also enjoys a long history of papermaking. Voith, the world's leading papermaking engineering firm, is based in this German state. Voith supplies local papermakers as they undertake international projects, as is the case of Palm's new factory in the United Kingdom. Wangner (a branch of Xerium Inc.), a producer of wire mesh for papermaking machines, has its head-quarters in Baden-Württemberg. The Papierzentrum, located in Gernsbach, is a key actor in the region's economic development as are the Papierm-acherschule Gernsbach, the Baden-Württembergische Papierverbände, the Geschäftsstellen-Gemeinschaft des für Baden-Württemberg zuständigen Arbeitgeberverbandes, and the Bildungsakademie Papier.

8.5   NICHE STRATEGIES, BRANDING, AND FLEXIBILITY

Family businesses have typically adopted niche market strategies, focusing production on special types of paper backed up by substantial know-how, since such products are less prone to global economic swings. These strategies usually have a high-value-added component. Graphic paper producers make high-value paper that can be either coated[19] or uncoated.[20] Other niches include thermal paper,[21] security paper,[22] fine paper,[23] filter paper,[24] and cigarette paper.[25] Yet, some FBs concentrate on more standardized types of production: tissue paper and case materials.

The niche strategy sometimes results from the firm's history or reflects the economic district in which the FB is located. Both history and economic district played a role for some fine paper producers, including the Bavarian firm Gmund, and the Catalan company J. Vilaseca, whose businesses are centuries old. In other cases, production specializations reflect more recent strategic decisions. Until the late 1980s, Ahlström had a highly diversified product range but then began concentrating on specialty papers, selling off its assets in newsprint and board. Factories in the Lucca district, as we have seen, have produced nothing but tissue paper since the mid-1960s.

Innovation and quality are crucial concerns in the niche strategy. Ziegler Papier, a Swiss family business, boasts that it "continues to pursue a niche policy based on top quality and innovative solutions." Occasionally, quality is synonymous with luxury. British firm James Cropper has incorporated the concept of "luxury" into its paper for packaging and high-quality stationery. Bavaria's Büttenpapierfabrik Gmund provides an extreme case of identification with luxury. In 1952, the owner opted to keep the business small and focus on specialty paper. Today, the firm produces luxury goods for world-market leaders (Tiffany, Louis Vuitton, Swaroski, and Hermès), using machinery developed in 1883, the oldest of its kind operating in Europe.

Very few FBs today produce low-quality printing paper or newsprint. Some FB newsprint producers encountered problems in the 1960s, but the use of recovered paper as raw material has ignited new hope for such FBs. Palm Papierfabrik exemplifies the success of this production choice. The Spanish firm Papelera Peninsular exemplifies the flip side. The owners, the Morenos, invested heavily in a new newsprint factory near Madrid in the early 1990s. Shortly after, the Swedish company Holmen acquired the mill. Other FBs produce corrugated board. Indeed, in 2009 a number of them were ranked very highly among European producers: SAICA (3rd), Hamburger (Prinzhorn, 4th), Europac (6th), and Palm (7th).

Branding is a key tool for creating product differentiation and, hence, obtaining a competitive advantage, as the tissue-paper industry illustrates.[26] Tissue producers have expanded internationally partly by purchasing brands in the markets they sought to enter. Sofidel acquired labels such as Softis and La Trefle (France), Onda and Volare (Romania), Soft & Easy (Poland), and Yumy (Turkey). Brands are also important to stationery firms with their own papermaking factories. Exacompta Clairefontaine has the Clairefontaine, Rhodia, and Quo Vadis brands; Hamelin has Oxford (a leading notebook producer) and Canson (following its takeover in 2007), and the Italian firm Pigna has the Pigna 1870. Until the early 1990s, Gmund only produced fine papers; since then it has introduced new machinery and expanded its product range to include the Alezan and Mohair brands, among others.

Most FB-owned factories have either a small or medium production capacity. This gives them considerable flexibility to adapt to customer requirements. James Cropper is thus able to adapt the color of its cardboard to customer orders more readily than larger factories. Some firms compete via vertical integration, seeking to reduce their exposure to market cycles and generate economies of scale. This strategy is characteristic of firms specializing in stationery, packaging, and paper for corrugated cardboard boxes.[27]

Occasionally, national mergers and takeovers boost international expansion. The merger between Marchi and Burgo, two traditional Italian firms dedicated to the production of medium- and high-quality graphic paper, best exemplifies this. Burgo was the leading national producer followed closely by Marchi. The search for synergies began in the 1980s with a number of joint investments. Burgo, however, lost its family ownership in 2000, and the two companies merged in 2004, becoming the Burgo Group in 2007, a leading firm in southern Europe managed by the Marchis. Fedrigoni is another example: it acquired Fabriano, which the Italian state owned, in 2002.

8.6   FROM SALES TO INVESTMENT

FBs can become global through licensing, exporting, and foreign direct investment (FDI).[28] In line with the Uppsala stage model, most of the firms analyzed here have used exporting (trading on average about 50 percent of their total sales) as their main path to internationalization. Consequently, exporting has enabled these FBs to acquire certain capabilities. Their export customers, in turn, are determined largely by three factors: culture/language, geographical proximity, and paper type. Van Houtum illustrates the influence of language in determining export markets. The Dutch tissue-paper producer developed key markets in the former Dutch colonies Aruba and Surinam. Likewise, Gomà Camps, the Spanish tissue-paper producer, utilized its Portuguese branch to export to North Africa and to Portuguese-speaking African countries. As a result, Gomà Camps established commercial branches both in Morocco and Angola. Concerning geographical proximity, southern European firms focus their export markets in this same broad region while German and Austrian companies prefer to target Central and Eastern Europe. Paper type can also determine the export market; thus, standard producers principally target Europe, while specialty paper firms target more distant markets.

Customer types largely dictate the means of export. FBs with a business-to-consumer (B2C) orientation are more likely to build commercial networks than those with a more business-to-business (B2B) orientation. There are thus two main avenues for exporting: outsourcing through sales agents and/or using the firm's own sales network. Logically, smaller companies prefer the first method as they can avoid increasing fixed costs. In strategic markets, however, firms typically use their own sales offices or branches to avoid high transaction costs.[29] To this end, some firms have set up new commercial branches in Eastern Europe and Asia.[30] Besides their own sales systems, some FBs maintain impressive networks of sales agents.

A second path towards international expansion is FDI. Indeed, some family papermaking businesses have utilized FDI to establish themselves as "pocket multinationals." The Italian company Fedrigoni was pioneering in this, setting up a factory in South Africa in 1948 that remained operational until 1964. Early projects typically embraced joint ventures as the means to invest abroad. For example, Bowater established a joint project in 1959 to produce pulp and newsprint in New Zealand to supply the Australian market. However, it was more usual to acquire existing factories than to set up new ones to keep the investment low. This was Bowater's strategy when entering continental European markets in the late 1950s. Ahlström also began its international expansion by buying a factory in Italy in 1963. Torras Hostench, owned by an old Catalan papermaking family, also bought a factory in Brazil in the 1970s.

FDI has increased rapidly over the last three decades. In 1985, 17 percent of Ahlström's staff was based outside Finland; by 1998, the figure had climbed to 73 percent. Today, Ahlström operates 39 production sites in 13 different countries. During the early 1980s, the Irish company Jefferson Smurfit saw the United States as its strategic investment destination, but by the late 1980s it began to expand across continental Europe. At that time, the Smurfit family also had assets in Latin America.

The actual location of investment also depends on the firm's home country. Firms aim to distribute FDI geographically in a way that avoids agency problems and keeps logistics costs low. Gradually, global FBs can invest in more distant countries. Southern European FBs have typically invested in neighboring areas. The Spanish firms SAICA and Europac have invested in France and Portugal. Italian firms have set up factories in Spain and France. German and Austrian firms have invested in Central and Eastern Europe. The Austrian firm, Mayr-Melnhof, has invested in Germany, the Netherlands, Slovenia, Bulgaria, Ukraine, and Turkey. Latin America has also been targeted for investment, for example, by Fedrigoni, which opened the group's first factory outside Europe in Brazil in 2009, while Mayr-Melnhof acquired a major stake in the largest Chilean folding carton manufacturer in 2010.

Typically, sales offices that initially succeed lead to future investment. Cartarie Tronchetti opened a commercial office in Spain in 1999, and then in 2005 the Tuscan firm set up a new factory in the country. Tronchetti followed a similar strategy in France, opening an office there in 2000 and now building a factory. It also purchased a factory in Poland in 2001. Papierfabrik Palm began to export newsprint to the United Kingdom in 1995 through its UK sales office. As a result, Palm identified a gap for new newsprint machines and opened a new newsprint factory in Norfolk in August 2009, representing the main UK investment in the paper industry over the last decade.

Family-run tissue-paper firms have also been particularly dynamic in their foreign investments because of their product's high transport costs and market growth. The Tuscan firms again illustrate this best. Kartogroup and Cartoinvest attempted pioneering, but ultimately unsuccessful, international operations. Sofidel began to expand its international production throughout the 1990s, opening factories in France, Germany, Poland, the United Kingdom, Greece, Turkey, Romania, Croatia, and Spain. In 2010, Sofidel was the second-largest European tissue-paper producer after SCA. The driving force behind its expansion has been the growth of the major distribution chains (such as Carrefour). The Lucart Group (the Cartiera Lucchese Group until 2009) has been running production operations in France since 1998. Lucart acquired Georgia-Pacific Italia in January 2012. Industrie Cartarie

Tronchetti also has two fairly new factories: one in Spain (2005) and the other in Poland (2008). It also plans to open a new factory in France. Outside Italy, other tissue producers have been able to expand internationally. Gomà Camps, the Catalan firm, set up industrial branches in France and Portugal in the late 1990s. WEPA, the German group owned by the Krengels, has industrial assets in Spain, Italy, France, and Poland. The expansion resulted from the takeover in 2009 (completed in 2010) of the Kartogroup assets in Italy and France. The Krengels have contacted a local partner, Gomà Camps, to invest in Spain, while the growth of German discount stores (Aldi and Lidl) has spurred the group's expansion.

The producers of corrugated board have largely chosen to set up or acquire paper mills and cardboard factories on account of vertical integration. The Austrian Mayr-Melnhof has assets in 14 countries (with cardboard production units in three—Austria, Germany, the Netherlands—and paper-converting factories in Tunisia, Turkey, Jordan, Russia, Poland, and Ukraine, among others). Spain's improved performance in the recovered paper market has now made two FBs that produce corrugated board using recovered paper count among Europe's main producers: SAICA and Papeles y Cartones de Europa S.A. (Europac). Since 2002, SAICA has owned a paper factory in France and operated different points of production for corrugated cardboard boxes. In 2006, it bought the British box-converting factories of International Paper, the world's biggest papermaking firm. Two years later, SAICA did the same with SCA's paper-converting assets in Italy and the United Kingdom. In mid-January 2012, SAICA Paper opened a new paper mill in the United Kingdom, near Manchester. Recently, it has shifted its targets to Eastern Europe. Thus, in late 2011, SAICA Pack acquired 49 percent of a Polish corrugated board factory in a joint venture with the German firm Thimm. Likewise, Europac has acquired a number of Portuguese firms during the privatization of its public assets (Gescartão, "PORTUCEL Embalagem" and "PORTUCEL Viana"). The firm's international expansion continued in France in 2008 and Portugal in 2009.

One foreign investment strategy is simply to purchase one's competitors. In 2001, Ahlström bought one of its main competitors in the Iberian market, the Spanish firm Papelera del Besós, a filter-paper producer. SAICA and Europac have also adopted this approach. An alternative is to purchase a complementary firm. Papierfabrik August Koehler, which concentrated all of its industrial assets in Germany, initiated its international growth by absorbing the Katz Group in 2009. Katz is a leading beer coaster manufacturer and has industrial locations abroad (in the United Kingdom and the United States).

Some internationalization projects, however, met with failure, for example, that of Spanish firm Torras Hostench, which included the purchase of assets in Brazil and Belgium and collapsed in the 1970s crisis. After suspending payments in 1982, Torras was bought by the Kuwait Investment Office in 1986. Today, it forms part of LECTA, a group specializing in high-quality printing papers. Cartoinvest constructed a factory in Catalonia in the early 1990s, while Kartongroup invested in Spain in 2002; however, SCA purchased Cartoinvest in 2002, and WEPA bought Kartongroup in 2008, except for its Spanish factory, which a local group acquired in 2009.

8.7 FINANCIAL SUPPORT, FAMILY OR PROFESSIONAL MANAGEMENT

The main avenues European papermaking FBs take to finance their growth in global markets include utilizing their own high reinvestment rates, becoming listed, or obtaining financial support from banks or other firms.

The majority of the families discussed here own from 30 to 100 percent of their company shares. Such rates of family ownership facilitate high rates of reinvestment with the aim of safeguarding company independence. Wolfgang Palm claims that "all the money made by the business is reinvested."[31] Typically, reinvestment alone is not sufficient to promote international expansion, so most firms register as public limited companies to access nonfamily capital on the stock market. One potential path is to draw on a foreign partner's share capital. For example, the Spanish firm Alier obtained financing from the Austrian company Patria, which acquired a 30 percent share in the company in 1990; however, the venture proved unsuccessful. Joint ventures with locally based partners are another means of financing a foreign investment (and reducing the risks associated with lack of knowledge of the new market). Thus, WEPA signed an agreement with Gomà Camps when building a factory in Spain, and the Portuguese branch of Gomà Camps bought share capital in AMS, a Portuguese tissue producer, in 2009. Yet, perhaps the main path for financing growth is via the credit market. Miquel y Costas & Miquel, the Catalan cigarette-paper producer, saw its family structure undermined when the Banco Exterior de España financed its expansion during the 1960s. Fedrigoni turned to a pool of Italian banks, led by Unicredit Banca de Empresa, to finance its takeover of Cartiera Miliani Fabriano in 2001. It then borrowed heavily in 2007 from the same banks to finance its growth. Today, Fedrigoni is owned by Unione di Banche Italiane. The European Investment Bank supported SAICA's investment in a new UK factory. In mid-2011, Friesland Bank Investments bought a majority of shares in van Houtum, the Dutch tissue-paper producer. Finally, Pamplona Capital Management, a private equity fund, supported WEPA's expansion by purchasing 34.83 percent of its shares in early 2010 following an increase in its share capital, while the three Krengel brothers each retained holdings of 21.72 percent.

A second option is to become listed. Most FBs in this study are not publicly quoted, and few of the largest papermaking companies have traded on the stock market to finance their internationalization, though Ahlström (listed since 2006) and Europac (since 1998) are among them. Very few small FBs are listed; often, taking measures to become listed is the first step to losing family ownership.

In most instances, the concentration of ownership among just a few family members safeguards the company's family status. Firms with more dispersed ownership appear more vulnerable to losing family ownership and are perhaps more likely to employ a nonfamily management structure. This happened at Ahlström, which had 200 family-member shareholders at one time. The firm's ownership model began to shift during a restructuring process in the 1980s and 1990s.[32] During the early twenty-first century, Ahlström finally dismantled the family business structure. Yet, the family links remain, since after going public its main shareholder, with a 10.02 percent share, is Antti Ahlström Perilliset, a private holding company Ahlström family members (heirs of Antti Ahlström) own. Other family members retain small stakes. Ziegler Papier's case was similar, with more than 70 Ziegler family members being shareholders at one point.

Intergenerational transitions mark critical periods in the life cycles of FBs, when family tensions are prone to rise. Often, such moments constitute opportunities to change management structures or even to sell the business. For example, Scheufelen was sold to the Finnish group Powerflute in 2009, when the fifth generation was entering the business. In early 2011, the Dutch company Papier Excellence (owned by the Asian Sinar Mas Group) purchased Scheufelen. Giesecke & Devrient (owner of Papierfabrik Louisenthal since 1964) was nearly sold following the death of Sigfried Otto, who had refounded the family group in 1948. However, Verena von Mitschke-Collande purchased the 50 percent share held by her sister Claudia Miller, resolving the conflict. An FB charter can eliminate such problems since it gives the firm stability and provides it a more solid basis for growth in international markets. The Spanish firm SAICA, for example, signed a family charter, subject to periodic revision, in 1988.

Typically, family members manage papermaking FBs (e.g., a Nusse family member handles Exacompta Clairefontaine; a Jass, Adolf Jass; Isidro Rincón, Europac; a Balet family member, SAICA; and a Cropper manages James Cropper, etc.). Over the years, however, nonfamily members have been appointed to manage the business. Nevertheless, family members' qualifications tend to increase from generation to generation. Frequently, they hold college degrees in engineering, economics, and business, and/or MBAs and PhDs.[33] Some firms apply a protocol to ensure that family members taking up managerial positions receive proper training. Thus, some firms require family members to hold a university degree and to be competent in one or more foreign languages. In some instances, young family members are sent to be trained at other firms before entering the FB. Bernhard Ziegler, until recently co-owner and manager of Ziegler Papier, helped set up a number of new paper factories in various countries. Thomas Prinzhorn worked for two years in a U.S. papermaking firm. Wolfgang Palm gained experience in a U.S. paper factory before joining the FB. The same was true of Balet family members at SAICA. Krister Ahlström, CEO at Ahlström from 1982 to 1998, had a successful career outside the FB before joining the firm. Moreover, after leaving Ahlström, he became vice-chairman of Stora-Enso, a leading Scandinavian pulp and papermaking company.

The firms with the fewest family-member shareholders are more likely to be managed by nonfamily. Although Kirster Ahlström initiated the reorganization of Ahlström, a nonfamily member was appointed CEO in 1999. Tronchetti introduced professional management when it began to expand internationally. The Tronchettis recruited a managerial team from Tuscan engineering firms with experience in global markets.

When FBs are sold, the new ownership and management structures tend to be one of three types: papermaking MNEs, other FBs, and managers from nonfamily businesses. The Cartoinvest's acquisition by SCA exemplifies the first type; Peterson & Sohn AS, the second. The Norwegian firm founded by Momme Peterson was sold in 2006 to a group of families already involved in the paper and pulp business (Paulsrud, Haglund, etc.). Ziegler Papier also fits into this category. The Zieglers wanted to sell but maintain a family ownership model. Subsequently, the Kuttler-Freys, a family with deep roots in the same region as the Ziegler mill, acquired and managed the Swiss firm. Cartiere Paolo Pigna represents the third type. Until recently, the Pigna family was the main shareholder, and then CEO Giorgio Jannone increased the company's subscribed share capital.

8.8   CONCLUDING REMARKS

FBs can be as internationalized and successful as any other kind of firm, as demonstrated by the European papermaking sector. Today, many FBs are among the leading firms in this sector and some are market leaders in their respective niches and have established themselves as veritable multinationals. Yet, just like other types of firms, some FBs have also failed in their internationalization bid.

The main factor ensuring the survival of FBs in the new global economy is their capacity to respond to new challenges. FBs have turned many of their typical characteristics to their advantage to compete successfully in global markets, such as their history and longevity (indicating the commitment to the firm's future), their know-how, the dynamic forces operating in their respective industrial districts, their adoption of niche market strategies, the flexibility of their production, expert branding, and their horizontal and vertical integration. All in all, papermaking FBs have developed a productive system founded on small and medium-sized production units characterized by a high degree of flexibility. Therefore, they primarily produce paper with considerable value added. In most instances, their productive specialization closely reflects their historical background; papermaking firms provide good examples of marked path dependence. Very few firms produce more standardized types of paper, having shifted production to these lines only quite recently. Crucially, the majority of European papermaking FBs today utilize their location as part of a cluster or within a given industrial district. Thus, Europe's papermaking firms clearly demonstrate that there is room for FBs in global business.

NOTES

1. This chapter forms part of the broader research project "Origins and Development of the Exporting Industrial Districts, 1765–2008: An Economic History Approach" directed by Jordi Catalan (Ministerio de Ciencia e Innovación) (HAR-2009–07571).
2. Casson, 1999, 13.
3. Colli, 2010, 23.
4. Fernández and Nieto, 2005, 77.
5. Kontinen and Ojala, 2010, 98.
6. Puig and Fernández Pérez, 2009, 464.
7. Colli and Rose, 2007, 197.
8. Coleman, 1958, 245.
9. Jones, 2007, 147.
10. Ibid., 149.
11. CEPI comprises the papermaking firms of Austria, Belgium, the Czech Republic, Finland, France, Germany, Hungary, Italy, the Netherlands, Poland, Portugal, Romania, the Slovak Republic, Slovenia, Spain, Sweden, the United Kingdom, Norway, and Switzerland.
12. Berghoff, 2006a.
13. Colli, Fernández Pérez and Rose, 2003.
14. Howorth, Rose and Hamilton, 2008, 235.
15. Gomà Camps (1758), Van Gelder Zonen (1783), Papierfabrik Louisenthal Gesellschaft (1818), Koehler Papierfabrik (1807), and M. Peterson & Søn (1801).
16. James Cropper (1845), Ahlström (1851), Kübler & Niethammer Papierfabrik Kriebstein AS (1856), Exacompta Clairefontaine (1858), Papierfabrik Palm GmbH & Co. (1872), Cartiere Paolo Pigna (1856/1870), Ziegler Papier AG (1861), Cartiera Carma (1873), and Alier (1886).
17. Grupo Lucart (1932), SAICA (1943), Van Houtum BV (1935), Cartiere del Polesine (1945), and WEPA (1948).
18. Mayr-Melnhof (1950), Industrie Cartarie Tronchetti (1952), Mauro Benedetti (1954), Papierfabrik Adolf Jass (1960), Pro-Gest Group (1973). The Marchi family, the owners of the Burgo Group, with business interests in silk, invested in papermaking in 1949.
19. Kübler & Niethammer Papierfabrik, Papierfabrik Scheufelen GmbH.
20. James Cropper, Ziegler Papier.
21. Diagramm Halbach GmbH, Blumberg GmbH.
22. J Vilaseca SA, Papierfabrik Louisenthal Gesellschaft, Fedrigoni.
23. Pigna, Cordenons.
24. Ahsltröm, Omniafiltra, Cartiera del Torano.
25. Miquel y Costas & Miquel, Delfort Group.
26. The tissue-paper producers sell their products via different brands. Papergroup: Tenerella; Euro Vast Spa: Fior di Carta, Rotolotto, and Bravo; Van Houtum BV: Satino; Sofidel: Regina; Carma: Bulkysoft and Tuscany; Gomà

Camps: Olimpic; WEPA: Sammy; Lucart: Grazie and Smile; ICT: Foxy; Cartindustria Veneta SRL: Soft Flower.

27. Imbalaggi Piemontesi SRL, Europac, SAICA, Papierfabrik Palm GMBH & Co., Cartiere del Polesine, Pro-Gest, Mauro Benedetti, Papierfabrik Adolf Jass, Peterson AS, Meyr-Melnhof.

28. Graves and Thomas, 2008.

29. The Swiss company Ziegler and the British firm James Cropper have sales branches in the United States. Papierfabrik Palm has its own offices in Italy, France, and the United Kingdom. LEIPA owns sales companies in the United Kingdom, France, Poland, and Romania and keeps local representatives in 22 countries. Exacompta Clairefontaine has commercial branches in several European countries.

30. Kunert Gruppe has set up offices in Indonesia and Thailand. The Italian firm, Pigna, runs a dense network in southern and Eastern Europe, Australia, Singapore, and Brazil. Ahlström has sales branches in 25 countries, maintaining a strong presence in East Asia. Koehler, owned by the Furler family, has sales offices in London, Paris, Milan, New York, and Shanghai. Fedrigoni set up a branch in Hong Kong in 2006 and has eight distribution centers in Europe. Büttenpapierfabrik Gmund has sales offices in the United Kingdom and France. It also owns three shops in Germany, one in Innsbruck, and another in Tokyo.

31. *Paper Technology* 50, no. 4 (October 2009): 11.

32. Ojala and Pajunen, 2006, 182.

33. Austrian Thomas Prinzhorn, owner of Prinzhorn Holding, has degrees in engineering and business from Harvard. Wolfgang Palm, CEO of Papierfabrik Palm, studied economics at the University of Mannheim. Adolf Jass, founder of Papierfabrik Adolf Jass, was trained as an economist. Hubert Schrödinger, CEO and co-owner of LEIPA Georg Leinfelder, has degrees in law and economics and a PhD in economics. Robin Huesmann, also a member of the family that owns LEIPA, holds a degree in engineering. Girolamo Marchi, CEO of Burgo Group, has a degree in law and an MBA from Columbia University.

9 The Feltrinellis—Going Global with the Timber Trade
How to Build a Fortune Using a Scarce Resource (1854–1942)

Luciano Segreto

Feltrinelli. If you go to Italy, sooner or later, you will find a bookstore with this name. There are more than one hundred of these bookstores in the country. The year 2012 was the fortieth anniversary of the mysterious death of Giangiacomo Feltrinelli, the controversial publisher who created the publishing house in 1954 with his prestigious family name but who moved during the 1960s toward the extreme left wing of the Italian political spectrum. He died in an attempted terrorist attack placing a bomb in a high-voltage electric facility on the periphery of Milan. Up until then, the family name had been associated with long-established and prosperous entrepreneurial activities. The family's spectacular success appeared to be continuing into the next generation when the Feltrinelli publishing house produced two bestsellers in the late 1950s: Boris Pasternak's *Dr. Zhivago*, which won him a Nobel Prize for literature, and Tomasi di Lampedusa's *The Leopard*, which became an international success in part due to Luchino Visconti's movie with Burt Lancaster's fantastic performance as the Count of Salaparuta. When young Giangiacomo (b. 1926) reached adulthood at the end of the Second World War, the Feltrinellis were unanimously considered one of the most important families in Italian capitalism alongside the Agnellis, Pirellis, Volpis, Orlandos, Bredas, and Falcks, among others. Of these, only the steel-producing Falcks, who had arrived in Lombardy in the early 1830s, and the Feltrinellis were already in their third generation.

The literature on family capitalism is quite extensive and often centered on the paradigmatic, rise, apogee, and decline of dynasties similar to the narrative presented in Thomas Mann's novel *Buddenbrooks*.[1] Nevertheless, most of this literature deals with industrial and/or financial dynasties rather than commercial ones.[2] It is very rare in American or European economic history to find examples of families successfully forming diversified family business (FB) groups at the height of their national economy such as those that can be found in many emerging markets today. Yet the Feltrinellis did just that in their third generation, defying the Buddenbrooks stereotype.[3]

The Feltrinelli family business group provides a unique case study of a multinational FB that operated in the international timber trade. This sphere of economic activity has been neglected because standard accounts of the industrial revolution in Europe stress how materials such as iron, steel, and later aluminum substituted for timber. Yet timber is one of the most important commodities in the history of economic development: it has long been used in railways, telegraph and telephone networks, and in the construction industry.[4] The family behind the firm provided the glue for the efficient organization of the core timber business but also for its later diversification strategy. Family relations also helped bridge the complexities of the timber sector across different, fairly undeveloped areas in Europe. Thus, the Feltrinelli case sits at the intersection of family business, international business, and business history.

One complexity of the timber trade was that, between the eighteenth and the twentieth century, two different market and business structures dominated the continent. On the one hand, the largest European market, based in London, took in imports mostly from the Baltic area and from Russia, while Liverpool and later Cardiff received the bulk of ships and timber arriving from North America (the United States and Canada).[5] The different legal systems and a bewildering array of local, formal, and informal customs regulating the use of the forests and the exploitation of this natural resource in different regions then added to the complexity. It wound up being easier, for example, for London-based merchants, after first attempting in the seventeenth and eighteenth centuries to establish their agencies in Sweden, Norway, or Russia, to eliminate their foreign branches, simply leaving the country and moving their firm to Russia or a Nordic country.[6]

After the big London fire of 1666, timber merchants seceded from the carpenters' corporation, which until that time had encompassed all business activities using timber, and became one of the most prestigious groups of social and professional elites. In London at the end of the eighteenth century, there were 128 timber merchants, but only 3 of them were located in the city. During the nineteenth century, their number increased considerably, so that by 1911 there were 180.[7] Their offices were located on some of London's most prestigious streets, such as Bishopsgate and Greenchurch, Feenchurch, and Cannon Streets. The trade's business organization was based on a widespread group of local timber merchants, some of whom were originally the foreign branches of big British importers that later became independent. These merchants had contacts with the owners of the forests and defined a FOB (freight/free on board) price for the raw material. Free delivery on board the buyer's vessel was the most usual way to conduct international trade prior to the development of modern communications (e.g., up to the early nineteenth century). Most often, buyers would charter or personally take a vessel to the exporting port and purchase the goods directly on site. Timber was then cut and shipped to London, where it was stocked in a growing area, which eventually moved from Lambeth down to the Surrey Commercial Docks (known now as the Surrey Quais) in the Thames bends.

Until the mid-nineteenth century, timber merchants dominated the market because they could mediate between foreign timber suppliers and local purchasers. They received timber from the Baltic ports during the summer while sitting in their offices and waiting for their clients.[8] Later, when competition increased, timber was sold at public auctions in the Baltic Hall of the South Sea House.[9] Slowly, a system based on sales without reserve took shape, which obliged sellers to sell the goods for the best offer, whereas beforehand they had had the option to refuse. This democratized the whole timber merchant community. Auctions typically occurred after dinners at which excellent wines were offered in large quantities.[10]

In Britain, a country known for its market liberalism, the evolution of business activities in this sector engendered a sophisticated division of labor and specialization with great variation among professional and economic profiles. This specialized system made it impossible to reduce the business and distribution chain from the forest to the boarding ports, and finally to the London and British market.

However, a very different market and business structure operated in Central and Southern Europe. The legal infrastructure was not altogether different from the Scandinavian and the Baltic area, where there were many possibilities among the local owners of the forests (landlords, peasants, local communities, old knights' orders, monasteries, the state, etc.). Yet the decisive difference was Central and Southern Europe's weaker structure of local entrepreneurship and more rudimentary, fragmented markets. Timber merchants were unable to coordinate the entire commercial structure from the production areas to the consumption markets in Germany, France, and Italy. Various national companies, like Feltrinelli, had to move to a multinational strategy quite quickly, which became even more feasible once the railway system reached a large part of the Austro-Hungarian Empire. Relatively young timber trading companies were thus transformed into international and/or multinational firms with rather complex organizational structures, including offices and agencies in many local areas where timber was available.

Most of these companies were FBs. Not surprisingly, family members constituted the primary, if not exclusive, human capital they needed to operate and further develop their strategies. The family provided a relatively flat hierarchy for processing the information necessary for success, which was complex and copious. The low market transparency resulting from local traditions and national constraints greatly affected day-to-day operations and the firms' manner of doing business, especially in Central–Eastern Europe but also, to some extent, in the Baltic area, the extreme north of Russia (in the White Sea area, centered in Archangel). They had to respond swiftly to opportunities, and social and cultural actors like families were able to do so. Especially in these less developed areas, wealthier merchants like the Feltrinellis helped provide the necessary business liquidity for local timber merchants. Forest landowners, particularly aristocratic ones, were also important families in the region who knew how to interact appropriately with other reputable families. Family members were the best representatives for local dealers in this more personalized business world; independent agents would not have generated the same degree of trust. Total commitment, personal sacrifice, and full-time availability were the main ingredients for an activity that implied moving around in search of new business opportunities. Information given by family members was certified reliable to the rest of the family. Moreover, considering that the transportation network was relatively poorly developed until the early twentieth century and that much of the timber was located in very isolated areas, family links were essential to establishing continuity and a long-term strategy that depended upon maintaining existing agreements and developing new ones. Of course, all these virtues generated by family trust could also transform into weaknesses. If a family's "human capital" was not sufficiently broad or competent in business, or if there were succession issues, then the delicate equilibrium created over many years of activity could diminish a firm's competitiveness, interfere with projects, and reduce the family's capacity to work as a supra- or multinational actor.

Italy's national timber resources were structurally weak, never exceeding two-thirds of total consumption. This shortage triggered the development of strategies based on imports that pushed Italian timber merchants abroad.[11] The Feltrinellis stemmed from the area around the Garda Lake, on the eastern border between Lombardy and Veneto. This familiar site was favorable for the family's timber business because it offered easy access to the Trentino forests (which until 1918 were part of the Austro-Hungarian Empire). At the same time, the family quickly realized that only by transferring the firm's headquarters to Milan, closer to major timber consumers, would it truly be able to develop its range of activities.

Ditta Fratelli Feltrinelli (Feltrinelli Brothers Company) was established in 1854 as a limited liability firm by five out of the twelve sons and daughters of Faustino and Maria Feltrinelli: Carlo (1819–1857), Antonio (1823–1863), Pietro (1825–1909), Angelo (1827–1900), and Giacomo (1829–1913). Antonio was the only one who had a university education (he studied civil engineering); Pietro was a priest but had a very good mind for business; Angelo was involved in small commercial activities in Gargnano (where he also became mayor in the 1880s) on the west bank of the Garda Lake. The firm's mastermind was the youngest brother, Giacomo, who started his career by selling charcoal and olive oil around the Garda Lake. Just three years after the company's founding, in 1857, Giacomo left the Garda area and settled in Milan, the dynamic economic center of Lombardy, then part of Austria-Hungary, opening the firm's first big warehouse not far from a main railway station. The railway link between Verona and Milan had just opened three years previously as part of a larger project to connect Milan with Venice. Thus, timber could reach Milan after being shipped by boat from the northern part of the Garda Lake, where it came from the Trentino valleys, to another railway station in Desenzano. In just a few years, the firm not only achieved prominence in Milan, where industrial and demographic developments in the 1860s–1870s increased the demand for timber, but also established a wide network of clients in the whole of Northern Italy, from Venice to Turin, and also, though more slowly, in Central and Southern Italy.

Italy's timber deficit increased greatly in the subsequent decades. Imports grew even more heavily during industrialization, which began in the 1870s–1880s and accelerated swiftly after the second half of the 1890s. Between 1878 and 1913, timber imports swelled from 574,300 tons to 1,347,800 tons. At the end of this period, only 12–14 percent of the timber sold was crude, the rest—making up between 60 and 80 percent of total Italian imports, including Trentino—was sawed.[12]

The weak, if not fully absent, entrepreneurial structure in many Austrian forest areas forced Italian merchants to establish agencies and offices there. In the early 1870s, the Feltrinelli firm established a branch in Villach, a village in a strategic position in Carinthia, some 40 kilometers (approximately 25 miles) from Klagenfurt, where the Austrian railway network had permitted timber shipping on the river from different valleys of the region since 1864 but also linked Tyrol to vast consumption markets from Vienna to Ljubljana, Trieste; after 1873, the railway reached Tarvisio, thanks to the construction of a bridge over the Drava to Northern Italy. The Villach branch rapidly became a platform for coordinating a complex range of activities, which included networking with local authorities for research and negotiating permission to cut trees in some forests, industrial initiatives such as sawing the timber, and shipping and commercial activities connected with exports to Italy.[13] Because of the intensity of contacts, it became absolutely necessary for at least one prominent family member to spend a large part of the year there.

The peculiarity of the timber trade, combined with the Feltrinellis' very aggressive and long-term, forward-looking strategy, spurred the firm to engage in an internationalization process that was quite rare for Italian firms, and especially for FBs in that period. In contrast to Siemens, which also went global utilizing the family as a strategy,[14] the Feltrinellis focused on classic merchant activities rather than offering new products but substituted for the lack of entrepreneurship by offering a bridge for local timber suppliers to areas of high demand. The speed with which the Feltrinelli firm transformed itself into a multinational enterprise was extraordinary. Yet, the multinationalization strategy was a necessary but not sufficient factor in the firm's success: for decades, Feltrinelli remained one of the biggest European timber firms.

The Feltrinellis' success in obtaining rights to cut trees in the Austrian forest resulted from rather sophisticated information management, good commercial organization, persuasive salesmen, a strong financial position based on a high level of liquidity, and, above all, discretion, which using human resources from the same family was made possible. In the first generation, Giacomo headed the firm in the family division of labor. The deaths of two of the co-founding brothers—Carlo in 1857 and Antonio in 1863—forced the remaining members to adapt. Giacomo was the real leader, running the main activities from Milan, but he traveled all around the Alps and into new high-potential areas. Angelo cooperated with him but always remained in Gargnano when he became the mayor of the village. Angelo also managed the warehouse in Desenzano. These brothers also utilized other family members, such as brothers-in-law or, in some cases, even nephews (their sisters' sons) as agents or representatives. A key issue for the firm's success was that family members alone circulated crucial business information.

Like many long-standing FBs, the Feltrinellis began training and socializing the second generation in the business early on. Consequently, succession was a lengthy, evolutionary process of relevant "pre-business" knowledge transfers and learning.[15] Young family members were integrated at age sixteen or seventeen and attained formal positions in their early twenties. The key figures in the second generation were Giovanni (1855–1896), Carlo's second son, and Giuseppe (1854–1930), the only son of Angelo. Giovanni, in particular, became the real successor of his uncle, Giacomo, because he was involved in the most important old and new firm businesses. Also, thanks to his young age, Giovanni traveled extensively around the Alps and in the other undeveloped areas where the firm traded timber and the transportation infrastructure was still partly under construction. In any case, his physical presence on site was decisive, especially during sales auctions and forest evaluations. Giuseppe was more active in managing the firm from Milan, a task that had grown increasingly complex after 1880 because the company managed a series of warehouses in the most important Italian towns (Milan, Genoa, Rome, Naples, Messina, Bari, etc.) and the Austrian and Slovenian branches became increasingly significant. Altogether, the firm's staff in the early 1890s numbered just under eight hundred—a figure that would seem uncommonly high even in the labor-intensive and mature textile industry at the time.

The firm's sustained good performance gave it tremendous liquidity, which it utilized to develop a virtuous cycle of growth in the timber trade. In the very complicated timber market, paying cash was a common tactic for eliminating competitors. Especially during public auctions, but also in private negotiations with representatives of local communities, the Feltrinelli firm achieved significant savings by offering an immediate, somewhat discounted payment instead of promising more three or six months later, as many competitors proposed. Because there were numerous hazards in the sector (sending the timber to the consumption markets, the economic difficulties in local or national markets, currency exchanges, weather, etc.), making later payments risky, timber sellers and forest owners often preferred immediate payment.

The "high liquidity effect" was even more important in Feltrinelli's diversification with its hidden prerequisite of wide family-member involvement, which provided contacts and opportunities in other sectors. Giacomo Feltrinelli began this process as early as in the 1870s, making real estate and housing construction investments in central areas in Milan, not far from the new central station. In diversifying, the firm usually established a partnership with other entrepreneurs who added particular skills (knowledge of a sector, contacts, previous interests in the same area, and other factors) useful for the success of the project. Rarely did the partners make a sizable investment, at least relative to the Feltrinellis. Acting as a sort of venture capital investor, Giacomo Feltrinelli involved the firm in the railroad business, which was one of the most promising and lucrative sectors between the 1870s and 1890s, especially in Southern Italy, where the network was not completed until the end of the nineteenth century. One strategic reason for this involvement was the firm's connections to the timber supply. Any firm interested in winning a contract or a subcontract to build a portion of the railway network managed by one of the big railway companies had to demonstrate its ability to finance the project. Once Feltrinelli had a contract, it, as a timber company, also gained the right to deliver the wooden ties for the track. Bundling the financing of its railroad construction company with the sale of timber products was important for the development of the business. For instance, Feltrinelli signed a contract in 1873 to deliver wooden ties for the coming Gotthard Line in Switzerland, thereby gaining a good reputation with the Gotthardbahn Gesellschaft, which was managing the whole project. This reputation probably contributed to the engineer Daniele Comboni, an entrepreneur working in public works and construction, joining the firm. Comboni belonged to one of the richest families of Limone del Garda, a village not far from Gargnano. In 1879, a new company, Comboni Feltrinelli & Co., was set up to build a 27-kilometer (16-miles) track in Switzerland from Lugano to Bellinzona, which also included a series of tunnels, the 1,700-meter (ca. 1-mile) Monte Ceneri among them.[16]

These successful initiatives in Switzerland opened the door to other international railway projects. Some were linked directly to the timber trade, as when Feltrinelli built some tracks for transporting timber to consumption centers or to ports for shipping in Greece and Macedonia in the 1880s. Other ventures related more to the high professional and technical profile the firm offered, as when Feltrinelli constructed a railroad line between Marienbad and Georgenstadt in the Austro-Hungarian Empire in the 1890s. In this case, Feltrinelli followed its typical organizational strategy by establishing a special joint venture company with a partner. This railway became one of the most crucial in the area because it linked spa centers (the most important being Karlsbad, today's Karlowy Vary) and also a very strategic coal area to the industrial consumption zones.

Feltrinelli's effective use of its accrued financial liquidity generated opportunities for diversifying into other sectors, and especially banking, in 1889. Giacomo Feltrinelli had previous experience in the banking sector but principally to become a part of Milan's influential circle in the business community: in the early 1870s, he had been a member of the board of directors of the Banca Popolare di Milano. In the same decade, he had also become a member of the local Chamber of Commerce and was one of the executive members of the organizing committee for the industrial exhibition that took place in Milan in 1881.[17] Banks offered the firm a strategic way to diversify into further industrial sectors and allowed it, to some extent, to manage the liquidity of the timber firm. So, in 1889, the Feltrinellis became involved in two different banks.

First, they helped found the Banca Unione Italiana together with other, mainly foreign shareholders of rather high repute—Banque Fédérale of Bern, the Berlin International Bank, the bank houses Dreyfus and Ehringer (both of Basel), the Bank of Winterthur, the Schweizerische Union Bank of Sankt Gallen, the Banque de Constantinople, the Anglo-Österreichische Bank in Vienna, two of the most important private banks, Vonwiller and Vogel in Milan, and the Banca Torino. This important new bank had an ambitious program of financing industrial firms and servicing the debt of the Italian government. However, the timing was poor, as the Italian economy had begun to suffer on account of real estate speculation in the mid-1880s, and some banks that were deeply involved sustained significant losses. That Giovanni Feltrinelli was the general secretary of the bank confirms the family's leading role in this unfortunate investment. In 1892, less than three years after it was founded, the bank was liquidated, with shareholders receiving 80 percent of their investment. Although this outcome was unfavorable, it was much better than the fate of the largest shareholder of Banca Unione Italiana, the Berlin International Bank, which had gone into bankruptcy one year earlier.[18]

Second, Giacomo Feltrinelli and his family firm, along with two partners, Costantino Colombo and Carlo Pasquinelli, in 1889 also set up a private bank bearing the name of the two partners, Banca Feltrinelli, Colombo & Co. The partners ran the day-to-day business on the ground floor of a house Giacomo had bought in 1867, in Via Romagnosi, where the timber firm's central office was also located. Giacomo and his nephew Giovanni, who was probably supposed to be the successor of the dynasty's founder, made the core strategic investment decisions. Like many other private banks in Milan, Banca Feltrinelli, Colombo & Co. engaged in financing and trading in the silk sector, which had been one of the most important and lucrative sectors for Milan and Turin banks since the early nineteenth century. They supported crude silk producers during production and acted as intermediaries in the international trade of the product, which was largely exported to France but also to some other industrial European countries.[19] With a private bank at their disposal, the Feltrinellis could best manage and redirect the high liquidity of the core timber business and also of the various initiatives in other sectors. The bank became the financial hub of the diversified family business group and placed the family among the region's business elites.

The firm also diversified in their home region, Garda Lake, in various capacities, acting both as philanthropists and entrepreneurs. The Feltrinellis' expanding involvement in Milan's social and economic activities never threatened their ties to this area, where their investments served the double purpose of helping Garda Lake's economic and social development and exploiting good business opportunities that their knowledge of local networks made possible. In the mid-1890s, the family joined the Società di Navigazione del Garda, the firm that ran the lake's navigation company, along with some Milanese and Swiss entrepreneurs, Mangili, the biggest Italian import-export company, and Maraini, who controlled the navigation company on Lake Lugano in Switzerland. Finally, the Garda Lake in the 1890s was becoming one of the most attractive tourist areas for wealthy German and Austrian families, who spent their holidays in the southern Alps. Giovanni Feltrinelli led the family into preparing tourist development schemes with some local hotel entrepreneurs.[20]

Yet another—and the most important—diversification initiative was an investment in a cotton-spinning factory. Since the late 1880s, Giacomo Feltrinelli had been in contact with some local industrial entrepreneurs and *brasseurs d'affaires*, businessmen with strong ties to the local and national political elites with constituencies in eastern Lombardy. Since 1878, the textile industry had been among Italy's most protected, and protective tariffs rose even further after 1887. Nevertheless, risks in the sector remained high because it was overcrowded; only under special conditions was it possible to succeed. This perhaps explains why Giacomo Feltrinelli did not accept the first proposal he received from one of these local businessmen in 1888–1889. In the mid-1890s, however, he accepted when one of the most famous and admired technicians of the Italian cotton industry, Vittorio Olcese, presented another project proposal. Between 1894 and 1895, Feltrinelli and Olcese jointly bought an old eighteenth-century aristocratic palace in Campione, a small village some 10 kilometers (approximately 6 miles) north of Gargnano, and established Cotonificio Feltrinelli in March 1895. All family members, including brothers- and sisters-in-law and their children, participated in this new, limited liability company, with no fewer than 15–20 holding shares. The Feltrinelli family owned 29 of the 54 capital shares, each valued at 25,000 lire—a high price, especially for less wealthy, extended family members. The extended family's involvement signaled that the whole family was committed to the new venture. By bearing a good portion of the risk and showing its long-term commitment, the family could attract new investment if needed. This was another way that family reputation could anchor new investments at home or abroad.

At the same time, as Fear's contribution to this volume shows, moving abroad requires FBs to reorganize, and the original timber trade firm, the Feltrinelli Company, was no exception. It was split into two companies: one for the domestic Italian investments, and the other for the international ones. Moreover, the three surviving founders, Giacomo, Pietro, and Angelo, decided to separate the company's Central-North warehouses from those in Southern Italy. The first two brothers managed the northern activities, while Angelo and his son Giuseppe handled the southern branches; the Austrian branches went to Giacomo and Pietro, while those in what is now Slovenia remained joined with the Southern Italian branches. Financial and real estate assets were also included in the division, which was supposed to distribute the firm's huge commercial structure equally among the brothers. Some years later, Giuseppe, however, claimed that his father Angelo had accepted a very unbalanced division of the total assets simply to avoid litigation with his brothers. But the real problem was the contrast between the management styles of Giuseppe and Giovanni, the supposed future leader of the FB group. This unequal division of the family assets caused controversy within the family—common to many FBs in varying stages of growth—as two cousins and other stepbrothers repeatedly broached the subject. However, their uncles and father decided for them since it was impossible to find a compromise.

Unfortunately, Giovanni, favored to succeed his uncle and founder of the dynasty, Giacomo, died in June 1896, leaving a wife and four very young sons. Giacomo then stepped into the father role for Giovanni's family. True to family tradition, he suggested the educational strategy for each of the four grandnephews. Giovanni's two oldest sons, Carlo and Giuseppe, particularly occupied his attention. Giacomo decided that a business school (a *Handelsschule* along the lines of the German model) in Bolzano (then Bozen) in South Tyrol would best prepare them for inclusion in the FB. Although Giacomo considered Giuseppe, familiarly known as Beppi, the most brilliant of the four, Carlo, the oldest one, who had a melancholic character but also a stronger commitment to the FB, was finally "chosen" to be the real inheritor of the family fortunes.

All the brothers became involved in the FB at a very young age except for the youngest, Antonio (nicknamed Tonino); he was also the only one to receive a university degree—in law. In the family division of labor, Carlo specialized in banking and financial activities, Beppi followed the Austrian business, the group's most important international business, and the third brother Pietro (Pierino, as the family called him) was sent off quite young to handle the Transylvanian trade in Sibiu, coinciding with the expansion of business in this area. In 1906, they founded a new company, the Società Italo-ungherese per l'industria forestale (Italian-Hungarian Industrial Forest Company) in Fiume (Rijeka). Again, all branches of the family invested and cooperated in it although it remained under the strict control of Giacomo and his nephew Francesco (Giovanni's brother) and other grandnephews. Since 1902, the Feltrinelli firm had had some contracts to exploit one of Europe's richest forest areas in eastern Transylvania, but then it was divided between the Austro-Hungarian Empire and the Kingdom of Romania. In 1906, the firm reached an agreement with the Universitas Saxorum (*Sächsische Universität* in German), an old institution founded by the Teutonic Knights to manage the real estate and particularly the huge forests they owned around Nagy Talmacs (today's Talmaciu). This was a small village 15 kilometers (or 9.5 miles) south of Hermanstadt (today's Sibiu), an old German enclave in a Hungarian- and Romanian-speaking territory.[21] These complicated Old World relations and fractured markets go a long way toward explaining why family members had to be present on the ground there and why a multinational firm arose rather than a trading company along the London model.

These developments in the timber trade increased the firm's international commercial network. From Nagy Talmacs, the timber, once cut and prepared for shipping, had two different ways to reach the market: by train or ship. Utilizing the Hungarian and the Austrian railway network, the timber could travel west as far as Trieste and Italy. By ship, it could be transported on the Danube as far as the Romanian ports of Galatz and Braila. From both these ports, it could then be shipped to many Mediterranean countries. It took the Feltrinellis three to four years to establish the relevant infrastructure, including the cableway and the railway network that allowed timber to reach the sawmill. But once the business was up and running, the firm was able to enlarge its client network from Constantinople to Izmir, from Palestine to Egypt, from Southern Italy to Marseille and Sète (on the French Mediterranean coast), Spain, and Morocco. The FB created the commercial conduit that linked the dark mountainous forests of Transylvania with sunny Mediterranean cities.

Prior to the First World War, the Feltrinelli firm's reputation spread all around the Mediterranean coasts. The Milan headquarters controlled the strategic coordination of the different branches (with the most centralized control focusing on corporate finance). Despite the large family banking business, Feltrinelli's international presence revolved around its long-established timber trade activities in Austria and its promising new investments in Transylvania, Hungary, and the most important Romanian ports on the Danube. Typical of the family tradition, three of Giovanni's four sons got involved in the FB around 1908–1910 (Carlo in the banking activities, Beppi in Austria, based in Villach, and Pierino in Hermanstadt), while the youngest one, Tonino, studied law. Coordinating the firm through personal relations and central family finance made it highly effective.

However, the centrality of personal family relations in the firm's coordination made it vulnerable in the face of family tragedy. Key members of the family died from natural causes or in tragic ways, which, with other dramatic family events, destabilized the company for decades just as it was consolidating its new international organizational profile. In 1909, Pietro, one of the founders, passed away of natural causes; in January 1913, Pierino shot himself in Nagy Talmacs, just one month before the death of his granduncle Giacomo, the head of the group; in June 1918, Beppi died after many years of being a morphine addict; and in 1918, Carlo was jailed for six months after being accused of trading with the enemy. He had been a member of the board of directors of a cotton company that had exported cotton and silk waste to Switzerland, which was then shipped to Germany for use in armament production.

Giacomo Feltrinelli's last will crowned Carlo, Giovanni's oldest son, the new leader of the FB group. Although he was not the majority shareholder of the firm or family bank, he effectively inherited the leading role; the involvement of the other partners, such as his brother Tonino, his mother, and his uncle Francesco, was limited. Only Francesco was active in firm business, and he, too, died in 1923. Despite his law degree and a formal position as firm CEO, Tonino had little to do with the FB. Of all the Feltrinellis, he perhaps best represents the third-generation Buddenbrooks syndrome as his main interests were art history and collecting paintings; he even ventured into painting himself when he discovered an artistic streak in his late thirties, managing to get his own work displayed in some important Italian exhibitions in the 1920s and 1930s.

Thus, the progressive concentration of power and responsibilities in a single person, Carlo, resulted more from a series of tragic events than from a real family business strategy. Nevertheless, in early 1919, Carlo presented a very lucid scheme for reorganizing the group. He felt it necessary to create a family holding, to be placed in neutral Switzerland, with a large majority of the timber firm's shares; the commercial activities were to be reorganized according to the different national markets: an Italian firm for the trade activities in Italy, and two distinct firms, one for Austria and another for Romania, where the group had its main economic activities; the family bank was to be transformed into a joint-stock company with a new name in order to hide the family's direct interests and involvement. Carlo also assumed that a managerialization process should be launched and/or fostered in all of the group firms.

His uncles (Francesco and Giuseppe, his father's stepbrother) and his brother Tonino accepted most of Carlo's ideas for this strategic reorganization except for the most important one—the family holding—which was never established. The new structure included the Società anonima per l'industria ed il commercio del legname (for the commercial and industrial activities in Italy), the Gebrüder Feltrinelli for Austria, and the Società Anonima Forestale Feltrinelli for Romania, whose legal headquarters remained in Rijeka (then Fiume), which had belonged to Italy since 1919 in consequence of the new postwar borders. A new bank was established, Banca Unione, with the family as the main shareholder, but several industrial and financial partners also participated, including Credito Italiano, Italy's second-largest bank.

Gradually, the group was transformed into a sort of "one-man company" after the two uncles Francesco and Giuseppe died in the 1920s, the Feltrinelli heirs grew less involved in the business, and Tonino developed his artistic interest. This was exactly the opposite of what the FB had been until then. Carlo became not only the leader of the family group but one of the most powerful men in the Italian economy. He sat on more than fifty companies' boards of directors, both in Italy and abroad. He was so respected and important as a European banker that he was nominated to represent Italy as a board member of the German Reichsbank in 1924 according to an agreement between Germany and the Allies. After 1924, a complex system of block syndicates (pyramiding) among the most important shareholders of Credito Italiano also made him the biggest shareholder of this bank, though he could technically have been considered an owner because one of his financial firms owned the majority of the holding company that controlled the bank.

Problems in the company emerged when Carlo Feltrinelli and his family were accused of illegally exporting capital and equities to Switzerland and of keeping some 250 kilograms (551 pounds) of gold ingots in a Swiss bank. He was asked to resign from all the boards he sat on of the firms controlled by IRI (the state holding company), the most important being his chairmanship of the Credito Italiano after the bank was placed under IRI control in 1933. As a moderate liberal, Carlo himself had never been really close to the fascist regime and was politically far away from Mussolini's rhetoric. But, as the chairman of Credito Italiano and the main shareholder of the biggest and most powerful Italian electric firm (Edison), he had been part of the interest group close to the fascist government. It was the government's desire to demonstrate its impartiality during the Depression, and particularly concerning the alleged fiscal fraud, that explains its harsh attitude toward Carlo in forcing him to resign this position.

Carlo Feltrinelli's dramatic death in 1935, probably because of a cerebral hemorrhage, reopened the succession issue for the FB. His failure to establish a Swiss holding with all the controlling or majority shares—one of his original intentions in restructuring the organizational design—meant that the destiny of the group was most probably in Tonino's hands. After 1938, Tonino also inherited his mother's group and bank shares, making him the new majority owner of Fratelli Feltrinelli (with 51.4 percent) as well as, through this company, of the Banca Unione; in Forestale Feltrinelli he held 59.7 percent of the equity. Tonino's personal relations with both Carlo's young widow Giannalisa and her oldest son, Giangiacomo (born in 1926), were bad.

In the absence of a legal mechanism that would have limited the decision-making power of one family member over the others—a mechanism that might have been adopted in the Swiss holding company statutes had it been established—Tonino symbolically wrote the last page of the dynasty's story. In March 1936, three months after Carlo's death and after a series of litigations with his sister-in-law, he wrote his last will, which donated his entire fortune, including the majority of the Feltrinelli group firms' shares, to the most important cultural institution of the country, the Royal Academy of Italy.[22] Without the personal capacity or desire to play the role of entrepreneur, Tonino fostered the group's managerial structure over the next six years, increasing the autonomy of the managers, many of whom had been working for the family group for more than twenty years. Tonino also decided to bequeath one of the most important firms inside the group, the Feltrinelli per l'Industria ed il Commercio della Masonite, to the managers. This company had been set up in 1935 with the license to use the U.S. Masonite Corporation's patent for producing hardboard made of steam-cooked, pressure-molded wood fibers and ranked among the most successful firms in this industrial segment for decades.

The exploitation of the family's human resources was the firm's most important strategy for three generations. However, a series of traumatic events forced the next generation into the core business without the necessary professional and psychological preparation. The progressive concentration of power in one single person weakened the group structure at the most delicate times. Despite these critical family transition moments, the FB group always performed well, if not extremely well. Its oligopolistic position in Italy and its international reputation acquired from long-term accomplishments made it successful in a sector where high professionalism, strong liquidity, and efficient networking were key strategies.

From the early 1920s, the Feltrinelli group suffered the depletion of its most important human resources, its family, followed by a crisis of succession. Despite its seeming adherence to the Buddenbrooks pattern, however, it is nonsensical to assume that a family firm is fated to dissolve in the third generation. Nevertheless, better distribution of responsibilities might have helped the firm to diversify and reorganize. Italy's managerial culture was very limited, existing only in large FBs like the Feltrinelli group, the vast majority of its economy being made up of small and medium-sized FBs and state-owned companies. Yet the Feltrinelli firm's performance was better than one could have expected. The timber trade was well organized.

In addition to internal family issues, external factors played a role in the firm's fate in the 1920s and 1930s. The Soviet Union made a comeback as a critical actor in the timber trade in the late 1920s, and the sector was cartelized in the 1930s, reinforcing the role of the largest firms such as the Feltrinelli group. Then, the Second World War and nationalizations across Eastern Europe destroyed most of the group's international structure (such as its investments in Romania and trading activities in Yugoslavia). As family members were largely absent from the timber business, managers ran the Feltrinelli group until Giangiacomo Feltrinelli changed the core business from timber to publishing and paradoxically became a member of the Italian Communist Party. He replicated the business culture based on the one-man company of his uncle Carlo, but this story has to wait to be told by another business historian.

NOTES

1. Many scholars apply the Buddenbrooks name to this pattern in the life cycle of family firms. See Rose, 1993, 127–129. For a critical rereading of the Buddenbrooks saga applying business history to the novel, see Allende, 2009.
2. Landes examines family dynasties that worked in the banking, automotive, and mining and steel industries: Landes, 2006. Also James considers only entrepreneurial families involved in steel: James, 2006. For a general overview, see Colli, 2003.
3. This contribution is based on my book, Segreto, 2011. Unless otherwise noted, the implicit reference is this work.
4. Timber is never even mentioned in David S. Landes's masterpiece Landes, 1969.
5. Williams, 1966, 104–106.
6. Cf. Söderlund, 1952, 50–51.

7. "1873–1923," *Timber Trade Journal. Jubilee Issue*, 30 May 1923, 5–6 e; *The Timber Trade of the City of London*, ibid., 25 March 1911, 1–7.

8. "1873–1923," *Timber Trade Journal. Jubilee Issue*, 30 May 1923, 5–6 e.

9. This was the old headquarters of the South Sea Company, which was bought in 1857 by the Baltic Sea Company and founded in 1744 by merchants and ship owners, who used to meet to discuss prices and freight charges at the Virginia and Maryland Coffee House. See http://www.balticexchange.com.

10. Auctions took place in the evening after "a good dinner, good wine, and good humor" as "people were more prone to be generous after an enjoyable meal than before." Methods of defining the price of a single lot were based on a special candle that was supposed to remain lit for 1–2 minutes. The last offer before the candle burned out would win. Stobart, 1927, 67.

11. Dr. Lyons, "Forest Areas in Europe and America, and Probable Future Timber Supplies," *Timber Trade Journal*, 18 October 1884, 258.

12. Segala and Serpieri, 1917, 17–20, 33–34.

13. Cf. *Die Kammer für Handel, Gewerbe und Industrie in Klagenfurt 1851–1926*, 1926, 33–34. *Kammer der Gewerblichen Wirtschaft für Kärnten*, 1953, 351–352. Fräss-Ehrfeld, 1999, 268–269.

14. See Lubinski (in this volume.)

15. Lambrecht, 2005. Fernández Pérez and Puig, 2004.

16. Archives of the Swiss Federal Railsways (Bern), SHESBB, VGB_GB_SBBGB03_032_02; Caizzi, 2007. Ceschi, 2005, 152.

17. Decleva, 1881. Crepax, 1991, 270.

18. Archives of the Chamber of Commerce of Milan, roll 186. Foundation G. Feltrinelli, Archives of the Feltrinelli Family, papers of Giovanni Feltrinelli, III.1–b. 1, file 6/1. Hertner, 1984, 83.

19. Angeli, 1982. Piluso, 2000, 526–530. Segreto, 2012.

20. Paris, 2007. Ogliari, 1987.

21. Teutsch, 1907. Schneider, 1990, 152–153, 372 and 379–383. Stoila, 2008, 158.

22. This was the name the fascist regime gave to the Accademia dei Lincei, Italy's oldest cultural academy. The fortune Tonino left this institution more than doubled its already generous budget.

10 Becoming Global, Staying Local

The Internationalization of Bertelsmann, 1962–2010

Hartmut Berghoff

Founded in Gütersloh, a small town in Eastern Westphalia, in 1835, Bertelsmann had grown to a medium-sized Protestant, all-German publishing and
printing business by 1950, when it employed a workforce of 400 people,
all based in Gütersloh. In 2010, by contrast, Bertelsmann's staff numbered
101,058, with two-thirds of them employed outside Germany. Bertelsmann
is now the largest European media company, generating approximately two-
thirds of its annual revenue abroad.[1]

Despite its tremendous growth, however, Bertelsmann AG remains in many
ways a family business. It was family-led for five generations by members of
the Bertelsmann family from its founding until 1887, and then by members
of the Mohn family until 1981,[2] when Reinhard Mohn (1921–2009), who
had led the company since 1947, withdrew from his formal position as CEO.
Nonetheless, the family remains heavily involved. For one thing, Reinhard
Mohn continued to take part in all strategic decisions almost until his death,
and several fifth- and sixth-generation family members have served on the
supervisory board, although managers without kinship ties to the Mohns have
led Bertelsmann and no family member has been on the executive board since
that time. Moreover, the powerful BVG (Bertelsmann Verwaltungsgesellschaft)
is half-comprised of family members. This six-person administrative body
possesses all the voting rights in the Bertelsmann AG Annual General Meeting and, since 1999, it has selected the members of the supervisory board,
made recommendations to the supervisory board for the CEO, and decided
on general guidelines of financing and on the company's statutes. In other
words, it has a central position with far-reaching authority. To be sure, the
three external managers—in 2010 the former Thyssen CEO, the Vice President of Nestlé, and the chairman of the BASF supervisory board—provide a
formidable counterpoise to the family, but the family still has the final say on
account of a complex pyramidal structure that distributes voting rights. All
in all, Bertelsmann is still de facto family-owned and supervised, although the
family's power is moderated by outside experts.[3]

By the 1990s, the medium-sized family printing and publishing house
of 1950 had been transformed into a major international player. In 2010
it had five divisions: 1) RTL Group: television, radio, and TV production;

2) Random House: book publishing; 3) Gruner + Jahr: magazine publishing; 4) Arvato: media, communication and other services; and 5) Direct Group: book and media clubs and bookstores. In 2009, Random House and Direct Group had by far the highest international orientation with more than four-fifths of their revenue coming from outside Germany. RTL, with almost two-thirds, was slightly above the company's average, while Arvato and Gruner + Jahr were below average but still generated more the half of their income abroad. This transformation occurred in six phases.

1. 1950–1961. In 1950, Bertelsmann began its club strategy, founding the book club "Lesering" in Germany. The record club "Schallplattenring" followed in 1956. Bertelsmann bought licenses for top-selling titles and sold them in high volume at low prices. The German law designed to maintain retail sales prices for books did not apply to book clubs so that Bertelsmann was able to exploit this loophole and turn millions of customers into regular readers.

2. 1962–1969. In the 1960s, Bertelsmann transferred this business model to other countries, first of all to Western Europe and Latin America. Bertelsmann also learned to reap economies of scope by using its existing facilities for printing and distribution for third parties. The music business became highly successful in Germany.

3. 1969–1981. In this phase, Bertelsmann kept expanding its clubs and printing activities geographically and also entered totally new fields like magazine publishing, acquiring Gruner + Jahr, the leading German magazine publisher. In the late 1970s, Bertelsmann became a major player in the U.S. market when it bought 51 percent of Bantam Books and invested heavily in the music business.

4. 1981–1991. Overexpansion and problems of succession led to a brief crisis, and then growth picked up again. Bertelsmann acquired RCA Records as the music business boomed, and the Bertelsmann Music Group (BMG) became one of the world's majors. The acquisition of Doubleday, the second-largest U.S. publisher, turned Bertelsmann into one of the largest publishers of English books. When European broadcasting was deregulated in the 1980s, Bertelsmann began to build up the largest commercial TV and radio network in Europe.

5. 1991–2002. In the 1990s, Bertelsmann's TV business took off, and the internationalization of all other fields progressed at high speed. In 1998, the company bought Random House and restructured it into one division with all Bertelsmann imprints. What was to become Arvato, the service division, benefitted from the general trend toward outsourcing. It offered integrated services from supply-chain management to customer relations (call centers), from distribution to accounting and IT services. The digital revolution began to affect more and more media, but Bertelsmann failed to keep up with upstart pioneers like Amazon and Google and to become a leading media-IT company.

6. 2002–2010. In this period, Bertelsmann refocused on its core competencies and sold or wound down many of its loss-generating Internet activities. It also divested itself of the music business due to the massive challenge of free music downloads. The club business entered the final stage of its product cycle, and an increasing number of clubs were sold. The most dynamic divisions up to the present have been RTL and Arvato, which have pulled the company back into growth and profitability.

10.1   KEY QUESTIONS AND THEORETICAL MODELS OF INTERNATIONALIZATION

The Uppsala model of internationalization states that future multinationals develop competitive advantages in domestic markets before they move abroad. Then they start exploring new opportunities in places where the geographical and "psychological" distance is relatively small to minimize the insecurities that result from cultural as well as legal and political differences.

In her classic study that lay the foundation of the resource-based view of firms, Edith Penrose distinguished between objective and experiential market knowledge. Objective knowledge concerns information that can be taught, acquired by reading, or bought from consultants. Experiential knowledge, on the other hand, relies on personal experience; it is market-specific and cannot be transferred from one foreign country to another. Consequently, people who have this specific knowledge and relationships are key players in the internationalization process.[4]

The Uppsala model presents the sequence of events in internationalization as follows: First, the firm begins to penetrate foreign markets by occasionally exporting its products via independent intermediaries like import merchants. As the volume grows, the firm eventually internalizes this exchange by employing representatives, opening sales offices, starting joint ventures with local firms, and finally by setting up production sites.[5] Mira Wilkins has suggested a six-stage model of corporate internationalization in which occasional exports are the beginning from which more regular exports, an exclusive representation outside the firm's structure, and finally foreign direct investment (FDI) in the form of service and then finally production facilities develop. In the end, the foreign subsidiary assumes increasing independence.[6]

Although these models are not specific to family firms, can they be applied to them? Do family firms have characteristics that either encourage or discourage internationalization and explain their specific approaches to foreign markets? In the general academic debate, the family firm used to be classified as an obsolete model, especially for a large company, because families seem to lack the financial and human resources to manage companies beyond a certain size. Meanwhile, the debate has highlighted the comparative advantages of family firms, increasingly describing them as a flexible and efficient institution. New Institutional Economics, for example, stresses family firms' lower transaction costs, as well as their ability to rely on motives beyond short-term economic gain and to mobilize qualities like loyalty, intrinsic motivation, emotional rewards, and long-term commitment.[7]

Research on family firms has long been conducted largely apart from research on corporate internationalization, but in recent years, these neighboring disciplines have begun to talk to each other. Initial studies suggest that the flexibility of family firms plays an important role in the internationalization process. Moreover, family members, who are regarded as possessing more integrity and, above all, as being more permanent players than managers, can be pivotal in opening doors through their personal contacts. One Australian entrepreneur, for example, claimed, "Being a family-run business helped secure contracts in Asia."[8] The stability and longevity usually associated with family firms also supports the incremental and cumulative process of internationalization, in which networking, learning, knowledge transfers, personal relations, and long-term perspectives seem to be key components.[9]

Research on family firms has shown how the family itself, in many cases, has become a vehicle of internationalization, such as when relatives have founded or managed foreign subsidiaries. The brothers Werner, Carl, and William Siemens personally connected their young firm's operations in nineteenth-century Germany, Russia, and England.[10] Such kinship ties reduce transactional uncertainties. Family members have also been instrumental in processes of knowledge and skill transfers and acted as cultural mediators. They have displayed remarkable integrative capabilities linking distant regions and spanning continents and used network resources like trustful cooperation and credit.[11] Some family networks have grown huge and comprised hundreds—in extreme cases thousands—of members dispersed over large geographical areas.[12]

Another facilitating factor for internationalization in family firms is family harmony as it "encourages family members to reinvest their dividends in the business and take a long-term perspective."[13] Vipin Gupta calls one of four family-business internationalization modes the "network extension pathway," wherein already existing "footholds and relationships" enable a firm, through the family members and trusted employees, "to extend the family business into new geographies."[14] As families regularly have more offspring than top positions in their company, founding foreign subsidiaries can help prevent family conflicts. There are many elaborate models, but these should suffice to discuss the extent to which Bertelsmann conformed to or deviated from these theoretical pathways to family-firm internationalization.

10.2   THE ANATOMY OF BERTELSMANN'S INTERNATIONALIZATION

To dissect the anatomy of Bertelsmann's internationalization process, some statistics are helpful. Table 10.1 row 1 shows that international markets were not significant before the 1960s, whereas they were of paramount

Table 10.1 Internalization Parameters. Bertelsmann 1950–2009

	1950	1960	1971/72	1980/81	1990/91	2000/01	2009
1. Revenue outside Germany as percentage of total revenue	≤ 3%[4]	≤ 5%[4]	27.4%	48.6%	62.9%	69.4%	64.5%
2. Number of employees outside Germany	0	0	?	12,151	24,387	50,019	66,053
3. Quota of employees outside Germany	0	≤ 2%[4]	24.8%[3]	40.4%	54.1%	60.9%	64.1%
4. Number of foreign countries with essential, consolidated Bertelsmann firms[1]	0	0	14	15	33	49	41
5. Number of foreign nationals among top executives/from 1971 on executive board	0	0	0	1 (Austria)	1 (Austria)	1 (USA)	1 (Austria)
6. Number of foreign nationals on supervisory board (board existed only since 1971)	–	–	1 (Italy)	0	0	3 (CH, Can, Belg)	2 (UK, Norway)
7. Capital quota of foreign shareholders	0	0	0	0	0	25.1%[2]	0

[1]Without associated firms, portfolio investments.
[2]With effect from July 6, 2001, that is, just after the end of the 2000/01 reporting period.
[3]1973/74. No prior information available.
[4]Estimates. Mainly sales in German-speaking countries.

Sources: Bertelsmann Annual Reports.

importance by the 1980s. In rows 2 and 3, the number and percentage of employees outside Germany over these periods tell the same story and make clear that the growth was not export-induced. The share of value creation and employment outside Germany also grew. The export stage simply did not take place. Books are too culturally sensitive to be simply exported across language boundaries, even if they are translated. Exports to Austria and Switzerland did occur prior to the foundations of subsidiaries in these countries, but they never played any significant role. Row 4, which only includes the numbers of countries with "essential" firms mentioned in the annual reports, shows that Bertelsmann engaged in FDI in ever more countries from 1962.

Table 10.2 shows where Bertelsmann has concentrated its internationalization efforts—on the advanced consumer markets in the Western world. In the last few years, the focus has even narrowed down to Europe as the U.S. market has declined in importance following the sale of all U.S. magazines in 2005 and BMG-Sony in 2006. This underrepresentation of the world's most advanced consumer society also has to do with legal restrictions inside the United States. The Communications Act of 1934 still limits foreign ownership of broadcast facilities, preventing RTL, for example, from running channels in the United States.

Bertelsmann remained a very German company at the top as it has had few foreign executives.[15] Returning to Table 10.1, Row 5, we can see, if we remove Austrian Egmont Lüftner from the foreigner bracket as well as American Peter Olson, the son of a German mother, that there has been no single "truly international" member of the executive board. The board's language is still German today. Peter Olson, board member from 2001 to 2008, however, is a rather international figure. With a law degree and an MBA from Harvard, he had worked in Japan for Dresdner Bank and in Germany for an American bank before he joined Bertelsmann in 1987. The supervisory board is also dominated by Germans, particularly former top managers from Bertelsmann and other leading German companies, and the family presence increased after 2006. Under German codetermination laws, several seats have to go to representatives of the works council and one to a representative of the middle management. In 2009, family, employee

Table 10.2 Bertelsmann Sales by Countries, 1990–2009

	1990/91	2000/01	2009
Germany	37.0%	30.6%	35.0%
Other European Countries	35.9%	31.5%	47.7%
USA	20.9%	32.2%	12.5%
Others	6.2%	5.7%	4.8%

Sources: Bertelsmann Annual Reports.

representatives, and the former Bertelsmann CEO had the majority of the 14 seats while there were only two non-German members.

The composition of Bertelsmann's boards does not reflect the multinational scope of the corporation. Up to 2011, none of the CEOs in office had any prolonged managerial experience abroad. While family firms typically appoint either family members or long-serving employees to its top positions, at Bertelsmann, the family was not present on the executive board after 1981, nor did it ever play a strong role as a vehicle for internationalization. Only one of Mohn's six children entered a management position in one of the foreign subsidiaries. Nonetheless, for the top management at Gütersloh headquarters, trustful and cordial relations with the family have remained of paramount importance. More than in managerial firms, Bertelsmann expects a certain cultural fit and a deep-seated loyalty, as well as an intimate understanding of the family's priorities. The career of Hartmut Ostrowski, CEO from 2008–2011, demonstrates just how long it can take to develop the requisite degree of mutual trust to bridge the family and the corporate sphere at Bertelsmann. Born in nearby Bielefeld, Ostrowski studied business administration at Bielefeld University and, at age 25, joined Bertelsmann immediately after graduation in 1982. Apart from a short stint at the German branch of the U.S. bank Security Pacific, he not only spent his entire career with Bertelsmann but also in Germany. In fact, he worked most of his life within a 10-mile radius of his birthplace.

Throughout its history, Bertelsmann has been almost 100 percent self-financed, mainly through ploughed-back profits, a growth-restricting preference typical of family firms that seek to avoid the influence of external stakeholders. For a long time, the family hardly withdrew any earnings from the company, certainly reflecting a predisposition for growth, and foreign shareholders simply did not exist (see Table 10.1, Row 7). At two important junctures, however, the family did allow minority stakes by outsiders: First, when Bertelsmann, which was transformed into a joint-stock company in 1971, bought Gruner + Jahr in several steps from 1969 onwards, it had to resort to a share swap, conceding 11.5 percent of its shares to German publisher Gerd Bucerius. Then, in 2001, Bertelsmann swapped shares with Belgian tycoon Albert Frère to raise its share in RTL to 67 percent in exchange for a 25.1 percent stake in Bertelsmann. This second share swap, in particular, highlighted the problems of outside influence, so that the company eventually bought back all externally held shares in 2006. Although the family had retained firm control, there were suddenly outside shareholders with their own agenda on the supervisory board. The representatives of Frère were very different from Bucerius, who had had personal ties to the Mohn family. Now, revolutionary changes were discussed like going public. The partial opening up to external—in this case also foreign—capital and the attempt of then CEO Thomas Middelhoff to leave behind the conservative principles of the Mohn family contributed to Middelhoff's resignation in 2002. In 2006, the company bought back all externally held shares.[16] In 2009, Bertelsmann was de facto 100 percent family owned, although legally the Bertelsmann foundation held 77.4 percent and the family only 22.6 percent.

In sum, Bertelsmann AG bore many qualities that some academics consider to be structural elements that disfavor internationalization: its funding was principally internal, its top decision makers were nationally recruited, and it was supervised by a family with strong local roots and little international experience. Such near identity of private wealth and business stakes is said to breed a distinct conservatism that favors allegedly safe niches and deters risky investments in unknown territories, supposedly making family firms "reluctant internationalizers."[17] Bertelsmann, however, is a powerful example to the contrary as it had a strong internationalization of management and capital below the level of the corporate center, that is, the Bertelsmann AG, which is organized as a management holding. In 2008, it had 1,086 subsidiary companies (915 fully consolidated), 51 joint ventures, and 120 associated firms.

One foundation of Bertelsmann's management philosophy has been the principle of decentralization, as the annual report clearly stated in 2009 in reflecting on the firm's core values in its 175th year:

> decentralization is an essential part of our culture, and together with the structure of our company, it forms the secret of our success. (. . .) We used the decentralized power of our company to act quickly . . . each division . . . in its own way. Once again, the entrepreneurs who make up Bertelsmann's "company of entrepreneurs" acted decisively, aided by their close proximity to their markets and to their customers. (. . .) Our operating businesses are run by managers who act as entrepreneurs: They enjoy considerable independence and bear full responsibility . . .[18]

Although printed on glossy paper, this report is not merely a slick PR statement but a clear-cut policy best suited to the diversity of the corporation's operations and regional outreach. A strong centralization have would have been extremely counterproductive. Reinhard Mohn, to his great merit, understood this from the beginning, combining central control with freedom of action in decentralized profit centers. This approach opened up many opportunities for foreign managers and foreign capital to become part of Bertelsmann. However, what these company statements do not admit is that the emergence of Bertelsmann as a decentralized multinational firm was neither the result of a grand masterplan nor a smooth process.[19]

10.3   "WHAT'S THE POINT OF GOING TO SPAIN?" BERTELSMANN'S FIRST FOREIGN MARKETS

Had Bertelsmann followed the Uppsala model of internationalization, it would have begun to expand its business outside of Germany first by turning to neighboring markets. Yet Spain was the first site of substantial FDI and the company's first foreign book club in 1962, while neighboring countries like Austria, Holland, Belgium, France, and Denmark got such clubs only later, with Denmark as late as 1973. The choice of Spain came as such a surprise, especially as the country was outside the European Economic Community (EEC), that the company published an article in its journal to clarify "What's the point of going to Spain?" In short, the article presented this step as one of moderate investment and minimal risk because of the Spanish partner company's (Vergara) capital, sales experience, and existing demand. In addition, Vergara's main shareholder, the plastic producer Aiscondel, was well equipped with capital. At the same time, the article maintained that Spain in 1961, though under Franco's dictatorship, displayed "stunning similarities to Germany around 1950": it was liberalizing and the standard of living was rising, while there were still significant reserves in the labor markets making it "easy . . . to recruit reliable salesmen and workers." Moreover, Spain would be "forced to come to an arrangement with the EEC," and it held the promise of "exceptional opportunities," especially given the rising Spanish-speaking population in the world, which at that time comprised 100 million people.[20]

Mohn did not have a clear globalization strategy, as this article implied, and he had not even initiated the joint venture. Vergara's owners, impressed by Bertelsmann's club, had established a first contact at the Frankfurt book fair and then paid a visit to Gütersloh,[21] just as the spectacular growth of the German book clubs—from zero (1950) to 2.5 million members (1960)— and the postwar catch-up demand for books had leveled off. The Spanish book market was underdeveloped in many ways: Many small towns had no libraries or bookshops in the 1960s, yet as illiteracy and poverty declined, the reading public expanded. Vergara believed that Bertelsmann's direct-marketing system was perfectly geared to serving this emerging mass market. The same rationale applied to the potentially giant Latin American market, the natural export area for books produced in Spain.

Despite the strong potential of the Spanish market, the choice of this country as a first foreign market also brought complications. Although the Franco dictatorship had been trying to modernize Spain after decades of stagnation since establishing the Plan de Estabilización in 1959,[22] liberalization was far from complete in 1962. In fact, profit transfers were not allowed until a decree was passed in 1963, and majority ownership by foreign entities was still forbidden, despite the friendlier framework for foreign investors in many sectors including publishing. Therefore, Bertelsmann and Vergara had to utilize legal sophistication and local partners to give the Spanish venture the appearance of being all Spanish. Bertelsmann bought a 50 percent stake in Vergara in 1962, and the subsequent founding of "Vergara, Círculo de Lectores" in Barcelona looked like an all-Spanish venture, at least on paper. The official founders and managers were Spanish nationals. No shares were directly held by Bertelsmann.[23] To supply the Círculo a large bookbindery and a printing factory, Industria de la Encuadernación, were set up in 1962 with a similar legal construction. Thus, Bertelsmann did not appear in the Constitution Writing of both companies created in 1962 but controlled them through Vergara.

In 1963 a nationwide system of agencies was build up. Books were delivered by messengers on motorbikes who were also sales representatives and money collectors. One "messenger" attended to 150 customers. The club targeted, just as in Germany, the mass market and clients who would traditionally not buy books. Membership fees were modest, and members were overwhelmingly women of the lower middle class.

Despite these fast advances, conflicts emerged in the first months. Given the high capital needs of the club, it seems that Aiscondel lost confidence in the project and Vergara ceased to be a useful instrument. In 1964, the name and the purpose of the printing company were changed. Printer Industria Gráfica emerged as a holding company. Arcadia Verlag, a Swiss publishing subsidiary of Bertelsmann, now gradually bought up shares in it. At the same time, Printer itself acquired shares of "Círculo de Lectores" until it owned 100% in 1966.[24] Also in 1963–1964, Bertelsmann installed a new management team of mixed nationality at Circulo, and Arnold Schmitt became general manager. In 1964 Bertelsmann had assumed sole responsibility. In May 1965, Schmitt assembled a Board of Directors. Members were José Esteve and Eduardo Nolla. The latter was an important figure in the Spanish publishing sector with excellent relationships to the Franco government. Nolla was in fact General Secretary of the Instituto Nacional del Libro Español (INLE). Founded in 1941, it was responsible for publishing policies, commercial protection, and censorship. This close tie to a high-ranking cultural official proved to be a great advantage. It helped circumvent many of the problems foreign companies faced and, above all, participate in subvention programs. Franco's development plans for the publishing sector aimed at increasing exports to Latin America, which dovetailed with ambitions to restore the Hispanidad, that is, the unity of the Spanish-speaking world and the Spanish influence in Latin America.

Bertelsmann enormously benefitted from this policy. Between 1969 and 1979, the Circulo founded clubs in Mexico, Colombia, Venezuela, Argentina, and Ecuador, Uruguay, Costa Rica, Peru, and Panama. The top management was of German, Spanish, and indigenous origin. Some managers were of mixed nationality, expats or children of immigrants. Mohn set some ground rules in 1967. Together with three top managers from Circulo (Schmitt, Larrio, Esteve), he traveled to Mexico to hire "local managers." Then these were "sent to Barcelona for training." Besides, Spanish managers had to support them and "be in Mexico for a prolonged time. Once local management will be capable of doing their job by themselves, we can prepare work on the next country."[25] A pattern was set. First the new clubs were part of Circulo but then operated more or less independently. Colombia had the most successful club with 924,000 members and 3,000 messengers in 1984.

In most Latin American countries with the exception of Colombia, Bertelsmann initially owned 100 or close to 100% of the clubs. For some years, joint ventures were agreed on in Ecuador, Brazil, Argentina, and Mexico, mostly with Latin American investors and publishers. Just as in Spain the "support of the cultural public authorities"[26] was vital. Although a factory was built in Colombia in 1977 to supply also neighboring countries, in the early 1980s most output was still printed in Spain. In 1983, Círculo de Lectores was the second-largest publishing exporter in Spain. Economically, the performance of most Latin American clubs was disappointing. Only Colombia constantly earned net profits. Many countries were hit by high unemployment and inflation. Thus the import of books from Europe did not create sufficient if any yields. There were also problems with local managers and authorities. Bertelsmann began its retreat from the Latin American market in 1980.[27] The Circulo had 1.1 million members in 1975. In the early 1980s, when the concentration of the Spanish publishing sector started, Bertelsmann was one of the leading publishing and printing groups. In 1971 it had bought 50% of Vergara and in 1977 49% of Plaza y Janés, one of the most important Spanish publishers. As intermediaries, Bertelsmann used Printer Industria Gráfica and the Spanish instrument company Nadinver.[28] In 1982 Bertelsmann acquired 100% of Plaza y Janés again through Printer. This transaction required a permit by the Spanish government. Later, Bertelsmann expanded its position in the Spanish-speaking market through the acquisition of Debate (1994), Lumen (1997), and Sudamericana (1998), the largest Argentinean publisher.

The Circulo was headed by Arnold Schmitt from 1963 to 1976 together with a predominately Spanish team. In 1969, he thanked Mohn for the chance to receive from Gütersloh organizational knowledge, investment funds, and "constant improvements of my salary." At the same time there was no unwanted interference from headquarters and no "smart alecky corporate bureaucracy stifling" local initiatives.[29] Schmitt was succeeded by Gerhard Greiner (1976–1980), and Hans Meinke from 1980–1997. Meinke was born in Palma de Mallorca (Spain), went to school in Spain and attended university in Germany. In 2001 Fernando Carro took over. He was born in Barcelona, where he attended the German School. He then went to college in Germany, and worked within Bertelsmann for publishers in Germany and in Spain. In 2006 he became global head for all club activities. In 2010 50% of Círculo was sold to the Spanish publisher Planeta Group and Carro moved into Circulo's supervisory board.

Bertelsmann maintained the pattern set in the early Spanish and Latin American clubs, treating them primarily as local ventures rather than as "objects of cultural imperialism." As the annual report of 1979/80 put it, Bertelsmann set up "specific programs for each country," buying licenses from publishers of those countries and leaving "sole responsibility for the program ... with the editorial office in the respective country."[30] This made sense from a marketing point of view, but in Latin America, the number of licenses from national publishers was relatively small. In Europe, most licenses were indeed bought from publishers of the respective country.

Being local was essential for many reasons, including cultural acceptability. An extreme example of such a case was the founding of the club "Meilat-Moadan, Israel Letarbut" in Israel, where a German media company was viewed with understandable suspicion. It was founded as a joint venture with Keter Publishing (Jerusalem) in 1980, had exclusively Israeli management, and included Hebrew literature in its program. Yet the book club failed despite Bertelsmann's efforts to make the club culturally acceptable, though primarily for business rather than cultural reasons. It closed in 1988 because of two peculiarities of Israeli economic policy. First, the club was not allowed to sell its books cheaper than any bookstore and second and much worse, high inflation coincided with a price freeze on books.[31]

Given the geographical and cultural proximity, it is perhaps not surprising that the largest and most successful of Bertelsmann's book clubs was France Loisirs, founded in France in 1970 together with the large publisher Presses de la Cité, each partner having a 50 percent stake. Yet this venture also had its problems and got off to a shaky start: There was strong opposition from French book dealers and publishers, as well as internal problems, high debts, and a management crisis. As Bertelsmann reported 10 years later, "Although it looked as though the club did not stand a chance, it achieved a breakthrough under new, predominantly French management"[32] garnering 2.9 million members, 186 stores, and 300 million DM in sales by 1980. To be sure, Bertelsmann filled a number of key positions in the French club with French people, yet the claim of French predominance is exaggerated in this case, which, in fact, highlights another feature of Bertelsmann's corporate culture: entrusting relatively young managers with lots of responsibility. The club's general manager was Walter Gerstgrasser, an Italian from the German-speaking region of South Tyrol, who had joined Bertelsmann in 1970. After only nine months and in his mid-30s, he was put in charge of France Loisirs in 1971. The head of the program's department was another German, Karsten Diettrich. Gerstgrasser turned France Loisirs into the biggest (5.4 million members in 1992) and most profitable of Bertelsmann's clubs.[33] The fact that since 1981 French law allowed the club to offer its members a significant price advantage proved crucial. Gerstgrasser also used France as a springboard to other francophone countries. Clubs were opened in Quebec, Switzerland, Belgium but a campaign to reach out for Algeria in 1980 and then all of the Maghreb came to nothing. In 2001 Bertelsmann acquired 100 percent of the capital and sold the club in 2011.

In their heyday, the clubs had almost 29 million members in 36 countries. Like most Bertelsmann subsidiaries, they always had a strong local character, first of all in terms of the selection of book titles, but also—to varying degrees—in terms of management, political connections, and capital. The rules of the clubs were never uniform. Different legal requirements, book price regulations, as well as market and political conditions, required diverse solutions. As the examples above illustrate, many of the clubs started as joint ventures not only because of the family firm's notorious shortage of investment funds but also because it was seeking local knowledge and acceptance.

As for management, even the Germans in top positions abroad became locals in a sense. They stayed in their positions for a very long time and adapted to the culture of their new home countries. There was no systematic rotation of top personnel from one foreign subsidiary to another. Moreover, the down-to-earth culture of headquarters was continued in the subsidiaries, and experiential knowledge in local contexts was key. It required long tenures and the acculturation of deployed German managers as well as the integration of indigenous nationals. The Spanish example also demonstrates how becoming international coincided with staying local in a double sense, namely, remaining embedded in the home nation and even region and, at the same time, making extensive use of local resources in the host economy. Internationalization in this case amounted to a fusion of ownership advantages (especially the club model) and locational advantages (especially cultural and social capital, as well as political connections).

10.4   A "EUROPEAN-AMERICAN MEDIA COMPANY WITH GERMAN ROOTS"[34]: THE MAKING AND RUNNING OF RANDOM HOUSE

Bertelsmann began to pursue the internationalization of other parts of its business in the 1970s, focusing on its publishing. There were several reasons for the company to internationalize. One was a new barrier to further growth in Germany in two revisions of the antitrust law introduced by the Social Democratic–Liberal coalition that had come to power in 1969. Having made media concentration a highly sensitive political issue, the government implemented scrutiny of large mergers in 1973 and the strict supervision of press mergers from 1976. After Bertelsmann had bought Gruner + Jahr in 1972–1973, it had become one of the Federal Republic's largest magazine publishers. With the new government oversight, it became all but impossible for Bertelsmann to make any more major acquisitions inside Germany after the incorporation of Gruner + Jahr so that it stepped up foreign book and record clubs and began internationalizing its music business. Under the Ariola label, it set up subsidiaries in the Netherlands, Belgium, and Luxembourg (Ariola Benelux) in 1969, as well as in Spain in 1970, France in 1973, the United States in 1975, and Mexico and the United Kingdom in 1977. Other reasons to internationalize included the collapse of the Bretton Woods system of fixed exchange rates in 1971 and the oil shocks of 1973–1974 and 1978–1979, which caused inflation and unemployment to soar. Stagflation along with sharp swings in the exchange rates put a heavy burden on the international economy. In this context, it made sense for Bertelsmann to diversify geographically.

In 1975 Bertelsmann's publishing division comprised 25 firms and groups in Germany and one in Switzerland. The move of headquarters from

Gütersloh to the important literary marketplace Munich in 1972 and the restructuring of the division by the new head Ulrich Wechsler in 1975 were signs of growth to come. In 1977 Bertelsmann bought Goldmann, a major paperback publisher, and a couple of other German firms in the following years. The first major step abroad was again into Spain, by now familiar territory.[35] In the same year, 1977, the aforementioned 49 percent of Plaza y Janés was acquired. Later the same year Bertelsmann landed a major coup that propelled the company all of a sudden into the sphere of major international publishers. It bought a 51-percent stake in Bantam books, the world's largest paperback publisher, which was, while based in the United States, also active in Canada, the United Kingdom, Australia, and New Zealand, for an estimated $36 to $50 million. Bertelsmann had bought the shares from the Agnelli group (Fiat) along with a 30% stake in the Milan-based Fratelli Fabbri Editori.[36] There was no long-term strategic planning preceding this deal. While the contracts for Fratelli Fabbri Editori were being prepared, the Agnelli group mentioned that it wanted to sell Bantam too. As Wechsler reflected on the transaction: "Acquisitions can only be planned to a limited degree (. . .) Luck and chance play an important part."[37]

This unplanned acquisition of Bantam, in the end, turned out very well for Bertelsmann, but it could have been otherwise. Just as the theoretical literature on family firms suggests, personality and trust played key roles. CEO Reinhard Mohn's sensitivity and modesty, as well as the trust-enhancing family tradition of the company reaching back into the nineteenth century, helped the new business partners overcome initial suspicion to develop a good relationship.

Immediately after signing the contract, Mohn flew to New York to meet Bantam CEO Oscar Dystel and his managers, but the atmosphere was "icy," and they gave him "a harsh welcome." Reflecting on the encounter, Mohn attributed their coldness to the fact that Dystel was Jewish and saw in him "a representative of a murderous regime, one with the audacity to act like the owner of an American publisher." Mohn quickly realized that he would have to devote considerable effort to making the relationship with Dystel work: "We looked at each other. It was clear to me at that very instant that I'd have to ignore my calendar. . . . Over the next five days and nights, Oscar Dystel, his managers and I discussed matters. We became friends."[38] The two men discovered a lot of common ground. They had started making their names about the same time: Mohn had founded his first book club in 1950 while Dystel had taken over as Bantam's general manager in 1954. Mohn talked about his youth in Nazi Germany and his war experiences, including two years in a POW camp in Kansas from 1944 to 1946. He emphasized the fair and liberal treatment he had received there and the culture of individual responsibility he encountered among Americans, which struck him as a positive countermodel to the authoritarian traditions of his homeland and contributed to his enthusiasm about U.S. management methods.

The relationship between Dystel and Mohn was crucial to making the deal work. Many leading figures in New York's publishing industry were of Jewish descent, and objections to a German takeover and to Germans in general loomed large. The contact between Mohn and Dystel eased Bertelsmann's start in New York, although many objections remained in place. It also helped that Mohn trusted the existing management and initially refrained from sending over managers from Germany. Wechsler explained his company's hands-off approach in 1977: "I don't think it is necessary for one of us to go to New York. It is sufficient to pay regular visits and have talks . . . every six to eight weeks."[39] With the trust Mohn put in him and the two men's friendship, Dystel stayed on until his retirement in 1980.

As in the Bantam case, Mohn's personality and the family tradition of the company proved to be assets in initiating many of Bertelsmann's early deals during an era when the image of the "ugly Germans" was still vivid. In the late 1960s, Bertelsmann's first attempts to found a book club in France had failed, but a second initiative succeeded because, according to Mohn, he and Pressé de la Cité's CEO, Sven Nielsen, got along with each other. Having lived in France since 1924, the Danish bibliophile had experienced the German occupation and was married to a member of the French resistance. To be sure, Nielsen was certainly not the natural partner for a German who had fought in the Wehrmacht, yet the two developed a trusting relationship leading to "years of cooperation" that came to be some of Mohn's "most cherished professional memories." In Mohn's estimation, Nielsen had been "a reliable friend all those years" who had shown him "that contracts . . . have their place in professional life, but they cannot replace personal integrity, mutual trust and respect." Although the two drafted a detailed contract, Mohn noted, "never once" did they have to refer to the agreement.[40]

By 1980, when Bertelsmann bought the remaining 49 percent of Bantam, the company's publishing division had made great strides in internationalization, with autonomy and local knowledge and connections proving to be vital components in the process. More than half of turnover, which had skyrocketed from 81 million DM in 1971–1972 to 634 million DM in 1980–1981, was generated abroad. Now in possession of 24 separate publishing houses, 5 of which were located outside of Germany, the company reorganized the publishing division into several subdivisions that reported to the division headquarters in Munich, although the operation units remained in the respective countries. As long as the imprints met their financial targets, they enjoyed a high degree of autonomy. Bertelsmann recruited managers locally or simply retained the previous management, foregoing the systematic exchange of foreign for German managers in order to capitalize best on local knowledge and connections—most of all, personal relations to literary agents and authors—that were and still are so crucial to the business.

Bertelsmann's internationalization of publishing from the late 1970s onwards differed strongly from the expansion of its clubs in the 1960s. In the earlier period, Bertelsmann had aimed for organic growth with modest investments, building up businesses from scratch in many countries. In the later period, by contrast, it made capital-intensive acquisitions that brought about huge leaps in growth. After such purchases, it took the company several years to regain liquidity and credit before it could take its next major step as it paid for them partly out of its free cash flow, bank credits, and bonds, only issuing its first bond ($200 million) in 1986.[41] After acquiring the remaining 49 percent of Bantam in 1980, Bertelsmann had to wait until 1986 to buy Doubleday and Dell/Delacorte for an estimated $475 million and then until 1998 to take over Random House for an estimated $1.4 billion.

Each of the acquisitions increased Bertelsmann's overall size, which improved its economies of scale and scope but also gave rise to high restructuring costs. With the acquisition of Doubleday and Dell/Delacorte in 1986, Bertelsmann became the second-largest publisher in the United States and was able to merge the logistics, distribution, and administration of its U.S. publishing and printing operations. The acquisition made Bertelsmann strong in both the hardcover and paperback markets, which meant it could contract for both with authors and coordinate its advertising accordingly. In negotiations with agents, authors, booksellers, and other publishers, increased size meant increased leverage. On the other hand, the restructuring included replacing most of the management of the newly acquired firms by Bantam, selling off Doubleday's chain of bookstores and its printing plant, and sharply curtailing its publishing program. These steps were necessary because the rising advances paid to star authors and the high discount for chain retailers had cut into profits.

The purchase of Random House (founded 1925–1927) in 1998 then made Bertelsmann the largest publisher in the world. With 23 percent of the world's trade books—nontechnical books for general readers—and $1.8 million in revenue, it was double the size of the next largest house, Simon & Schuster. This merger took many Americans by surprise, "rais[ing] the usual outrage about media concentration, with a dose of cultural xenophobia thrown in."[42] One factor contributing to the furor was the Jewish origin of many authors and publishers; some of the acquired imprints like Pantheon (founded in 1942 in the United States) and Schocken (founded in 1945 in the United States), in fact, had been set up by exiled Jewish publishers. Also originally a Jewish family company, Alfred Knopf (founded 1915) has been part of Random House since 1960.

Despite the company's tremendous new size—and its commanding presence in the U.S. book market since its acquisition of Bantam in 1977—Bertelsmann was virtually unknown outside the industry, primarily because it kept using the brand names it had acquired. In a decentralized structure, it simply made no sense to push a strong umbrella brand. Thus, although Bertelsmann acquired a staggering number of imprints, it did not institute a sweeping policy of consolidation and centralization. While general functions like distribution, finance, marketing, production, and rights management were centralized, the individual imprints enjoyed a high degree of editorial autonomy, even though some restructuring and mergers of subdivisions and imprints occurred.

This strategy was not surprising, given Reinhard Mohn's vision—already outlined in a speech in New York in 1978—of how to structure a huge media concern, which stressed the need to preserve the comparative advantages of small, localized structures:

> The assessment of literature and contact with authors are tasks which only a handful of finely-attuned persons can master. The . . . advantages of a large company are of little use for such work. On the contrary, we find out again and again that the routine of a large company inclines to suffocate the creativity needed for the editorial work. In part, this inability . . . can be attributed to the easily comprehended fact that extremely sensitive and creative staff do not find the necessary working requirement in large companies. . . . [T]here is also the flaw that the feedback of market experience which is so necessary for the development of the powers of judgement . . . is not felt with . . . sufficient intensity in a large company. . . . [L]iterature . . . must take national characteristics into account . . . , so that the possibility for international cooperation turns out to be very limited. . . . For the same reason we can observe . . . that . . . professional know-how . . . stops when it comes to the frontiers of a country.[43]

The builder of a giant corporation was singing the gospel of the small firm. In fact, he aimed to combine the advantages of size, economies of scale and scope, with the flexibility and creativity of small and medium-sized enterprises. In plain words, Mohn highlighted the importance of proximity to markets, the strength of small units, the crucial role of human resources with local knowledge, and the cultural sensitivities of media products.

After 1998, Bertelsmann then folded Random House and Bantam Doubleday Dell into one firm. The integration of procurement, sales, and distribution alone brought tremendous economies of scale and scope. A warehouse was built that had space for 100 million volumes and could handle deliveries of 1 million books a day. Although Bertelsmann generally maintained and respected the individual imprints, it did subject the new publishing operation to massive streamlining. Prior to the deal, Random House's performance had been disappointing, despite its outstanding reputation for literary quality.

Around this time, Bertelsmann developed a new corporate image, presenting itself as a "European-American media company with German roots,"[44] and took a number of steps that accorded with this. In 2001, it renamed its *Book AG* book division *Random House* and transferred its headquarters to New York, not least because North America now accounted for 71.6 percent of its sales. Even the company's German-language publishers (8.9 percent) had to report to New York from that point on. The decision to use the name of an acquired company for the book division again reflected Bertelsmann's principle of decentralization, yet it also hinged on marketing considerations: Random House is a global brand name recognized in different cultures and does not reveal German ownership at first glance. It also appointed former banker Peter Olson as the CEO of Random House in 1998 and adopted International Accounting Standards (IAS) in 2001 in accordance with the company's new self-description.

Yet Bertelsmann's "European-American" claim was greatly exaggerated. No other division transferred its headquarters abroad, and the corporate center remained in Gütersloh. The relocation of the book division was exceptional and due to media producer's indispensable need to be close to authors and customers.

At first glance, the relocation of the book division appears to conform to Mira Wilkins's sixth stage of internationalization, when foreign subsidiaries grow more independent and a polycentric structure emerges. But, in fact, the theory that subsidiaries start as puppets on the string of the mother company and only gradually take matters into their own hands does not play out in the case of Bertelsmann, where the subsidiaries had a high degree of independence from the start. Yet, the philosophy of decentralized leadership did not grant divisions and subdivisions total autonomy. They had to coordinate their policies with Gütersloh and—above all—to deliver satisfactory financial results. Without them, these subsidiaries or their top personnel sooner or later disappeared, and literary traditions per se did not count much.

Whenever imprints missed financial targets, Bertelsmann suspended the principle of nonintervention with individual divisions. Prior to the acquisition of Random House, when Bantam Doubleday Dell had been in the red, Gütersloh had taken stringent measures, appointing Peter Olson CFO, who later became CEO of Random House. Perceived as an "outsider" and a "numbers person," Olson had implemented a severe cost-cutting operation and sold or closed down all units but the core book business. He did not, however, "interfere with the creative side" of this business but employed a hands-off strategy that, as he explained in an interview, was linked to financial performance: "If they meet their financial obligation to the company, they will have autonomy."[45] In fact, Bertelsmann made a point of finding top managers from outside the publishing industry. Another example was Jack Hoeft, the CEO of Bantam Doubleday Dell from 1989 onwards, who was brought on board from Coca-Cola. According to Olson, Random House took a "financial approach" to the book world. People in the trade with a more traditional, literary outlook saw in him "some kind of demonizing pariah."[46]

At the same time, in line with Mohn's vision, literary traditions were important as long as they helped the bottom line, so insiders with a literary background were also needed. Ann Godoff, a kind of star in New York's literary scene, attracted authors to Random House by paying mammoth advances, such as $5 million to Salman Rushdie. When she failed to match those advances with sufficiently big sales, Olson fired her in January 2003 and merged her division (Trade Group) with another (Ballantine), which dismayed many observers. Immediately after Godoff's downfall, Penguin offered to build up her own imprint, Penguin Press, and about 30 authors followed her, which again underlines the importance of personal resources in this business.[47]

Five years later, Olson himself left when Random House was not performing as well as it should have. Between 2006 and 2008, sales had declined by 11.6 percent and profits by 24.7 percent.[48] The book clubs Columbia House und Bookspan that had been acquired in 2005 performed disastrously and were sold in 2008. On top of this, the financial crisis of 2007–2009 set in.[49] The new CEO, Markus Dohle, restructured Random House by merging five subdivisions into three. About 350 jobs were cut. After stagnation in 2009, the availability of 20,000 e-book titles in 2010 helped usher in a considerable rebound in sales and profits. Considering the structural problems publishing in general is now experiencing, Random House has a very strong market position. Since 1998, Random House has garnered 18 Pulitzer Prizes and a long list of National Book Awards. In 2009, it put out 15,000 new titles and sold 500 million books worldwide. In 2011, Random House comprised more than 120 editorially independent imprints and publishing companies in 19 countries whose books are sold in almost every country in the world.

10.5 CONCLUSION

These two case studies of the internationalization of Bertelsmann divisions have demonstrated clear limitations to the Uppsala and the Wilkins models. Neither in the club nor in the publishing business were exports the starting point. In accordance with the models, however, Bertelsmann, used the domestic market as a training ground, only crossing national borders after finding successful business models in Germany and then hitting upon obstacles to further domestic growth. It skipped the models' export phase, mainly because books are culturally sensitive products and the German-language market is too small. The size of language markets also help explain why Bertelsmann's internationalization pathway did not start in neighboring countries but in Spain, with access to the giant Spanish-language market. Another reason was that entry barriers to the English-speaking world market were much higher. In the developing Spanish market, a newcomer like Bertelsmann with little capital could hope for success.

A factor completely missing from any of the models that also played a role in Bertelsmann's choice of Spain was opportunity, and sometimes mere chance. The "network extension pathway" did not contribute to it at all. Neither family members nor long-serving employees set up foreign subsidiaries. Relatives were either not interested or not capable, and long-serving employees were not available in sufficient numbers as the company was growing so fast. Instead, Bertelsmann entrusted young ambitious managers from Germany, the host country, or third countries with this task. The only family member who played an active role was Reinhard Mohn, who opened doors by building up strategic friendships and personally supervising the first subsidiaries and selecting their managers.

Contrary to what Wilkins's model predicts, the subsidiaries enjoyed considerable independence from the start as Mohn favored a decentralized structure. The result was ample leeway for foreign subsidiaries but definitely not a polycentric corporation. Overarching strategic decisions remained the prerogative of Gütersloh. When financial returns were disappointing, decentralized units regularly hit upon the limits of their freedom, experiencing intervention, reorganization, an exchange of managers, or even disinvestments, as was the case in Latin America.

The family-owned and -controlled structure of the company neither inhibited nor fueled internationalization. It set financial constraints but did not lead to risk aversion. The family always had the power to withdraw capital from the company but they minimized dividend payouts for decades, thus helping growth and internationalization. However, both might have been even faster had Bertelsmann opened itself up to capital markets. In this respect, the usual growth restrictions of family firms remained in place.

Despite the enormous international scope of its operations, Bertelsmann remained a German company in terms of its top management and capital structure. On the second and third level of the corporate hierarchy and structure, there was much more multinationalism. Joint ventures made the injection of foreign capital—often necessary for legal and/or monetary reasons—possible. In most cases, Bertelsmann conceded only minority shares to outside investors, limiting outside power over the subsidiaries and shutting out external influence on the Bertelsmann holding apart from 2001 to 2006. Bertelsmann, thus, has always remained a true family firm.

Top management remained locally grounded in Germany and Gütersloh, but the managers of the several hundred foreign subsidiaries were, likewise, locally grounded in their respective countries. Local knowledge and connections, legal and political restrictions were of paramount importance, so the top foreign managers were often recruited within the host countries, immigrated into the host countries for good, or came from families with mixed nationalities.

Although local managers did not always produce the desired results and manifest conflicts between the center and the periphery occasionally erupted, the local-grounding approach worked overall. Mohn's entrepreneurial vision encouraged people to try out their ideas. His belief in decentralization and his promotion of initiatives from below precipitated an impressive growth dynamic. For him, becoming global and staying local was no contradiction at all.

NOTES

1. This contribution is based largely on Berghoff, 2010.
2. Johannes Mohn (third generation) was the son-in-law of Heinrich Bertelsmann (second generation) and took over in 1887 because Heinrich had no surviving sons. Friedländer and Bühler, 2002, 26–34.

3. Berghoff, 2013.
4. Penrose, 1959.
5. Johanson and Vahlne, 1990.
6. Wilkins, 1974, 416–422.
7. Casson, 1999. Puig and Fernández Pérez, 2009. Berghoff, 2006a. Lubinski, 2010.
8. Australian family entrepreneur, quoted in Graves and Thomas, 2008, 163.
9. Casson, 2000. Kogut and Zander, 1993. For a summary of this literature, see Casillas, Acedo and Moreno, 2007, especially 73–93. Fernández Moya, 2010.
10. See Lubinski (this volume.)
11. Berghoff, 2001. Berghoff and Spiekermann, 2010.
12. Markovits, 2000.
13. Graves and Thomas, 2008, 162.
14. See Gupta (this volume.)
15. This was not exceptional even among large German firms. Daimler-Benz had no foreigners on its executive board until 1997 and no foreign shareholders until 1972. Grunow-Osswald, 2006, 454–455.
16. Bucerius's shares had been inherited by the Zeit Foundation in 1995 and were bought back between 1999 and 2003. Lindner, 2010.
17. Gallo and Sveen, 1991.
18. Bertelsmann AG Annual Report 2009 (English version), 25 and 33.
19. For similarities with Unilever, see Jones, 2002.
20. *Bertelsmann Illustrierte* 1962.4, 4–5.
21. Ribera, 2008. Lokatis, 2010.
22. This section draws heavily on extensive information provided by Maria Fernández Moya. I am very grateful for her kind and open cooperation.
23. Nicolás Surís Palomé (Vergara's CEO) bought 160 shares on behalf of Vergara; Juan Pujol Borotán and Pedro Pararols Riere bought 19 each. *Archivo General de la Administración* (Alcalá de Henares, Madrid), Culture Section, Instituto Nacional del Libro Español, *Registro de empresas editoriales*, Box 60; and information provided by Unternehmensarchiv Bertelsmann AG (hereafter UA BAG).
24. Ibid., and Constitution Writing, July 20, 1962; Notary: José Vall Serrano, Protocol: No. 2952 (Barcelona).
25. UA BAG 0006/63, Letter Mohn to Schmitt, July 6, 1967.
26. Bertelsmann AG Annual Report 1979/80, 26.
27. Bertelsmann AG Annual Report 1980/81, 27–28, and UA BAG, Memo by Andreas Knura, "Die Clubaktivitäten von Bertelsmann in Lateinamerika 1967–1993."
28. Letter from Plaza y Janés to the General Manager of Book and Libraries, Nov. 30, 1977. *Archivo General de la Administración* (Alcalá de Henares, Madrid), Culture Section, Instituto Nacional del Libro Español, *Registro de empresas editoriales*, Box 6.
29. UA BAG 0046/69, Letter Schmitt to Mohn, Dec. 30, 1969.
30. Bertelsmann AG Annual Report 1979/80, 26.
31. Bertelsmann AG Annual Report 1978/79, 13 and Lokatis, 2010, 161.
32. Bertelsmann Report 1980/14, 10.
33. He remained at its helm until his death in 1992. See Lokatis, 2010, 162.
34. *Bertelsmann Management News* 64 (1998): 4.
35. There had been small subsidiaries in Austria and Switzerland prior to 1977.
36. Füssel, 2010. Greco, 1997, 64–72.
37. "Interview Ulrich Wechsler," *Bertelsmann Report* 101 (Oct. 1977): 5–12, 6.
38. Mohn, 2009, 71–72. See also UA BAG 0046/513, Letter Mohn to Dystel, Oct. 31, 1982. This friendship is not mentioned in *Reminiscences of Oscar*

Dystel, 1986. Transcript of an interview, Columbia University, Oral History Research Office, American Entrepreneurs Project, RLIN number NXCP88-A113. It confirms the initial conflict and Mohn's visit.

39. "Interview Ulrich Wechsler," *Bertelsmann Report 101* 1977 (Oct. 1977): 5–12, 11.
40. Mohn, 2009, 69–70.
41. Berghoff, 2010, 40–43, 49–53, and 58–49. *New York Times*, Sept. 27, 1986, and Mar. 24, 1998.
42. *Time Magazine*, Apr. 6, 1981. http://www.time.com/time/magazine/article/0,9171,988089,00.html (retrieved March 25, 2013)
43. UA BAG 0007/692, Lecture Reinhard Mohn at the German-American Chamber of Commerce in New York, Jan. 14, 1978. See also Füssel, 2010, 114–119.
44. Bertelsmann Management News 64 (1998), 4.
45. All quotes from *New York Times*, July 20, 2003. http://www.nytimes.com/2003/07/20/magazine/20RANDOM.html?pagewanted=1 (retrieved March 25, 2013).
46. Peter Olson, quoted in *New York Times*, July 20, 2003. http://www.nytimes.com/2003/07/20/magazine/20RANDOM.html?pagewanted=1 (retrieved March 25, 2013).
47. *New York Magazine*, Mar. 26, 2001, and July 20, 2003. http://nymag.com/nymetro/arts/features/4506/ and http://www.nytimes.com/2003/07/20/magazine/20RANDOM.html?pagewanted=1 (retrieved March 25, 2013)
48. Bertelsmann AG Annual Report 2007, 26, 66, and 2008, 52. Exchange rate effects and the general downturn of U.S. consumer spending were among the causes.
49. Olson also had serious health problems in 2007. *Buchmarkt*, May 8, 2008.

Part IV
Inside the Family

11 "This Sad Affair"

Separation, Sentiment, and Familism in a Nineteenth-Century Family Multinational

Andrew Popp

11.1 INTRODUCTION

Distance and geography can have profound, unsettling effects on people's lives. The relevant management literature has treated psychic and cultural distance as an effect in international business, particularly in Multinational Enterprises (MNEs). But what of emotional distance—of affect—in international business? This chapter explores that question through the case of T. E. Thomson and Co., a nineteenth-century British family MNE. It will examine experiences of death, romance, and dispute in the early history of the firm. All organizations carry an emotional charge, but family firms might be considered particularly emotionalized arenas. But if that is so, then they might also provide the opportunity for distinctive responses to this emotionality. The case suggests a reconsideration of where we draw the boundary between the "family" and what we might call family-like effects in the family firm; just as emotion spilled over from the family to inundate the firm, so it also spilled over the family, strictly defined, to sweep up nonfamily members. In turn, responses to difficulties, whether of family or nonfamily members, were colored by family-like qualities.

In exploring emotional distance, I build on the psychic/cultural distance concepts only obliquely. The psychic/cultural distance concepts assume that the expatriate employee takes "home" along in the form of ingrained prejudices, norms, values, and behaviors, creating a distance manifested in apartness from the immediately present "host" environment—creating the possibility of dissonance. Reconciling home and host cultures requires adjustment and learning on the part of the expatriate individual.[1] Failure or difficulty in adjusting can lead to negative consequences that impact firm performance. With emotional distance, it is instead precisely the problem that the expatriate cannot take home with her. She is bereft of home emotionally, as she is physically. For family members of family MNEs, overseas postings not only mean separation from "home" as an abstract constellation of national cultural values, norms, behaviors, and institutions but also separation from the hearth of the family home and the web of affective relations that encircle it. It is in some ways a sacrifice of family to the family firm.

This separation can be of real consequence for both family and firm and is a dilemma unique to family firms.

A further unique aspect of the emotional dimensions of family firms may be their ability to develop family-like relationships and affects that encompass more people than those defined as family members by birth or marriage, a familism created as a further layer to the emotional dynamics of the family firm. This familism appears as an extension to and is inseparable from the "familiness" of the family firm.[2] It is a style or approach to relationships that grows out of the firm's rootedness in family. One obvious familistic relationship created in family firms, especially perhaps family MNEs, is that of *in loco parentis*. Fathers and fathering will run through this story; a father "unmanned" by the death of his son, the firm stepping in as father to an errant employee, and to act as a stern seat of paternal authority.

This chapter does not build constructs. Emotions will always overspill and elude any construct we erect to contain them. Despite their universality, emotions are, in the experiencing of them, always unique, idiosyncratic, contingent, and inseparable from particular concrete relations. They are lived out and need to be studied as such with an emphasis on the particular and the fine-grained, directing us towards the methods of microhistory. Thus, having surveyed the literature and introduced the case firm, we will explore three separate vignettes that brought the emotional life of the family MNE to the fore. The first of these involved the death in India of John Shaw, the eldest son of John Shaw, the principal founding partner of T. E. Thomson and Co. This event seemed to threaten the very survival of the firm for reasons both financial and emotional. The remaining two vignettes are lighter—one involved an employee making an unsuitable match among the expatriates of Calcutta, the other an employee disputing his salary—and highlight how the familiness of the firm created a style of familism that was evoked during moments of high emotion.

11.2   EMOTIONS IN FAMILY FIRMS AND INTERNATIONAL BUSINESS

It is only recently that emotions in family firms have begun receiving sustained attention.[3] Emotions in the context of MNEs and international business have hardly been considered at all. All organizations and the lives they contain create, magnify, and distort emotions, but family firms are often emotional arenas of a particular tenor and intensity. Brundin and Sharma, who, quoting Coleman, define emotions as "feelings and their 'distinctive thoughts, psychological and biological states, and range or propensities to act,'" have conceptualized the emotional dimensions of family firms as resulting in "emotional messiness" (EM).[4] EM is the product of the family firm's hybrid nature, resulting from the combination of two incompatible systems (family and firm), and underpinned by generalized mechanisms of *psychological ownership* and *psychological contracts*. The effects of EM are mediated by the "emotional intelligence" of key actors, thus determining whether messiness produces positive or negative "familiness." Thus, the EM construct remains firmly located within the well-known "familiness" concept, which posits that family firms possess a unique set of resources and capabilities generative of either advantage or disadvantage.

A related conceptual development within family business studies is that of "emotional ownership" (EO), as proposed by Nicholson and Björnberg.[5] Though drawing on extensive qualitative empirical work, this concept, like that of EM, draws on universalized psychological models (in this case, of attachment and identification) in combination with a belief in the distance between family and firm as entities belonging to essentially separate systems. As with the EM concept, EO is psychological in orientation and concerned with illuminating "the psychological processes that are encompassed" by the family firm.[6] Both models are then psychological rather than emotional and, to an extent, aim to provide a toolkit with which emotions within family firms can be managed or even harnessed. This is a tidy version of messiness. Emotions are to be controlled. Barbara Murray, for example, identifies an "emotionality-rationality dilemma" and claims that this "uneasy marriage of emotionality and rationality [can be] managed through the ability of the family to communicate."[7] Finally, the treatment of emotions in family business heretofore tends strongly to be ahistorical and acultural. Increasingly, work in the history of emotions is revealing the extent to which, instead, the experience of emotions shows profound variation across time and space.[8]

Discussion of emotion within the international business literature is largely restricted to work concerned with cultural distance and, in particular, expatriate reactions and adjustment to international assignments.[9] For example, Leung et al. note that "we do not know much about how emotional antagonism against other cultural groups affects trade patterns and intercultural cooperation in a business context."[10] There is an interesting subtext here; as in the family business literature, "emotion" often appears to function largely as a synonym for "unreason." Emotions are dangerous, and responses to them should be directed towards their management. Gabel et al. even argue that technical skills are less important to the success of international assignments within MNEs than "the ability to control emotions."[11] Messiness is again corralled within the orderliness of construct building and rational, reasoned management. However, if social scientists are uncomfortable acknowledging the emotional complexity of international business, then managers, with their depth of firsthand experience, are all too aware that the emotions involved are not only those of accommodation to an alien culture but are also those of grappling with separation from affective bonds. As one senior MNE manager reported to Gabel et al., "Our screening cycle includes accounting for emotional balance of people who are outside of their environment *and* away from their families."[12] Another informant concluded that what "often prevents people from adapting is their fear or their homesickness. They miss their family and friends . . . and that can happen in New York, in Sydney or in La Paz."[13] As the last sentence hints, emotional difficulties in international business may result as much from the sheer fact of separation as from the typical focus of the literature: the degree of cultural distance experienced.

A combined reading of the emotional messiness/ownership and cultural distance/adjustment literatures might suggest family firms possess a particularly striking positive advantage of familiness in dealing with the problems of overseas postings and careers in that their typically strong emotional bonds provide the commitment and emotional stability necessary for successful adjustment. However, such a reading remains trapped in a mechanistic and reductive conceptualization of the relationship between firms, families, and the separation that internationalization necessarily implies.

Emotions in family firms require reconceptualization. In part, this means an historicization of the subject. The family business literature treats "family" as an almost entirely unproblematic concept. It does not often ask what is meant by "family," or whether that meaning is shared between or even within nations and cultures. It does not ask whether or how the meaning of family might have changed over time; thus, it (along with much business history writing on family firms) ignores the extremely extensive literature on the history of the family, a literature that documents considerable change over time, even within single cultural settings.[14]

At the same time, we have doubts about the assumed universality of the psychological models that underpin work on emotions in both the family business and international business fields. Historians are naturally attuned to difference, context, and contingency; generalizability always butts up against the specific and particular. There is an ongoing dialectic between continuity and change, the local and general, structure and agency. In response, we adopt a view of emotions as subtle, complex, experiential phenonema that are historically situated and thus filtered through the "emotionologies" of their day. Emotionologies, a concept developed by Stearns and Stearns, refers to the standards and norms that surround a given emotion (e.g., romantic love) in a society at a particular point in time.[15] Emotionologies filter, mediate, and help express underlying emotional experiences. They have the advantage of being much more readily available to the historian than lived emotional experiences, which are necessarily transient, ephemeral, and unrecorded.

The microhistorical approach, with its double movement between the micro and the macro, the particular and the common, seems promising for the historical study of emotions in given situations. In putting this microhistorical method to work, we use personal and business correspondence as our primary source (buttressed with extensive business archives). Letters are typically used in relatively straightforward ways by business historians (i.e., as unproblematic statements of fact), though Boyce's recent study of business cultures in one firm is a notable exception.[16] However, letters are subtle literary creations, and they are increasingly read as such by historians working across a number of fields but particularly in family and gender history. Especially relevant to our study are David A. Gerber's studies of immigrant letters and those "interpersonal relations, by which interaction between family, kin, and friends are maintained and regulated by correspondents in the absence of opportunity for physical proximity and conversation."[17] Thus, it is important to heed his warning that we be alert to "what is not made explicit, and is hidden or held back, and the untruths that are told, in historical personal correspondence" and that "the weighty emotional context of this correspondence does not necessarily dictate transparency in immigrant letters." Equally, we note his characterization of nineteenth-century transatlantic families as "rendered especially vulnerable by separation."[18] Crucially, Gerber talks of the "many unanticipated sources of continuity in [the] emotional needs" of the immigrant adrift in a strange and foreign land.[19] Still, as Stott's work shows, many nineteenth-century families were able to survive and persist through the pressures imposed by separation and often did so through correspondence.[20]

11.3   T.E. THOMSON AND CO.

T.E. Thomson and Co. was established in Calcutta, India, in 1834. Named after its first manager, Thomas Edward Thomson, the firm was the creation of the parent partnership of Shaw and Crane. John Shaw and Henry Crane had been in business since 1815 as partners in a hardware factoring firm based in Wolverhampton in the heart of the bustling Black Country industrial district, to the north of Birmingham. Prior to forming the partnership with Crane, which was to last until 1848, Shaw had been in business on his own account since 1805, having begun his working life as an apprentice around 1800. John Shaw died in 1858, but the firms he founded, John Shaw and Sons and T.E. Thomson and Co., both survived him to become independent multigenerational family firms, retaining that status until the late twentieth century. During their long histories, the conjoined firms underwent considerable geographical and sectoral diversification, a process arguably sparked by the events of 1834. Though not well known, John Shaw and Sons/T.E. Thomson and Co. were extremely long-lasting family MNEs.

The status of the firms in relation to each other and as a multinational family firm requires clarification. T.E. Thomson and Co. was nominally independent but was entirely the creation of Shaw and Crane, very largely controlled by them from England, and almost certainly also very largely owned by them (surviving contracts demonstrate that Thomson ran the Indian concern as a direct employee of Shaw and Crane). Though somewhat unlike other examples of the type, particularly in the social, economic, and geographic origins of its promoters, as well as in its aims and activities, the firm is best thought of as a free-standing company. It was created for the specific purpose of furthering and extending Shaw and Crane's ongoing Indian trade via a shift from an export mode to a business model based on a combination of import/export and retailing, founded on direct investments in assets in India; in its early years, at least, it did not have even a nominal United Kingdom presence separate from the offices of Shaw and Crane. As noted, business correspondence reveals that though Thomson necessarily had some discretion (e.g., in his purchases of goods for return to England), Shaw and Crane attempted to retain as much control as possible. This tight linking of ownership and control between the two nominally independent firms cements the combined operation's status as an MNE, as it owned and controlled assets in more than one country. In time, Thomson and Co.'s operation grew very considerably in geographic scope, first in the "Country trade" across Southeast Asia, via third-party merchants, and eventually by way of offices in Australia, South Africa, and elsewhere.

Shaw and Crane was organized as a partnership. John Shaw, the older man, had first established the business, and Crane had initially worked for him as an employee. Shaw was decidedly the senior partner and held the largest stake in the firm. He had married in 1813, and his wife Elizabeth played a very important if informal role in the firm. She kept an eye on the warehouse and its operations when John was on selling trips, liaised with Crane, passed information to her husband, dealt with some remittances and debts, and on occasion met clients, both at Wolverhampton and on her own journeys to see her family in Lancashire. Her work for the firm would probably now be entirely invisible were it not recorded in the many private letters she wrote to John. As Eleanor Hamilton has argued, women's contributions to entrepreneurial family firms are often vital but neglected in historical and family business research.[21] There is no doubt that John depended very heavily on Elizabeth for practical, moral, and emotional support. They were in business together and recognized this situation as a means to nurturing the life of their family.[22] At the same time, John was frequently alone at home: his letters reveal him shouldering much of the burden of childrearing and other domestic matters, such as employing and monitoring servants, tending to produce grown in the garden, and purchasing items for the family home; he operated very comfortably in the supposedly feminine domestic sphere. The Shaws' family and business lives were intimately and intricately bound together.[23]

John and Elizabeth started a family soon after marrying. Their first child, also John, was born in 1815, followed by Thomas in 1818, Elizabeth in 1819, Edward Dethick in 1821, Mary in 1823, and, finally, Richard in 1827. Thus, John Jr. was nineteen and being readied for entry into the firm in 1834, the year the Indian business was launched. For example, a letter written by Elizabeth to her husband in the summer of 1834 records how Crane had left their eldest son in charge of some business matters over the previous two days and clearly invested great trust and responsibility in him: ". . . yesterday he gave him a long invoice to write that has taken him till today at noon . . . he [John] was by himself most of the time yesterday and this morning [the warehouse] was quite deserted—He found Mr Crane's keys left in his drawers."[24] Though John Jr. was to meet a tragic death in India in 1839, transgenerational succession was handled successfully; the firm of Shaw and Sons had been entirely passed to the next generation prior to John Shaw's death in 1858. The archives contain no explicit discussion of succession, but there seems to have been a clear intent to ensure the continuation of the firm beyond the individual life cycle.[25] Indeed, the next generation proved more than able to take the firm forward in its development and, despite adopting limited liability status in the late 1880s, it remained an independent family business until the late twentieth century. Our study catches the firm during its transitions from a simple partnership located solely in the domestic economy to one that was both multinational and much more clearly oriented around the Shaw family.

John Shaw had been in business for nearly thirty years before launching the Indian concern. His approach to business, which he often found a trying, worrying world, might be characterized as steady and cautious. He perfected routines and took no more risks than were inevitable for a concern whose stock in trade was buying and selling, much of it on credit. He was suspicious of relying on others and looked to God and Providence for protection. Crane was brought into the business as a known and trusted lieutenant but does not seem to have injected a greater dynamism. Indeed, Elizabeth Shaw, though she liked Crane, also thought him a dilettante when it came to work, which he seemed to view almost as a plaything. In this context, the move to India seems surprisingly out of character, but, in fact, it too followed a cautious evolutionary path, embarked upon in 1827 when Shaw and Crane received a letter from Sheffield-based correspondents offering them the opportunity to begin an export trade to India. They took this opportunity, doing steady business over the next few years, though all of it relied entirely on a network of third parties such as merchants, shipping agents, and London acceptance houses. This trade carried some risks—of cargos lost at sea or remaining unsold at their destinations—but was as hedged about as possible, betraying John's characteristic risk aversion.

The world of Anglo-Indian commerce was engulfed in tumult in 1830 following the collapse that year of leading Calcutta-based merchant house Palmer and Company.[26] Amid the intricate ties of credit, patronage, and dependence knitting together the English merchant community in Calcutta lay a fatal weakness, so that by 1834 all other British firms in the city had followed Palmer into bankruptcy. It was into this vacuum that Shaw and Crane stepped with the formation of T.E. Thomson. We have elsewhere analyzed this move from the perspective of both a stages model of internationalization and as an example of the making present of entrepreneurial opportunity.[27] No doubt, these perspectives help shed light on the *process* of internationalizing the firm and on what was thus *created*. However, *motivations* remain more obscure. In this context, it is revealing to highlight family life cycles and demographics.[28]

By 1834, John was a middle-aged man. It seems counterintuitive that he would embark on a risky new adventure at this stage, having achieved a degree of comfort and even security. However, he (and Crane) had a family of boys coming to maturity. These conditions may have rendered him willing to accept a limited, controlled degree of risk exposure in order to forge a vehicle to take his sons' careers forward. The result was a decisive move into multinational business.

11.4   SEPARATION IN AN EARLY NINETEENTH-CENTURY FAMILY FIRM

The Shaw family was inured to separation. During courtship and throughout his marriage to Elizabeth, John had undertaken regular selling journeys that took him away from home for extended periods of time.[29] On the tenth anniversary of their marriage, Elizabeth calculated that she and John had spent fully four years of that span apart. Moreover, John's peripatetic work had brought him a bride from far away. When she married, Elizabeth left her family in Lancashire to move south to the Midlands. But she worked hard to maintain the bonds with her birth family through correspondence and frequent visits home. Separation and its emotional burden were built into this marriage and the entrepreneurial life that supported it from the outset; the letters between John and Elizabeth are full of a yearning ache for what is absent. Family offered the necessary bulwark against the demands placed on it by the family firm.

However, in turning to the experience of the early pioneers of international family business, it is important to recognize the historical context within which separation occurred. Available transportation and communication technologies imposed a terrible burden of delay, uncertainty, and outright peril. For Shaw, Crane, and Thomson travel time—whether for humans or letters—between England and India was a minimum of three months. One simple exchange of letters took six months to complete. Hitherto, business historians have been largely concerned with the impact of such elongated lines of communication on the ability of early MNEs to maintain meaningful, sustained control over subsidiaries. But we must bear in mind also the very real isolation imposed on expatriate employees. Thomson was the first to bear the brunt of this isolation. Letters to him from home are full of business concerns, naturally, but they are also solicitous of his well-being and happiness. Crane in one letter to Thomson relates a Sunday evening gathering at home in Wolverhampton and supposes "you sometimes think of us. How soon have half a dozen years past [sic] away," displaying a sympathetic imagining of Thomson's experience.[30] Perhaps he hoped it would provide the consolation of fellow feeling. Yet he also reveals a sense of surprise at the elapse of time, acknowledging that the separation must seem near permanent; half a dozen years already. Time apart was measured in years, decades, rather than weeks or months. On another occasion, Crane expresses his regret to Thomson that he had not had "an opportunity of seeing your young ones."[31] What is left unsaid in this straightforward message has great poignancy. International business imposed the most painful separations on servants, friends, and family.

For John and Elizabeth, during the early years of their partnerships in life and work, a deeply affectionate and loving marriage had provided the framework within which separation could be faced and coped with. Internationalization via the vehicle of T. E. Thomson, in which some key actors were not family by either blood or marriage, presented a more complex picture. However, as we shall see, John, Henry, Elizabeth, and the others were able to draw on their own earlier experiences and practices in order to exercise a broadened familism that extended to a care for nonkin members. In some senses, the firm was then a synonym for the contemporary household, which made space for both kin and nonkin, such as friends, lodgers, and servants, as part of a single affective unit.[32] Though terribly, almost irrevocably, separated, the members of this unit remained tied by bonds far stronger than those of pecuniary self-interest or collective profit maximization.

11.5 THREE VIGNETTES: DEATH, BETROTHAL, AND DISPUTE

There is no more profound and disturbing emotional experience than bereavement. Prolonged separation may have imposed its own burdens, but this was nothing compared to the tragedy that befell the Shaw family and firm in 1839. John had always shown a cautious and risk-averse approach to business, and he extended that attitude to the Indian "adventure." In his response to the first letter to make its way back to England from Thomson in Calcutta, he betrayed some excitement, admitting, "I do believe we have let open the finest field for commercial pursuits that we could have thought of," and yet tempered it thus: Thomson, he reported to Elizabeth, was "quite elated with success. Hope he may not be too sanguine. He has sent us orders which will amount to I should think six to eight thousand [pounds] but as this is such an unexpected sum I think it will be well to send about half for present."[33] However, the threat and peril posed by the venture into multinationalism proved to be much more direct and traumatic than the financial losses anticipated by John.

The story of the death in India of John and Elizabeth's eldest son at the age of twenty-four has a simple universal pull. We are struck by the difficulty and delay in communicating the terrible news. John's death was first reported in a letter from Thomson dated 10 November 1839 that did not survive. John appears to have become ill and died over a very short period in late October. Thomson's letter was not received in England until late January 1840. The first known response is a letter from Crane sent on the last day of that month.

The impact of the news on family and friends at home can still be felt with great immediacy in Crane's fragmented, broken prose:[34]

> Your [letter] has spread gloom around. I scarcely know what to write to you, especially [as] Mr Shaw having by this mail addressed you . . . it is the worst blow that ever the Calcutta concern met with and when Mr Shaw will get over it I do not know. Since the receipt of the letter from you on 31st October last [and] also one from poor John of the same date he has done everything in his power for the Calcutta concern[.] what he will do in the [coming] months I cannot tell he is at present so unnerv'd that he scarce knows what to do, it is a most unfortunate affair, he was worth to you almost a piece of Gold of his own weight and had he been able to stand the climate it would I doubt not have been a capital thing for the concern.[35]

Shock, regret, uncertainty, and sadness are intermingled in a confused out-pouring. Crane vividly conveys the impact on the unnerved father and yet still flits uneasily between his own grief and a presiding concern about its impact on the concern. A future that had looked full of promise had been at a stroke rendered deeply uncertain.

Crane goes on to discuss the circumstances of John's death, which, though unclear in detail, are stark enough in outline. Nineteenth-century India was notorious for claiming expatriate European lives, and Crane's reference to the climate suggests that John was among this sad toll. Having presumably begun to show signs of illness and fever, he had quit the unhealthy conditions found on the coast at Calcutta for Meerut, in the state of Uttar Pradesh, where slightly cooler, cleaner airs might have been expected at that time of the year. Inevitably, decisions are reviewed, the possibility of responsibility, however painful, necessarily raised: "I do not blame anybody for the part they took in getting him out [of Calcutta] nor do I see any blame that can be laid for his going to Meerut it having decidedly a better climate than Calcutta."[36] Having tried to absolve Thomson of any sense of guilt, Crane continues his letter in what now seems an almost heartless vein: "the arrival of the next mail is look[ed] for with anxiety however he is gone and cannot be restored. I do not know what effect this may have." It is soon evident that Crane is simply doing whatever is necessary to stop a personal tragedy from sowing the seeds of a commercial disaster.

> One thing is quite clear that we must try to keep the concern all right during the [duration of] Mr Shaw's feelings on the late event, do not act in a hurry respecting the information he may have written you under excited feelings, but I know nothing of what he has said.[37]

Beyond the sense of John Shaw's pain that they convey, these lines reveal something important about the nature of control and decision making at this hybrid family firm/partnership. First, lines of communication clearly remained highly personal and far from coordinated or integrated. Both Shaw and Crane had written to Thomson, each without knowledge of what the other had said and possibly giving conflicting instructions. Whereas the circumstances were exceptional, the wider archives suggest that this practice was far from unknown. Although this might have caused confusion, there is a sense in which the informality of communications may also have proved a valuable safety mechanism. Reading between the lines, it seems that the elder John Shaw had been put beyond the power of reason and rational decision making. Crane feared what Shaw might have written and warned Thomson not to act on it. Organized as a "pure" family firm, with John Shaw as the sole principal, the Indian concern might not have survived this crisis. At the same time, if "familiness" was a weakness here, the elder Shaw simply too pained by the loss to function properly as a businessman rather than a grieving father, then a wider familism was activated as a substitute. Crane was almost a part of the Shaw family, with whom he had worked and socialized for very many years, and was able to write with decision *and* deep, heartfelt sympathy.

Still, part of the decisiveness required was to look to the future, and Crane returned again to practical matters:

> . . . send home all the money you can, you see Mr Shaw now says suppose Mr Thomson's life should sigh [expire?] what will become of us. I think you should make your will if you have not done so yet and also hand us a copy . . . and try to place us in the most [secure] position on this point for you must see it will be to the advantage of the concern for us to know in case of need what is likely to be done so we should not be thrown into confusion.[38]

John Shaw, in his stricken state, saw only the possibility of disaster piling upon disaster, against which Crane searched for protection. Crane ended his letter, the entirety of which amounted to a desperate attempt at containment, emotionally and practically, on the simplest of notes: "be sure [to] take care of yourself for that is of all the greatest importance."[39] Once again, the familism of this family firm surfaced to buttress its members against the emotional toll of separation.

The whole episode is most poignant. Moreover, the effects were to last for years. John Shaw clearly struggled to recapture his earlier excitement for and engagement with the Indian business, and his inertia appeared to threaten the business itself. In a letter of March 1840, Crane reported to Thomson, "I don't know when he [Shaw] will overget this sad affair and it will I fear make sadly against us in this concern."[40] As late as March 1843, Crane was forced to write to Thomson in the frankest possible terms:

> Your letter received last month though pretty stiff is scarcely stiff enough for Shaw has only put part [of an order received] in hand and at present

none of Griffin's hoes . . . you must continually keep pushing him on . . . I am very much vexed Shaw does not continue supplying as he ought to do but I cannot persuade him.[41]

If Crane was able to reassure Thomson that he was not to blame for what had happened, then perhaps John Shaw was unable to do the same for himself. The commercial ambition manifested through Thomson and Co. had brought success but also sorrow. Had the price paid simply been too high for John and Elizabeth, always both truly loving and devoted parents, to bear?

The loss of any child is a grievous blow, but the circumstances under which it came to the Shaws undoubtedly complicated its effects. First, the younger John died as a servant and agent of the firm's ambitions for overseas growth. It was that alone that took him to India and his untimely death. Second, it was that same service to the family firm that ensured he died so far from home, a point reinforced most movingly when Crane reported to Thomson that "Mr Shaw still continues [to be] trouble[d] about not getting John's things."[42] John and Elizabeth could not be with their eldest son as he lay ill, at his death, or at his funeral, nor even visit his grave. Their geographical separation provided a faint echo of a far wider emotional abyss. Absence in life was mirrored by a more profound absence in death.

Further evidence hints at how the Shaws' contemporaries, friends, and acquaintances readily accepted the inseparability of family and commerce and inward emotion and outward engagement with the world of industry and trade. In a letter to Crane penned in April 1840, just months after the loss of John, Ben Walton, a Black Country supplier to both Shaw and Crane and Thomson and Co., suddenly broke off from mundane business concerns to relate an experience he had had with the Shaws:

> We had visits from some of the principal ladies of the town and neighbourhood [to view a new line in furniture] . . . With the rest of the visitors we had Mr and Mrs Shaw who very much admired them, little did they think at the time that their son would never see them. Mr Shaw spoke with the greatest delight upon the pleasure it would be to his son to see so good a specimen of the manufactures of his native town.[43]

For Walton, it seemed natural to understand family, firm, manufactures, trade, and emotions such as delight, pride, and pleasure, as the inseparable interwoven threads of a single tapestry.

The crisis of John's death seems to have shifted a number of balances within the firm: Crane, who had once treated the business almost as a hobby, took a firmer grasp on Thomson and Co. as his partner retreated into prolonged grief. He was helped in this by the way in which the firm operated in a wider familistic framework within which the owners and managers continued to work sympathetically with the emotions of all those involved as they encountered the realities of an expatriate career. This was most starkly highlighted by the younger John's death, but examination of two less serious incidents demonstrates how this empathetic, affective style of management ran throughout every dimension of the firm's experience of internationalization.

If a son's death had underscored the centrality of fathers, fathering, and fatherhood within the family and the firm, then that aspect was mirrored in these further cases. Almost all we know of the first case is contained in a single letter from Crane to Thomson concerning the actions of Powell, a young assistant to Thomson in Calcutta:

> Yesterday I had a visit from Mr Powell in reference to your letter of the 10th of November. I had no intimation of its content till he arrived on Saturday night last, he is most completely knocked down by the contents of his son's letters which state more than perhaps even you were aware[,] in as much as he states his intention to marry the girl in January[.] he is quite silent about who or what she is and you do not state any thing in that respect. Mr and Mrs Powell are in great distress and the long time that must lapse before any particulars can be obtained makes them most unhappy. If when you receive this he is married there is an end to it[,] if he is not and you consider the connection improper please on my account do all you can to prevent it, if the girl is respectable and him to blame then do not interfere.[44]

Immediately striking is the extent to which the "long time that must elapse" in communications added materially and significantly to Mr and Mrs Powell's "great distress." This was an unavoidable reality of early international business until the advent of an effective global telegraph system from the last third of the nineteenth century onwards. In a later letter, the same Powell reminds Turner, a fellow employee, of the "nine years . . . [that] have elapsed since we both left England."[45] At that time, an overseas posting was probably best considered as being close to permanent emigration.

Subtler but arguably more important is the way in which the firm easily slipped into the role of acting *in loco parentis*. The firm, rooted in family, generating an operative sense of familism, was able to substitute for family. Realizing that they lacked sufficient parental authority themselves, Mr and Mrs Powell recognized in the firm a natural alternative locus of paternal stricture, and Crane reacted without surprise or reluctance to their understanding of the proper ordering of these relationships.

However, if familism could generate gentle paternal authority, then it could also, like "real" families, generate jealousy, spite, and even malice. When in 1849 a dispute over salary broke out between the aforementioned Powell and Turner, Thomson's replacement as head of the Calcutta business, we see a similar intermingling of relationships across the porous, overlapping borders of family, firm, friends, kith and kin, for which convenient, dichotomous oppositions are inappropriate. First, though, the case allows us to tie up some loose ends. At the heart of the dispute was Powell's sense of entitlement to an increase in salary that, as both men acknowledged, had been sanctioned by "Mr Shaw."[46] However, Turner felt unable to act "were I ever so much disposed to . . . until Estate [Thomson's] affairs are wound up and the books balanced."[47] This was written in 1849, three years after Thomson's death; Thomson had clearly failed to heed Crane's desperate pleas of early 1840 that he order his affairs so that the firm would be in a better position to meet any further calamitous events.[48] Also striking is the extent to which Thomson's personal affairs were bound up with those of the firm. In pressing his claim, Powell asserted that his current salary would "not feed my children's mouths, nor enable me to clothe them."[49] It seems likely that the marriage that had so alarmed his parents at home in England had gone ahead.

The details of the dispute (contained in an exchange of letters between Turner and Powell and one long, self-justificatory letter from Powell to his mother) are now unimportant. Powell appears to have been a difficult malcontent, Turner a high-handed and partial manager. More interesting is the relational framework within which what was, after all, a purely managerial issue was played out. Again, this was characterized by the extensive blurring of boundaries between families and firm. First, several of the young male employees lived and ate together at the business premises, providing a simulacrum of family life and, likely, a breeding ground for petty resentments.[50] Second, we have seen that Powell's desired increase in salary was sanctioned by Mr Shaw—Powell repeated this several times as though it were not simply a managerial decision but a more personal, and more valuable, dispensation from a paternal figure. Moreover, he claimed that Mr Kay, another young employee in dispute with Turner, had been given a promise that the firm would provide him with board and lodging by "Mr Shaw and Mrs S." The inseparability of firm and family in Powell's mind is clear, for Mrs Shaw had no formal role whatsoever within the business and yet he highlighted her promise as significant and meaningful.[51] This was a promise within a structure of emotional relationships rather than a structure of organizational authority.

Critically, it was to an arena of overlapping familial relationships, rather than those of organizational hierarchy, that Powell looked for a resolution of his problems. He had all his letters to and from Turner copied and sent them to his "dear Mamma" in England:

> [s]o that if Turner should dare to implicate me as having anything to do with Mr Kay's affairs . . . , then and not otherwise, I trust my father will wait on Mr Shaw with them and also this letter so that Mr Shaw may be able to judge after the plain statement I have made and from the tenor of my letters to Mr Turner whether I am guilty or not in the matter. I would at once have written to Mr Shaw, but was unwilling to intrude on his time.[52]

An expanded, emotionally loaded sense of family—what we have called here familism—remained the primary field within which these events played themselves out.

11.6 CONCLUSIONS

In their introduction to this volume, the editors note that "How families 'embed' the firm in its emotional strategies and generational life cycle and how firms can rely—or not—on family members is a major variable for understanding firm strategy."[53] This case exemplifies that claim. In some ways, what we have presented are only snapshots that in themselves resonate little beyond the obscure lives they briefly illuminate. Yet they demonstrate how the evolution and development of the family firm can never be divorced from the emotions of all of those brought within its orbit. Critically, those emotional entanglements, a complex admixture of sentiment and strategy, were made more complex by the experience of physical separation and emotional distance unavoidable for early family MNEs.

In a natural, unprompted response, the firm developed and drew on an expanded sense of familism that encircled kith and kin, friends and family, alike. Familism bound the firm, gave it strength and resilience, and both propelled the firm overseas and enabled it to cope with the very real trials it was to meet there. At the same time, familism bound members in a web of relationships that in demanding duty, debt, obligation, and honor could pull them in multiple, sometimes contradictory, directions. Family and familism were no simple boon to the ambitions of the nascent multinational. Nor were they a mere "resource" on which the firm could unproblematically draw. This chapter ends then with a simple plea: that we recognize the immediacy and complexity of emotions in family firms and acknowledge that separation did not simply attenuate those emotions but instead lent them even greater meaning and significance.

NOTES

1. Black and Mendenhall, 1991. Gabel, Dolan and Gerdin, 2005. Shenkar, 2001.
2. Habbershon and Williams, 1999.
3. Brundin and Sharma, 2012. Jenkins, Brundin and Wiklund, 2010. Nicholson and Björnberg, forthcoming.
4. Brundin and Sharma, 2012.
5. Nicholson and Björnberg, forthcoming.
6. Ibid.
7. Murray, 2002, 75.
8. Frevert, 2011.
9. Bonache, 2005.
10. Leung, Bhagat, Buchan, Erez and Gibson, 2005, 357.
11. Gabel, Dolan and Gerdin, 2005, 377.
12. Ibid., 387. Emphasis added.
13. Ibid., 388.
14. Popp and Holt, forthcoming-a.
15. Stearns and Stearns, 1985.
16. Boyce, 2010.
17. Gerber, 2005, 315.
18. Ibid.

19. Ibid., 317.
20. Stott, 2006.
21. Hamilton, 2006.
22. Popp, 2012.
23. Ibid.
24. Shaw Ms. No. 75, Elizabeth Shaw to John Shaw, 12 August 1834.
25. Owens, 2002.
26. Webster, 2005.
27. Popp, 2011. Popp and Holt, forthcoming-b.
28. Finn, 2010.
29. Popp, 2009.
30. DB/24/B/450. Assorted Correspondence, 1839–1846. Archives of T. E. Thomson and Co. Wolverhampton Archives and Local Studies (hereafter WALS). All Shaw and Thomson archives are publicly accessible.
31. DB/24/B/WALS.
32. Vickery, 2009.
33. Shaw Ms. No. 26, John Shaw to Elizabeth Shaw, 20 September 1835.
34. This and other letters cited in this chapter were written informally, often without regard to punctuation and capitalization. I have edited them lightly, adding bracketed punctuation, for reader comprehension but have left many errors uncorrected to give a better sense of the original documents.
35. WALS DB/24/B/450; Assorted Correspondence, 1839–1846.
36. Ibid.
37. Ibid.
38. Ibid.
39. Ibid. Thomson was destined to die in India.
40. Ibid.
41. Ibid.
42. Ibid.
43. Ibid.
44. Ibid.
45. DB/24/B/461. Letters between Powell and Turner, 1849. WALS.
46. Ibid.
47. Ibid.
48. Unsurprisingly, Powell was intensely frustrated: "Three years have elapsed next month since Thomson died and the books are not yet closed and for all I know it may be another three years before they are . . . [yet] the last conversation we had you said 'that although Mr Shaw had sanctioned an increase for yet you considered that the concern would not bear it without any reference whatever to the books being closed or not.' " Ibid.
49. Ibid.
50. Powell describes one employee, Mr Weston, as a "low bred meddling toady whose fawning flattery of Turner is his only recommendation." Ibid.
51. Powell goes on to say that "I think Mr Shaw will hesitate a little before he upholds Turner in his harsh treatment of Kay." Later in the same letter, he returns to the same point, asking "what think of that for the carrying out of Mr Shaw's words to Kay that everything should be done to make him comfortable." Powell seems to have placed real trust in Shaw's word. Ibid.
52. Ibid.
53. Introduction (this volume.)

12 Two Countries, One Home, One Occupation

Italian Ice Cream Parlors as a Family Business in Germany, 1900–Today[1]

Anne Overbeck

Whether as chimneysweeps, construction workers, or stonemasons, Italian migrants have been traveling back and forth between Germany and Italy for over a century. Italian ice cream makers and their family businesses, however, are the most numerous and prominent in the German public's perception. During the German *Wirtschaftswunder* or "Economic Miracle," a phase of intense economic growth, ice cream parlors sprang up in every German village and suburb. The *Eiscafé Venezia* was a standard element of the German business landscape and—with minor adjustments—has remained so up to today. Even though most Germans remember the 1950s as the period when Italian ice cream parlors were established in Germany, their history goes back much further. Since the middle of the nineteenth century, gelatieri have been selling their products all over Europe, especially in Germany. Some families have managed to maintain their businesses into the fourth or fifth generation.[2] Remarkably, over this extended period the trade succeeded in keeping over 80 percent of the ice cream parlors in the hands of relatively few families, all of whom stem from two small valleys in the Dolomites. Family and family networks, thus, have been extremely important to these businesses' success. Historian Sylvia Junko Yanagisako put it poignantly: ". . . labor is never abstract, but is always provided by people with particular social identities and histories."[3] This is especially applicable to the Italian ice cream makers as family and business life are almost inseparable for them. This fusion influences almost every aspect of their private lives, including their attitudes towards success and education, and even their leisure activities. It has enabled this group to keep a monopoly on the ice cream making business over many decades and to establish Italian ice cream as a brand name, but it has also restricted the next generation's career choices.

12.1 FROM PUSHCART TO PARLOR: THE ORIGINS OF THE ITALIAN ICE CREAM TRADE

The ice cream making trade was in many ways "born global." From the beginning, the gelatieri traveled to foreign countries and territories to sell their products during the summer, returning to their home villages during the winter.

Ice cream making is a family business (FB)—but a broader regional identity encompasses the FB that ties the Italian gelatieri together. Up to the present (2012), 80 percent of all Italian ice cream makers in Germany stem from two small valleys in the Dolomites in northern Italy—the Zoldo and Cadore Valleys. The trade can be traced to the mid-nineteenth century.

Until 1866, these two valleys belonged to the kingdom of Lombardo-Venetia, forming part of the Habsburg Empire. When the first ice cream makers left home to sell their product in other countries, they went to other parts of the Habsburg monarchy—to Austria and Hungary. Their business only made a profit during the summer months. During the winter, they returned to their villages and worked in lumber agriculture. Over the next several decades, the gelatieri spread further north and east. By around 1900, the first ice cream trolleys appeared in the streets of the Ruhr area in Germany, which was then booming because of the expanding steel and coal industries. At that time, selling ice cream was a mobile business for Italians. They produced ice cream at two or three central sites and then sold it via small pushcarts throughout the city. This system proved to be very efficient. Ice cream making required bulky, expensive equipment that was hard to obtain, and production was time-consuming and strenuous. Yet the few production sites managed to provide ice cream for an entire city. Usually, one family owned these sites and employed younger family members as vendors until they opened their own businesses in another city. At that time, ice cream making was an exclusively male business. Women and children remained at home in the villages in northern Italy. Only in the winter months were the families together.[4]

World War I stopped the business for a while, but by the late 1920s, the gelatieri had returned in greater numbers to Germany and the Netherlands. This time they converted their formerly mobile businesses into permanent ice cream parlors because new commercial restrictions and laws increasingly prohibited selling ice cream via pushcarts, for example, stipulating that ice cream could not be sold to children under the age of sixteen and forbidding pushcarts near schools and playgrounds.[5] In Vienna, one of the centers of the Italian ice cream trade at the turn of the twentieth century, ice cream carts were prohibited entirely on two grounds: Keeping ice cream cold enough had always been a challenge, so that buying ice cream from these carts always entailed the danger of catching paratyphus, today called salmonella. More important, local authorities intended the restrictions to protect German and Austrian businesses from the mobile competition. The regulations forced the gelatieri to find new business methods, with profound consequences for their families. The period of centralized production was over. The men who had previously worked as pushcart vendors now had to produce their own ice cream in their individual parlors. From this point on, the women joined their husbands, traveling north to work as waitresses and clerks in the parlors. The children, however, remained in Italy and lived with relatives.[6]

The 1930s—not the 1950s as is commonly believed in Germany—was the first great era of expansion for ice cream parlors in Germany.[7] Many families opened their first parlors in the Ruhrgebiet then because, not only had the

Figure 12.1 The Zoldo Valley, 1930s
© LWL-Industriemuseum Zeche Hannover, Bochum, Germany

Figure 12.2   Giovanni Martini in Recklinghausen, Germany, 1910s
© LWL-Industriemuseum Zeche Hannover, Bochum, Germany

economic crisis increased poverty in their home villages, but the political ties between Hitler's Germany and Mussolino's Italy made the two countries grow closer. Consequently, the split between Germany and Italy in 1943 was also a rupture for many gelatieri, whose businesses had prospered since the 1930s. Many parlors closed after the invasion of Italy; others were lost during the wartime bombing raids. Remarkably, the first gelatieri returned to Germany to reopen their business in wooden shacks or partially destroyed buildings just a few months after the end of World War II. Many ice cream making families had already planned to reopen their businesses when they left for Italy. They did not sell their inventory but stored it with neighbors to be ready to set up shop again as soon as things calmed down.[8]

The 1950s and 1960s were a period of intense economic boom in Germany, the so-called *Wirtschaftswunder* (Economic Miracle). This new prosperity allowed Germans to travel, leading to a surge in tourism—mainly to Italy and Austria. Italy was not only a popular holiday destination but was also glorified in numerous popular songs, movies, and journals. Together, prosperity and Italy's popularity allowed Italian ice cream parlors to succeed throughout Germany. The boom also caused many families who had been working in the Netherlands and Belgium to move to Germany. With almost every German suburb now having its own parlor, the Italian valleys of Zoldo and Cadore experienced a new wave of migration.[9] Ice cream parlors have grown less profitable since the 1990s, causing ever more families to close their parlors, but an astounding number (about 3,500 across Germany) were still up and running in 2009.[10]

Figure 12.3   Parlor of Giovanni de Lorenzo in Witten, Germany, 1960s
© LWL-Industriemuseum Zeche Hannover, Bochum, Germany

Family and family networks always provided the backbone for this growth and helped to bridge the "psychic distance" between the home valleys and country of business in many ways. First, families passed on production knowledge from generation to generation. After finishing school—around age 14—younger family members went abroad to learn the trade with their parents or close relatives until they could open their own businesses. Second, relatives also taught them local regulations and how to deal with local German authorities. Finally, family networks in the home valleys produced and exported almost all ingredients and other supplies, such as furniture and technological equipment: three of the four main suppliers were located in Zoldo and Cadore.[11] The employees at these suppliers were particularly important in setting up new parlors as they worked throughout Germany and could provide information about where ice cream parlors were still lacking. This knowledge about how to deal with the German authorities, how to buy store equipment, and where to open businesses gave the gelatieri from Zoldo and Cadore a competitive advantage over other Italians coming to Germany during this time. The tightknit network kept outside competition to a minimum.[12] Here, it is crucial to understand the importance of the valleys in keeping the system alive. Whereas the different families had little contact during the summer months, they lived next door to one another in the winter, when they coordinated the business in Germany. They discussed new businesses, gave advice on new parlors, and hired new apprentices. Often, these discussions occurred at family gatherings—weddings, funerals—and simply at the local bars. Trade fairs and other official meetings were of limited importance, which excluded competitors from other regions from participating in such decision making. The only official trade fair for gelatieri in Germany— one of the central annual events for gelatieri from Zoldo and Cadore—was established in the 1960s in Belluno, at the foot of the Zoldo valley mountains. It is held in late autumn, after most parlors close for the winter. Though it is open to the public, the fact that it is held in Italy signals the dominance of Italian ice cream makers from this region in the German market.[13]

12.2   IT STAYS IN THE FAMILY: THE ICE CREAM MAKING BUSINESS AND FAMILY LIFE

Family and family networks not only explain the long-lasting success but also the limitations of Italian ice cream parlors in Germany. What Silvia Junko Yanagisako highlights for family businesses in general also applies to the gelatieri:

> Family and kinship processes, relations, and sentiments are crucial for the production and reproduction of all forms of capitalism, whether family capitalism or nonfamily capitalism. Family capitalism, however, brings more clearly into view these processes, relations, and sentiments.[14]

Figure 12.4 Valeriano Lazzarin at His Parents' Parlor in Iserlohn, Late 1960s
© LWL-Industriemuseum Zeche Hannover, Bochum, Germany

The ice cream making business dominated every aspect of the gelatieri's family life. It helped determine one's choice of life partner, the schooling of the children, and how to fill leisure hours. The border between Germany and Italy and the seasonal migration kept the system alive over the decades.

Gender roles clearly influenced the trade. In the beginning, only men were involved. Yet when permanent parlors replaced pushcarts, women were needed as waitresses and financial and personnel managers; the children stayed at home and were raised by their grandparents.[15] Consequently, children and the elderly were the only inhabitants of the Italian villages in the summer. If no grandparents were available, children attended boarding schools. In the 1950s and 1960s, several schools were established that catered exclusively to gelatieri. In Zoldo, for example, a boarding school was founded in Zoldo Alto that was open only in spring and autumn and was used as a senior citizen center during the winter when the children were with their parents.[16]

Gelatieri were slow to adopt new gender roles and changes in business responsibilities. Traditionally, women worked as waitresses while men were the formal owners who represented their businesses to the outside world. Men also made the ice cream, at first because it was very strenuous physical labor, and later because it was family tradition. For instance, when the umbrella organization of the Italian ice cream makers in Germany "Uniteis" was founded in 1969, its members were exclusively men, all from the Cadore and Zoldo valleys. Until the late 1980s, the few women who ran their own shops only did so because their husbands had died. Today, 15 percent of

Figure 12.5   Valeriano Lazzarin at School in the Zoldo Valley, Early 1960s
© LWL-Industriemuseum Zeche Hannover, Bochum, Germany

Uniteis members are women, and women run and own 9 percent of the ice cream parlors in Germany.[17]

Not despite of, but because of, the separation of the family members for almost half the year family life stands front and center for many gelatieri. For the children, the summer separation from their parents guaranteed that they would have strong ties to the Italian villages. Until they started their first job, Germany was foreign to them, even though their family had worked there for decades. Also, one's choice of spouse was a choice for or against the traditional lifestyle. Of the 32 gelatieri we interviewed, 27 had married someone from the same valley (2 had divorced). The remaining 5 had married Germans. Germany had become their focal point, and their binational children went to German schools.[18]

It is indicative of the system's reliance on family rather than outside institutions that German as a foreign language is not part of the school curriculum in Zoldo and Cadore, although almost everybody in the valleys has worked in Germany at some point. Learning German at school in preparation for professional life was not considered necessary, as the family would fill that role when it became relevant, thereby tying the next generation's future in the trade to the family structure. Once in Germany, gelatieri rarely established closer ties to the new country, not least because they had no time. They worked during the summer months seven days a week, sometimes 10–12 hours per day, limiting their social environment to coworkers—who usually stemmed from those villages as well—and customers. There was

Figure 12.6   Grandparents and Children During the Summer, Zoldo Valley, 1940s
© LWL-Industriemuseum Zeche Hannover, Bochum, Germany

little spare time to build a social life in Germany, so many ice cream makers speak and write very little German, even though their families have been working in Germany for three or four generations.[19]

If Italy were not relatively close to Germany, the families would not have had the opportunity to maintain a strong tradition of back-and-forth migration. This makes this seclusion from the host culture possible and draws a strong contrast between the winters and the summers. Beginning in the 1950s, the income from ice cream parlors was sufficient for families to live off of year-round. Rather than take a second job in the winter, family members enjoyed family time as they reunited after a summer away. Weddings and baptisms were traditionally held in winter to allow all family members to participate.[20]

The contrast between the gelatieri's living conditions in Germany and Italy provides another indicator of their personal values. In Germany, many gelatieri live in small, barely furnished apartments with few personal effects or decorations above or close to their parlors. In their home villages, however, they build big, luxurious houses decorated with family photographs and personal furnishings.[21]

A key factor in understanding the gelatieri's work ethic is that they consider their trade to be artisanry, in contrast to other migrants who saw their jobs as transitional occupations or stepping stones to success in the new society. Families stuck with the ice cream trade as long as they could make a sufficient living. It was as much part of their identity as their connections to their home villages.[22]

This sense of identity also explained the skepticism or indifference many gelatieri felt towards traditional education. They did not value university education, as it would lead to an estrangement from traditional family ways. Many gelatieri children who pursued a different career recounted the difficulties of loosening family ties and working against their families' expectations. Not until the 1990s did a shift in the traditional lifestyle emerge. As parlors became less profitable, many in the younger generation were not willing to endure the stress of running their parents' businesses. Still, when interviewed, the young adults who chose a different profession feel they have to justify their decision.[23]

Family and kinship practices formed the basis for the long-standing success of Italian gelatieri in Germany. Seasonal, cross-border migration, lack of interest in life outside the ice cream parlors, and the separation of family during the summer guaranteed that the younger generation had strong ties to the Italian valleys and that the artisan tradition and family business continued. Yet these also prevented family members from moving up in society by pursuing a university education. They, likewise, inhibited the development of closer ties to Germany, which remained almost exclusively a work domain.

12.3 WORKERS' BARRACKS AND ICE CREAM PARLORS: THE GERMAN IMAGE OF THE ITALIAN GELATIERI IN THE 1950s AND 1960s

Family networks strongly influenced the durability of these businesses because they supplied knowledge, material resources, and staff. Yet the gelatieri's conduct of family life also had unintended but positive consequences for the way they were perceived, especially in Germany during the 1950s and 1960s.

The overwhelmingly positive image of Italian ice cream parlors is one of their surprising characteristics, especially when contrasted with the strong anti-Italian currents exhibited toward Italian "guestworkers" arriving in Germany at the same time. As previously noted, Germany experienced an economic boom—the *Wirtschaftswunder*—in the mid-1950s, spurred by the growth of heavy industries—like coal and steel—in the Ruhr area in North Rhine–Westphalia. By the mid-1950s, the German workforce was insufficient for these growing industries, which threatened to curb the boom. Accordingly, the German government signed a Recruiting Agreement with Italy in 1955, in which Italian "guestworkers" initially received contracts with limited rights and maximum two-year terms to work in Germany. Given the agreement's short-term nature, no integration and inclusion policies or special support structures were implemented. This prompted a sudden migration wave of young, mostly southern Italian men to Germany—right when the popularity of Italian ice cream parlors peaked.[24] The stark differences in the public perception of these two groups provide interesting insights into how Italian ice cream established itself as a brand.

In contrast to many other ethnic minority workers, Italian gelatieri did not cater to their own community but almost exclusively to the larger German population. For their economic survival—and, even more, because they were selling a product German confectioners had been making for decades—they needed a positive image. Four factors converged to enable Italian gelatieri to turn their product into a unique brand in Germany: the economic boom, the glorification of Italy as a vacation destination, the emerging youth culture, and the gelatieri's social isolation outside their parlors.[25]

After the currency reform of 1948, ice cream parlors opened up all over Germany—in city centers and suburbs, large towns and small villages. They became a meeting point for youth and a symbol of the nation's economic prosperity, which coincided with Italy establishing itself—alongside Austria—as a top vacation destination. This resulted in the glorification of all things Italian: the nation, weather, and people. Accordingly, many popular songs and movies thematized or were set in Italy. In this context, Italian ice cream parlors allowed Germans returning from vacation to relive their vacation memories at home and those left behind the opportunity to get a taste of the experience.[26]

In addition, the parlors provided needed meeting places for the newly emerging youth culture. Most youths were too young to gather in pubs, and parents disapproved of their visiting those places. Traditional German coffeehouses, by contrast, were too conservative and boring to catch young people's interest. Ice cream parlors, and also the milk bars popular at the time—modern businesses with long opening hours—filled the gap between the pubs and the traditional coffeehouses. A newspaper article from 1959 sums up the public image of these venues:

> Hot rhythms from the jukebox, teenagers with snappy haircuts and hip clothing . . . But appearances are deceiving. No, here no wild dance is planned, but rather boys and girls spoon from their delicious ice cream bowls quite properly . . . to entertain themselves quite decently and inoffensively.[27]

The parlors were a hybrid mix of hip meeting place and Italy, with Italians positively perceived. In interviews, the gelatieri described positive experiences with Germans. This seems astounding at first, as many of the Italian guestworkers who went to work in the coal mines or steel plants had rather negative experiences with the German population.[28]

Social position and family life distinguished these two groups. The gelatieri, as entrepreneurs and small business owners, occupied a higher social position and garnered more respect than the guestworkers, who were seen

Figure 12.7 Italian Guestworkers in Herne, Germany, 1960s
© LWL-Industriemuseum Zeche Hannover, Bochum, Germany

as part of the working class.[29] The different family life of the guestworkers and gelatieri, in turn, influenced their respective social environments, along with their leisure habits and activities. The gelatieri already had a stable if limited and confined social family network in the new country. During the summer, the employees often worked shifts of more than 12 hours, seven days a week. As leisure time was rare, they had very little contact with their German environment outside of work. Many guestworkers, by contrast, had no such family network. In the early years of the program, they were mainly young unmarried men who planned to work in Germany for a couple of years and eventually return to Italy. Clear-cut shifts in the coal mines and steel factories gave them ample leisure time. After work and on the weekends, they attended German bars and dance parlors or met friends at train stations or other public places. Thus, they were more visible and had a much stronger presence than the gelatieri. Discord erupted when guestworkers tried to meet young women at local dances, but gelatieri did not attend these events in the first place. Although the gelatieri interacted more often with Germans, these interactions were set customer-salesperson conversations. The guestworkers' contact with their German environment was more public and in less structured situations with more potential for conflict and misunderstanding.[30]

Above all, contact between Italian men and German women was frowned upon. Whereas songs and movies portrayed Italian men as romantic and temperamental, it was considered indecent to have actual contact with

Figure 12.8   Salvatore Fiore and His Wife at Their Parlor in Castrop-Rauxel, Germany, 1960s
© LWL-Industriemuseum Zeche Hannover, Bochum, Germany

Italian men, whether guestworkers or gelatieri. All the binational couples we interviewed talked about the complications and conflicts they endured within their families and at work at the beginning of their relationships. Ulla Renon's case is typical.[31] When she started dating an Italian ice cream maker from the shop next door, her employer scolded her for spending time with a *Spaghettifresser*[32] and insinuated that her boyfriend had negatively influenced her work ethic. Her father refused to meet her boyfriend and discouraged her from being seen with him publicly to spare himself the embarrassment of his daughter being an *Itaker Liebchen*.[33] The positive image of Italy and Italian men worked only when the two cultures kept a certain distance. When contact became too close, other stereotypes of Italian men as lazy, unreliable, and slovenly came to the fore.

In sum, the German perception of gelatieri was much more positive than that of Italian guestworkers. This positive assessment resulted from the social space the parlors provided and their representation of an escape to a romantic vision of Italy. It was only maintained as long as the Italians working there kept their distance from their German customers outside the parlor. The tightknit family networks and long working hours minimized contact between gelatieri and Germans and, thus, also helped distinguish them from Italian guestworkers and upheld the positive stereotypes about Italy that fostered the Italian-ice-cream-parlor brand.

12.4   BLURRING THE LINES: CHANGES IN THE TRADE, 1990–TODAY

Gelatieri are just one of many groups with a migration background who have come to work in Germany over the centuries—as seasonal workers, guestworkers, or permanent immigrants. Yet what sets the gelatieri from the Zoldo and Cadore valleys apart is the endurance of their lifestyle of seasonal work between Italy and Germany over more than a century and, in contrast to other seasonal workers, for example, in construction and stonemasonry, the prominent role they play in German public perception. Family and family ties lie at the heart of this long-lasting success and correspond to the large share of the Italian ice cream business held by a limited number of families.

The German public still has a very positive image of Italian ice cream parlors. The parlors boomed along with the German economy and coincided with Italy's heyday as a glorified vacation destination. The gelatieri used this general positive perception to establish Italian ice cream as a unique but decentralized brand, which has survived up to today. Nevertheless, outside of the parlors, encounters between Germans and Italians were difficult, as the conflicts with Italian guestworkers that came to Germany at the same time attest.

Since the 1990s, the gelatieri's traditional lifestyle has been weakening. Many gelatieri still stick to their traditional way of life, close their shops during the winter, and send their kids to school in Italy. But more and more families are now centering their lives around their businesses in Germany, not least because they can no longer afford to close for several months or employ seasonal workers while they are away. Also, cheaper flights and faster cars have made it possible for them to remain connected to their valleys through repeated short visits rather than season-long stays.

In addition, it has become difficult to recruit the next generation of gelatieri. Many young people are now severing their ties to the family tradition, seeking less strenuous, time-consuming jobs than taking over their parents' businesses. These days, other migrants—especially people of Turkish or Portuguese descent—are running many ice cream parlors. Italian ice cream as a brand remains strong, however, as these parlors still bear Italian names despite their ownership. Uniteis e.V. remains ambivalent to this development as it both ensures the survival and even the expansion of the Italian ice cream brand and risks weakening what defines and distinguishes it.[34]

The Italian valley anchor was essential to coordinating the family business abroad throughout most of the twentieth century. This literal "home base"—where international business decisions were made—provided the gelatieri from the Zoldo and Cadore valleys with a distinct advantage over competitors, which enabled them to monopolize this segment. The fraying family ties since the 1990s go hand in hand with a general weakening of the Italian ice cream making trade. The business is opening up to new contenders outside the family circle, as the younger generation of Italians from these valleys increasingly consider alternate careers. But for the remaining families, and there are still more than 3,500 across Germany, family and family networks still constitute the base of the trade.

NOTES

1. This chapter is based on research conducted in the context of an exhibition project for the LWL-Industriemuseum Zeche Hannover in Bochum in 2009. http://www.lwl.org/LWL/Kultur/wim/portal/S/hannover/Ausstellungen/.
2. There is little historical research on this topic, except by Dutch historian Frank Bovenkirk. In addition, Edith Pichler has conducted some studies on Italian ethnic communities, and the Organization of Italian Ice Cream Makers in Germany (Uniteis e.V.) has published some popular science articles. A book by Maren Möhring on ethnic food in Germany comparing Italian ice cream makers and pizza restaurants is in production. Bovenkerk and Ruland, 1992; Bovenkerk, 2004; Panciera, 1999; Pichler, 1997; Powell, 2005; Vio, 1999.
3. Yanagisako, 2002, 5.
4. Bovenkerk, 2009. Overbeck, 2009.
5. From the *Speiseeisverordnung* (ice cream regulation) of the city of Witten in 1910. In *Polizeiverordnung betreffend den Verkauf von Speiseeis*, Witten 1910, ULB Münster, 4*Ik-5372-5.
6. Campanale, 2009. Panciera, 1999, 5–12.
7. Almost all interviewed families had opened their first parlor in Germany in the 1930s, for example, Eiscafé Majer in Dortmund, founded in 1933, Eiscafé de Lorenzo in Witten, founded in 1930, and Eiscafé Pieruz in Dinslake, founded in 1938.
8. Interview by Anne Overbeck with Ezio Cordella, Goima di Zoldo, 2009; and with Gabriella Gamba, Forno di Zoldo, 2009.
9. The Dortmund yellow pages exemplify the fast growth of these businesses. Between 1951 and 1961, the number of listed parlors rose from 4 to 26; Stadt Dortmund: Adressbuch der Stadt Dortmund, 1951 and 1961.
10. Homepage of the Organization of Italian Ice Cream Makers in Germany (Uniteis e.V.), http://www.uniteis.com/pagine_de/uniteis_notizie.htm; interview by Anne Overbeck with Ezio Cordella, Goima di Zoldo, 2009; and with Gabriella Gamba, Forno di Zoldo, 2009.
11. Novarredo, the biggest supplier in northern Germany, was founded in 1959 by two former ice cream makers from the Zoldo Valley. In the south, two similar firms with owners from Cadore were established.
12. During our project, we found only one Italian parlor owner (out of 40 interviewed) who had originally come to Germany as a "guestworker" from southern Italy.
13. Interviews by Anne Overbeck with Ezio Cordella, Goima di Zoldo, 2009; Gabriella Gamba, Forno di Zoldo, 2009; Aduo Vio, Bochum, 2009.
14. Yanagisako, 2002, 13.
15. Panciera, n.d.
16. Schroeter, 2009.
17. Panciera, n.d.
18. Campanale, 2006, 34–52.
19. Ibid., 27–34. Interview by Anne Overbeck with Augusta Corte Levou and Maria-Theresa Mayer, Dortmund 2009.
20. Schroeter, 2009, 28.

21. During the project, we also traveled to the Zoldo Valley to conduct interviews and see the differences in the living situations between Germany and Italy. Schroeter, 2009, 27.
22. In 2009, the German Chamber of Commerce and Trade officially recognized ice cream making as an artisanal trade. The Organization of Italian Ice Cream Makers in Germany (Uniteis e.V.) had aimed for this since the 1970s to make the trade more attractive to the younger generation.
23. Several sociologists and behavioral scientists connect Italian parents' skepticism towards formal educational and state institutions to their children's lack of success at school, see, for example, Auernheimer, 2006, 67. Boos-Nünning, 1991. Diehl, 2002.
24. The continuing demand for workers prompted the German government to sign further Recruiting Agreements, in 1960 with Spain and Greece, in 1961 with Turkey, in 1963 and 1964 with Morocco, in 1965 with Tunisia, and finally in 1968, with Yugoslavia. From 1955 to 1973, about 14 million foreign workers were recruited to Germany. About 11 million went back to their home countries. The others remained in Germany permanently. In the following years, many brought their families to Germany; Rieker, 2003, 17–26.
25. Andersen, 1997, 65–117. Osses and Asfur, 2005, 7–15.
26. Stirken, 1998.
27. "Heiße Rhythmen aus der Musikbox, flottfrisierte und salopp gekleidete, 'Halbwüchsige' . . . . Aber der Schein trügt, hier wird kein, 'Ringelpietz' veranstaltet, sondern die Jungen und Mädchen löffeln recht gesittet aus ihren köstlichen Eisbecher (. . .) um sich in aller, 'Zünftigkeit' harmlos zu amüsieren." In "Eis a la Valentino ist bei den 'boys and girls' die kalte Mode. Ein ganzes Dorf macht Gelato," *Westfalenpost Iserlohn*, 23 and 24 May 1959.
28. Rieker, 2003, 53–63.
29. Overbeck, 2009, 12. Interview by Anne Overbeck and Katharina Vollmert with Salvatore Fiore, Castrop-Rauxel, 2009.
30. Overbeck, 2009, 12. Interview by Anne Overbeck and Katharina Vollmert with Salvatore Fiore, Castrop-Rauxel, 2009. Rieker, 2003, 83–99, 113–121.
31. Interviews by Anne Overbeck with Ulla Renon, Marl, 2009; with Giancarlo de Mario, Bottrop, 2009; interview by Anne Overbeck and Katharina Vollmert with Salvatore Fiore, Castrop-Rauxel, 2009.
32. Meaning "spaghetti-eater," this is a common derogatory term for Italian migrants to Germany.
33. This is a derogatory term for German women dating Italian men.
34. Panciera, n.d.

13 When Du Pont Entered Mexico (1902–1928)

How the Network Played the Game

Liza Lombardi

During the nineteenth century, Du Pont de Nemours expanded its activities throughout the United States mostly by supplying black powder, dynamite, and smokeless powder to the American government.[1] The company started to sell its products abroad at the beginning of the twentieth century, especially to the Canadian and Mexican governments.[2] By 1910, the company operated a joint venture in Canada with Nobel Industries[3] and owned a nitrate field in Chile that provided it with raw material.[4] During World War I, it supplied the British and the French with gunpowder and other explosives.[5] After the war, Du Pont entered into negotiations in pursuit of various international investment opportunities in China, Cuba, Chile, and Japan.[6] Concerning Mexico, the company received a variety of investment propositions, but, initially, none of them captured the company's attention.

Du Pont's most important Mexican investment opportunity was the buyout of an explosives company: the Compañia Nacional de Dinamita y Explosivos (CNDE), founded in 1901, which operated as a state monopoly. Although Du Pont was not initially interested in this investment, it did eventually purchase the company. In doing so, it dealt with a variety of actors: Mexican businessmen, American bankers, the former director of the company, and then with the new owner of CNDE, the Nobel France group. In all the correspondence remaining from these negotiations, Du Pont's presidents and members of the board, apart from Coleman du Pont, successively refused the offer to buy out the CNDE. They considered it fundamentally unsound: a judgment that was borne out by the Compañia's uninspiring performance from 1901 to 1915 and the factory's closure in 1915. In contrast, the Chilean and the Canadian investments, undertaken jointly with Du Pont's European competitors, were profitable from the beginning.[7]

It is therefore surprising, after all these refusals, that Du Pont decided to invest in Mexico in 1925 by buying the CNDE plant with the intention of reorganizing and reopening it. In this, Du Pont shared the governance equally with the American company Hercules.[8] With this Mexican and other foreign investments, Du Pont became a multinational in Wilkins's sense—that is, a firm that "extends over national borders to operate (to do more than export) under more than one national sovereign"[9]—at the beginning of the twentieth century.

In this chapter, I am interested in explaining how Du Pont made the decision to enter Mexico. I place primary emphasis on the company's status as a family firm. Du Pont can be considered a family firm from its foundation in 1802 until 1958: during this entire period, the family owned and managed the company, so it unambiguously fits Colli and Rose's definition of a family firm as one in which "the family owns enough of the equity to be able to exert control over strategy and is involved in top management positions."[10]

Indeed, Chandler and other scholars (Hounshell and Smith, for example) have demonstrated how the Du Pont family firm changed its structure, organization, and management between its foundation in 1802 and the 1920s: The company expanded its activities throughout the United States in the nineteenth century; then, in 1902, it underwent a complete reorganization, changed its structure, and improved its management. In 1921, Du Pont adopted what Chandler named the multidivisional structure, once again reorganizing its production and management activities.[11] But neither Chandler nor Hounshell and Smith considered another important turning point in the history of Du Pont: 1958. In this year, the last historical member of the family left the board of directors. By "historical members of the family," I mean Coleman (chairman of the Executive Committee between 1902 and 1915) and his cousin Pierre (chairman between 1915 and 1919), who were both behind the complete reorganization of the company in 1902,[12] as well as Pierre's brothers Irénée (chairman between 1920 and 1925) and Lammot (chairman between 1926 and 1939).[13] Coleman and Pierre are naturally considered historical family members because of the role they played in 1902. Pierre is also considered a historical family member, along with his brothers Irénée and Lammot, because of the influence they had over the Executive Committee and the board of directors. Table 13.1 presents the positions held by the Historical Family Members during five decades.

The Mexican investment took place during the period of international expansion still largely controlled by key family figures (between 1915 and 1928) and is, thus, characteristic of how investments abroad were negotiated and operated under the family's governance.

Table 13.1   Positions Held by the Historical Family Members During Five Decades

	Chairman Executive Committee	Chairman Board of Directors	Honorary Chairman of the Board
Coleman	1902–1915		
Pierre	1915–1919	1919–1939	1946–1954
Irénée	1920–1925	(Vice Chairman) 1926–1939	1954–1958
Lammot	1926–1939	1940–1947	

Source: By the author.

The executive functions of the du Ponts gave the family an immediate role in the strategic direction the company took, but my case study of the Mexican investment also shows that the family's network was decisive in encouraging the key family decision makers to move forward with the deal. In particular, the three brothers shared a network of wealthy and influential friends, the most important of whom were Charles Sabin, the president of the Guaranty Trust from 1915 and a representative of the United States in the International Committee of Bankers for Mexico; Dwight Morrow, a partner at J.P. Morgan & Co. who would become the American ambassador to Mexico in 1927; and Thomas Lamont, one of J.P. Morgan & Co.'s most important partners and the president of the ICBM from 1918. Lamont, in particular, had strong interests in Mexico and staunchly encouraged the brothers to invest there. The three of them maintained important relations with the du Ponts: they were together in a political union and intertwined via numerous boards (General Motors, Cuba Cane Sugar Company, and various banks boards). In the private correspondence of the three brothers, these friends were involved in numerous exchanges of letters of invitation to stay in the du Pont family mansion in Cuba, dinner invitations, congratulations for the children's studies, and so forth. Even the wives of these wealthy men wrote to the brothers to discuss both private matters and business affairs.[14]

I present the case study as follows: The first part of this chapter presents the political and economic situation of Mexico before the Mexican Revolution—whose first troubles arose between 1910 and 1915—and its aftermath. This will shed light on the climate in which the initial discussions within the Du Pont Company about entering Mexico took place between 1902 and 1915, which are considered in part two. The third part considers the years after the revolution in Mexico and the political and economic environment in which the investment would be finalized, between 1915 and 1928 (discussed in part four).

13.1 THE POLITICAL AND ECONOMIC SITUATION IN MEXICO (1876–1915)

During the dictatorship of Porfirio Diaz (1876–1911), the so-called Porfiriato, Mexican industries developed primarily by means of foreign investments made by foreign industrial enterprises, entrepreneurs, and financiers with whom Diaz had connections. One of the most important sectors developed under the Porfiriato was the railroad industry. As historians Stephen Haber and Noel Maurer note, federal funds were not sufficient to finance the development of the railway network; in this context, Diaz welcomed and favored foreign investments. As a result, foreign investors came to control most significant Mexican industries through monopolies. Large American and European oil companies, railway industries, mineral extractive firms, and chemical companies became the major owners of Mexico's natural resources. Soon, a feeling spread that foreigners were dispossessing the nation of its soil, sub-soil, and economic development. It was in this feeling that the revolution would take root[15].

In the chemical industry, the CNDE was the most important foreign chemical enterprise in Mexico prior to the revolution. The French Société Centrale de Dynamite along with some Mexican businessmen established CNDE in 1901 in Durango. The CNDE had close links to key figures in Diaz's retinue: Julio Limantour, the finance minister's son, and Porfirio Diaz Jr., the President's son, sat on the company board. Following the explosives company's inauguration, the Mexican government decided to tax all imports of explosives and the use of dynamite, but it exempted CNDE products. The explosives producer thus became a state monopoly. However, there was one significant problem: the monopoly's output only satisfied 60 to 80 percent of the Mexican army's demand for dynamite, so it had to import explosives from the United States that were subject to the import tax.[16] Effectively, therefore, CNDE, Du Pont, Hercules, Apache, Atlas & Giant, and a number of German producers supplied the Mexican army.[17]

In 1914, President Carranza, who held the presidency from August 1914 to May 1920, defended nationalism for Mexico. In this vein, he decided to abolish various privileges, taxes, and trade contracts established during the Porfiriato. Of particular relevance for the chemicals (or explosives) industry was Carranza's decision to abrogate the decree of February 21, 1905, which had established the consumption tax on dynamite and industrial explosives and to tax only imports of dynamite, powder for mining, piroxiline, and cotton powder ($0.12 a kilogram, net weight). In 1915, he further modified the taxation of dynamite, reducing the import tax to one-third of its original value ($0.04 a kilogram).[18] These changes had a profound and negative effect on CNDE's monopoly, resulting in its closure in 1915.[19]

After 1915, such nationalist tendencies continued to grow in importance. For example, whereas oil had been one of the major exports prior to the revolution, the 1917 Constitution made it clear that natural resources were no longer legitimate objects for foreign investment; soil, water, mineral resources, and oil were declared national and inalienable properties in whose development only Mexican citizens were entitled to invest (art. 27). Although the federal government could grant concessions to private or commercial societies, resources had to be developed in a sustainable way.[20]

Another consequence of the nationalist tendencies was the nationalization of the private properties and activities of landed elites. This expropriation had a powerful impact on foreign investors as it threatened their investments in the country; the revolutionary conditions made them much less attractive. Statistics on flows of foreign direct investment (FDI) in Mexico reveal a significant deceleration of foreign (portfolio and/or direct) investment in new plants and equipment, even though inflows did not dry up altogether. The Mexican Revolution also occasioned various difficulties for existing foreign investments in Mexico, including American ones. The revolutionary (and successive) governments tended to nationalize foreign assets across the Mexican economy, especially in extraction activities. For example, the American Smelting and Refining Company's loss during the period from 1910 to 1920 was estimated at $674,449.[21]

13.2 DU PONT'S INITIAL NEGOTIATIONS TO BUY THE CNDE (1902–1915)

Du Pont's initial negotiations to invest in the Mexican CNDE took place in this politically and economically troubled era for Mexico. Yet the existing literature barely explores these discussions. Historians Graham Taylor and Patricia Sudnick speak about the negotiations for the investment between 1902 and 1907 and attribute the termination of the negotiations to the New York stock market Panic of 1907.[22] Alfred Chandler and Stephen Salsbury, in their book on Pierre S., provide important information on the initial negotiations around this Mexican investment, but they consider only the early stages of these discussions and also end their account in 1907.[23] Although the literature on the internationalization of family firms suggests that family governance should not impede the multinationalization process,[24] Chandler and Salsbury suggest otherwise in their analysis of the early internationalization of the Du Pont Company. In their view, the family link between Pierre and Coleman du Pont, cousins and chairmen of the board, was not of any help during the negotiations but actually hindered the process. Pierre had a very important influence on the board and knew that the members of the Executive Committee viewed him, as Chandler and Salsbury demonstrate, as their natural leader. When Coleman, during his chairmanship, was fighting to sell the idea of this investment in Mexico to the board, Pierre, treasurer by this time, actively gathered the board around his own view that investing in Coleman's project in Mexico would be uninteresting and unsound.[25] Finally, in general accounts of American investments in Mexico, notably the work of Mira Wilkins, there is no information on Du Pont's Mexican investment at all.[26]

In this section, I contest what Chandler and Salsbury claim about Pierre S.'s position in the initial negotiations. I also add information about this early stage of the Mexican investment from archives that were not available to Chandler and Salsbury in 1971, notably the archives of the CNDE. I then describe how the negotiations continued after 1907 using these now available primary sources.

Coleman du Pont, during his chairmanship, envisioned taking the company abroad. He was the only one on the board who really considered entering Mexico with an investment in the CNDE: he found the proximity and CNDE's tax-protected monopoly very enticing. Moreover, as the company was partly owned by the Société Centrale, head of the Latin group, Coleman hoped to arrange an entente with them to build a mammoth chemical company by merging the American group and the Latin group.[27]

Coleman entered into negotiations with José Yves Limantour (the Mexican finance minister) and P. Martinez del Rio (a prominent Mexican businessman) about a possible exchange of stock with a view to sharing control of the CNDE, or the potential outright purchase of the company to gain full control of it. In 1904, Coleman met Siegfried Singer, director of the Société Centrale, in St. Louis. The two businessmen shared the opinion that joining the American and Latin groups' efforts would make for interesting bargaining with the Anglo-German group. In the beginning, Pierre was not completely opposed to this idea. With John J. Raskob, the financial director of Du Pont as well as a close friend of the du Pont family, Pierre came to Paris and met with Singer and Limantour Jr. and considered various proposals: Du Pont could supply the west coast of Mexico until the railroads were built, or Du Pont could buy 10,000 of 14,000 shares and then control the CNDE. This agreement held great appeal for Coleman.[28]

However, Pierre feared that both the Latin group and the American antitrust lobby would react negatively to this deal. Furthermore, he did not want to enter Mexico because it seemed to him that the Mexican monopoly had not attained the results that the French and Mexicans had hoped for when they created it in 1901. Indeed, the Annual Reports of the CNDE demonstrated that between 1901 and 1905, the monopoly failed to make a profit, resulting perhaps from organization and setup costs and/or from two devastating explosions. In addition, it had insufficient capital such that, as company directors noted, financial reorganization would be essential for the production of explosives to continue being a going concern in Mexico. The directors would need some bankers' assistance. Finally, they admitted that the problems encountered in the production of explosives in Mexico and the distance between the directors and the plant made the management of the company difficult.[29]

Pierre and the other members of the board were aware of CNDE's poor performance and of the potential illegality of the trust with the Latin group. Consequently, they did not see anything positive about going to Mexico. Pierre influenced Barksdale, Haskell, and others rather easily. In fact, according to Chandler and Salsbury, he was the only person who would have been able to gather the board around Coleman, but he did the opposite instead.[30] This divergence between Coleman and Pierre marked the beginning of Coleman's alienation from the board. He was finally expelled from it in 1915 and sold all his company shares back to the family holding company, Christiana Securities.[31]

13.3   THE MEXICAN POLITICAL AND ECONOMIC CONTEXT (1915–1928)

In Mexico, FDI recovered quickly after the revolution largely, as Table 13.2 shows, as a result of the new foreign investments in the petroleum industry. By contrast, foreign investment in mining and extracting activities decreased

Table 13.2 U.S. FDI in Mexico, Selected Sectors/Years in Million USD

Total			Manufacturing			Petroleum			Mining and Extracting Activities		
1914	1919	1929	1914	1919	1929	1914	1919	1929	1914	1919	1929
587	644	709	10	8	6	85	200	206	302	222	248

Source: Wilkins, 1974, 31–55.

but nevertheless remained important relative to other sectors, whereas FDI in Mexican manufacturing, in particular, remained negligible.

Developments in FDI in these sectors (oil, mining, extracting, and manufacturing) after the revolution must be understood in the context of the financial events between 1918 and 1923 and the role of the International Committee of Bankers for Mexico (ICBM) in dealing with the Mexican sovereign debt crisis. The primary stated objective of the ICBM was to help to resolve the Mexican debt crisis. From 1914, Mexico was in default on its debt to American investors and to the American government. Indeed, the United States had invested more than $1 billion in the country since the end of the nineteenth century and, as already noted, American companies' investments in Mexico were threatened by the wave of nationalization. The American government was especially concerned about the future of American oil corporations' investments there.[32]

The ICBM was formed in 1918 with the support of the American State Department and the British Foreign Office. Thomas Lamont, who had become a partner at J.P. Morgan and Co. in 1911, was its president, and Charles Sabin was one of its members. Both men were friends with the du Ponts. Sabin's wife was in close contact with Pierre's, and, furthermore, they all were together in a political union and sat on the same boards.

Lamont was concerned with defending the interests of the more than 200,000 small bondholders who had taken on the Mexican debt when it was contracted in 1899. As a Morgan partner, Lamont had to defend the stability and prosperity of these securities and the repayment of the debt.[33] Historian Alan Knight holds that Lamont's position on the ICBM implies that he took on a sense of responsibility for the evolution of the relationship between the Mexican and American states, particularly between 1918 and the 1930s.[34]

In 1920, Adolfo de la Huerta became the Secretary of Finance and Public Credit. Thus, he traveled to New York in 1922 to meet with Lamont, Sabin, and the other members of the ICBM to negotiate the recognition and repayment of the Mexican government's debts. The *New York Times* referred to this event as the first step toward Washington's official recognition of the Mexican government. De la Huerta, representing the administration of then president Álvaro Obregón, recognized the debt ($500 million—split between debt to private interests and the U.S. government) and interest for servicing the debt ($280 million). He also negotiated a repayment schedule, which was to begin in 1928 and continue for a period of forty years. In the agreement, Lamont obtained the promise that the government would use oil taxes to establish a $30-million fund to cover the costs of servicing its debt. In this way, Lamont aimed to ensure the ongoing operation of American (or all foreign) oil corporations operating in Mexico. The Mexican government's recognition of its foreign debt also generated a substantial need for government funds. Mexico, with a relatively weak economy, thus had to appeal for FDI to be able to repay its debt.[35] But according to the table above, FDI did not go up much between 1919 and 1929. In return for recognizing its debt, the Mexican government gained official recognition in 1923 under the Bucareli Treaty, although the congresses of both countries never signed it. The ICBM did not participate in these negotiations but was indirectly involved in the preliminary talks about it.[36]

13.4   WHEN DU PONT ENTERED MEXICO (1915–1928)

It was in the mid-1910s that negotiations to acquire CNDE resumed at Du Pont. Around this time, Pierre received a number of invitations from American entrepreneurs to invest in Mexico. In 1916, he was courted to make investments in gold mining as well as in financial services among other propositions in Central and South America. Yet he refused categorically to enter into discussion of any of these investment opportunities without providing any explanations. Du Pont's finance director Raskob and Irénée received proposals as well but gave the same kind of terse responses as Pierre saying that they were not interested.[37]

Nonetheless, the possibility of acquiring the CNDE was revived between 1915 and 1916 with letters Pierre received from Charles Sabin. The banker introduced Tomas MacManus, a banker and Mexican official (Member of the Mexican Chamber of Deputy), to Pierre. Sabin recommended MacManus and supported his proposal to the chemical group. To Sabin, it was important (though the reasons were unclear at that time) that Pierre view investing in Mexico and in the CNDE as an opportunity that could become profitable over time. For his part, MacManus seemed to have close contact with the French director of the CNDE and knew that he was thinking of selling the company to Du Pont and thus giving the American group "the full control of the market for explosives in the Republic of Mexico," as he wrote to Pierre in March 1916.[38] In the same letter, MacManus acknowledged that the political situation in Mexico was not satisfactory but that order would eventually be restored and lead to large-scale resumption of business, "especially in mines and railway construction . . . requiring explosives in like proportions."[39] Pierre replied to MacManus that this proposition had been made "several times" to the American company but that it was not possible for Du Pont to consider entering Mexico because of the unattractiveness of the Mexican market.[40]Sabin and Lamont, working with the ICBM, of course, hoped that the economic conditions of Mexico would improve.

At the same time, although American government officials discouraged Du Pont, it was already apparent that the Mexican government was growing more open toward American investments in general. In 1916, the American Secretary of War Newton D. Baker advised Pierre to stop exporting ammunition and explosives to Mexico because of the risk that they could be used against American people or interests.[41] In November that same year, Calderon, the Du Pont branch office manager in Mexico, wrote Pierre about the "inimical attitude" the Mexican government displayed toward the chemical group and hoped it would disappear.[42] On the other hand, in June 1919, Pattuson, a Du Pont official, wrote Irénée, then president of Du Pont, that, according to local experts, Carranza's government was apparently favorably disposed toward Du Pont.[43] Then, in 1921, after more shifts in the leadership of Mexico, Francis A. Cooch, Trust Officer of the Equitable Trust Company in Wilmington, wrote Irénée about a close contact of Obregon's administration, Colonel J. O. Ramos, who could be of interest for the purpose of Du Pont buying the CNDE.[44]It seems surprising that Du Pont entered Mexico after having denounced this investment as weak and unsound for so many years. The company's 1925 Annual Report sought to explain the shift with reference to Mexico's "enormous mineral resources" and the opportunity they afforded "for the development of an explosives industry." In light of these facts, the report explained, Du Pont had been looking at Mexico as "a possible location for a new commercial explosives unit" for "some time" and, thus, when the opportunity had arisen during the year, it had arranged "to acquire the only plant located in Mexico and . . . in conjunction with another American explosives company, organized the Cia Mexicana de Explosivos, to acquire and operate it."[45]

Yet the path to this decision was still a rough one, with Irénée continuing to be hesitant after Nobel France director Paul Clemenceau proposed a deal in April 1924. Nobel France held more than 75 percent of the voting shares of the Société Centrale, which still owned the inactive CNDE.[46] Clemenceau proposed to lease the CNDE to Du Pont for a period of ten years, during which Du Pont would be able to completely reorganize the Mexican plant at its own expense in anticipation of earning 50 percent of its profits.[47] Lammot du Pont, vice president by this time, came to France to negotiate with Clemenceau and then found the proposition attractive. He cabled Irénée to seek his agreement on a somewhat altered proposal in which the stockholders would pay for the reorganization and would also bear the loss of the operation in the event of a new Mexican Revolution: "[. . .] if Du Pont will become the operator of the plant for account of the present stockholders, then it would be expected that the present stockholders would put up the money to rehabilitate the plant and they would also stand the loss of the operations."[48]

Despite Lammot's enthusiasm for the proposal, Irénée found it "unfortunately not as interesting as I hoped and expected it would be," as he wrote Clemenceau in October 1924. A commission that had investigated the plant had sent him a report concluding that the plant's location would impede the attainment of low production costs and that dynamite imports undermined the domestic production of the country. The commission's overall assessment was definitive: the CNDE would lose money if it were to be revived. A Du Pont investment in the CNDE remained an unsound idea. Consequently, Irénée expressed his regret and decision not to lease the plant because the arrangement was "not feasible" in concluding his letter to Clemenceau.[49] Clemenceau then expressed his disappointment in this "final refusal to our lease proposition" in his reply to Irénée.[50]

Nonetheless, in 1925, the deal was approved. Du Pont, under Irénée's direction, bought the CNDE and agreed to share control of it with Hercules (50 percent), the American chemical company that had been part of the Du Pont group at the beginning of the twentieth century. The conditions of the purchase were outlined in correspondence between Clemenceau and Irénée: Du Pont would buy the CNDE based on a ten-year lease that would eventually give the chemical group full control over it. Exactly as in the proposal by Clemenceau in April 1924, Du Pont would be allowed to reorganize and modernize the company as much as it chose but now agreed to do so at its own expense.[51]

What had brought about this seemingly sudden change of heart? Comparing the process of this Mexican investment to other foreign investments, it becomes clear that friends of the three brothers, including Thomas Lamont and Charles Sabin, among others, played a significant role, particularly as bankers, in many of them. When Du Pont chose to invest in Chile in 1921, Charles Sabin, Thomas Lamont, Dwight Morrow, and others formed a committee to promote the country, to advertise Du Pont of Bayer and B.A.S.F.'s prospects there, and to propose a financial arrangement. In Cuba in 1915, Charles Sabin sold the shares of one of the most important sugar factories to Pierre, Irénée, and Lammot. Irénée would chair the Cuban Cane Sugar Corporation in 1930, and Thomas Lamont would join him in 1933. In China, Lamont proposed a financial deal to help Pierre establish a dye plant in the region of Shanghai in 1919.[52] Likewise, concerning the Mexican investment, it is clear from a report from 1928 written by Du Pont director W. Farmer that Pierre, Irénée, and Lammot benefited from the work of Lamont, Sabin, and the ICBM (on which both of them held prominent roles) in Mexico:[53] the U.S. government's recognition of the new Mexican government was necessary for Du Pont to enter the country, and the ICBM had generated incentives for the Mexican government to welcome American investments.

Other changes in the conditions of the investment that must have swayed Irénée's decision are also apparent from this report. For one thing, Du Pont had persuaded the Mexican Tariff Commission to reduce the tariffs on three materials necessary for explosive products. These tax decreases would lead to total annual savings of about $160,000: the duties on glycerin, nitrate of soda, and cartridge shell paper would be reduced from 6 to 3 cents (representing $75,000 annual savings); to one-tenth the previous rate ($35,000 annual savings); and from 15 to 0.5 cents ($50,000 annual savings), respectively. Moreover, the report emphasized that the Mexican government was willing to maintain friendly relations with the United States and to continue its important efforts to encourage American FDI in the country. The "inimical attitude" Calderon had feared back in 1916 seemed to have softened.[54]

A final factor that may have tipped the scales in favor of the Mexican investment was the prominence of the J.P. Morgan & Co. in Mexico (with its strong ties to Thomas Lamont). First, most of the American FDI that had come into Mexico since the end of the revolution came from companies somehow intertwined with the Morgan bank. For example, the American Smelting and Refining Company, which had been established in Mexico in 1895, rebounded quickly after the revolution with profits from an important contract concluded during World War I with the European Allies through J.P. Morgan. It reinvested some of these funds in Mexico after the war. General Electric opened a lamp factory in Monterey during the negotiations between Lamont and de la Huerta. Similarly, J.P. Morgan &Co. had provided a loan enabling the $2,500,000 merger of sugar interests covering properties located near Tampico. Finally, General Motors entered Mexico between 1925 and 1927,[55] with Pierre chairing GM's board and his brothers as directors of the automobile company and, thus, probably bearing some responsibility for GM's investment in Mexico. All these American investments in Mexico reassured Du Pont that the country was catching up, at least in its credibility, with other foreign nations as attractive places for FDI.[56] With Du Pont's ties to J.P. Morgan & Co. executive Lamont, and the bank's own loans to Mexico dating back to 1899, the bank's heavy involvement in FDI in Mexico during this period and Du Pont's decision to invest there are hardly surprising: it was important that American investments and capital return to Mexico to help the country recover a tax base sufficient for repaying its debt.[57]

Whereas the influence of Lamont, Sabin, and other personal acquaintances on the du Ponts' decision to invest in Mexico is well established in the archival evidence as presented here, Du Pont executive Farmer's 1928 report was rather vague on the question of "personal contacts": "It does not seem worthwhile to tabulate the former acquaintances we renewed and new ones we made. Suffice it to say that we contacted broadly and with the best quality in caliber. The consensus of facts and opinions obtained from there are reflected herein."[58] Farmer's vague reference here pertains to various actors: Charles Sabin, who gave Du Pont a connection in Mexico to understand better the political and economic climate; Thomas Lamont, whose work permitted the Mexican government to be recognized, enabling Du Pont to imagine making an investment there; and to Dwight Morrow. Connected to J.P. Morgan & Co. as a former partner, Morrow, as mentioned above, was a close friend of the brothers and had been involved in their investment in Chile in 1921. He also happened to be the U.S. ambassador to Mexico (1927–1930) when Du Pont negotiated opening a new plant in Mexico in 1928, this time to produce rayon, an artificial textile fiber. He proposed to help Du Pont in any way he "properly could in connection with this plan."[59] Farmer was then put into contact with the ambassador in 1928 to tackle the matter directly in Mexico. Although Morrow may not have been a good advisor, Farmer came back to the United States with a report sufficiently clear to permit the company to invest in Mexico.[60]

13.5   CONCLUSION

Chandler and Salsbury ended their account of Du Pont's potential investment in Mexico in 1907, long before Du Pont actually wound up purchasing the CNDE in 1925. The continuation of the story presented here demonstrates that, although Coleman was the first to envision taking the company abroad and specifically into Mexico, it was Pierre and Irénée who finally led the company to the Mexican and other foreign investments after Coleman had been expelled from the board. In taking this big step, Pierre and Irénée conferred with one another, as well as, of course, Lammot, and then they discussed it with their friends—Thomas Lamont, Charles Sabin, and Dwight Morrow—simultaneously taking their work into account.

These wealthy and important bankers and businessmen worked together on several Du Pont's investments abroad whenever such investments were of interest to them (common or not). Moreover, their private lives were intertwined: their children were friends, their wives were connected, they spent holidays together in Cuba, and so forth. Consequently, the network was connected to the family not merely through the businessmen and bankers. This situation fits with the idea that Casillas et al. put forward: the relationships of a family can have a strong impact on the internationalization process of a family firm.[61] The letters exchanged, the information gathered, and especially the reports commissioned make it clear that these bankers and friends of the historical family members exerted the greatest influence on the brothers' decision to invest in Mexico. In addition, they show that the three brothers worked jointly between 1915 and 1928.

In a tumultuous era for Mexico, Du Pont reinforced the nation's multinationalization by buying back a state monopoly. This case study illustrates the role social networking can play in the internationalization of a family firm. Even though the brothers running the company wanted to expand in the United States rather than Mexico, their network of friends/businessmen/bankers, seeking investments in Mexico, made them reconsider, however indirectly, by positively changing Du Pont's perception of the economic environment for American investments in Mexico, among other things. Other case studies on Du Pont have shown that this network continuously influenced the du Ponts between 1915 and the 1950s (in Chile, in Cuba, in China, etc.). Only after 1958 when the last historical family member left the board would there be a complete change of governance along with different sorts of networks and investment considerations.

NOTES

1. Black powder made of sodium nitrate was the initial explosive produced and sold by Du Pont. Lammot du Pont, the grandson of Eleuthere Irénée (the founder of the company) and the father of Pierre S., Lammot, and Irénée, improved it in 1857 by substituting potassium nitrate for sodium nitrate. In the 1880s, he persuaded his family to produce dynamite. Smokeless powder was used in firearms and was intended primarily for the military market; the company started to sell it in important quantities in 1902. Hounshell and Smith, 1988.

2. Quantities unspecified in the archives; Hagley Museum and Library, Du Pont's Annual Report, 1905.

3. Canadian Explosives Industries Ltd. (45 percent shares for Du Pont, 55 percent for Nobel) then jointly organized the production and sale of explosives in Canada. Hagley Museum and Library, Du Pont's Annual Report, 1910.

4. Hagley Museum and Library, Du Pont's Annual Report, 1915.

5. Quantities unspecified in the archives; Hagley Museum and Library, Du Pont's Annual Reports, 1915–1919.

6. The negotiations with Chile would lead to the joint construction with Nobel and Atlas of a factory in 1923. In Cuba, Du Pont would not erect any plants, at least until 1957 when it began constructing a neoprene factory. However, this was interrupted by the Cuban Revolution. In China, Du Pont invested in dyes during the 1930s but divested this very soon because the company was not profitable. Finally, the factory in Japan would never be built.

7. Archives du Monde du Travail, Roubaix, France: file 65 AQ: explosives industries, Annual Reports of the Société Centrale, 1903–1915.

8. Hagley Museum and Library, Du Pont's Annual Report, 1925.

9. Wilkins, 1986, 81.

10. Colli and Rose, 2007, 194.

11. Hounshell and Smith, 1988. Chandler, 1962. Chandler, 1977.

12. Pierre and Coleman decided to buy back Du Pont de Nemours when the former director of the company, Eugene Du Pont, died in 1901. With no direct successor, the family thought to sell back Du Pont to Laflin and Rand. Chandler, 1962, 55–57.

13. Hagley Museum and Library, Du Pont's Annual Report, 1958.

14. Hagley Museum and Library Archives: Acc. 1662, Acc. 473, Acc. 228, Acc. LLMS-10/A.

15. Maurer and Haber, 2007.

16. Haber, 1989. Marichal, 1995.

17. The German companies are unspecified in the archives. In 1923, two years before the acquisition, Du Pont sold the greatest amount ($3,105,650) of merchandise to the Mexican government; Apache had the second-highest sales ($2,127,000), and Hercules the third-highest ($800,000). Between 1913 and 1923, Hercules had lost some of its market share, but the company used to sell a lot more than Du Pont to Mexican officials. Before 1918, its turnover was as much as ten times that of Du Pont (Hagley Museum and Library, Statement about Du Pont's sales in Mexico, 1913–1923, Acc. 1662, Box 20).

18. Venustiano Carranza's Decree on the CNDE, May 8, 1915 and October 6, 1915, Hagley Museum and Library, Acc. 1662, Box 46.

19. Haber and Razo, 1998, 113.

20. The Constitution of 1917 was the third Mexican Constitution (the previous two had been formulated in 1824 and 1857). It reinstated several of the 1857 principles, in particular those about secularism, social and labor protection,

238 *Liza Lombardi*

and the limitation of foreign interests. See Archives du Crédit Agricole, Paris, France, DEEF73437/0002 Be.13.76 3001: Files about the French explosives societies and their relations with Mexico, Boletin Mexico relaciones exteriors.

21. Wilkins, 1974, 38.
22. Taylor and Sudnick, 1984, 39.
23. Chandler and Salsbury, 1971, 166–167.
24. Casillas, Acedo and Moreno, 2007. Casillas, Moreno and Acedo, 2010.
25. Chandler and Salsbury, 1971, 171.
26. Wilkins, 1974.
27. Chandler and Salsbury, 1971, 177.
28. Chandler and Salsbury, 1971, 177.
29. Archives du Monde du Travail, Roubaix, France: file 65 AQ: explosives industries, Annual Reports of the Société Centrale, 1903–1912.
30. Chandler and Salsbury, 1971, 168.
31. Pierre regarded Coleman as a detractor, fearing that Coleman might sell his shares to some German competitors. Christiana Securities was a holding company that owned most Du Pont stock and aimed to work against the impression that Du Pont was a major trust. Nonetheless, during these years, Christiana Securities was chaired by the chairmen of Du Pont. Chandler and Salsbury, 1971, 335.
32. Harrison, 1988, 22–27.
33. The *New York Times* referred in numerous articles to Lamont's work in Mexico, reviewing reports of the ICBM and Mexican government meetings. The committee's composition is described in these articles, as well. See, for example, "Unite to Protect Mexican Holdings," *New York Times*, February 24, 1919, 1–4.
34. Knight, 1987, 133.
35. "Huerta Will Meet Bankers Here Soon," *New York Times*, April 4, 1922, 36.
36. Smith, 1963. Smith, 1993.
37. Hagley Museum and Library, Acc. LLMS-10/A, Acc. 228, Acc. 473.
38. MacManus to Pierre, March 4, 1916, Hagley Museum and Library, Acc. 1662, Box. 35.
39. Ibid.
40. Pierre to MacManus, March 6, 1916, Hagley Museum and Library, Acc. 1662, Box 35.
41. Baker to Pierre S., March 22, 1916, Hagley Museum and Library, Acc. 1662, Box 35.
42. Calderon to Pierre, November 10, 1916, Hagley Museum and Library, Acc. 1662, Box 35.
43. Pattuson to Cauffiel and Irénée, June 15, 1919, Hagley Museum and Library, Acc. 1662, Box 35.
44. Cooch to Irénée, December 5, 1921, Hagley Museum and Library, Acc. 1662, Box 46.
45. Hagley Museum and Library, Du Pont's Annual Report, 1925: 7–8.
46. By the way, Paul Clemenceau was the brother of Georges Clemenceau, "the Tiger," Président du Conseil between 1906 and 1909 and again between 1917 and 1920. Paul had been strategically placed at the head of Nobel Industries France during the war so that he could help the French government in its war against the Triple Alliance.
47. Clemenceau to Irénée, April 26, 1924, Hagley Museum and Library, Acc. 1662, Box 20.
48. Lammot to Irénée, April 29, 1924, Hagley Museum and Library, Acc. 1662, Box 20.

49. Irénée to Clemenceau, October 20, 1924, Hagley Museum and Library, Acc. 1662, Box 20.
50. Clemenceau to Irénée, November 5, 1924, Hagley Museum and Library, Acc. 1662, Box 20.
51. Fisher to Irénée, "Advice of Actions," May 14, 1925, Hagley Museum and Library, Acc. 1662, Box 20.
52. Hagley Museum: LLMS/10, Hagley Museum and Library, Acc. 473.
53. This report was written after the CNDE buyout from the perspective of reinvesting in Mexico. Farmer was the director of Du Pont Rayon in Buffalo, New York.
54. Report to the Board, "Interests in Mexico," May 19, 1928, Hagley Museum and Library, Acc. 542, Box 818.
55. Corey, 1930, 448.
56. Report to the Board, "Interests in Mexico," May 19, 1928, Hagley Museum and Library, Acc. 542, Box 818.
57. Gonzales, 2002, 197.
58. Report to the Board, "Interests in Mexico," May 19, 1928, Hagley Museum and Library, Acc. 542, Box 818.
59. D. Morrow to W. S. Carpenter, March 13, 1928, Hagley Museum and Library, Acc. 542 Series II part 2, Boxes 818.
60. D. Morrow to W. S. Carpenter, March 13, 1928, Hagley Museum and Library, Acc. 542 Series II part 2, Boxes 818.
61. Casillas, Moreno and Acedo, 2010.

Contributors

Hartmut Berghoff is Director of the German Historical Institute in Washington, DC, and Professor of Economic History at the University of Göttingen in Germany. His fields of expertise are the history of consumption, business history, and immigration history. Most recently, he has coedited *Decoding Modern Consumer Societies* (Palgrave Macmillan, 2012) and *Doing Business in the Age of Extremes. Essays on the Economic History of Germany and Austria* (Cambridge University Press, 2012). For a full CV and a complete list of publications, consult http://www.ghi-dc.org/Berghoff.

Jeffrey Fear is the newly appointed Professor of International Business History at the University of Glasgow, Centre for Business History. He holds a PhD in history from Stanford University and has previously taught at the University of Pennsylvania, the Harvard Business School, and the University of Redlands. He is on the editorial board of the *Business History Review* and *Essays in Economic and Business History*. He writes on small and medium-sized business multinationals, international cartels, and management history. His articles have appeared in the *Business History Review*, *Jahrbuch für Wirtschaftsgeschichte*, the *Oxford Handbook of Business History*, the *Handbook of Organizational Learning*, and *Big Business and the Wealth of Nations*, among others.

Paloma Fernández Pérez has a PhD in history from the University of California at Berkeley and is Professor of Economic History at the University of Barcelona. She is coordinating a team of 21 scholars from 11 countries in research that studies the origins and evolution of large family businesses in Latin America and Spain. Her research interests are family business, innovation, entrepreneurial networks, and lobbies. She has published *El rostro familiar de la metrópolis* (Unicaja, 1997) and *Un siglo y medio de trefilería en España* (Barcelona, 2004), has edited with P. Pascual *Del metal al motor* (Bilbao, 2007), and has published articles in *Business History*, *Enterprise & Society*, *Business History Review*, *Revista de Historia Industrial*, *Revista de Historia Económica*, and *Investigaciones* *de Historia Económica.* She is a principal researcher for a project on entrepreneurial networks in Spain and a member of the Centre d'Estudis Antoni de Capmany.

Vipin Gupta (PhD, Wharton School) is Professor and Codirector of the Global Management Center at California State University San Bernardino. He has made significant contributions to the science of culture, sustainable strategic management in the emerging markets, managing organizational and technological transformations, and entrepreneurial and women's leadership, and is a pioneer in the field of culturally sensitive models of family business around the world. He has authored or edited 16 books, including the seminal GLOBE book on culture and leadership in 62 societies, 11 on family business models in different cultural regions, 2 on organizational performance, 1 on the MNCs in China, and an innovative strategy textbook. He has published about 150 articles as book chapters and in academic journals, such as the *Journal of Business Venturing, Journal of World Business, Family Business Review, International Journal of Cross-Cultural Management,* and *Asia-Pacific Journal of Management,* among others. Dr. Gupta has been a Japan Foundation fellow, and a recipient of the Society for Industrial Organizational Psychologists' coveted "Scott M. Myers Award for Applied Research—2005."

Miquel Gutiérrez Poch is Associate Professor at the University of Barcelona. His research focuses on the papermaking industry in a long-term perspective (from the eighteenth century to the present). He is part of a research team focusing on clusters and industrial districts. He has published more than ten articles and a couple of books about the history of papermaking. His current book project deals with the success of a cigarette papermaking firm in global markets and its niche market strategy.

Susanne Hilger is Professor of Economic and Social History at the Heinrich Heine University in Düsseldorf. Her research interests are industrial and business history of the nineteenth and twentieth centuries, the history of Americanization, as well as the history of family businesses. Her recent publications include *Kleine Wirtschaftsgeschichte von Nordrhein-Westfalen* (Greven, 2012) and the coeditorship of *Wirtschaft—Kultur—Geschichte: Positionen und Perspektiven* (Franz Steiner Verlag, 2011). Her current research project is about the "success factor" of family in European business in times of globalization.

Taeko Hoshino is Executive Research Fellow at the Institute of Developing Economies-JETRO in Japan and was Visiting Researcher of Centro de Estudios Sociológicos of El Colegio de México in Mexico for two years until August 2012. Her research interests include development problems of emerging countries and the role of family business groups in the development of the national economy, taking Mexico as a research field. She has published in such journals as *Developing Economies* and *Ajia Keizai*. She is the author of *Industrialization and Private Enterprises in Mexico* (Institute of Developing Economies, 2001) and contributed a chapter, "Business Groups in Mexico," to *The Oxford Handbook of Business Groups*, edited by A. Colpan, T. Hikino, and J. Lincoln (Oxford University Press, 2010). Her most recent research deals with the global production network of the automotive industry and local firms' possibility of entering the network, focusing on the Mexican case.

Liza Lombardi is a PhD candidate at the Paul Bairoch Institute of Economic History of the University of Geneva. Her research interests are family business, internationalization, and networks. In her dissertation, "When Du Pont Went Global (1915–1975): How the du Pont Family Built an Empire Abroad," supervised by Prof. Youssef Cassis (European Institute, Florence), she intends to demonstrate that family firms could be big business and could go global during the twentieth century. The manuscript will be finalized in Fall 2013.

Christina Lubinski is Research Fellow at the German Historical Institute in Washington, DC. Her first book based upon her dissertation deals with corporate governance changes in German family firms since the 1960s and won the Prize for Business History by the Germany Society of Business History. As Harvard Business School Newcomen Fellow in 2010–2011, she compared German and U.S. family firms with a special focus on the process of internationalization. She has published on family business and multinationals in *Business History Review, Enterprise & Society*, and the *Journal of Family Business Strategy*. Her most recent research deals with German and U.S. companies in India since 1900 and asks how they dealt with the challenges of political risk.

Anne Overbeck is a Doctoral Fellow at the Max Planck Institute for the History of Science in Berlin. She is part of the Junior Research Group "Family Values and Social Change: The U.S.-American Family in the 20th Century" at the University of Münster sponsored by the German Research Foundation. Since 2010, she has been working as a museum curator running her own curating agency, *dingedurchdenken-Projekte für Kultur und Wissenschaft*. Her research interests include migration history, American history, and gender studies. She is working on a PhD thesis on the concepts of African American motherhood and her publications include *Eiskalte Leidenschaft: Italienische Eismacher im Ruhrgebiet* (Klartext, 2009) and "The Enemy Within: African-American Motherhood and the Crack Baby Crisis," in *Family Values and Social Change: The American Family in 20th Century USA*, edited by Isabel Heinemann (Campus, 2012).

Andrew Popp is Professor of Business History at the University of Liverpool Management School. His research interests have focused on a range of issues in British business history, including industrial districts, regional business networks, and social capital; cultural representations of business; traveling salesmen; and, most recently, entrepreneurship and family business. He has published on these and other topics in *Business History, Enterprise & Society, Business History Review, Economic History Review*, and *Entrepreneurship and Regional Development*. In 2012, he published *Entrepreneurial Families: Business, Marriage and Life in the Early Nineteenth Century* (Pickering and Chatto). He is an Associate Editor at *Enterprise & Society*.

Luciano Segreto is Professor of Business History in a Global Economy and of Financial History at the University of Florence. He is the Chairman of the Cultural Memory Council of the Institute for Corporate Cultural Affairs and a member of the Scientific Council of the Maison des Sciences de l'Homme d'Aquitaine. His research interests are family business, international financial relationships, and banking history. Among his most recent publications are *Europe at the Seaside: The Economic History of Mass Tourism in the Mediterranean*, edited by L. Segreto, C. Manera, and M. Pohl (Berghahn Books, 2009); *Credito Emiliano 1910–2010. Dalle radici agricole alla diffusione nazionale* (Laterza, 2010); *European Business: Corporate and Social Values*, edited by H. Bonin and L. Segreto (Peter Lang, 2011); *I Feltrinelli. Storia di una dinastia imprenditoriale, 1854–1942* (Feltrinelli, 2011), a book that was deemed the best book of 2012 by the Italian Society for Contemporary History; and *European Business and Brand Building*, edited by L. Segreto, H. Bonin, A.K. Kozminski, C. Manera, and M. Pohl (Peter Lang, 2012).

References

Allende, Fermín. (2009). Poor Thomas Buddenbrook! Family Business in Literature. *Business and Economic History On-Line,* 7, http://www.h-net.org/~business/bhcweb/publications/BEHonline/2009/allende.pdf.

Ampalavanar Brown, Rajeswary (Ed.). (1995). *Chinese Business Enterprise in Asia.* London: Routledge.

Amsden, Alice, & Hikino, Takashi. (1994). Project Execution Capability, Organizational Know-How and Conglomerate Corporate Growth in Late Industrialization. *Industrial and Corporate Change, 3*(1), 111–147.

Andersen, Arne. (1997). *Der Traum vom guten Leben: Alltags- und Konsumgeschichte vom Wirtschaftswunder bis heute.* Frankfurt a.M.: Campus.

Anderson, Ronald C., & Reeb, David M. (2003). Founding-Family Ownership and Firm Performance. Evidence from S&P 500. *Journal of Finance, 58*(3), 1301–1328.

Angeli, Stefano. (1982). *Proprietari, commercianti e filandieri a Milano nel primo Ottocento: il mercato delle sete.* Milan: Angeli.

Arkin, Anthony J. (1981). *The Contributions of the Indians to the Economic Development of South Africa, 1860–1970—Income Approach.* PhD diss., University of Durban-Westville, Durban.

Aspe, Pedro. (1993). *Economic Transformation: The Mexican Way.* Cambridge, MA: MIT Press.

Astrachan, Joseph H., Klein, Sabine B., & Smyrnios, Kosmas X. (2002). The F-PEC Scale of Family Influence. A Proposal for Solving the Family Business Definition Problem. *Family Business Review, 15*(1), 45–58.

Auernheimer, Georg. (2006). Schüler und Eltern italienischer Herkunft im deutschen Schulsystem. In M. Libbi (Ed.), *Berufliche Integration und plurale Gesellschaft.* Cologne: Versus-DGB Bildungswerk NRW.

Ausschuß zur Untersuchung der Erzeugungs- und Absatzbedingungen der deutschen Wirtschaft. (Ed.). (1930). *Die deutsche Schuhindustrie: Verhandlungen und Berichte des Unterausschusses für allgemeine Wirtschaftsstruktur.* Berlin: Mittler.

Barca, Fabrizio, & Becht, Marco (Eds.). (2002). *The Control of Corporate Europe.* Oxford: Oxford University Press.

Barney, Jay. (1991). Firm Resources and Sustained Competitive Advantage. *Journal of Management, 17*(1), 99–120.

Basly, Sami. (2007). The Internationalization of Family SME: An Organizational Learning and Knowledge Development Perspective. *Baltic Journal of Management, 2*(2), 154–180.

Bat'a, Jan. (1951). *A Study of Migration.* Washington, DC: White House.

Bat'a, Tomáš. (1992). *Knowledge in Action: The Bat'a System of Management.* Amsterdam: IOS Press.

Baumol, William J. (1990). Entrepreneurship: Productive, Unproductive, and Destructive. *Journal of Political Economy, 98*(5), 893–921.

Beauchamp, Ken G. (2001). *History of Telegraphy*. London: Institution of Electrical Engineers.

Bell, Jim, McNaughton, Rod, & Young, Stephen. (2001). 'Born-Again Global' Firms: An Extension to the 'Born Global' Phenomenon. *Journal of International Management* 7(3), 173–189.

Berghoff, Hartmut. (2001). Marketing Diversity: The Making of a Global Consumer Product—Hohner's Harmonicas, 1857–1930. *Enterprise & Society, 2*, 338–372.

———. (2004). *Moderne Unternehmensgeschichte: Eine themen- und theorieorientierte Einführung*. Paderborn: Schöningh.

———. (2006a). The End of Family Business? The Mittelstand and German Capitalism in Transition, 1949–2000. *Business History Review, 80*(2), 263–295.

———. (2006b). *Zwischen Kleinstadt und Weltmarkt. Hohner und die Harmonika 1857–1961. Unternehmensgeschichte als Gesellschaftsgeschichte* (2). Paderborn: Schöningh.

———. (2010). From Small Publisher to Global Media and Service Company: Outline of the History of Bertelsmann, 1835 to 2010. In Bertelsmann AG Corporate History (Ed.), *175 Years of Bertelsmann: The Legacy for Our Future* (pp. 8–83). München: C. Bertelsmann.

Hartmut Berghoff (2013): Blending Personal and Managerial Capitalism: Bertelsmann's Rise from Medium-sized Publisher to Global Media Corporation and Service Provider, 1950–2010, Business History, DOI:10.1080/00076791.2012. 744584.

Berghoff, Hartmut, & Spiekermann, Uwe. (2010). Immigrant Entrepreneurship: The German-American Business Biography, 1720 to the Present—A GHI Project. *Bulletin of the German Historical Institute, 47*(2), 69–82.

Black, Edwin. (2004). *Banking on Baghdad: Inside Iraq's 7,000-Year History of War, Profit and Conflict*. Hoboken, NJ: John Wiley & Sons.

Black, J. Stewart, & Mendenhall, Mark. (1991). The U-Curve Adjustment Hypothesis Revisited: A Review and Theoretical Framework. *Journal of International Business Studies, 22*(2), 225–247.

Bonache, Jaime. (2005). Job Satisfaction Among Expatriates, Repatriates and Domestic Employees: The Perceived Impact of International Assignments on Work-Related Variables. *Personnel Review, 34*(1), 110–124.

Bonaglia, Federico, Goldstein, Andrea, & Mathews, John A. (2007). Accelerated Internationalization by Emerging Markets' Multinationals: The Case of the White Goods Sector. *Journal of World Business, 42*, 369–383.

Boos-Nünning, Ursula. (1991). Berufswahlprozesse und Berufsberatung griechischer, italienischer, portugiesischer und türkischer Jugendlicher. *Deutsch lernen, 4*, 322–358.

Bovenkerk, Frank. (2004). *Ijscomannen en schoorsteenvegers: Italiaanse ambachtslieden in Nederland*. Amsterdam: Self-Published.

———. (2009). By Belluno in die ganze Welt. Die Geschichte der italiensichen Eismacher in Europa. In A. Overbeck & D. Osses (Eds.), *Eiskalte Leidenschaft: Italienische Eismacher im Ruhrgebiet* (pp. 14–23). Essen: Klartext.

Bovenkerk, Frank, & Ruland, Loes. (1992). Artisan Entrepreneurs: Two Centuries of Italian Immigration to the Netherlands. *International Migration Review, XXVI*, 927–939.

Boyce, Gordon. (2010). Language and Culture in a Liverpool Merchant Family Firm, 1870–1950. *Business History Review, 84*(1), 1–26.

Bracke, Thierry, & Fidora, Michael. (2012). The Macro-Financial Factors Behind the Crisis: Global Liquidity Glut or Global Savings Glut? *North American Journal of Economics and Finance, 23*, 185–202.

Brändle, Judith (Ed.). (1992). *Die Bat'a-Kolonie in Möhlin: eine Ausstellung im Architekturmuseum in Basel vom 3. Oktober 1992 bis 22. November 1992*. Basel: Schweizer Architekturmuseum .

Braun, Bianca. (2009). *Erfolgreich jenseits der Börse: Was führende Familienunternehmen auszeichnet.* Zurich: Orell Fuessli.

Bräutigam, Petra. (1997). *Mittelständische Unternehmer im Nationalsozialismus: Wirtschaftliche Entwicklungen und soziale Verhaltensweisen in der Schuh- und Lederindustrie Badens und Württembergs.* Munich: Oldenbourg.

Brundin, Ethel, & Sharma, Pramodita. (2012). Love, Hate, and Desire: The Role of Emotional Messiness in the Business Family. In A. Carsrud & M. Brännback (Eds.), *Understanding Family Businesses: Undiscovered Approaches, Unique Perspectives, and Neglected Topics* (pp. 55–72). New York: Springer.

Buckley, Peter J. (2009a). Business History and International Business. *Business History, 51*(3), 307–333.

———. (2009b). *Foreign Direct Investment, China and the World Economy.* Basingstoke: Palgrave.

Bühlmann, Elisabeth. (1999). *La Ligne Siemens. La Construction du Télégraphe Indo-Européen, 1867–1870.* Bern: Peter Lang.

Cabrera-Suárez, Katiuska, Saá-Pérez, Petra De, & García-Almeida, Desiderio. (2001). The Succession Process from a Resource- and Knowledge-Based View of the Family Firm. *Family Business Review, 14*(1), 37–48.

Caizzi, Bruno. (2007). *Suez e San Gottardo; a cura di Carlo G. Lacaita; con un testo di Giovanni Vigo.* Lugano: G. Casagrande.

Calof, J. L., & Viviers, W. (1995). Internationalization Behavior of Small and Medium-Sized South African Enterprises. *Journal of Small Business Management, 33*, 71–79.

Campanale, Laura. (2006). *I gelatieri veneti in Germania: Un'indagine sociolinguistica.* Frankfurt a.M.: P. Lang.

———. (2009). Die Eisdiele als multikulturelles Babel. Eine linguistische Studie. In A. Overbeck & D. Osses (Eds.), *Eiskalte Leidenschaft: Italienische Eismacher im Ruhrgebiet* (pp. 46–53). Essen: Klartext.

Casillas, Jose C., & Acedo, Francisco J. (2005). Internationalization of Spanish Family SMEs: An Analysis of Family Involvement *International Journal of Globalisation and Small Business, 1/2*, 134–151.

Casillas, Jose C., Acedo, Francisco J., & Moreno, Ana M. (2007). *International Entrepreneurship in Family Businesses.* Cheltenham: Edward Elgar.

Casillas, Jose C., Moreno, Ana M., & Acedo, Francisco J. (2010). Internationalization of Family Business: A Theoretical Model Based on International Entrepreneurship Perspective. *Global Management Journal, 3*(2), http://globalmj.eu/2010/2012/2009/internationalization-of-family-businesses-a-theoretical-model-base-on-international-enterpreneurship-perspective/.

Casson, Mark. (1999). The Economics of the Family Firm. *Scandinavian Economic History Review, 47*(1), 10–23.

———. (2000). *Economics of International Business: A New Research Agenda.* Cheltenham: Edward Elgar.

Cekota, Anthony. (1968). *Entrepreneur Extraordinary: The Biography of Tomas Bat'a.* Rome: Edizioni Internazionali Sociali .

Ceschi, Raffaello. (2005). *Ottocento ticinese: la costruzione di un cantone* (5). Locarno: A. Dadò.

Chadwick, Leslie, Ghafoor, Shahzad, Khail, Fukaiha Kaka, Khan, Uzair Farooq, & Hassan, Faiza. (2011). Globalization of SMEs Process. *Interdisciplinary Journal of Contemporary Research in Business, 4*(2), 859–882.

Chanda, Nayan. (2006). Indians in Indochina. In K. S. Sandhu & A. Mani (Eds.), *Indian Communities in Southeast Asia* (pp. 31–45). Singapore: Institute of Southeast Asian Studies.

Chandler, Alfred D. (1962). *Strategy and Structure. Chapters in the History of the Industrial Enterprise.* Cambridge, MA: M.I.T. Press.

——. (1977). *The Visible Hand. The Managerial Revolution in American Business*. Cambridge, MA: Belknap Press of Harvard University Press.

Chandler, Alfred D., & Salsbury, Stephen. (1971). *Pierre S. Du Pont and the Making of the Modern Corporation*. New York: Harper & Row.

Chen, Ling, Dong, Jiyang, & Hull, Yue Xu. (2009). Exploring the Internationalization Pathways of the Chinese Family Firms: A Case Study of Six Firms in Zhejiang Province. *Paper presented at Inaugural CEA (Europe) and 20th CEA (UK) Annual Conference July 23–24, 2009, Dublin, Ireland*.

Chetty, Sylvie, & Blankenburg Holm, Desiree. (2000). Internationalisation of Small to Medium-Sized Manufacturing Firms: A Network Approach. *International Business Review, 9*(1), 77–93.

Chikugo, Koij. (1991). *Bat'a: The Czech Example of Welfare Capitalism*. PhD diss., State University of New York, Albany.

Child, John, Faulkner, David, & Pitkethly, Robert. (2000). Foreign Direct Investment in the UK 1985–1994: The Impact on Domestic Management Practice. *Journal of Management Studies, 37*(1), 141–166.

Chrisman, James J., Chua, Jess H., & Sharma, Pramodita. (2005). Trends and Directions in the Development of a Strategic Management Theory of the Family Firm. *Entrepreneurship Theory and Practice, 29*(5), 555–575.

Chrisman, James J., Chua, Jess H., & Steier, Lloyd P. (2003). An Introduction to Theories of Family Business. *Journal of Business Venturing, 18*(4), 441–448.

Church, Roy. (1993). The Family Firm in Industrial Capitalism. International Perspectives on Hypotheses and History. *Business History, 35*(4), 17–43.

Coase, Ronald H. (1937). The Nature of the Firm. *Economica, 4*, 386–405.

Coleman, Donald C. (1958). *The British Paper Industry, 1495–1860: A Study in Industrial Growth*. Oxford: Oxford University Press.

Colli, Andrea. (1998). Networking the Market. Evidence and Conjectures from the History of the Italian Industrial Districts. *European Yearbook of Economic History, Vol. 1* (pp. 75–92). Aldershot: Ashgate.

——. (2003). *The History of Family Business 1850–2000*. Cambridge: Cambridge University Press.

——. (2010). Family Firms in European Economic History. *Social Science Research Network* http://ssrn.com/abstract=1583862.

——. (2011). Business History in Family Business Studies. From Neglect to Cooperation? *Journal of Family Business Management, 1*(1), 14–25.

Colli, Andrea, Fernández Pérez, Paloma, & Rose, Mary B. (2003). National Determinants of Family Firm Development? Family Firms in Britain, Spain, and Italy in the Nineteenth and Twentieth Centuries. *Enterprise & Society, 4*(1), 28–64.

Colli, Andrea, & Rose, Mary B. (2003). Family Firms in Comparative Perspective. In F. Amatori & G. Jones (Eds.), *Business History Around the World at the Turn of the Century* (pp. 339–352). Cambridge: Cambridge University Press.

Colli, Andrea, & Rose, Mary B. (2007). Family Business. In G. Jones & J. Zeitlin (Eds.), *The Oxford Handbook of Business History* (pp. 194–218). Oxford: Oxford University Press.

Colpan, Asli M., & Hikino, Takashi. (2010). Foundations of Business Groups: Towards an Integrated Framework. In A.M. Colpan, T. Hikino & J.R. Lincoln (Eds.), *The Oxford Handbook of Business Groups* (pp. 15–66). Oxford: Oxford University Press.

Colpan, Asli M., Hikino, Takashi, & Lincoln, James R. (Eds.). (2010). *The Oxford Handbook of Business Groups*. Oxford: Oxford University Press.

Conrad, Sebastian. (2010). *Globalisation and the Nation in Imperial Germany*. Cambridge: Cambridge University Press.

Corey, Lewis. (1930). *The House of Morgan: A Social Biography of the Masters of Money*. New York: G.H. Watt.

Coviello, Nicole, & Munro, Hugh. (1997). Network Relationships and the Internationalisation Process of Small Software Firms. *International Business Review,* 6(4), 361–386.

Crepax, N. (1991). La Camera di commercio di Milano durante gli ultimi decenni dell'Ottocento. In C. Mozzarelli & R. Pavoni (Eds.), *Milano Fin de Siecle E Il Caso Bagatti Valsecchi.* Milan: Guerini.

Davidoff, Leonore. (1995). 'Where the Stranger Begins.' The Question of Siblings in Historical Analysis. In L. Davidoff (Ed.), *Worlds Between. Historical Perspective on Gender and Class.* New York: Routledge.

Davidoff, Leonore, Doolittle, Megan, Fink, Janet, & Holden, Katherine. (1999). *The Family Story. Blood, Contract and Intimacy 1830–1960.* London: Longman.

Davis, James H., Schoorman, F. David, & Donaldson, Lex. (1997). Toward a Stewardship Theory of Management. *Academy of Management Review, 22*(1), 20–47.

De Clercq, Dirk, Sapienza, Harry J., & Crijns, Hans. (2005). The Internationalization of Small and Medium-Sized Firms. *Small Business Economics, 24,* 409–419.

Decleva, Enrico. (1881). Milano industriale e l'esposizione del 1881. In F. Brioschi (Ed.), *L'Italia industriale nel 1881.* Milan: Hoepli.

Deeg, Richard. (1999). *Finance Capitalism Unveiled: Banks and the German Political Economy.* Ann Arbor: University of Michigan Press.

Devinat, Paul. (1930). Die Schuhfabrik Bat'a. In Internationales Arbeitsamt. (Ed.), *Studien über die Beziehungen zwischen Arbeitgebern und Arbeitnehmern, Vol. 1* (pp. 235–286). Geneva: Internationales Arbeitsamt.

Die Kammer für Handel, Gewerbe und Industrie in Klagenfurt 1851–1926. (1926). Klagenfurt: Verlag der Kammer für Handel, Gewerbe und Industrie.

Diehl, Claudia. (2002). Die Auswirkungen längerer Herkunftslandaufenthalte auf dem Bildungserfolg türkisch- und italienischstämmiger Schülerinnen und Schüler. *Zeitschrift für Bevölkerungswissenschaft, 27*(2), 165–185.

DiMaggio, Paul J., & Powell, Walter W. (1983). The Iron Cage Revisited: Institutional Isomorphism and Collective Rationality in Organizational Fields. *American Sociological Review, 48*(2), 147–160.

Ding, Yuan, Zhang, Hua, & Zhang, Junxi. (2007). Private vs State Ownership and Earnings Management: Evidence from Chinese Listed Companies. *Corporate Governance, 15*(2), 223–238.

———. (2008). The Financial and Operating Performance of Chinese Family-Owned Listed Firms. *Management International Review, 48*(3), 1–22.

Dubreuil, Hyacinthe. (1936). *L'Exemple de Bat'a: La libération des initiatives individuelles dans une entreprise géante.* Paris: Bernard Grasset.

Dunning, John H. (1979). Explaining Changing Patterns of International Production: In Defence of the Eclectic Theory. *Oxford Bulletin of Economics and Statistics, 4*(4), 269–295.

———. (1993). *The Globalization of Business. The Challenge of the 1990s.* London: Routledge.

———. (1997). *Alliance Capitalism and Global Business.* London: Routledge.

———. (2001). The Eclectic (OLI) Paradigm of International Production: Past, Present and Future. *International Journal of the Economics of Business, 8*(2), 173–190.

Dyer, W. Gibb Jr. (1986). *Cultural Change in Family Firms. Anticipating and Managing Business and Family Transitions.* San Francisco: Jossey-Bass.

———. (1989). Integrating Professional Management into a Family Owned Business. *Family Business Review, 2*(3), 221–235.

Ehrenberg, Richard. (1906). *Die Unternehmungen der Brüder Siemens. Erster Band.* Jena: Gustav Fischer.

Eifert, Christiane. (2006). Succession Patterns in German Family Firms in the 20th Century. *Paper presented at the International Economic History Conference, Helsinki, Finland, August 21–25.*

Eisenhardt, K.M., & Martin, J A. (2000). Dynamic Capabilities: What Are They? *Strategic Management Journal, 21*(10–11), 1105–1121.

Epple, Angelika. (2010). *Das Unternehmen Stollwerck: Eine Mikrogeschichte der Globalisierung.* Frankfurt: Campus Verlag.

Erdély, Eugen. (1932). *Bat'a: Ein Schuster erobert die Welt.* Leipzig: Kahler.

Fan, Yiu-Kwan. (1998). Families in the 21st Century: The Economic Perspective. *HKCER Letters, Vol. 50* (May), http://www.hkcer.hku.hk/Letters/v50/fan.htm.

Fear, Jeffrey. (2001). Thinking Historically About Organizational Learning. In M. Dierkes, A. Berthoin Antal, J. Child & I. Nonaka (Eds.), *Handbook of Organizational Learning* (pp. 162–191). Oxford: Oxford University Press.

———. (2003). *Banking on Germany? HBS Case 9–703–028* (Publication date: Apr. 18, 2003).

———. (2005). *Organizing Control: August Thyssen and the Construction of German Corporate Management.* Cambridge, MA: Harvard University Press.

———. (2012). Straight Outta Oberberg: Transforming Mid-Sized Family Firms into Global Champions 1970–2010. *Jahrbuch für Wirtschaftsgeschichte/Economic History Yearbook, 53*(1), 125–169.

Feldenkirchen, Wilfried. (1994). *Werner von Siemens: Inventor and International Entrepreneur.* Columbus: Ohio State University Press.

———. (1999). *Siemens, 1918–1945.* Columbus: Ohio State University Press.

Fernández, Zulima, & Nieto, Maria J. (2005). Internationalization Strategy of Small and Medium-Sized Family Businesses: Some Influential Factors. *Family Business Review, 18*(1), 77–88.

Fernández Moya, María. (2010). A Family-Owned Publishing Multinational: The Salvat Company (1869–1988). *Business History, 52*(3), 453–470.

Fernández Pérez, Paloma, & Puig, Núria. (2004). Knowledge and Training in Family Firms of the European Periphery: Spain in the Eighteenth to Twentieth Centuries. *Business History, 46*(1), 79–99.

———. (2009). Global Lobbies for a Global Economy. The Creation of the Spanish Institute of Family Firms in International Perspective. *Business History, 51*(5), 712–733.

Fernández Pérez, Paloma, & Rose, Mary B. (Eds.). (2010). *Innovation and Entrepreneurial Networks in Europe.* New York: Routledge.

Finn, Margot. (2010). Anglo-Indian Lives in the Later Eighteenth and Early Nineteenth Centuries. *Journal of Eighteenth-Century Studies, 33*(1), 45–65.

Franzke, Stefanie, Grohs, Stefanie, & Laux, Christian. (2004). Initial Public Offerings and Venture Capital in Germany. In J.P. Krahnen & R.H. Schmidt (Eds.), *German Financial System* (pp. 233–260). Oxford: Oxford University Press.

Fräss-Ehrfeld, Claudia (Ed.). (1999). *Lebenschancen in Kärnten 1900–2000: ein Vergleich.* Klagenfurt: Verlag des Geschichtsvereines für Kärnten.

Frevert, Ute. (2011). *Emotions in History—Lost and Found (Natalie Zemon Davies Annual Lecture Series).* Budapest: Central European University Press.

Friedländer, Saul, & Bühler, Hans-Eugen. (2002). *Bertelsmann im Dritten Reich.* München: C. Bertelsmann.

Füssel, Stephan. (2010). The Bertelsmann Book Publishing Companies, 1945–2010. In Bertelsmann AG Corporate History (Ed.), *175 Years of Bertelsmann: The Legacy for Our Future* (pp. 84–129). München: C. Bertelsmann.

Gabel, Racheli Shmueli, Dolan, Shimon L., & Gerdin, Jean Luc. (2005). Emotional Intelligence as a Predictor of Cultural Adjustment for Success in Global Assignments. *Career Development International, 10*(5), 375–395.

Gallo, Miguel Angel, & Sveen, Jannicke. (1991). Internationalizing the Family Business: Facilitating and Restraining Forces. *Family Business Review, 4*(2), 181–190.

Gankema, Harold G.J., Snuif, Henoch R., & Zwart, Peter S. (2000). The Internationalization Process of Small and Medium-Sized Enterprises. An Evaluation of Stage Theory. *Journal of Small Business Management, 38*(4), 15–27.

Garrido, Celso. (1999). El caso mexicano. In D. Chudnovsky & A. López (Eds.), *Las multinacionales latinoamericanas: Sus estratégias en un mundo globalizado* (pp. 167–258). Buenos Aires: Fondo de Cultura Económica.

Gatti, Alain. (2004). *Chausser les Hommes qui vont pieds nus: Bat'a Hellocourt, 1931–2001. Enquête sur la memoire industrielle et sociale.* Metz: Ed. Serpenoise.

Gerber, David A. (2005). Acts of Deceiving and Withholding in Immigrant Letters: Personal Identity and Self-Presentation in Personal Correspondence. *Journal of Social History,* 39(2), 315–330.

Gersick, Kelin E., Davis, John A., Hampton, Marion McCollom, & Lansberg, Ivan. (1997). *Generation to Generation. Life Cycles of the Family Business.* Boston: Harvard Business School Press.

Gerslová, Jana. (2003). Tomas Bat'a—Der 'tschechische Ford'. In U.S. Soenius (Ed.), *Verbinden—Bewegen—Gestalten: Unternehmer vom 17. bis zum 20. Jahrhundert* (pp. 295–311). Cologne: Rheinisch-Westfälisches Wirtsch.-Archiv.

Gerslová, Jana. (2011). 'Der Schuster, der die Welt erobert': Die tschechoslowakische Firma Bat'a als Paradefall eines innovativen Unternehmens (1894–1948). In P. Berger, P. Eigner & A. Resch (Eds.), *Die vielen Gesichter des wirtschaftlichen Wandels Beiträge zur Innovationsgeschichte* (pp. 277–311). Vienna: LIT.

Gibb Dyer, W. (1989). Integrating Professional Management into a Family Owned Business. *Family Business Review,* 2(3), 221–235.

Gidoomal, Ram. (1997). *The UK Maharajahs: Inside the South Asian Success Story.* London: Nicholas Brealey.

Ginalski, Stéphanie. (2010). Business Elites and Family Capitalism: The Case of the Swiss Metallurgy Industry During the 20th Century. Paper presented at the European Business History Association Conference, http://www.ebha.org/ebha2010/code/media_167606_en.pdf.

Ginwala, Frene. (1977). *Indian South Africans.* London: Minority Rights Group Report, no. 34.

Godley, Andrew. (2001). *Jewish Immigrant Entrepreneurship in New York and London 1880–1914. Enterprise and Culture.* Basingstoke: Palgrave.

Gonzales, Michael J. (2002). *The Mexican Revolution, 1910–1940.* Albuquerque: University of New Mexico.

Gordon, Grant, & Nicholson, Nigel. (2008). *Family Wars: Classic Conflicts in Family Business and How to Deal with Them.* London: Kogan Page.

Graf, Ulrich. (2000). Kaba: Entscheidungen überprüfen und allenfalls korrigieren. In E. Brauchlin & P. Hauser (Eds.), *Mittelgrosse industrielle Unternehmungen erfolgreich im globalen Wettbewerb* (pp. 29–37). Bern: Paul Haupt.

Granovetter, Mark S. (1973). The Strength of Weak Ties. *American Journal of Sociology,* 78(6), 1360–1380.

Graves, Chris, & Thomas, Jill. (2005). Internationalization of the Family Firm: The Contribution of an Entrepreneurial Orientation. *Journal of Business and Entrepreneurship,* 17(2), 91–113.

———. (2006). Internationalisation of Australian Family Businesses: A Managerial Capabilities Perspective. *Family Business Review,* 19(3), 207–224.

———. (2008). Determinants of the Internationalization Pathways of Family Firms: An Examination of Family Influence. *Family Business Review,* 21(2), 151–167.

Gray, Colin. (1997). Managing Entrepreneurial Growth: A Question of Control? In D. Deakins, P. Jennings & C.M. Mason (Eds.), *Small Firms: Entrepreneurship in the Nineties* (pp. 29–46). London: Paul Chapman.

Greco, Albert N. (1997). *The Book Publishing Industry.* Mahwah, NJ: Lawrence Erlbaum.

Grunow-Osswald, Elfriede. (2006). *Die Internationalisierung eines Konzerns: Daimler-Benz 1890–1997.* Vaihingen: IPA Verlag.

Guillén, Mauro F. (2000). Business Groups in Emerging Economies: A Resource-Based View. *Academy of Management Journal, 43*(3), 362–380.

Gutmann, Joachim. (2000). Einführung: Intuition und Strategie. In J. Gutmann & R. Kabst (Eds.), *Internationalisierung im Mittelstand: Chancen-Risiken-Erfolgsfaktoren* (pp. xv–xxiv). Wiesbaden: Gabler.

Habbershon, Timothy G., & Williams, Mary L. (1999). A Resource-Based Framework for Assessing the Strategic Advantages of Family Firms. *Family Business Review, 12*(1), 1–25.

Haber, Stephen H. (1989). *Industry and Underdevelopment: The Industrialization of Mexico, 1890–1940.* Stanford, CA: Stanford University Press.

Haber, Stephen, Maurer, Noel, & Razo, Armando. (2002). Sustaining Economic Performance Under Political Instability: Political Integration in Revolutionary Mexico. In S. Haber (Ed.), *Crony Capitalism and Economic Growth in Latin America: Theory and Evidence* (pp. 25–74). Stanford, CA: Hoover Institution Press.

Haber, Stephen, & Razo, Armando. (1998). Political Instability and Economic Performance: Evidence from Revolutionary Mexico. *World Politics, 51*(1), 99–143.

Hamilton, Eleanor. (2006). Whose Story Is It Anyway? Narrative Accounts of the Role of Women in Founding and Establishing Family Businesses. *International Small Business Journal, 24*(3), 253–271.

Hannah, Leslie. (1983). From Family Firm to Professional Management. Structure and Performance of Business Enterprise. *Zeitschrift für Unternehmensgeschichte, 28*(2), 120–125.

Hansen, Roger. (1971). *The Politics of Mexican Development.* Baltimore: Johns Hopkins University Press.

Harrison, Benjamin T. (1988). *Dollar Diplomat: Chandler Anderson and American Diplomacy in Mexico and Nicaragua, 1913–1928.* Pullman: Washington State University Press.

Haunschild, Ljuba, Hauser, Christian, Günterberg, Brigitte, Müller, Klaus, & Sölter, Anja. (2007). *Die Bedeutung der außenwirtschaftlichen Aktivitäten für den deutschen Mittelstand: Gutachten im Auftrag des Bundesministeriums für Wirtschaft und Technologie (IfM-Materialien Nr. 171).* Bonn: Institut für Mittelstandsforschung.

Haunschild, Ljuba, & Wallau, Frank. (2010). *Die größten Familienunternehmen in Deutschland (IFM-Materialien Nr. 192).* Bonn: Institut für Mittelstandsforschung. http://www.ifm-bonn.org/assets/documents/IfM-Materialien-192.pdf.

Hauser, Christian. (2006). *Aussenwirtschaftsförderung für kleine und mittlere Unternehmen in der Bundesrepublik Deutschland: Eine empirische Analyse auf der Basis der ökonomischen Theorie des Föderalismus* (1. Aufl.). Wiesbaden: Deutscher Universitätsverlag.

———. (2007). *Mittelstand in Deutschland: Eine Einführung (Vortrag anlässlich des 6th Russian German Young Leaders Forum am 15.06.2007 in Hamburg).* www.ifm-bonn.org/assets/documents/C-Hauser-15–06–2007.pdf.

Headrick, Daniel R. (1981). *The Tools of Empire. Technology and European Imperialism in the Nineteenth Century.* New York: Oxford University Press.

Heim, Peter. (2000). *Königreich Bally: Fabrikherren und Arbeiter in Schönenwerd.* Baden: Hier und Jetzt.

Heimerzheim, Peter, & Siegwerk AG (Eds.). (2007). *In(k)novation: 100 Jahre Siegwerk-Innovation [1906–2006].* Cologne: Geschichtsbüro-Verlag.

Hennerkes, Brun-Hagen, & Pleister, Christopher (Eds.). (1999). *Erfolgsmodell Mittelstand: 12 Unternehmer geben Einblicke in ihr Denken und Handeln.* Wiesbaden: Gabler.

Henning, Karl Wilhelm. (1949). *Tomas Bat'a: Eine betriebswirtschaftliche Untersuchung.* Hanover: Weidemann.

Hertner, Peter. (1984). *Il capitale tedesco in Italia dall'Unità alla prima guerra mondiale: banche miste e sviluppo economico italiano.* Bologna: Il Mulino.

———. (1989). Financial Strategies and Adaptation to Foreign Markets: The German Electro-Technical Industry and Its Multinational Activities 1890s to 1939. In A. Teichova, M. Lévy-Leboyer & H. Nussbaum (Eds.), *Multinational Enterprise in Historical Perspective* (pp. 145–159). Cambridge: Cambridge University Press.

Hier spricht der Chef. (1953). *Der Spiegel, 22,* 16–19.

Hilger, Susanne. (2008). 'Globalization by Americanization'—American Companies and the Internationalization of German Industry after World War II. *European Review of History, 15 (Special Issue: Americanization in Europe in the Twentieth Century 2008),* 375–402.

Hilsum, Lindsey. (2005). *We Love China.* London: Granta.

Himbara, David. (1994). *Kenyan Capitalists, the State and Development.* Boulder, CO: Lynn Rienner.

Hiralal, Kalpana. (2001). *Indian Family Businesses in the Natal Economy, 1890–1950.* PhD diss., University of Natal.

Hlavková, Veronika. (2006). Aufbau der Bat'a-Filialen in den 30er Jahren des 20. Jahrhunderts in Afrika. *Acta musealia, 2,* 9–10.

Hollenstein, Heinz. (2005). Determinants of International Activities. Are SMEs Different? *Small Business Economics, 24,* 431–450.

Hommel, Ulrich, & Schneider, Hilmar. (2003). Financing the German Mittelstand. *EIB Papers, 8*(2), 53–90. http://hdl.handle.net/10419/44828.

Hoshino, Taeko. (1996). Privatization of Mexico's Public Enterprises and the Restructuring of the Private Sector. *Developing Economies, 34*(1), 34–60.

———. (2001). *Industrialization of Private Enterprises in Mexico.* Chiba: Institute of Developing Eonomies–Japan External Trade Organization.

———. (2002). Mekisiko: CEMEX no Takokuseki Kigyōka to Semento Sangyō no Sekaiteki Saihen. In T. Hoshino (Ed.), *Hatten Tojōkoku no Kigyō to Gurōbarizēshon* (pp. 19–68). Chiba: Ajia Keizai Kenkyūjo.

———. (2005). Executive Managers of Large Mexican Family Businesses. *Institute of Developing Economies (IED) Discussion Paper, 40,* 1–42.

———. (2006). Estructura de la propiedad y mecanismos de control de las grandes empresas familares en México. In M. de los Angeles Pozas (Ed.), *Estructura y dinámica de la gran empresa en México: Cinco estudios sobre su realidad reciente* (pp. 112–176). Mexico: El Colegio de México.

———. (2010). Business Groups in Mexico. In A. M. Colpan, T. Hikino & J. R. Lincoln (Eds.), *The Oxford Handbook of Business Groups* (pp. 424–455). Oxford: Oxford University Press.

Hounshell, David A., & Smith, John K. (1988). *Science and Corporate Strategy.* Cambridge: Cambridge University Press.

Howorth, Carole, Rose, Mary B., & Hamilton, Eleanor. (2008). Definitions, Diversity and Development: Key Debates in Family Business Research. In M. Casson, B. Yeung, A. Basu & N. Wadeson (Eds.), *The Oxford Handbook of Entrepreneurship* (pp. 225–247). Oxford: Oxford University Press.

Hoy, Frank, & Verser, Trudy G. (1994). Emerging Business, Emerging Field. Entrepreneurship and the Family Firm. *Entrepreneurship Theory and Practice, 19*(1), 9–23.

International Family Enterprise Research Academy. (2003). Family Firms Dominate. *Family Business Review, 16,* 235–239.

Internationales Arbeitsamt. (Ed.). (1930). *Die Arbeitsbedingungen in einem rationalisierten Betrieb: Das System Bat'a und seine sozialen Auswirkungen.* Berlin: Internationales Arbeitsamt Genf, Zweigamt Berlin.

James, Harold. (2006). *Family Capitalism: Wendels, Haniels, Falcks, and the Continental European Model.* Cambridge, MA: Belknap Press of Harvard University Press.

Janjuha-Jivraj, Shaheena. (2006). *Succession in Asian Family Firms*. New York: Palgrave Macmillan.

Jayaram, Narayana. (2004). Introduction—The Study of Indian Diaspora. In N. Jayaram (Ed.), *The Indian Diaspora: Dynamics of Migration* (pp. 15–43). New Delhi: Sage.

Jenkins, Anna S., Brundin, Ethel, & Wiklund, Johan. (2010). Grief or Relief? Emotional Responses to Firm Failure. *Frontiers of Entrepreneurship Research, 30*(1), 1–15.

Jensen, Michael C., & Meckling, William H. (1976). Theory of the Firm. Managerial Behavior, Agency Costs and Ownership Structure. *Journal of Financial Economics, 3*(4), 305–360.

Johanson, Jan, & Vahlne, Jan-Erik. (1977). The Internationalization Process of the Firm: A Model of Knowledge Development and Increasing Foreign Market Commitments. *Journal of International Business Studies, 8*(1), 23–32.

———. (1990). The Mechanism of Internationalisation. *International Marketing Review, 7*(4), 11–24.

John, Richard R. (2010). *Network Nation. Inventing American Telecommunications*. Cambridge, MA: Belknap Press of Harvard University Press.

Jones, Geoffrey. (1996). *The Evolution of International Business: An Introduction*. London and New York: Routledge.

———. (2002). Control, Performance, and Knowledge Transfers in Large Multinationals: Unilever in the United States, 1945–1980. *Business History Review, 76*(3), 435–478.

———. (2005). *Multinationals and Global Capitalism: From the Nineteenth to the Twenty-First Century*. Oxford: Oxford University Press.

———. (2007). Globalization. In G. Jones & J. Zeitlin (Eds.), *The Oxford Handbook of Business History* (pp. 141–168). Oxford: Oxford University Press.

Jones, Geoffrey, & Khanna, Tarun. (2006). Bringing History (Back) into International Business. *Journal of International Business Studies, 37*, 453–468.

Jones, Geoffrey, & Lubinski, Christina. (2012). Managing Political Risk in Global Business: Beiersdorf 1914–1990. *Enterprise & Society, 13*(1), 85–119.

Jones, Geoffrey, & Rose, Mary B. (1993). Family Capitalism. *Business History (Special Issue on Family Capitalism), 35*(4), 1–16.

Jones, Marian V., Dimitratos, Pavlos, Fletcher, Margaret, & Young, Stephen (Eds.). (2009). *Internationalization, Entrepreneurship and the Smaller Firm: Evidence from Around the World*. Cheltenham: Edward Elgar.

Kahn, Joel A., & Henderson, Douglas A. (1992). Location Preferences of Family Firms. *Family Business Review, 4*(3), 271–282.

Kallai, Paul. (1936). *Die wirtschaftliche Lage und Entwicklungstendenzen der deutschen Schuhindustrie unter besonderer Berücksichtigung der Bat'a-Schuhwerke*. PhD diss., University of Geneva.

Kammer der Gewerblichen Wirtschaft für Kärnten (Ed.). (1953). *Kärntens gewerbliche Wirtschaft von der Vorzeit bis zur Gegenwart*. Klagenfurt: J. Leon.

Kaplinsky, Raphael, & Morris, Mike. (2009). Chinese FDI in Sub-Saharan Africa: Engaging with Large Dragons. *European Journal of Development Research, 21*(4), 551–569.

KfW Bankengruppe. (2009). Auslandsinvestitionen im Mittelstand: Märkte, Motive, Finanzierung. Wirtschafts-Observer online, *43*(Jan.). http://www.kfw.de/kfw/de/I/II/Download_Center/Fachthemen/Research/Wirtschaft2.jsp.

Khanna, Tarun, & Palepu, Krishna. (1997). Why Focused Strategies May Be Wrong for Emerging Markets? *Harvard Business Review, July-August*, 41–51.

Khanna, Tarun, & Palepu, Krishna. (2000). Is Group Affiliation Profitable in Emerging Markets? An Analysis of Diversified Indian Business Groups. *Journal of Finance, 55*(2), 867–891.

Khanna, Tarun, & Yafeh, Yishay. (2007). Business Groups in Emerging Markets: Paragons or Parasites? *Journal of Economic Literature, 45,* 331–372.

Kipping, Matthias, & Üsdiken, Behlül. (2007). Business History and Management Studies. In G. Jones & J. Zeitlin (Eds.), *The Oxford Handbook of Business History* (pp. 96–119). Oxford: Oxford University Press.

Kisch, Egon Erwin. (1969). Schuhwerk. In B. Uhse & G. Kisch (Eds.), *Prager Pitaval—Späte Reportagen—Gesammelte Werke in Einzelausgaben II* (pp. 415–428). Berlin: Aufbau-Verlag.

Kleedehn, Patrick. (2007). *Die Rückkehr auf den Weltmarkt: Die Internationalisierung der Bayer AG Leverkusen nach dem Zweiten Weltkrieg.* Stuttgart: Franz Steiner Verlag.

Klein, Gary D. (1986). *South Africans of Gujarati-Indian Descent: Cultural, Structural and Ideological Dynamics Within Their Community.* PhD diss., Temple University. Available at http://jdc.jefferson.edu/gsfp/1/.

Klein, Sabine B., Astrachan, Joseph H., & Smyrnios, Kosmas X. (2005). The F-PEC Scale of Family Influence. Construction, Validation, and Further Implication for Theory. *Entrepreneurship Theory and Practice, 29*(3), 321–339.

Klich, Ignacio, & Lesser, Jeff (Eds.). (1998). *Arab and Jewish Immigrants in Latin America: Images and Realities.* London: Routledge.

Klingan, Katrin, & Gust, Kerstin (Eds.). (2009). *A Utopia of Modernity—Zlín: Revisiting Bat'a's Functional City.* Berlin: Jovis.

Knight, Alan. (1987). *U.S.-Mexican Relations, 1910–1940: An Interpretation.* San Diego: Center for U.S.-Mexican Studies.

Knight, Gary, & Cavusgil, Tamer S. (2009). *Born Global Firms: A New International Enterprise.* New York: Business Expert Press.

Kobrak, Christopher, & Hansen, Per. H. (Eds.). (2004). *European Business, Dictatorship, and Political Risk, 1920–1945.* New York: Berghahn Books.

Kock, Carl J., & Guillén, Mauro F. (2001). Strategy and Structure in Developing Countries: Business Groups as an Evolutionary Response to Opportunities for Unrelated Diversification. *Industrial and Corporative Change, 10*(1), 77–113.

Kocka, Jürgen. (1999). The Entrepreneur, the Family, and Capitalism: Examples from the Early Phase of German Industrialization. In J. Kocka (Ed.), *Industrial Culture and Bourgeois Society: Business, Labor, and Bureaucracy in Modern Germany, 1800–1918* (pp. 103–138). New York: Berghahn Books.

Kogut, Bruce, & Zander, Udo. (1993). Knowledge of the Firm and the Evolutionary Theory of the Multinational Corporation. *Journal of International Business Studies, 24*(4), 625–645.

———. (2003). A Memoir and Reflection: Knowledge and an Evolutionary Theory of the Multinational Firm 10 Years Later. *Journal of International Business Studies, 34,* 505–515.

Kolbeck, Christoph, & Wimmer, Rudolf (Eds.). (2002). *Finanzierung für den Mittelstand: Trends, Unternehmensrating, Praxisfälle.* Wiesbaden: Gabler.

Köll, Elizabeth, & Goetzmann, William N. (2005). The History of Corporate Ownership in China: State Patronage, Company Legislation and the Issue of Control. In R.K. Morck (Ed.), *A History of Corporate Governance Around the World. Family Business Groups to Professional Managers* (pp. 149–184). Chicago: University of Chicago Press.

Kontinen, Tanja, & Ojala, Arto. (2010). The Internationalization of Family Businesses: A Review of Extant Research. *Journal of Family Business Strategy, 1*(2), 97–107.

Kumar, Nagesh. (2008). Internationalization of Indian Enterprises: Patterns, Strategies, Ownership Advantages, and Implications. *Asian Economic Policy Review, 3*(2), 242–261.

La Porta, Rafael, Lopez-de-Silanes, Florenco, & Shleifer, Andrei. (1999). Corporate Ownership Around the World. *Journal of Finance, 54*(2), 471–517.

Lambrecht, Johan. (2005). Multigenerational Transition in Family Businesses: A New Explanatory Model. *Family Business Review, 18*(4), 267–282.

Landes, David S. (1969). *The Unbound Prometheus: Technological Change and Industrial Development in Western Europe from 1750 to the Present.* Cambridge, UK and New York: Cambridge University Press.

———. (2006). *Dynasties: Fortunes and Misfortunes of the World's Great Family Businesses.* New York: Viking.

Langenscheidt, Florian, & Venohr, Bernd. (2010). *Lexikon der deutschen Weltmarktführer.* Cologne: Deutsche Standards Editionen.

Lansberg, Ivan. (1988). The Succession Conspiracy. *Family Business Review, 1*(2), 119–143.

———. (1999). *Succeding Generations. Realizing the Dream of Families in Business.* Boston: Harvard Business Review Press.

Larçon, Jean-Paul (Ed.). (2009). *Chinese Multinationals.* Hackensack, NJ: World Scientific.

Le Bot, Florent. (2005). La 'famille' du cuir contre Bat'a: Malthusianisme, Corporatisme, Xenophobie et antisemitisme dans le monde de la chaussure en France, 1930–1950. *Revue d'historie moderne et contemporaine, 52,* 131–151.

Lee, Keun, & Kang, Young-Sam. (2010). Chinese Business Groups in China. In A. M. Colpan, T. Hikino & J. R. Lincoln (Eds.), *The Oxford Handbook of Business Groups* (pp. 210–236). Oxford: Oxford University Press.

Lee, W. Robert (Ed.). (2011). *Commerce and Culture: Nineteenth-Century Business Elites.* Farnham, Surrey; Burlington, VT: Ashgate.

Leff, Nathaniel H. (1978). Industrial Organization and Entrepreneurship in the Developing Countries: The Economic Groups. *Economic Development and Cultural Change, 26*(4), 661–675.

Léhar, Bohumil. (1960). *Dejiny Batova Koncernu (1894–1945).* Prague: Státní nakladatelství politické literatury.

———. (1963). The Economic Expansion of the Bat'a Concern in Czechoslovakia and Abroad (1929–1938). Translated by Roberta F. Samsour. *Historica, 5,* 147–188.

Leibinger, Berthold. (2010). *Wer wollte eine andere Zeit als diese: Ein Lebensbericht.* Hamburg: Murmann.

Leung, Kwok, Bhagat, Rabi S., Buchan, Nancy R., Erez, Miriam, & Gibson, Christina B. (2005). Culture and International Business: Recent Advances and Their Implications for Future Research. *Journal of International Business Studies, 36,* 357–378.

Lindner, Erik. (2010). Reinhard Mohn and Gerd Bucerius: An Entrepreneurial Friendship. In Bertelsmann AG Corporate History (Ed.), *175 Years of Bertelsmann: The Legacy for Our Future* (pp. 208–237). München: C. Bertelsmann.

Lipartito, Kenneth, & Morii, Yumiko. (2010). Rethinking the Separation of Ownership from Management in American History. *Seattle University Law Review, 33*(4), 1025–1063.

Loane, Sharon, & Bell, Jim. (2009). Clients as a 'Hidden' Resource in Rapid Internationalization. In M. V. Jones, P. Dimitratos, M. Fletcher & S. Young (Eds.), *Internationalization, Entrepreneurship and the Smaller Firm: Evidence from Around the World* (pp. 91–105). Cheltenham: Edward Elgar.

Lokatis, Siegfrid. (2010). A Concept Circles the Globe: From the Lesering to the Internationalization of the Club Business. In Bertelsmann AG Corporate History (Ed.), *175 Years of Bertelsmann: The Legacy for Our Future* (pp. 132–171). München: C. Bertelsmann.

Lubinski, Christina. (2010). *Familienunternehmen in Westdeutschland: Corporate Governance und Gesellschafterkultur seit den 1960er Jahren.* München: C. H. Beck.

———. (2011). Path Dependency and Governance in German Family Firms. *Business History Review, 85*(4), 699–724.

Lutz, Martin. (2011). *Siemens im Sowjetgeschäft: Eine Institutionengeschichte der deutsch-sowjetischen Beziehungen 1917–1933*. Stuttgart: Steiner.

Mager, Peter. (1999). Respekt vor fremden Kulturen. In B.-H. Hennerkes & C. Pleister (Eds.), *Erfolgsmodell Mittelstand: 12 Unternehmer geben Einblick in ihr Denken und Handeln* (pp. 199–219). Wiesbaden: Gabler.

Mani, A. (2006a). Indians in Jakarta. In K. S. Sandhu & A. Mani (Eds.), *Indian Communities in Southeast Asia* (pp. 98–130). Singapore: Institute of Southeast Asian Studies.

———. (2006b). Indians in Northern Sumatra. In K. S. Sandhu & A. Mani (Eds.), *Indian Communities in Southeast Asia* (pp. 46–97). Singapore: Institute of Southeast Asian Studies.

Marek, Martin. (2009). Stav bat'ovského bádáni: od meziválecné publikacni tvorby po soucasné odborné studie [The State of Bat'a Research: From Interwar Publications to Contemporary Scholarly Studies]. *Casopis Matice moravské, 128*(2), 413–443.

Marichal, Carlos (Ed.). (1995). *Las inversiones extranjeras en América Latina, 1850–1930: Nuevos debates y problemas en historia econòmica comparada*. Mexico City: El Colegio de México.

Markovits, Claude. (1999). Indian Merchant Networks outside India in the Nineteenth and Twentieth Centuries: A Preliminary Survey. *Modern Asian Studies, 33*(4), 883–911.

———. (2000). *The Global World of Indian Merchants, 1750–1947: Traders of Sind from Bukhara to Panama*. Cambridge: Cambridge University Press.

Maurer, Noel, & Haber, Stephen. (2007). Related Lending and Economic Performance: Evidence from Mexico. *Journal of Economic History, 67*(3), 551–581.

McNeil, William H. (1963). *The Rise of the West: A History of the Human Community*. Chicago: University of Chicago Press.

Meyer, Klaus, & Skak, Ane. (2002). Networks, Serendipity and SME Entry into Eastern Europe. *European Management Journal, 20*(2), 179–188.

Michler, Inga. (2009). *Wirtschaftswunder 2010: Deutschlands Familienuntrnehmer erobern die Weltmärkte*. Frankfurt: Campus Verlag.

Miller, Danny, Steier, Lloyd P., & Le Breton-Miller, Isabelle. (2003). Lost in Time: Intergenerational Succession, Change and Failure in Family Business. *Journal of Business Venturing, 18*(4), 513–531.

MOFCOMs (Ministry of Commerce People's Republic of China). (2010). Statistical Bulletin of China's Outward Foreign Direct Investment (Published since 2003).

Mohn, Reinhard. (2009). *A Global Lesson: Success Through Cooperation and Compassionate Leadership*. New York: Crown.

Moravčiková, Henrieta. (2009). Die Architektur des Bat'a-Konzerns als Faktor der Modernisierung: Beispiel Slowakei. In W. Nerdinger (Ed.), *Zlín: Modellstadt der Moderne* (pp. 148–158). Berlin: Jovis.

Morck, Randall K. (2003). Agency Problems in Large Family Business Groups. *Entrepreneurship Theory and Practice, 27*(4), 367–382.

Morck, Randall K. (Ed.). (2005). *A History of Corporate Governance Around the World: Family Business Groups to Professional Managers*. Chicago: University of Chicago Press.

Morck, Randall K., Shleifer, Andrei, & Vishny, Robert. (1988). Management Ownership and Market Valuation. An Empirical Analysis. *Journal of Financial Economics, 20*, 293–316.

Morck, Randall, Wolfenzon, Daniel, & Yeung, Bernard. (2005). Corporate Governance, Economic Entrenchment, and Growth. *Journal of Economic Literature, 43*, 655–720.

Morgan-Thomas, Anna, & Jones, Marian V. (2009). Post-Entry Internationalization Dynamics. Differences Between SMEs in the Development Speed of Their International Sales. *International Small Business Journal, 27*(1), 71–97.

Murray, Barbara. (2002). Understanding the Emotional Dynamics of Family Enterprises. In D. E. Fletcher (Ed.), *Understanding the Small Family Business* (pp. 75–93). London: Routledge.

Musteen, Martina, Francis, John, & Datta, Deepak K. (2010). The Influence of International Networks on Internationalization Speed and Performance: A Study of Czech SMEs. *Journal of World Business, 45*, 197–205.

Naldi, Lucia, & Nordqvist, Mattias. (2009). Family Firms Venturing into International Markets: A Resource Dependence Perspective. *Frontiers of Entrepreneurship Research, 28*(14), article 1. Available at: http://digitalknowledge.babson.edu/fer/vol28/iss14/21.

Nerdinger, Winfried (Ed.). (2009). *Zlín: Modellstadt der Moderne*. Berlin: Jovis.

Nicholson, Nigel, & Björnberg, Asa. (2012). Emotional Ownership—The Next Generation's Relationship with the Family Firm. *Family Business Review 25/4*, 374-390.

Nickles, David Paull. (2003). *Under the Wire: How the Telegraph Changed Diplomacy*. Cambridge, MA: Harvard University Press.

Nie, Winter, Xin, Katherine, & Zhang, Lily. (2009). *Made in China: Secrets of China's Dynamic Entrepreneurs*. Singapore: John Wiley & Sons (Asia).

Nolan, Edward Henry. (1858). *The Illustrated History of the British Empire in India and the East, from the Earliest Times to the Suppression of the Sepoy Mutiny, in 1859*. London: J. S. Virtue.

O'Sullivan, Mary, & Graham, Margaret B. W. (2010). Moving Forward by Looking Backward. Business History and Management Studies. *Journal of Management Studies, 47*(5), 775–790.

Ogliari, F. (1987). *La navigazione sui laghi italiani*. Milan: Cavallotti.

Ojala, Jari, & Pajunen, Kalle. (2006). Two Family Firms in Comparison: Ahsltröm and Schauman During the 20th Century. In J.-A. Lamberg, J. Näsi, J. Ojala & P. Sajasalo (Eds.), *The Evolution of Competitive Strategies in Global Forestry Industries: Comparative Perspectives* (pp. 167–189). Dordrecht: Springer.

Okoroafo, Sam C. (1999). Internationalization of Family Businesses. Evidence from Northwest Ohio, USA. *Family Business Review, 12*(2), 147–158.

Organisation for Economic Cooperation and Development (OECD). (1996). *The Knowledge-Based Economy*. Paris: OCDE/GD(96)102. http://www.oecd.org/dataoecd/51/8/1913021.pdf.

———. (1997). *Globalisation and Small and Medium Enterprises (SMEs)*, V. 1, Paris: OECD Publishing.

———. (2012). OECD Review of Telecommunication Policy and Regulation in Mexico. http://dx.doi.org/10.1787/9789264060111-en.

Osses, Dietmar, & Asfur, Anke. (2005). *Neapel, Bochum, Rimini: Arbeiten in Deutschland, Urlaub in Italien*. Essen: Klartext.

Overbeck, Anne. (2009). So kam das Eis ins Ruhrgebiet: Italienische Eismacher im Ruhrgebiet 1900–2009. In A. Overbeck & D. Osses (Eds.), *Eiskalte Leidenschaft: Italienische Eismacher im Ruhrgebiet* (pp. 30–37). Essen: Klartext.

Oviatt, Benjamin M., & McDougall, Patricia P. (1994). Toward a Theory of International New Ventures. *Journal of International Business Studies, 25*(1), 45–64.

Owens, Alistair. (2002). Inheritance and the Life-Cycle of Family Firms in the Early Industrial Revolution. *Business History, 44*(1), 21–46.

Panciera, Donata. (1999). *Wie das Eis entstand—la storia del gelato: Vom Zeitalter der Speiseeiserzeuger zur MIG—All époea de gelatieri alla Mostra Internazionale del Gelato*. Verona: Uniteis.

———. (n.d.). Handwerklich hergestelltes Speiseeis. Geschichtlicher Überblick. http://www.uniteis.com/pagine_de/Handwerklich_hergestellte_Speiseeis/Geschichtlicher_Uberblick.htm.

Paris, I. (2007). Economia e mercato nell'area gardesana negli ultimi cinque secoli, il caso di Desenzano. In S. Onger (Ed.), *Il mercato del lago: Desenzano del Garda in età moderna e contemporanea* (pp. 71–80). Grafo: Brescia.

Patel, Zarina. (1997). *Challenge to Colonialism: The Struggle of Alibhai Mulla Jeevanjee for Equal Rights in Kenya.* Nairobi: Modern Lithographic (K).

Penrose, Edith Tilton. (1959). *The Theory of the Growth of the Firm.* Oxford: Oxford University Press.

Philipp, Rudolph. (1928). *Der unbekannte Diktator Thomas Bať a.* Vienna: Agis.

Pichler, Edith. (1997). *Migration, Community-Formierung und ethnische Ökonomie: Die italienischen Gewerbetreibenden in Berlin.* Berlin: Parabolis.

Pietrobelli, Carlo, Rabellotti, Roberta, & Sanfilippo, Marco. (2010). *The Marco Polo Effect: Chinese FDI in Italy.* International Economics (IE) Programme Paper IE PP 2010/04. www.chathamhouse.org.uk.

Piluso, G. (2000). Il mercato del credito a Milano dopo l'Unità. Struttura e dinamiche evolutive. In G. Conti & S. L. Francesca (Eds.), *Banche e reti di banche nell'Italia postunitaria, II. Formazione e sviluppo di mercati locali del credito.* Bologna: Il Mulino.

Plakoyiannaki, Emmanuella, & Deligianni, Ioanna. (2009). Growth and Learning Spillovers from International Markets. Empirical Evidence from Greek Firms. In M. V. Jones, P. Dimitratos, M. Fletcher & S. Young (Eds.), *Internationalization, Entrepreneurship and the Smaller Firm. Evidence from Around the World* (pp. 37–52). Cheltenham: Edward Elgar.

Pomeranz, Kenneth. (1997). "Traditional" Chinese Business Forms Revisited: Family, Firm and Financing in the History of the Yutang Company of Jining, 1779–1856. *Late Imperial China, 18*(1), 1–38.

Popp, Andrew. (2009). From Town to Town: How Commercial Travel Connected Manufacturers and Markets in the Industrial Revolution. *Journal of Historical Geography, 35*(4), 642–667.

———. (2011). From Wolverhampton to Calcutta: The Low Origins of Merchant Enterprise. In R. Lee (Ed.), *Commerce and Culture* (pp. 37–60). Aldershot: Ashgate.

———. (2012). *Entrepreneurial Families: Business, Marriage and Life in the Early Nineteenth Century.* London: Pickering & Chatto.

Popp, Andrew, & Holt, Robin. (forthcoming-a). Emotion, Sensibility, and the Family Firm: Josiah Wedgwood and Sons. *Business History.*

Popp, Andrew, & Holt, Robin. (2013). The Presence of Entrepreneurial Opportunity. *Business History 55/1, 9-28.*

Porter, Michael E. (1998). Clusters and the New Economics of Competition. *Harvard Business Review, Nov-Dec,* 77–90.

Poutziouris, Panikkos Zata, Smyrnios, Kosmas X., & Klein, Sabine B. (Eds.). (2006). *Handbook of Research on Family Business.* Cheltenham: Edward Elgar.

Powell, Marilyn. (2005). *Ice Cream: The Delicious History.* New York: Overlook Press.

Poza, Ernesto J. (1989). *Smart Growth: Critical Choices for Business Continuity and Prosperity.* San Francisco: Jossey-Bass.

Prasad, S. B. (1999). Globalization of Smaller Firms. Field Notes on Processes. *Small Business Economics, 13,* 1–7.

Puig, Núria, & Fernández Pérez, Paloma. (2009). A Silent Revolution: The Internationalisation of Large Spanish Family Firms. *Business History, 51*(3), 462–483.

Ribera, Francesc. (2008). Círculo de Lectores. In F. Ribera (Ed.), *Los número uno en España* (pp. 89–101). Barcelona: Dobleerre Editorial.

Rieker, Yvonne. (2003). 'Ein Stück Heimat findet man ja immer': Die italienische Einwanderung in die Bundesrepublik. Essen: Klartext.

Rivoli, Pietra. (2009). The Travels of a T-shirt in the Global Economy: An Economist Examines the Markets, Power, and Politics of World Trade (2nd ed.). Hoboken, NJ: John Wiley & Sons.

Rommel, Günter. (1995). Simplicity Wins: How Germany's Mid-sized Industrial Companies Succeed. Boston, MA: Harvard Business School Press.

Rose, Mary B. (1993). Beyond Buddenbrooks: The Family Firm and the Management of Succession in Nineteenth-Century Britain. In J. Brown & M.B. Rose (Eds.), Entrepreneurship, Networks and Modern Business (pp. 124–143). Manchester: Manchester University Press.

Rose, Mary B. (Ed.). (1995). Family Business. Aldershot: E. Elgar.

Roth, Kurt. (1932). Das System Bat'a. PhD diss., University of Würzburg.

Sachse, Carola. (1990). Siemens, der Nationalsozialismus und die moderne Familie: Eine Untersuchung zur sozialen Rationalisierung in Deutschland im 20. Jahrhundert. Hamburg: Rasch und Röhring.

Salas-Porras, Alejandra. (1998). Estrátegias de las empresas mexicanas en sus procesos de internacionalización. Revista de la Cepal, 65, 133–153.

Sandhu, Kernial Singh. (2006). The Coming of the Indians to Malaysia. In K.S. Sandhu & A. Mani (Eds.), Indian Communities in Southeast Asia (pp. 151–189). Singapore: Institute of Southeast Asian Studies.

Santiso, Javier. (2008). La emergencia de las multilatinas. Revista de la Cepal, 95, 7–30.

Schmid, Walter. (1939). Die wirtschaftliche Entwicklung der C.F. Bally A.G. und der Bally Schuhfabriken A.G. in Schönenwerd, mit besonderer Berücksichtigung des Exportproblems. PhD diss., University of Bern.

Schneider, Ben Ross. (2009). A Comparative Political Economy of Diversified Business Groups, or How States Organize Big Business. Review of International Political Economy, 16(2), 178–210.

Schneider, Friedrich. (1990). Talmesch, die Sächsische Gemeinde in Siebenbürgen, Rumänien, Vol. 1: Von der Gründung bis zum Beginn des Zweites Welkrieges 1939. Wiesbaden: Self-Published.

Schroeter, Barbara. (2009). Die Heimat der Gelatieri—die Geschichte des Zoldo Tals. In A. Overbeck & D. Osses (Eds.), Eiskalte Leidenschaft: Italienische Eismacher im Ruhrgebiet (pp. 24–30). Essen: Klartext.

Schröter, Harm. (1993). Aufstieg der Kleinen: Multinationale Unternehmen aus fünf kleinen Staaten vor 1914. Berlin: Duncker & Humblot.

Schulte Beerbühl, Margrit. (2007). Deutsche Kaufleute in London: Welthandel und Einbürgerung 1660–1818. München: Oldenbourg.

Schulze, William S., Lubatkin, Michael H., & Dino, Richard N. (2003). Toward a Theory of Agency and Altruism in Family Firms. Journal of Business Venturing, 18(4), 473–490.

Schulze, William S., Lubatkin, Michael H., Dino, Richard N., & Buchholtz, Ann K. (2001). Agency Relationships in Family Firms: Theory and Evidence. Organization Science, 12(2), 99–116.

Schwenger, Rudolf. (1928). Das 'System Bat'a'. Soziale Praxis, 37, 1137–1142.

Scott, John D. (1958). Siemens Brothers, 1858–1958. An Essay in the History of Industry. London: Weidenfeld and Nicolson.

Segala, Giacomo, & Serpieri, Arrigo. (1917). Il legno greggio. Produzione—commercio—regime doganale. Roma: Tip. nazionale Bertero.

Segreto, Luciano. (2011). I Feltrinelli: storia di una dinastia imprenditoriale (1854–1942) (1). Milano: Feltrinelli.

———. (2012). Private Bankers and Italian Industrialization. In Y. Cassis & P. Cottrel (Eds.), The World of Private Banking (pp. 177–203). London: Ashgate.

Shane, Scott, & Venkataraman, Sankaran. (2000). The Promise of Entrepreneurship as a Field of Research. *Academy of Management Review, 25*(1), 217–226.

Sharma, Pramodita. (2004). An Overview of the Field of Family Business Studies. Current Status and Directions for the Future. *Family Business Review, 17*(1), 1–36.

Shenkar, Oded. (2001). Cultural Distance Revisited: Towards a More Rigorous Conceptualization and Measurement of Cultural Differences. *Journal of International Business Studies, 32*(3), 519–535.

Simon, Hermann. (2009). *Hidden Champions of the 21st Century: Success Strategies of Unknown World Market Leaders.* Dordrecht: Springer.

Smith, Robert Freeman. (1963). The Formation and Development of the International Bankers Committee on Mexico. *Journal of Economic History, 23*(4), 574–586.

Smith, Robert Freeman. (1993). Thomas W. Lamont: International Banker and Diplomat. In T. J. MacCormick & W. LaFeber (Eds.), *Behind the Throne: Servants of Power to Imperial Presidents, 1898–1968* (pp. 101–125). Madison: University of Wisconsin Press.

Söderlund, Ernst Frithiof (Ed.). (1952). *Swedish Timber Exports, 1850–1950: A History of the Swedish Timber Trade, edited for the Swedish Wood Exporters' Association.* Stockholm: Swedish Wood Exporters' Association.

Statistical Department India Office. (1867). *Statistical Abstract Relating to British India from 1840 to 1865. Compiled from Official Records and Papers Presented to Parliament.* London: George E. Eyre and William Spottiswoode.

Stearns, Peter N., & Stearns, Carol Z. (1985). Emotionology: Clarifying the History of Emotions and Emotional Standards. *Journal of Social History, 90*(4), 813–836.

STIHL. (2002). *75 Jahre wegweisend: 1926–2001.* Ludwigsburg: STIHL.

Stirken, Angela. (1998). *Eisdiele: "Komm mit nach Italien . . . !".* Bonn: Stiftung Haus der Geschichte der Bundesrepublik Deutschland.

Stobart, Thomas J. (1927). *The Timber of the United Kingdom, Vol. 1.* London: C. Lockwood & Son.

Stoila, G. (2008). *Talmaciu: Intre miturile istoriei si realitatile contemporane.* Sibiu: Editura Adalex.

Story, Dale. (1986). *Industry, the State, and Public Policy in Mexico.* Austin: University of Texas Press.

Stott, Greg. (2006). The Persistence of the Family: A Study of a Nineteenth-Century Canadian Family and Their Correspondence. *Journal of Family History 31*(2), 190–207.

Sturm, Hanspeter. (1967). Salamander. *Tradition 12,* 309–333.

Sudrow, Anne. (2010). *Der Schuh im Nationalsozialismus: eine Produktgeschichte im deutsch-britisch-amerikanischen Vergleich.* Göttingen: Wallstein.

Tagiuri, Renato, & Davis, John. (1996, Original: 1982). Bivalent Attributes of the Family Firm. *Family Business Review, 9*(2), 199–208.

Tang, Yee Kwan. (2009). Networks and the Internationalization of Firms: What We Believe and What We Might Have Missed. In M. V. Jones, P. Dimitratos, M. Fletcher & S. Young (Eds.), *Internationalization, Entrepreneurship and the Smaller Firm: Evidence from Around the World* (pp. 106–122). Cheltenham: Edward Elgar.

Tavares, Márcia. (2007). Outward FDI and the Competitiveness of Latin American Firms. In R. Grosse & L. F. Mezquita (Eds.), *Can Latin American Firms Compete?* (pp. 45–65). Oxford: Oxford University Press.

Taylor, Graham D., & Sudnik, Patricia E. (1984). *Du Pont and the International Chemical Industry.* Boston, MA: Twayne.

Teutsch, Friedrich. (1907). *Geschichte der Siebenbürger Sachsen für das sächsische Volk, Vol. 3.* Kronstadt: Verlag von Johann Gött

Tinker, Hugh. (1977). *The Banyan Tree: Overseas Emigrants from India, Pakistan, and Bangladesh.* Oxford: Oxford University Press.

Tsang, Eric W.K. (2001). Internationalizing the Family Firm: A Case Study of a Chinese Family Business. *Journal of Small Business Management, 39*(1), 88–94.

Vickery, Amanda. (2009). *Behind Closed Doors: At Home in Georgian England.* New Haven, CT: Yale University Press.

Vio, Aduo. (1999). *Gelato: Witho e Storia—Dalla Bibbia al 2000.* Belluno: Self-Published.

von Klaß, Gert. (1961). *Salamander: Die Geschichte einer Marke.* Wiesbaden: Verlag für Wirtschaftspublizistik.

Ward, John L. (1987). *Keeping the Family Business Healthy. How to Plan for Continuing Growth, Profitability, and Family Leadership.* San Francisco: Jossey-Bass.

———. (2004). *Perpetuating the Family Business: 50 Lessons Learned from Long-Lasting, Successful Families in Business.* New York: Palgrave MacMillan.

Weber, Klaus. (2004). *Deutsche Kaufleute im Atlantikhandel 1680–1830: Unternehmen und Familien in Hamburg, Cádiz und Bordeaux.* München: Beck.

Weber, Max. (1978). *Economy and Society: An Outline of Interpretive Sociology* (G. Roth & C. Wittich, Eds. Translated by Ephraim Fischoff et al. Vol. 1). Berkeley: University of California Press.

Weber, Wolfgang, & Kabst, Rüdiger. (2000). Internationalisierung mittelständischer Unternehmen: Organisationsform und Personalmanagement. In J. Gutmann & R. Kabst (Eds.), *Internationalisierung im Mittelstand: Chancen-Risiken-Erfolgsfaktoren* (pp. 8–12). Wiesbaden: Gabler.

Webster, Anthony. (2005). An Early Global Business in a Colonial Context: The Strategies, Management, and Failure of John Palmer and Company of Calcutta, 1780–1830. *Enterprise & Society, 6*(1), 98–133.

———. (2009). *The Twilight of the East India Company. The Evolution of Anglo-Asian Commerce and Politics, 1790–1860.* Rochester: Boydell & Brewer.

Weiher, Sigfrid von. (1990). *Die englischen Siemens-Werke und das Siemens-Überseegeschäft in der zweiten Hälfte des 19. Jahrhunderts.* Berlin: Duncker & Humblot.

Wenzlhuemer, Roland. (2013). *Connecting the Nineteenth-Century World: The Telegraph and Globalization.* Cambridge: Cambridge University Press.

Westhead, Paul, & Cowling, Marc. (1998). Family Firm Research. The Need for a Methodological Rethink. *Entrepreneurship Theory and Practice, 23,* 31–56.

Wilkins, Mira. (1970). *The Emergence of Multinational Enterprise: American Business Abroad from the Colonial Era to 1914.* Cambridge, MA: Harvard University Press.

———. (1974). *The Maturing of Multinational Enterprise: American Business Abroad from 1914 to 1970.* Cambridge, MA: Harvard University Press.

———. (1986). Defining a Firm: History and Theory. In P. Hertner & G. Jones (Eds.), *Multinationals: Theory and History* (pp. 80–95). Aldershot: Gower.

———. (1988). The Free-Standing Company, 1870–1914: An Important Type of British Foreign Direct Investment. *Economic History Review, 41*(2), 259–282.

Wilkins, Mira, & Schröter, Harm G. (Eds.). (1998). *The Free-Standing Company in the World Economy, 1830–1996.* Oxford: Oxford University Press.

Williams, David M. (1966). Merchanting in the First Half of the Nineteenth Century: The Liverpool Timber Trade. *Business History, 8*(2), 103–121.

Williamson, Oliver E. (1975). *Markets and Hierarchies: Analysis and Antitrust Implications.* New York: Free Press.

Wimmer, Rudolf, Domayer, Ernst, Oswald, Margit, & Vater, Gudrun. (2005). *Familienunternehmen—Auslaufmodell oder Erfolgstyp* (2). Wiesbaden: Gabler.

Wimmers, Stephan, & Wolter, Hans-Jürgen. (1997). *Situation und Perspektiven des industriellen Mittelstands in der Bundesrepublik.* Stuttgart: Schäffer-Poeschel.

Winch, Graham W. (2006). Drivers and Dynamic Processes for SMEs Going Global. *Journal of Small Business and Enterprise Development, 13*(1), 73–88.

Winkelmann, Thorsten. (1997). *Internationalisierung mittelständischer Zulieferunternehmen: Entscheidungen im Strukturwandel.* Wiesbaden: Gabler.

Wolfgang Mewes Beratergruppe Strategie (Ed.). (2000). *Mit Nischenstrategie zur Marktführerschaft: Strategie-Handbuch für mittelständische Unternehmen.* Zurich: Orell Fuessli.

Wong, Y. H., & Leung, T. K. P. (2001). *GUANXI: Relationship Marketing in a Chinese Context.* New York: International Business Press.

Wu, Shijin. (2009). *Chinese Multinationals in Historical Perspective: Organizational Capability, Entrepreneurship and Environment.* Saarbrücken: VDM Verlag.

Yanagisako, Sylvia J. (2002). *Producing Culture and Capital: Family Firms in Italy.* Princeton, NJ: Princeton University Press.

Yates, JoAnne. (1986). The Telegraph's Effect on Nineteenth Century Markets and Firms. *Business and Economic History, 15 (second series)*, 149–163.

Yeung, Henry Wai-chung. (2000). Limits to the Growth of Family-Owned Business? The Case of Chinese Transnational Corporations from Hong Kong. *Family Business Review, 13*(1), 55–70.

Zachary, Ramona K. (2011). The Importance of the Family System in Family Business. *Journal of Family Business Management, 1*(1), 26–36.

Zahavi, Gerald. (1983). Negotiated Loyalty: Welfare Capitalism and the Shoeworkers of Endicott Johnson, 1920–1940. *Journal of American History, 70*, 605–611.

———. (1988). *Workers, Managers, and Welfare Capitalism: The Shoeworkers and Tanners of Endicott Johnson, 1890–1950.* Urbana: University of Illinois Press.

Zahra, Shaker A. (2003). International Expansion of U.S. Manufacturing Family Businesses. The Effect of Ownership and Involvement. *Journal of Business Venturing, 18*(4), 495–512.

Zahra, Shaker A., & George, Gerard. (2002). Absorptive Capacity: A Review, Reconceptualization, and Extension. *Academy of Management Review, 27*(2), 185–203.

Zahra, Shaker A., & Sharma, P. (2004). Family Business Research. A Strategic Reflection. *Family Business Review, 17*(4), 331–346.

Zeleny, Milan. (1998). Bat'a System of Management: Managerial Excellence Found. *Human Systems Management, 7*, 213–219.

Zhang, Wenxian, & Alon, Ilan (Eds.). (2009). *Biographical Dictionary of New Chinese Entrepreneurs and Business Leaders.* Cheltenham: Edward Elgar.

Zhanming, Jin. (2009). Corporate Strategies of Chinese Multinationals. In J.-P. Larçon (Ed.), *Chinese Multinationals* (pp. 1–29). Hackensack, NJ: World Scientific.

Index

268   *Index*